The Gold Train

Ronald W. Zweig

The Gold Train

The Destruction of the Jews and the Looting of Hungary

wm

WILLIAM MORROW
An Imprint of HarperCollins*Publishers*

FIRST U.S. EDITION

Printed on acid-free paper

Library of Congress Cataloging-in-Publication Data
has been applied for.

ISBN 0-06-620956-0

02 03 04 05 06 BVG 10 9 8 7 6 5 4 3 2 1

Contents

List of Illustrations

(Photographic acknowledgements are given in parentheses)

1. Propaganda photo in Hungarian Fascist newspaper *Harc* (June 1944) showing confiscated Jewish valuables (*Hungarian National Library*)
2. Jews waiting to hand in their radios to the authorities, Budapest, May 1944 (*Bundesarchiv*)
3. Jew arrested outside the Budapest ghetto by Arrow Cross agents, December 1944 (*Yad Vashem Photo Archives*)
4. Árpád Toldi, in a 1944 gendarmerie publication (*author's collection*)
5. Wilhelm Höttl at Nuremberg, 1946 (*NARA, Washington, DC*)
6. Kurt Becher in 1944 (*Spiegel Archiv*)
7. Jewish-authored books collected for destruction at a Budapest papermill, June 1944 (*US Holocaust Memorial Museum Photo Archives.*)
8. Villagers looting Jewish property, after the removal of Jews to ghettos, April–May 1944 (*US Holocaust Memorial Museum Photo Archives*)
9. Official removal of household effects from formerly Jewish homes, April–May 1944 (*US Holocaust Memorial Museum Photo Archives*)
10. Members of the Szálasi government, 16 October 1944 (*no source*)
11. Gideon Rafael (Ruffer), 1947 Palestine Mandate pass (*Mrs Nurit Rafael*)

List of Maps

Acknowledgements

I stumbled across the Gold Train fifteen years ago while researching an entirely different subject in the Public Record Office in London. The Train appeared mysteriously in the files of the British Foreign Office, as something huge and sufficiently ominous to disturb the peace of the whole Middle East. Apparently it was important enough that an academic historian like myself, specializing in twentieth-century Jewish history, should have known all about it. But I had never heard of it, and was puzzled.

The originality of Foreign Office thinking did not surprise me, but the idea that gold and diamonds, looted from Hungarian Jews during the Holocaust, might undermine the relations between Arabs and Jews was unexpected and intriguing. That is how my personal voyage on the Gold Train began, and since then I have been trying to separate fact and fantasy in archives across six countries.

At the outset of this project in the late 1980s there were few relevant records available, but in the course of time public and private archival collections were opened to research in America, Britain, France, Hungary, Israel and Austria, and it became possible to piece together the complicated story presented here. It is generally believed that records automatically become available to research after a decent period of time had elapsed, but that is very far from the truth. There are many millions of documents relating to the Second World War and the Holocaust that are still classified, closed or simply missing. Recently governments have been willing to reconsider the need for continued secrecy about events that happened over fifty years ago. My own research benefited greatly from these new public policies.

In the United States, the Nazi War Crimes Disclosure Act of 1998, and the remarkable successes of the Interagency Working Group established to supervise the implementation of the Act, has forced every United States government agency to reconsider the secrecy classification of documents relating to the Second World War. At least 80 million documents are now being examined, and approximately 10 per cent of them have already been made available for research. At least two American intelligence documents cited in this text were opened only days before the research was completed. Crucial records of the French occupation forces in Austria relating to 'Trésor Hongrois' were suddenly and unexpectedly also opened to research.

Records that have been opened are sometimes suddenly closed again, as happened with some of the more important Hungarian records. Fortunately, the Hungarian government and the archives of the Holocaust memorial at Yad Vashem in Israel reached an agreement in April 2001 that reopened the files of the Hungarian war crimes trials. Post-war Hungary made a remarkable effort to try the people responsible for the catastrophe caused by Hungary's participation in Germany's war against her neighbours, against the Soviet Union and against her own Jewish community. The prosecution files and trial proceedings for over 30,000 war criminals are a rich source of information, and I have been able to make use of the relevant records.

Many of the events described here took place in Austria. I owe a particular debt of gratitude to Dr Thomas Albrich from the University of Innsbruck, friend and colleague, who helped me unearth the information on buried treasure in the Tyrol, challenged my views on a number of points, was a font of local lore and geography for the Vorarlberg–Tyrol regions and saved me from many errors. If any mistakes remain, Thomas Albrich is not to blame.

I owe many additional debts of gratitude, especially to archivists. Dr Greg Bradsher, the doyen of Holocaust-era asset records at the National Archives in College Park, Maryland, ensured that I did not miss too many relevant files. So too did Dr Richard Boylan, William Walsh, Dr Amy Schmidt and John MacDonald. Greg Murphy helped me trace missing documents in the National Archives when I was too far away to do so myself. The documentary and photo archivists of Yad Vashem in Jerusalem and the United States Holocaust Memorial Museum, together with the archivists of the American Jewish Joint

Distribution Committee in New York and in Jerusalem, the Central Zionist Archives in Jerusalem, the Central Archives for the History of the Jewish People, Jerusalem, the American Jewish Archives in Cincinnati, Ohio, and the Institut für Zeitgeschichte at the University of Innsbruck have all greatly contributed to this research.

Some of the surviving participants in the events described here were generous with their time and their collections of private papers, and they have been acknowledged in the relevant places in the text. I would particularly like to acknowledge the literary executors of the estate of Abba P. Schwartz. Schwartz played a central role in the last stage of the Gold Train story, as an employee of the international refugee organizations. The relevant files are missing from the archives of those organizations, but Schwartz's collection of private papers was exhaustively complete. His executors allowed me to save the papers from a warehouse, and they are now open to research in the Central Zionist Archives in Jerusalem.

Colleagues from Hungary have helped guide me through the historiography of the Hungarian Holocaust, and have advised on the accessibility of records. I owe debts of gratitude to Dr László Karsai and Dr Judit Molnár, from the University of Szeged. Neither of them have read the manuscript and cannot be assumed to share my conclusions. I have benefited from the help of a number of Hungarian graduate students who did the research that language barriers prevented me from doing myself. Péter Hegedüs, Alexandra Vincze, Mihály Riszovannij and Zsuzsa Shiri helped me understand Hungarian documents found in Budapest, Jerusalem and Washington. Alex Pataki translated as we travelled the route of the Gold Train through Hungary. Albane Noddings searched the archives of the Banque de France in Paris, and Judith Gallagher did the same in the Staatsarchiv, Vienna. My thanks to all of them. But I owe a special debt to three assistants – Michael Rosenfeld, Anna Kürti-Hamp and László Csősz – each of whom has made a major contribution to the research on which this book is based. They searched for records, translated them faithfully (sometimes more than once), and, most importantly, challenged my preconceptions as I began to piece together the huge documentary mosaic. I am grateful to each of them for their dedication to this project.

The Center for Advanced Holocaust Studies at the United States

Holocaust Memorial Museum, Washington, DC, and the Institute for Holocaust Studies at Yad Vashem, Jerusalem, awarded me visiting fellowships which allowed me to complete the research.

My wife, Hanna, frequently helped me in the archives. Professor Gabriel Gorodetsky of Tel Aviv University read the manuscript and made many helpful comments, as did my son, Eytan. Drs Leonard and Cynthia Glassman of Alexandria, Virginia, offered the hospitality of their home during my many visits to the National Archives of the United States. Jay Rosenberg prepared the maps. Kenneth Alford, with whose interpretation of the documents I have strongly disagreed, was nevertheless gracious enough to allow me full access to his document collection.

A few years ago I encountered Gabriel Schellinger in an archive in Jerusalem, reading the same Gold Train files that I had been working on. He had been a teenager in Budapest during the war, and witnessed at first hand many of the events described in this book. I was curious why a retired microbiologist would spend so much time pouring over the archival records. He replied that his family had lost all their possessions in the compulsory expropriations of 1944, and he was certain that the valuables had found their way to the Gold Train. He was not looking for any sort of restitution. but needed to know what happened to his parents' wedding rings. Gabriel passed away before this research was completed, but I would like to think that his question has finally been answered.

This project has taken many years, and my family has had to put up with my increasingly single-minded obsession as the story unfolded. To Eytan, Alon and especially my wife, Hanna, I offer this book as restitution.

R.W.Z
Jerusalem,
March, 2002

Abbreviations

Agency	Jewish Agency for Palestine
CGAAA	Commissaire Général des Affaires Allemandes et Autrichiennes
CIA	Central Intelligence Agency
CIC	Counter Intelligence Corps
Colmar	Colmar Archival Centre of the French Occupation of Germany and Austria
Congress	World Jewish Congress
CZA	Central Zionist Archives, Jerusalem
DEGOB	National Relief Committee for Deportees (Deportáltakat Gondozó Országos Bizottság)
HNA	Hungarian National Archives
IGCR	Intergovernmental Committee on Refugees
IRO	International Refugee Organization
JDC, or Joint	American Jewish Joint Distribution Committee
MAE	Archives du Ministère des Affaires Étrangères, Paris
MNSZP	Hungarian National Socialist Party (Magyarországi Nemzeti Szocialista Párt)
NA	National Archives, United States
OMGUS	Office of the Military Government, US Zone, Germany
OSS	Office of Strategic Services
PCIRO	Preparatory Commission of the International Refugee Organization
RSHA	Reichsicherheitshauptamt
SHAEF	Supreme Headquarters, Allied Expeditionary Force
SOE	Special Operations Executive

UNRRA	United Nations Relief and Rehabilitation Administration
USFA	United States Forces in Austria
USFET	United States Forces, European Theater
YVA	Yad Vashem Archives

Glossary

Bricha	'The Escape' – organization responsible for movement of Jews from eastern Europe to the American zones of occupation in Germany
Haganah	Jewish underground armed forces in British Mandate of Palestine
Mossad Le'Aliya Bet	Organization responsible for traffic of illegal immigrants to Mandatory Palestine
Palmah	Elite units of Jewish underground in Palestine

Maps

1. General map of Hungary with Soviet front in late December 1944, showing Debrecen, Szeged, Budapest, Székesfehérvár

2. Map of western Hungary showing route of train, December 1944: Budapest, Székesfehérvár, Zirc (Lókút/Óbánya), Győr, Sopron, Brennbergbánya

3. Sopron county, with Brennbergbánya and surrounding towns Kőszeg, Sopronkövesd, Sopronkőhida, Nagylózs

4. Route into Austria, March–April 1945: Brennbergbánya, Ágfalva, Wiener Neustadt, Wilhelmsburg, Wieselburg, Amstetten, Hallein, Hopfgarten

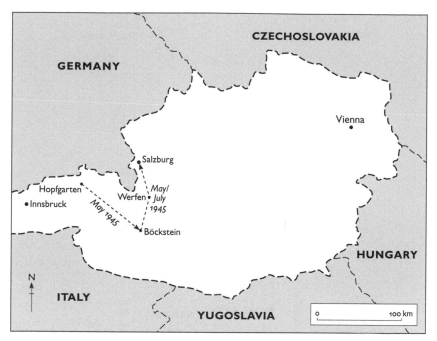

5. Route of May 1945: Hopfgarten–Böckstein, and of May–July 1945:
Böckstein–Werfen–Salzburg

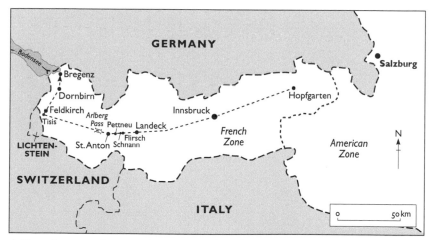

6. French zone of occupation: route of the lorries in Tyrol and Vorarlberg

7. Kingdom of Hungary 1867–1918

8. Hungary 1941

Introduction

> A society requires antecedents. Where these are not naturally at hand, where a community is new or reassembled after a long interval of dispersal or subjection, a necessary past tense to the grammar of being is created by intellectual and emotional fiat.
> – George Steiner, *In Bluebeard's Castle*, p. 1

Hungary is protected from the infiltration of other cultures by virtue of the uniqueness of the Magyar language. It is a barrier against incursion as effective as the Alps in protecting the Swiss. Foreign scholars of modern Hungarian history are also kept at bay by an additional obstacle – the complexity of Hungarian politics and its constantly shifting alliances. At the core of this complexity lie two unresolved issues: where is Hungary and who is a Hungarian? Hungary's borders changed radically three times within a 25-year period, and the make-up of the population changed accordingly. The only practical definition of a Hungarian was someone who spoke the Hungarian language. In the 'Vienna Accords' of 1940 Nazi Germany imposed border changes in south-eastern Europe that returned to Hungary the territories it had lost in the Treaty of Trianon in June 1920. Together with territory, Hungary also regained a large Jewish Magyar-speaking population. These people became the victims of ethnic cleansing in 1944. For a crucial four-month period (mid-March to late July 1944) the Holocaust in Hungary was directed by radical right-wing pro-German elements within Hungary. These Hungarian ethnic cleansers had adopted a racial definition of who was part of the Hungarian nation. The racial definition was borrowed from Nazi Germany, and it was exclusionary, unlike the cultural definition that was more widely accepted and more typically Hungarian.

In July 1944, when the administrative machinery of the Holocaust began to touch the Hungarian-speaking and totally Hungarian-acculturated Jews of the capital, Budapest, the traditional political leadership of Hungary regained control of 'Jewish policy' and dictated that the deportations to Auschwitz be stopped. Historians have offered many explanations for the sudden intervention of the Regent, Horthy, in July. In addition to the pressing diplomatic and political considerations that forced the Regent to act, Horthy wanted to restore a non-racial definition of Jews in Hungarian society. He considered that the fully assimilated Jews of the capital were 'good Hungarians'. So their fate was not to be Auschwitz.

However, there was an additional process at work in the Holocaust of Hungarian Jewry that ran parallel to the ethnic cleansing of the deportations. The expropriation and redistribution of Jewish assets in Hungary had almost universal support, because so many people benefited. It was an integral part of the ideology of the right-wing groups that came to the fore during the years of the Second World War. As opposed to the pro-German factions that sacrificed Hungarian interests in their devotion to the Third Reich, the *Hungarizmus* fascists wanted to preserve Jewish assets for Hungary. Differences over the fate of Jewish property between Germany and its Hungarian supporters and agents, who wanted the goods to benefit the Third Reich, and the Hungarian radical right, who wanted to keep Jewish wealth in Hungary, were a serious cause of tension between the two Axis countries. Ironically, the property of the Jews who were gassed in Auschwitz was considered to be part of the Hungarian national estate while the hapless owners were not.

In the last six months of the war, Hungary became a battlefield between the retreating forces of Hitler's Third Reich and the onward march of the Soviet Red Army. On 24 September 1944, Russian forces crossed Hungarian lines in occupied Romanian Transylvania. By October the fighting passed into Hungarian territory, and in early November the Red Army made its first (but unsuccessful) push towards Budapest, situated almost exactly in the middle of the country. In the face of these dramatic military developments, the German occupying forces imposed a new and more reliably pro-Nazi government led by the radical fascist Ferenc Szálasi. Immediately after coming to power on 16 October, the new government began to implement a scorched earth policy in the territories that were about to fall under Russian control. Food supplies and agricultural equipment, industrial stock and machinery, hospitals, cars and even horses, anything that could be moved, were loaded onto Danubian barges or fifty-wagon freight trains and taken across the western border of Hungary into Austria and Germany. The intention was to deprive the advancing Russians while at the same time strengthening the Third Reich in its last stand. From October 1944 until the first week of April 1945, when the Russians completed the occupation of all of Hungary, between three and eight 100-axle trains crossed the border daily. During these six months Hungary, by its own decision, gave away most of its economic resources.

The 'Gold Train' is the story of one train among the many, but it was entirely unlike all the others. This train was organized in secret, and took fourteen weeks to complete a journey that normally takes less than half a day. It was the culmination of years of planning and carefully organized plunder. This was not a flight in panic from the Red Army; it was an attempt to save something of the social revolution that the Hungarian ultra-nationalist and anti-Semitic right wing had brought about. The train carried a large part of the transportable wealth of the Jews who had lived within the enlarged borders of wartime Hungary. Gold, wedding rings, watches, jewellery, silverware, cash, stamp collections, cameras, binoculars, even Persian carpets and expensive furniture – enough to fill a freight train of almost fifty wagons.

The occupying German forces also plundered Hungarian Jewry. But the Germans did not have the time or the control of the countryside needed to plunder the Jewish middle class and the poorer Jews. The German experts in asset stripping and spoliation that accompanied the Wehrmacht when Germany occupied Hungary in March 1944 dealt exclusively with the wealthiest sectors of Jewish society, the largest industrialists, all of whom were able to buy their own safety. The story told here deals with the seizure of the transferable belongings of the majority of the Jews of Hungary, not of the wealthiest elite, but of the comfortably off, the middle class and the poor. How their possessions were taken from them and transported out of Hungary is one part of the events recounted here. The ultimate fate of these assets became a *cause célèbre* in the diplomacy of post-war reconstruction and refugee rehabilitation, and in internal Jewish affairs as well. The politics of dealing with recovered victim loot forms the second half of this study.

Like all historical accounts, this work is an attempt to rediscover the past. The passage of time, the passing of people involved, and the dispersal of records make any historical research difficult. The story of the Gold Train has, in addition to the vagaries of time, been clouded by myths concerning the fate of its fabulous missing cargo, myths that are still being actively propagated. The earliest account of the Gold Train, published in a Budapest newspaper in November 1945, set the tone for all subsequent tellings of the story: 'It goes beyond any novel of the Wild West, there is no detective story that comes even near to the fantastic history of the journey of the Gold Train.'[1] Myths about the Gold Train have also been encouraged by media images of Nazi gold and the exciting genre of post-war adventures. Hollywood was producing films about Nazi loot as early as 1948,[2] while the real story of the Hungarian Gold Train was still unfolding. One full-length feature film even told the story of a trainload of loot escaping into the territory of the Reich moments before the Allied liberation. *The Train*[3] presented a compelling image of a train carrying the whole artistic heritage of France worth an entirely unimaginable amount of money. Although it was not based on a specific historical event, this cinematic account and others like it helped to create the popular conception of trainloads of Nazi loot of fabulous value. When the story of the Hungarian Gold Train resurfaced in the 1990s it was strongly influenced by these images of drama and excitement skilfully created on film. In the popular reconstruction of the past, Hollywood is more important than history.

The real fate of the plundered assets of Hungarian Jewry was intentionally obscured in the immediate post-war years, and again more recently. Huge amounts of money are involved, and the claims concerning the train are still unresolved. (The most recent claim, for $5 billion, based on the missing assets of the Gold Train, was submitted to a New York court a few days before this Introduction was written.)

How and why these tendentious accounts have taken the place of what was once the widely known fate of the Gold Train is a story as interesting and as complex as the story of the train itself. Fantasies can become 'facts' with a weight and seriousness all their own.

But the boldest and most dangerous myths were those that inspired the perpetrators of ethnic cleansing. Two myths in particular condemned Hungarian Jewry to its fate: the fantasy that all Jews were wealthy, and an unrealistic belief in the possibility of seizing prosperity and economic well-being from one ethnic community and transferring it to another. But prosperity and well-being are fragile constructs, easily destroyed by the forces of history, and the notion that the glitter of gold and the lure of diamonds are immutable and last for ever is the greatest myth of all.

History can serve different political and commercial interests, and even today, three generations after the events described, the story recounted here remains alive. In the reconstructed memory of a community that was savagely abused during the war years, and intimidated and hounded in the post-war Communist era, the boundaries between fact and wishful thinking are often blurred. Newly available records make it possible to separate fact and fiction, and to lay to rest one of the unexplained dramas of the last days of the Second World War.

I

Hungary and the Jews

The Magyar-speaking people of the Habsburg Empire achieved independence in 1867, when Hungary and Austria were defined as equal but separate states under the Dual Monarchy. For the next fifty years the borders of the Hungarian state included the large majority of Hungarian-speakers. This population was spread widely through south-eastern Europe, in areas where other national minorities co-existed side by side with Hungarians, and the state also encompassed a very large, but mixed, population of non-Magyar national minorities. According to the census of 1910, there were 9,944,627 'Magyars' (i.e. Magyar-speaking people) in a total population of 18,264,533 – 54.4 per cent. This slender majority was achieved by including Magyar-speaking Jews (5.9 per cent of the population), and excluding Croatia-Slavonia.[1] In the jostling for power and influence within the country, the ruling Magyars had to be constantly alert to the fact that their numeric superiority might be challenged. As membership in a national minority was defined by spoken language, any community or ethnic group that adopted the Hungarian language was an asset in the Magyar struggle to maintain supremacy.

At the beginning of the nineteenth century there were 83,000 Jews in Hungary (twice as many as lived in France at the same time), but they represented only 1 per cent of the population. During the period up to 1914 the Jewish population grew rapidly as a result of immigration from eastern Europe. By 1848 there were 336,000 Jews in Hungary, and in 1910 there were over 911,000. The governments of the time encouraged this migration. In return, the Jews 'showed their gratitude by eager assimilation, ardent patriotism, and financial support of the government, and the party in power'.[2] As the Jews learned to speak Hungarian, they were counted as Magyars in the statistics. In fact, during the entire period Jewish immigration was the greatest single Magyar-speaking gain – a fact that defused any outspoken opposition to the rapid growth of the Jewish community. The government pursued a policy of aggressive Magyarization, increasingly enforcing the use of the Hungarian language in schools, in the press and in cultural institutions. The Jews participated willingly in this process, abandoning the German or Yiddish of their vernacular and adopting Hungarian culture with 'spontaneous eagerness'.[3] Although the Jewish community was divided on the extent of the cultural Magyarization to be adopted (might Hungarian replace Hebrew in religious services? would cultural assimilation be allowed to replace Jewish religious traditions?), both sections of the community, the modernizing 'Neolog' and the traditionalist 'Orthodox', wholeheartedly adopted Magyar nationalism and Magyar political aims. Hungarian Jewry closely identified with the state that offered them formal emancipation from the legal constraints which inhibited Jewish life elsewhere in Europe, as well as providing huge opportunities for economic and social progress.

The formal emancipation of Hungarian Jewry came shortly after Hungary achieved its own independence. In December 1867 Law XVII was enacted, which stipulated that 'The Israelite inhabitants of the country are declared to possess equal rights with the Christian inhabitants in the exercise of all civic and political functions. All laws, usages, and ordinances contravening this principle are hereby rescinded.'[4] In 1895 the Jewish religion was recognized as a 'received religion', giving it the same status as all other churches except the Roman Catholic, which enjoyed special privileges. (It is ironic that the founders of political Zionism in the 1890s, Theodor Herzl and Max Nordau, came from Hungary, because Zionism did not make significant inroads in Hungarian Jewish life until after the experiences of the Holocaust.)

As elsewhere during the nineteenth century, the Jewish population was highly urbanized. The 200,000 Jews who lived in Budapest in 1910 made up 20 per cent of the city's population (four times more than the proportion of Jews in Berlin). They were more heavily employed in the professions, trade and commerce than the rest of the population, and by 1910 every second Hungarian lawyer or physician was Jewish. Jews were particularly well represented in the media, both as journalists and as newspaper owners. While part of Hungarian Jewry prospered, real wealth was concentrated in the hands of a few hundred families. The great majority of the Jews, especially the immigrants in the north-east, 'lived in poverty, often abject poverty'.[5] After 1910 the Jewish community began to decline in numbers. Emigration from Hungary, together with assimilation (conversion to Christianity) and a declining birth rate, caused the community to shrink by about 30,000 in the years before 1930. But the Jews of Hungary continued to gain in prominence. Emperor Franz Josef elevated twenty-five families to baronial rank, and almost 300 others were ennobled. Hungary was a predominantly agricultural society, and life was defined by the social relationships of landowner, gentry and labourer. The Magyars did not favour commerce, and this created an imbalance which the Jewish community was able to correct. At all levels, from the local shopkeeper to the most powerful industrialists, the Jews played an increasingly prominent role in Hungarian economic life.

For most of the nineteenth century, the occasional outbursts of anti-Semitism did not disturb the growing Jewish community. They were local and sporadic, and were soon countered by the authorities. In 1875 a deputy in the Hungarian parliament formulated an anti-Semitic platform, but he was soon marginalized. In the general elections of 1884, seventeen members were elected on anti-Semitic platforms, but the anti-Jewish parliamentary group was one of the smallest in the lower house, and other parties treated them with contempt.[6] In 1895 the newly-formed Catholic People's Party (Katolikus Néppárt) adopted an anti-Jewish platform that was typical of a clerical and conservative party. 'Jewish liberalism' and socialism were targeted as 'destructive and anti-Christian'. But this was not a racial anti-Semitism, and Jewish converts to Catholicism were excluded from the anti-Semitic attacks. Further, the Jewish grandees were equally hostile to the progressive ideologies that had some support within the Jewish community. As the government opposed any outbursts of anti-Jewish feeling, and as the Hungarian population was generally tolerant, anti-Semitism had little impact prior to the First World War.[7] Nevertheless, certain patterns began to appear. The elections of 1884 showed that the strongest support for anti-Semitic politics came from areas with a large Swabian (i.e. Volksdeutsche) population. In addition to the antipathies that this German-speaking minority held specifically for Jews, it was indicative of a growing resentment of other ethnic minorities for the aggressive Magyarization policies of the government, with which the Jews were so closely identified. The Jewish-owned press and Jewish journalists of Budapest were strongly jingoistic and Magyar chauvinist. As a result, they became the target of a growing hostility among the other ethnic minorities spread across Hungary. By identifying so closely with the hegemonic Magyar half of the population, the Jews alienated the non-Hungarian other half. And within Magyar society, the anti-Semitism of the very influential Catholic church defined clear limits to the degree of Jewish acceptance in the broader society. The very success of Jewish integration and cultural assimilation in Hungary during the nineteenth century carried with it the threat of its reversal and of a more ominous future.

Two events immediately after the First World War transformed Hungarian political life, and also seriously undermined (although not yet destroyed) the mutually advantageous relations between Hungarian Jews and the Hungarian ruling class. As the war came to an end and the Habsburg Empire collapsed, Hungary declared itself a republic. At the same time, the national minorities of Hungary opted to break away and seek their own independence – a process which ended with Hungary's total dismemberment. For a brief period in 1919 a coalition of left-wing Social Democrats and Communists established a radical regime under the leadership of Béla Kun, who headed the Council of People's Commissars of the Hungarian Soviet Republic. This regime imposed a series of revolutionary reforms, including the abolition of titles and ranks, nationalization of all commercial enterprises employing more than twenty people, the separation of church and state, and the secularization of education. But this experiment in a Soviet-style system lasted only five months. The reforms were enforced by widespread violence, and the regime was soon overthrown by the intervention of Entente forces, and by Hungarian anti-Bolshevik groups led by Admiral Miklós Horthy out of Szeged and Count István Bethlen from Vienna. Béla Kun himself escaped to Moscow.

The brief experience with a revolutionary government (in which many Jews were prominent), and the success of the counter-revolutionary violence unleashed by Admiral Horthy's small army, were the formative political experiences in Hungary for the next twenty-five years. All Jews were vilified because of their role in Béla Kun's short-lived Soviet Republic (thirty-two of the forty-five commissars, including Kun himself, were Jewish or of Jewish origin),[8] and thousands of Jews and leftists were killed and robbed in the White Terror instigated by Horthy's troops.

The violence eventually subsided, and the conservative, nationalist and militarist world-view that was summed up as the 'Szeged Idea' (i.e. associated with the forces that Horthy gathered at the city of Szeged at the start of his campaign) became the ruling spirit of Hungary between the wars. Horthy, venerated by the middle classes as well as by the landowners as the saviour of Hungary, was appointed Regent. He had the right to convene and dissolve parliament, and the right to initiate or delay legislation. He was the commanding officer of the armed forces, and the prime minister was responsible to the Regent alone (in fact if not by law). For the entire period from 1920, Horthy enjoyed immense prestige and was able to use his authority to oversee all Hungarian governments, until the Germans finally deposed him in October 1944.

The second, definitive, development was the Treaty of Peace signed at Trianon on 4 June 1920. This harsh peace settlement after the First World War deprived Hungary of 71.4 per cent of her pre-war territory, and 63.5 per cent of her population. 'Trianon Hungary' was reduced to a population of 7,615,000, while 3,200,000 Magyar-speakers became subjects of neighbouring Romania, Czechoslovakia, Yugoslavia and Austria. The changes in the borders, and the imposed restrictions on the national pretensions of the Magyar state, were traumatic. Just as Horthy's counter-revolutionary victory over the experiment of Béla Kun shifted Hungary's internal politics sharply to the right, so the Treaty of Trianon determined Hungary's foreign policy for over a generation. There was a universal resolve not to accept the finality of the settlement. 'Nem, Nem, Soha!' – 'No, No, Never!' – was the mantra repeated at every public political occasion and in every classroom.[9] Hungary became an irredentist state, with the main foreign policy objective of revising the borders of 1920. Inevitably, Hungary was drawn into alliance with the other country keenest to revise the post-First World War peace treaties, that also felt a serious sense of grievance and frustrated national mission – Germany.

FASCISM IN HUNGARY

During the 1920s Hungary enjoyed a degree of prosperity. The ruling Party of National Unity (Nemzeti Egység Pártja, or NEP) combined social democratic, centrist and rightist splinter groups to form a stable political bloc that gave parliamentary backing to the prime minister, István Bethlen. Supported by a credible majority in parliament, and enjoying the support of the Regent Horthy, Bethlen was able to mobilize foreign capital that generated real economic growth. In 1920, the parliament passed a law of *numerus clausus*, limiting the proportion of Jews and other minorities in Hungarian universities – the first effectively anti-Semitic law in post-1918 Europe. Bethlen allowed the law to pass into oblivion, and at the same time his government ennobled a number of prominent Jewish personalities, who were also given seats in the upper house of parliament. Hungarian Jewry was not unduly affected by the law of 1920, and it was withdrawn eight years later.

But the idyll was short-lived. From 1930 Hungary was seriously affected by the great depression, and the prosperity of the 1920s vanished in the face of a sharp decline in wheat prices and industrial production. Hungarian politics now shifted dramatically to the right, and the issues of Trianon and the anti-Semitic and anti-Bolshevik themes of the 'Szeged Idea' came to the fore. Unemployment and declining prospects made more and more people look to the success of Italian fascism and the growing strength of the German National Socialist movement. Hitler's rise to power in January 1933 opened up the possibility of an alliance that would force a revision of the Treaty of Trianon.

In September 1932 the Regent appointed Gyula Gömbös as prime minister. Gömbös had been one of Horthy's most loyal supporters in the counter-revolution, in which he served as a junior officer. When he resigned his commission he entered politics as a member of the governing NEP. Soon, however, he founded a small 'Party of Racial Defence' dedicated to anti-Semitism. Gömbös became the focus of the political aspirations of all sectors within Hungary that were dissatisfied with Bethlen's policies. Bethlen's empathy with the Jewish grandees, and his willingness to honour the commitments to the Allies under Trianon, melded together in the minds of Gömbös's supporters.

During the four years of his government (1932–1936) Gömbös did not initiate any major reforms. Nevertheless, he transformed the political atmosphere, elevating the wild and often incoherent demagogy of the fringe radical parties to the status of prime ministerial pronouncements. It is difficult today to convey the incoherence, the breathtaking confusion, of political discourse among the Hungarian radical right wing. The mixture of Magyar chauvinism, racial anti-Semitism, anti-intellectualism, and populism in social policies (land reform, hostility to inherited privilege, etc.) encouraged an excited and theatrical rhetorical style. Gömbös's first address as prime minister was typical of the genre:

'I stand here before you as your Leader. I might lead you on a new path, but do not fool yourselves by expecting miracles. Our path will be a steep, rocky, thorny one, but I feel, I know, that it will lead us to the goal. Hungarians! My brothers! Ignite the candle of trust at the life-fire of my soul that burns for you, my nation! Spread this illumination!'[10]

Gömbös's heir to the leadership of the radical right was Ferenc Szálasi (whose role in the Gold Train saga will be discussed in Chapter 3). In 1940 Szálasi was released after two years in jail. When he began to talk in a similar and even more obscure manner, many of his followers asked if he had lost his mind in prison. During the war years Szálasi's ideological writings and speeches became even more incoherent. Nevertheless, in 1944 he became prime minister.

During the mid-1930s the radical right-wing parties failed to make any headway in parliament. The success of the National Socialists in Germany was not repeated in Hungary, and in the 1935 elections the extremist parties won only four out of 256 seats in the lower house.[11] In part, this is because Gömbös and his radical supporters had co-opted the NEP and the political centre, gaining complete control of that party by 1935. But it was also because so much of the reactionary and racist rhetoric of the extremist right-wing anti-Semitic parties had already been adopted by respectable society. Their inflammatory slogans were now commonplace. Although the Gömbös government did not introduce any radical legislation of its own, it did bring about a dramatic change in the staffing of the civil service and army. Politically reliable right-wingers were appointed to official positions throughout the country, and many of them were (like Gömbös himself) drawn from the German-speaking Swabian minority.[12]

Gömbös also realigned Hungarian foreign policy, and tried hard to build an alliance with Hitler and Mussolini. In June 1933, only a few months after Hitler became chancellor of Germany, Gömbös visited him in Berlin. Although the visit was secret at the time and concluded without any official statements, it was an important step in the forging of an Hungarian–German alliance. Shortly after the visit, the two countries signed an economic agreement which greatly increased their bilateral trade and encouraged Hungarian dependence on German manufactured goods (especially armaments) in exchange for Hungarian agricultural exports. Gömbös later informed his closest political associates that at their meeting Hitler had told the Hungarian prime minister of his designs on Czechoslovakia and encouraged his guest to believe that Hungary would be able to regain some of its northern territories lost at Trianon.[13]

In 1935 Gömbös visited Germany again, this time to confer with Hermann Goering, the Prussian Minister of the Interior and head of the police and Gestapo. German economic penetration of the Hungarian economy was proceeding rapidly, and German investors, tourists and Nazi party agents travelled throughout Hungary with increasing frequency. The Hungarian prime minister assured Goering that he would adopt the political system of the Third Reich as a model for Hungary, and would bring about this change in the near future.

Gömbös died a year later, before he could fulfil his promise to Goering. While he did not introduce any major political or anti-Semitic reforms, he laid the foundation for the fateful alliance between Hungary and Nazi Germany. He managed to transform the state apparatus, and changed the political atmosphere in Hungary by moving the centre far closer to right-wing extremist policies.

The prime ministers who came after Gömbös – Kálmán Darányi (1936–1938) and Béla Imrédy (1938–1939) – endorsed Gömbös's agenda: a German orientation in foreign policy and an anti-Semitic domestic policy. But there was one, ironic, break with the past. Whereas Gömbös was a self-confessed right-wing extremist and overtly hostile to the Jews, in fact he did little to implement any anti-Jewish policy. Darányi and Imrédy, on the other hand, who were believed to be closer to the conservative and 'sensible' school of Bethlen, each initiated significant anti-Jewish programmes. Both brought Hungary closer to the abyss of 1944.

On 5 March 1938 Darányi announced that Hungary would undertake a massive programme of rearmament. The government's new policy, known as the Győr Programme, was the result of constant pressure from the Hungarian army's General Staff. The generals wished to prepare Hungary for its 'historic role' in the forthcoming campaign against Bolshevism, arguing that Hungary's current military weakness was due to socialist and Jewish influence. A rapid expansion of Hungary's military strength was the inevitable consequence of the pro-German foreign policy pursued since Hitler came to power. At the same time, Darányi announced that the government would take strong steps against Jewish influence in economic and cultural life, and would ruthlessly repress any left-wing agitation.

Within a week, Germany occupied Austria and suddenly Hungary and the Third Reich shared a common border. Relations between the two countries continued to improve, and in November 1938 Hungary received the first of a series of territorial rewards as Hitler's loyal ally. Through the mediation of Italy and Germany, Hungary was able to re-annex the Magyar-speaking areas of Czechoslovakia. Other territorial gains were to follow.

The second part of Darányi's Győr Programme was a watershed for the Jewish community. (Randolph Braham, doyen of the historians of the Holocaust in Hungary, has described it as 'the beginning of the end of this once flourishing Jewish community'.)[14] Darányi's speech showed that his purportedly liberal-conservative government shared the anti-Semitism of the extremist radical parties and intended to express its views in legislation. He introduced a bill designed to reduce Jewish economic and professional life to 20 per cent of the overall national total. While the Jews were only 5 per cent of the population, they were disproportionately represented in the professions, and the 20 per cent quota was expected to cause 15,000 Jewish professionals to lose their jobs.[15] The law asserted that imposing restrictions on the Jews was 'a national duty'. It was introduced to parliament in April, one month after Darányi's Győr speech, and was debated in the lower house during nine sittings, from 8 to 15 May. Although the new policy met with some opposition in parliament,[16] its adoption became inevitable when the various Christian churches endorsed the legislation, which was enacted as Law XV (1938).

Darányi was replaced as prime minister by Béla Imrédy in May 1938, while the First Anti-Jewish Law was being debated in parliament. Imrédy, like Darányi before him, was brought to power by a conservative anti-radical right group, with the intention that he should block the growth of the extreme right-wing political factions. The anti-Jewish legislation was justified as a means of pre-empting the radical right. But the new prime minister had his own agenda: to deepen relations with Germany, and achieve closer coordination with German foreign policy. By the end of 1938 Imrédy was also planning a second anti-Jewish law, to tighten the restrictions on the Jews. Under his leadership, the governing party (now renamed Magyar Élet Pártja or MEP – the 'Party of Hungarian Life') began to advocate anti-Jewish policies normally associated with the extremists. Not only was the Jewish role in Hungarian economic life to be drastically reduced, but Jews were to be excluded from the political and cultural life of the nation as well. The central plank of the party's economic policy was 'supervision and liquidation of Jewish property without injury to production and national wealth'.[17] In line with his sympathy for the policies of Nazi Germany, Imrédy called on Hungary to participate in a 'Europe-wide solution of the Jewish question'.

Imrédy's initial public reputation was based on his success as Minister of Finance in the Gömbös government and later as head of the Hungarian National Bank. He was considered one of the best and the brightest of the economic managers of the period. By endorsing the anti-Jewish legislation of his predecessor and attempting to expand it into a policy of expropriating Jewish property as the pillar of a policy of economic reform, Imrédy gave credence to the intention of the radical right to seize Jewish material possessions as the catalyst of a new Hungarian prosperity. The illusion that despoiling a minority community would lead to the enrichment of the general community and to a new prosperity was to be a recurring theme in Hungarian political discourse, and a major cause of the events of 1944.

Ironically, opponents of Imrédy's pro-Axis policy decided to undermine the prime minister's credibility by circulating leaflets attesting to the fact that Imrédy was part Jewish. Horthy called on Imrédy to refute the 'accusations', but the prime minister was unable to disprove the documents that 'proved' some Jewish family ancestry. Accordingly, in mid-February 1939 Imrédy resigned. Horthy's own account of these events is particularly revealing. The ambivalent attitude of the Hungarian conservative political elite to the Jewish question is apparent from the Regent's memoirs, almost to the point of parody. Imrédy had to be dismissed, Horthy recalled, because of the prime minister's 'rabid anti-Semitism'. The fact that Imrédy was unable to disprove to Horthy the allegations about his Jewish ancestry was, according to the Regent, only the pretext.[18] As head of state, Admiral Horthy was the ultimate defender of the constitutional rights of Hungarian Jewry. The convoluted logic of this account of the dismissal of Imrédy was also the best example of the Hungarian establishment's confusion concerning its attitude towards the Jews.

THE RADICAL RIGHT

By the late 1930s Hungary was obsessed with the 'Jewish problem'. Jews were considered to be too numerous, too conspicuous, and too prosperous for their numbers in the overall population. Anti-Semites, in Hungary as elsewhere, often held contradictory beliefs without being concerned at the logical conflict. Thus the Jews were 'too predominant in Hungarian cultural life' while they were also foreign and detached from Hungarian ways; there were 'too many Jewish captains of industry, banking and commerce' while the Jews were also a Bolshevik threat. Their religion was obscurantist and insular yet they were a threat to the rule of Christendom in Hungary. But most significantly of all, the important role of the Jewish community in Hungarian life was an obstacle in the development of close relations with Nazi Germany. And increasingly, Hungarian opinion saw the ties with the Third Reich as Hungary's only option for revising the Treaty of Trianon and for keeping the Soviet Union at bay.

During the period from 1932 to 1936, Gyula Gömbös co-opted to the government programme many of the slogans and most of the agenda of the radical right parties. As a result, these parties remained small, with insignificant representation in parliament (a total of four seats between three parties of the right-wing fringe, in a lower house of 256 members).[19] There was no need to support a fringe party when the government promised to implement the popular policies of these parties. Finding themselves without any real mass support, the right-wing groupings spent most of their time in faction fighting and ideological controversy, fusing and splitting again with tiresome regularity. However, this situation was transformed by one man: Ferenc Szálasi.

Szálasi was a career officer and a member of the army General Staff. Of mixed Magyar, Slovak and Armenian background, Szálasi developed a political ideology that included a little of almost every volkish, racist and chauvinist thinking of his time. He had been strongly influenced by Turanianism, an exotic nineteenth-century pseudo-anthropology and etymology which argued that the Turkic Hungarian tribes were the original biblical Semites (and therefore Jesus was a Hungarian and the Bible was originally written in a Magyar-like language; accordingly, European Christian civilization was a gift of Hungarian culture). But he refined some of the wilder contemporary ideologies and attempted to find political answers to the problems of the multi-ethnicity of the Danubian basin. His solution was a state which he variously called the 'Carpathian-Danubian Great Fatherland' or the 'United Lands and the March of Hungaria' – a union of happy ethnic minorities ruled by Hungarians with the language of the latter as official language for 'the direction and leadership of the state'.[20] Szálasi believed that the Magyars had a unique role not only to rule the Danube region but to be a light and a model for civilizing the rest of Europe. The centrality of Hungary, its language, its experience and its duty, were all summed up in a Szálasi-coined term – 'Hungarism' (*Hungarizmus*). Hungarism was the distinctive characteristic of his ideology and of the movement he led – the Arrow Cross or *Nyilas*.

When Szálasi retired from the army, he launched his political movement with an appeal to public opinion in the name of 'God, peasant, citizen and soldier'. The platform of his movement included the restoration of the fatherland's old grandeur, the rejection of the Trianon Treaty, defaulting on all debts to non-fascist states, the assumption by the state of domestic debt (mainly agricultural), the elimination of all

Jewish influence, the 'eradication of the Jewish credit economy' and the establishment of the 'United Lands of Hungaria'.[21]

The originality of Szálasi's political thinking was a matter of the greatest consequence after 1935. His competitors on the right shared many ideas and objectives with Szálasi's programme, but they totally rejected his belief that Hungary alone had the task of leading southeastern Europe, or that Hungarism could be a model for the reorganization of Europe as a whole. Szálasi's opponents on the right believed that the pre-eminence which Szálasi accorded to Hungary belonged in fact to Germany, to the Third Reich and specifically to Adolf Hitler. Only through Hitler's leadership and Germany's victory, they believed, would Hungary be able to reclaim her own historic borders and rights, and Europe be protected from the Soviet Union. The groups who believed in the ideology of National Socialism and in the primacy of Germany called themselves 'National Socialist', as distinct from the *Hungarizmus* groups of which Szálasi's Arrow Cross was the most prominent.

A number of political figures were associated with the Hungarian National Socialist groups, but the only ones of relevance here are Count Fidél Pálffy, László Endre and László Baky. Pálffy, like most of the actors in this drama, participated as a young officer in the forces associated with Horthy in Szeged in 1919–1920 (he was a liaison officer between the counter-revolutionary forces and the French occupation forces). After he was demobilized he returned to his family estates, but lost them to Czechoslovakia when the border was redrawn at Trianon. In the depression of 1929–1930, he lost the small Hungarian estate he owned. By the 1930s Pálffy was an insolvent member of the aristocracy, and like other members of his class who were also financially embarrassed, he was drawn to radical fringe politics. Pálffy founded the United National Socialist Party (Egyesült Nemzeti Szocialista Párt), with its outspokenly pro-German Nazi style and platform.

The National Socialist groups merged and split, with each other, with other marginal groups, and even with Szálasi's growing Arrow Cross movement, according to the needs of extremist politics at the time. There is little point in recounting these twists and turns. The one consistent factor throughout the period from the late 1930s until the end of the war was their loyalty to Germany and the precedence they gave German interests over the immediate needs of Hungary. Berlin was fully informed of their activities, and ensured that their political groups always had the funds necessary to operate. This allowed them to forge special links to German intelligence – which, as we shall see, also has a role in the story of the Train. The Hungarian National Socialists were so dependent on funds from Berlin that they can fairly be labelled as German agents.

In addition to differences over the correct attitude to Germany, Szálasi and the National Socialists differed in the degree and nature of their hatred of the Jews. Szálasi shared the general dislike for the Jews. He distrusted cosmopolitanism, and often pointed to the Jewish prominence among Marxists. As his earliest political programmes showed, he blamed the Jews for the economic distress of the Hungarian peasants, and resented the Jewish role in the Hungarian economy. His solution was deportation of the Jews out of Hungary. But 'deportation', in Szálasi's usage, did not have the genocidal meaning it was to acquire in 1944. He simply wanted the Jews to leave. After he came to power in October 1944, his Arrow Cross movement was associated with very brutal, murderous attacks on the Jews of Budapest. There is no evidence that Szálasi himself inspired these attacks or that he shared the pathological hatred of the Jews that characterized the Hungarian National Socialists.[22]

Nevertheless, his party was clearly anti-Semitic, and this was one of the few principles of his intellectual world that was understood and shared by all his followers. The rest of his political theorizing was largely incomprehensible. In 1936 he published his thoughts under the title *Road and Goal* (*Út és cél*), from which the following is a fair sample:

The ideological foundation of Hungarism's national economy and work-order is Social Nationalism and its conscious practice. Only through the ideology and practice of Social Nationalism can the individual become a true national socialist . . . National Socialism means nationalist order in socialism, Social Nationalism means socialist order in nationalism, therefore: spiritual order in matter, material order in the spirit. The soul's order in the body, the body's order in the soul.[23]

Perhaps it is not surprising that by early 1937 his group was limited to only a few thousand members. Nevertheless, Szálasi was considered a risk to public security and he was arrested, together with his closest associates. In April that year his party was banned, as part of a general crackdown on pro-German parties following the death of Gömbös.[24]

The arrest and trial brought the fledgling movement a lot of free publicity, and made them appear more substantial than they really were. Middle-class elements began to be attracted to the movement, despite the street violence and demonstrations associated with the Arrow Cross. And other small radical groups sought out Szálasi. The most significant of these mergers, in light of subsequent events, took place in autumn 1937. László Endre had been sub-prefect of the Gödöllő district since December 1937. He ran for parliament in the elections of 1935 as an unendorsed candidate of the ruling NEP, but was badly defeated by the endorsed candidate. By summer 1937 he reappeared as the leader of the 'Race Protecting Socialist Party'. Shortly afterwards he met Szálasi, and became a quick convert to Hungarism. Together they formed a new party, combining Endre's group and Szálasi's proscribed party. The new party was called the Hungarian National Socialist Party, and Endre accepted Szálasi's unconditional leadership. (During 1944, Endre was one of the handful of Hungarian leaders most actively involved in the mass murder of Hungarian Jews. Given Szálasi's views on this matter, it is clear that Endre maintained a large degree of freedom of manoeuvre when the Germans actually occupied Hungary.) At the same time, one of the leaders of the Swabian German-speaking minority in Hungary, Ferenc Rothen, also joined Szálasi. The Swabians had been carefully cultivated by the German Foreign Office, as had other *volksdeutsche* communities throughout eastern Europe. By 1937 the Swabians were closely identified with Nazi policy, and it was inevitable that they should be attracted to the newly-created Hungarian party bearing the approved brand name 'national socialist'. Rothen was almost certainly a German agent, and the same is probably true of Endre.

The creation of the united party was announced on 23 October 1937. Szálasi addressed the enthusiastic crowd with an explanation of his social and economic policy, eschewing the stranger elements of Hungarism and his vision of the 'United Lands of Hungaria'. Instead, he talked about social structures in slogans which must have sounded revolutionary in a largely agricultural society like Hungary's, so conscious of caste and class:

Within the architecture of the people's community the peasant is the support of the nation, the worker is the builder of the nation, the intelligentsia is the leader and guide of the nation, the army is the defending power of the nation.

The three pillars of his policy, he explained, were the moral and spiritual pillars ('true belief in God, true love for Christ') and the material ('everything belongs to the people's community which is embodied by the state').[25] This later 'pillar' was not anti-materialist but rather hinted at a redistribution of wealth to the 'people's community' – i.e. to the real Magyars. It was one of the very few policy items on the Arrow Cross agenda that was consistently pursued.

Berlin began to take note of Szálasi as he gained prominence in Hungary. His trial and conviction were widely reported in the leading German press, and a 'brilliant future' was forecast for the man who would unite the various radical right-wing factions in Hungary.[26] But this public display of enthusiasm hid a deeper concern in Berlin. Szálasi was Hungarist and as such he would not be willing to place the interests of Nazi Germany over the interests of Hungary. There were other small political groups in Hungary that would have done whatever Berlin wanted, believing that the triumph of Nazism in Europe would serve the interests of Hungary in the long run. The group associated with Count Fidél Pálffy was the most significant of these slavishly pro-Berlin parties, and in 1937 they refused to join with Szálasi. Berlin's dilemma was that while Szálasi had the ability to mobilize the street, and perhaps even masses of Hungarians, Pálffy did not. Therefore Berlin had little choice but to back Szálasi, and finance him, in the hope that eventually they would be able to bend him to their will. This incongruity in Germany's policies to the radical right in Hungary remained alive until the very last moments of the Second World War. It underlies some of the most dramatic steps taken by the Germans in 1944. And, as will be shown, it explains some of the more mysterious turns taken in the story of the Gold Train.

The German interest in Szálasi, and the increasing material aid they provided to the radical right, was only one reason for a huge surge in support in Hungary for right-wing political parties in 1938 and early 1939. The fact that Germany suddenly acquired a common border with Hungary after the Anschluss in Austria, and the increasingly pro-German foreign policies of the Darányi and the Imrédy governments, lent an aura of respectability to the 'national socialist' character of the Arrow Cross. The first serious inroad that the party made into government circles was László Endre's appointment as sub-prefect of Gödöllő. The Győr Programme (March 1938) calling for rearmament, and also for restrictions on the Jews, lent added credibility to Szálasi's policy pronouncements. Uniformed Arrow Cross teams flooded Budapest and country towns with propaganda leaflets, and, mimicking the street violence that characterized the early stages of Hitler's rise to power in Germany, they attacked Jews and other targets.

Szálasi's party was quickly becoming a mass movement, and the government in Budapest became alarmed. In June he was arrested again, and in July 1938 the High Court sentenced him to three years' imprisonment for subversive activities against the state and the social order. At his appeal – which failed – in August, Szálasi made one of his more memorable public statements: 'You say that my theory is confused and incomprehensible. Why, God, too, created the world from chaos.'[27]

As long as the legally constituted government of Hungary complied with Germany's needs within reason, the authorities in Berlin were satisfied to keep the right-wing parties on a short leash. They performed two important services for Germany, by mobilizing mass support for anti-Bolshevik, anti-Jewish and pro-German policies within Hungary, and by keeping up the pressure on the government party to support such policies.

But Berlin was wary of them as potential candidates for government. It was fully cognisant of the Hungarian chauvinism of some right-wing circles, which could easily be turned against German interests. Also, these circles were too erratic and incompetent to be entrusted with government except as a last resort. These facts were clear to the specialists on Hungary in Berlin.[28] Nevertheless, two schools of thought developed on Hungarian affairs, each associated with a different agency. The German Foreign Office preferred to keep the radical right at a distance, while encouraging them in their mimicry of the Third Reich and cultivating the belief that Germany would assist them reach power when the time came. On the other hand, Himmler's *Sicherheitsdienst* maintained its own intelligence network in the

Balkans and paid particular attention to Hungary. The SS officer in charge of this Balkan network was Wilhelm Höttl. Höttl was a strong advocate of support for the non-Hungarist, extremely pro-German National Socialists, and he consistently supported them against Szálasi. Höttl (who will be introduced more fully in a later chapter), and his closest associate and friend in the Hungarian right wing, László Baky, both play key roles in the saga of the Gold Train.

At the same time as Endre was making his way among the radical right-wing groups, László Baky was beginning to play a strategic role in extremist politics. Baky was described by Miklós Lackó, the leading historian of the Arrow Cross, as 'the prototype of the morally depraved adventurer of sadistic disposition'.[29] As an army officer, Baky had fought with Horthy's troops in Szeged and had taken an active role during the White Terror that followed the collapse of Béla Kun's government. From 1925 he served as an officer in the Gendarmerie, and in the early 1930s he was given the task of monitoring the various right-wing factions on behalf of the authorities. In this role he often took part in right-wing demonstrations as an observer-informer for the police. After he resigned from official government service in 1937 or 1938 with the rank of major-general in the Gendarmerie, he was free to devote himself fully to the right-wing groups he had earlier been sent to observe, and became the 'intelligence officer' of the Arrow Cross movement. But he continued to act as an informer for the Hungarian police while at the same time acting as a paid agent of the Germans – specifically, of the security service of the SS. In 1939 he resigned from the Hungarist Party of Szálasi and became instead one of the leaders of Pálffy's Hungarian National Socialist Party.[30] Although he was on the Germans' payroll and was being paid for his politics, he also genuinely identified with the pro-German stance of Pálffy. And he certainly welcomed the virulent strain of anti-Semitism that emanated from Berlin.

While the local national socialist politicians enjoyed the support of Berlin, it was Szálasi's Hungarist Arrow Cross movement that attracted the masses. At the height of the party's popularity in 1939–1940, it had around 250,000 to 300,000 members.[31] During that time it became embroiled in the most significant miners' strike in Hungarian history, and was so successful in politicizing this mass industrial action that the party actually reversed its stand and withdrew support out of fear that the strike's success would provoke strong government steps against the Hungarist Party. The growth of the party was closely watched on all sides, and was not welcomed by the government of Budapest.

The Germans were also wary of their protégé. If the Arrow Cross movement attracted too many supporters and gained too much public support, it would eventually disrupt the good relations the German Foreign Ministry was cultivating with the Hungarian government and with the aristocratic, conservative and reactionary circles that supported the Regent Horthy. Berlin's support for a similar populist fascist movement in Romania, the Iron Guard, had encouraged that movement to a rashness that eventually led them into conflict with the ruling establishment. The leaders of the Iron Guard were arrested, and fourteen of them (including the party head) were executed. This in turn gave rise to public disturbances which lasted for years.[32] Neither Szálasi nor the German backers of the Hungarist Party and of the other radical right-wing groups were interested in such a situation developing in Hungary. Szálasi was a legalist and held very conservative views about how he would come to power. He never endorsed the notion of seizing power by force, and for most of the period under discussion he believed that he would be called by Horthy to save the Hungarian nation.

While Szálasi was locked away in jail, his successors faced the task of containing the radicalism of the party followers, allowing them to let off steam without provoking the authorities to take further steps against the Arrow Cross. This proved an impossible task. In December 1938 a demonstration in Budapest of some 10,000 Arrow Cross members from across the country led to serious rioting and street violence, the arrest of hundreds of the demonstrators and the death of one. In February 1939 party members attacked the famous Dohány synagogue with hand grenades, wounding twenty-two people. There were also other, minor, incidents during the winter of 1938–1939.

Shortly after the hand grenade attack the government acted, banning the Arrow Cross Hungarist Party. Many of the leading activists fled to Germany after warrants for their arrest were issued. Ironically, only Kálmán Hubay (who filled in as leader while Szálasi was in jail) and László Baky were not arrested or forced to flee. Both were considered 'responsible' leaders, while Baky was also a police informer. (And both, incidentally, were in German pay.) The government decree dissolving the party came into effect in February 1939.

The ban was short-lived. Within weeks most of the leaders were released, and Hubay and Baky undertook to steer the party to a 'disciplined, constitutional line'. In return, the government allowed the party to reorganize and rebuild itself, without the louder activist elements. In March the two leaders published a new party programme which was entirely palatable to the establishment. Szálasi's Hungarism was not mentioned, land reform was only alluded to indirectly as 'agrarian reform to increase production', and all other signs of earlier radicalism were removed. The only policy issue which reflected the older extremism was the new programme's 'irreconcilable' hostility to the Jews. They defined the Jews as a race, and called for a 'Hungarian state free from Jews'.[33] These were policies with which even the most conservative Hungarians could agree. It looked as if the ruling circles had triumphed. By dispersing the activist elements among the radical right and co-opting the policies of the less fanatic elements, the government and its aristocratic supporters believed they could not be outflanked by the extremists. Accordingly, the government called new elections for May 1939, rightly confident that they had little to fear. Although the Arrow Cross (no longer called the Hungarist Party) increased their representation from two seats to twenty-nine, and other right-wing splinter groups also did well, the government maintained its overall hold on the parliament with little difficulty.

The Arrow Cross reached a peak, but they had been tamed. From that moment on, their public support began to weaken. In September 1940 Szálasi was released from Szeged jail and the party once again was distracted by arcane ideological discussions and theorizing. Szálasi reappeared on the political stage with heightened prestige as a martyr of his movement, but he was even more incoherent than before.

ANTI-JEWISH LEGISLATION

The elections of May 1939 saw a dramatic growth in the strength of the radical right in parliament, and also in their public respectability. Five different racist, national socialist, 'Hungarist' parties increased their parliamentary representation. In the previous parliament they had been marginal; now they held 20 per cent of the seats. The Arrow Cross alone won twenty-nine seats (11 per cent), making it the largest party after the Party of Hungarian Life, the party of government. (The number of seats won does not reflect the actual popular vote, where the right wing did even better than in parliament. The Arrow Cross received 750,000 out of the 2,000,000 votes cast, while in Budapest they received more than twice as many votes as the Socialists, and almost as many as the government party.)[34] But the Party of Hungarian Life took over 70 per cent of the lower house, with 187 seats, and its control of the parliament was unquestioned.[35] The street violence of 1938 and early 1939 had been contained, and there was a general sense that the right-wing parties were no longer a threat to the stability of the regime.

There were a number of reasons for this success in stemming the growth of the fascist right. Foremost among them were the foreign policy achievements of the government. In November 1938 Germany and Italy supported Hungary's territorial claims against Czechoslovakia. For the first time Hungary was able to undo a clause of the Treaty of Trianon, by re-annexing the Magyar-inhabited areas of southern Slovakia and western Carpatho-Ruthenia. This area, known in Hungary as the Felvidék district, covered just over 4,630 square miles. The successful foreign policy which led to the return of this area to Hungary did much to enhance the government's standing.

In March 1939, Hungary was able to enlarge its borders once more when it annexed the rest of Carpatho-Ruthenia from Czechoslovakia (with Germany's blessing). As Hungary's borders expanded, so did its Jewish population. The Felvidék district contained 68,000 Jews in its overall population of 1,075,000, and the Carpatho-Ruthenian territory brought an additional 78,000 Jews in a total population of 700,000. And this focused public attention once again on the 'Jewish problem'.

The response of the Imrédy government to this renewed interest in the Jewish question was the second reason for the successful deflection of the right-wing activists: the government proposed another anti-Semitic bill to parliament, thus intensifying the step taken in 1938. In this way, too, the government outflanked the right wing, and responded to an increasingly belligerent domestic public opinion for which the Jews were easy prey.

Work began on drafting the second anti-Jewish legislation within months of the first anti-Jewish bill passing into law. It was conceived by Béla Imrédy, who took a sudden and dramatic turn towards right-wing and anti-Semitic policies after the re-annexation of Felvidék. As he told a party forum, the return of the northern province increased the number of Jews in Hungary, and their proportion of the population.[36] The new legislation revised the previous bill by adding a racial definition to the status of Jew, demonstrating the growing influence of German thinking on the Hungarian response to the 'Jewish problem'. The legislation was drafted by the Minister of Religious Affairs and Education, Count Pál Teleki. Teleki was a traditionalist and conservative, but he shared the hostility toward Jews that was now openly expressed in the most respectable circles. He personified the manner by which the Hungarian establishment responded to the threat of instability posed by right-wing parties by co-opting their policies and adopting the rhetoric they used.

Under the new legislation (Law IV, 1939), all Jews were banned from employment in the public sector (including teaching); no Jew could acquire Hungarian citizenship; no Jew could be elected to the upper house of the Parliament (except the official representatives of the Jewish community, whose membership was *ex officio*); no Jew could vote in elections unless his family had resided in Hungary continuously since 1867; and no Jew could be a candidate for a municipal post. These restrictions had symbolic importance more than any practical effect, as most Jews did not work in the public sector.[37] However, the law also imposed severe restrictions on the liberal professions in the private sector. The number of Jewish lawyers, doctors, journalists, engineers and actors was now limited to 6 per cent of their profession, while artists and journalists were, in addition, banned from positions of authority at their place of work. The quota for white-collar jobs in the business sector was set at 12 per cent. Further, Jewish owners of agricultural land could be forced to surrender their holdings 'without any limitations' (i.e. without meaningful compensation).[38]

While the law was being drafted, Imrédy was deposed as prime minister and Count Teleki, the minister responsible for preparing the bill, was appointed as his successor. The bill was discussed in public for months before the actual debate in parliament. The Jewish community lobbied strenuously for its defeat, and went to great lengths to prove its loyalty to the Hungarian state ever since 1849. (On one day of debate in the lower house, Jewish officer veterans filled the public gallery wearing their medals for valour on dress uniforms of mourning.) But it was all to no avail. Although voices were raised against the bill, the churches once again supported the anti-Jewish measures after they had demanded some rewording to protect converts to Christianity. The bill was passed with a large majority on 4 May 1939.

It was estimated that approximately 40,000 Jews lost their jobs as a result of the First Anti-Jewish Law. The Second Law was far more devastating, potentially affecting 250,000 Jews in Hungary as a whole. Indeed, within two years of the bill becoming law, 61 per cent of Jewish breadwinners in Budapest were unemployed.[39] But the bill was especially damaging to Jews in areas annexed from Czechoslovakia, both the 68,000 in the Felvidék province annexed the previous November and the 78,000 in the Carpatho-Ruthenian district annexed in March. Many of them were unable to prove Hungarian citizenship and were treated as aliens, with fatal consequences.

Despite the wave of unemployment created by the law, its actual impact on the economic well-being of the Jewish communities throughout Hungary varied. The circumstances of Jews in the countryside were very different from those of the urbanized community of Budapest, and the situation of Jews in the re-annexed areas was very different from that of their co-religionists in Trianon Hungary. Furthermore, the rigour with which the law was implemented fluctuated in the period up to the German occupation of March 1944. The law affected the poorer ranks of the Jewish community, the salaried workers and the unskilled. Those in commerce and industry managed to make ends meet by getting around the provisions of the law or taking advantage of loopholes.[40]

Fortuitously, while the Second Law was being drafted, debated and implemented, the Hungarian economy began to expand strongly. A government development plan saw public expenditure surge, and the rearmament promised in the Győr Programme absorbed all unemployment. Very soon Hungary faced a new situation of labour shortage, insufficient productive capacity and expanding prosperity. Ironically, under these new circumstances the productive capacity of Jewish enterprises became a vital asset to the national economy and to the rearmament efforts.[41] The result was that while the law could be used against the most economically vulnerable Jews, if it was implemented against the professional middle class, the blue-collar workers or the industrialists then the Hungarian economy would be hurt. Hungary faced the same dilemma that confronted the Nazis in Germany in the first five years after Hitler came to power. The Jews could not be eliminated from the national economy without causing a seriously negative effect on general economic welfare. Eighteen months after the law was enacted, Horthy wrote to Teleki, 'it is impossible to discard the Jews ... in one or two years and to replace them by incompetent, vulgar and boorish elements, because we could flounder. Such a project requires at least one full generation.'[42]

This led to a very selective implementation of the law, something that was reinforced after early 1943, when Germany's military defeats in North Africa and at Stalingrad encouraged second thoughts in Budapest. The law remained in force, and publicly it was constantly endorsed. But in practice it was only partly implemented. Jewish industrialists, medium-sized manufacturers, self-employed professionals and industrial manual workers (this latter group making up 30 per cent of the employed Jews in Budapest)[43] were largely unscathed by the legislation of 1939. Only the small entrepreneurs, the salaried white-collar workers and salaried professionals, and those previously employed in the media, were completely deprived of their livelihood. This large group was increasingly impoverished for at least two years before the German occupation of Hungary in 1944. By 1942, 300,000 people had to be financially supported by the Jewish community – a community whose overall resources were already shrinking.[44]

There are few reliable statistics for measuring the direct impact of the anti-Jewish legislation. Available data shows that the number of

Jews in the Hungarian economic elite had dropped from 28 per cent in 1937 to 17.5 per cent in 1943.[45] As to the broader Jewish public, there is ample impressionistic evidence that the discriminatory legislation was having a cumulative effect on their economic well-being. From 1941, the Ministry of the Interior ordered the provincial police to prepare monthly reports on political groups, on the supply situation, and on the ethnic minorities. These reports frequently discussed the state of the Jews in each Hungarian province, and of Jewish/non-Jewish relations. Many of these reports have survived, and they reflect the growing marginalization of the Jewish minority throughout the country. The police were not asked to report on the economic situation of the Jews; nevertheless a number of them did. While ten of the reports asserted that the financial situation of the Jews was 'good' in 1941/1942, only one positive report was made for 1943/1944. But twenty-two reports for the period 1941 to 1944 stated that their economic situation was 'bad'.[46]

At the end of August 1940 Hungary made yet another 'correction' to the Trianon borders. This time, with German and Italian backing, Romania was forced to hand back to Hungary most of Transylvania (40,000 out of a total 60,000 square miles). This territory, the north-western province of inter-war Romania, now became the north-east provinces of Hungary. A total of 164,000 Jews lived in the area reclaimed by Hungary. Ironically, they had closely identified with Hungarian culture during the fifty years up to the end of the First World War in 1918, and represented a very large percentage of the Hungarian-speakers on whose behalf Hungary's traditional claims for this region were based. But the Hungary to which this population was now returned, following the re-annexation of Transylvania, was a very different society from the one they had known. Within days of the Hungarian army moving in, the military administration applied all the anti-Jewish laws current in Hungary, as well as a spate of local initiatives designed to verify the citizenship status of Jews in the reclaimed areas. Tens of thousands lost their jobs, while others also lost their citizenship and were arrested.

The fourth and final territorial expansion at the expense of her neighbours came in April 1941, when Hungary participated in the German invasion of Yugoslavia. As a result, Hungary re-annexed a further 11,625 square miles, constituting three regions of which the most prominent were Bácska and Baranya. Out of a total population of 1 million, 14,202 Jews were added to the growing Jewish population under direct Hungarian control.

A significant number of refugees from Poland had found asylum in Hungary after the German invasion of that country in September 1939, and as many as 10 per cent of this latter group were Jewish – adding another 15,000 Jews to the overall total. (Braham states that the actual number of refugees might be closer to 35,000.)[47] The Jewish communities under Budapest's direct control now numbered 725,000, with an additional *circa* 100,000 'racially' Jewish converts to Christianity who were defined as Jews by the various anti-Semitic laws enacted up to 1944.[48] As Hungary's territory grew, so did the number of Jews under its control.

Pál Teleki committed suicide prior to the invasion of Yugoslavia, as he considered the invasion to be a dishonourable breach of Hungary's diplomatic commitments. He was replaced by László Bárdossy. The new prime minister identified the 'Jewish problem' as one of the most pressing issues facing his government, and as with every change of government in Hungary during the past few years (there had been many), Bárdossy tried to outdo his predecessors in the formulation of anti-Jewish measures. A third anti-Jewish law had been in preparation for some months by Teleki, and after his suicide Bárdossy pushed for the law's presentation to parliament. The new legislation was not titled 'anti-Jewish', as it dealt with general marriage laws. But its provisions were designed to bring Hungarian practice in line with the Third Reich's Nuremberg Laws. Part IV of the law ('The Prohibition of Marriages between Jews and Non-Jews') adopted a purely racial definition of Jewishness – anyone who had two grandparents born as Jews. The law banned marriage and sexual relations between racially defined male Jews and non-Jewish women. As this would have seriously affected the existing marriages of very many Hungarian Christians with Jewish ancestry, the churches vociferously opposed the law until a provision was included which allowed the Ministry of Justice to waive the rules in certain cases. Once this loophole was written into the law to protect those born Christian but with two Jewish grandparents, the law was adopted by parliament in August 1941.

Step by step the legal status of the Jews in Hungary was being reduced to the pariah status of the Jews in Germany. And, as a parallel and related development, Hungarian foreign policy was increasingly tied to the policies of Berlin.

The growing identification with the Third Reich, and the belief that Germany would win a quick victory over the Soviet Union, encouraged Hungary's military leaders to push for an effective Hungarian military role in the anti-Russian campaign. Within weeks of the German invasion of Russia in June 1941, the Hungarians committed some military and auxiliary units to the campaign. As a result, Hungary was at war with the Soviet Union. (Ironically, the auxiliaries were forced Jewish labour units.)[49] Eventually, the Hungarian Second Army, a total of 200,000 troops, was sent to the front. By the end of the year, Hungary found itself at war with Britain and the United States as well.

Once Hungary was at war, public enthusiasm and militancy expressed itself in heightened attacks against the Jews, who were blamed for every inconvenience caused by the hostilities. Shortages, rising prices, black marketeering – all these were said to be the fault of the Jews. The war also provided an excuse for some of the harshest steps yet taken against the Jewish community.

Many of the Jews in the four areas re-annexed during the previous three years did not have the documentation necessary to prove their right to Hungarian citizenship. In addition, as noted above, many Jews sought refuge in Hungary following the German occupation of Poland and, later, Russia. All aliens, including the alien Jews, came under the National Central Alien Control Office, and many of them lived in refugee camps run by this government agency. Once Hungary joined the hostilities against the Soviet Union as Germany's ally, the officials of the Alien Control Office received government approval (including that of Horthy) to transfer all the refugees into occupied Polish Galicia, adjacent to Hungary's border and under Hungarian military administration, but with a strong German presence. The refugee Jews (and, incidentally, some authentically Hungarian Jewish communities) were handed to the German authorities at a rate of 1,000 a day. By mid-August 1941, approximately 18,000 had been 'resettled'.

This was exactly the time when the German Einsatzgruppen were actively shooting Jews *en masse* in the territories occupied by the

Wehrmacht. The sudden transfer of Jews from Hungary was more grist to this evil mill. On 26 and 27 August, 14,000 of those expelled from Hungary were shot by units of the German SS at Kamenets-Podolsk, with the assistance of Ukrainian units as well. But some escaped and managed to return to Hungary with eyewitness accounts of what 'resettlement' really meant. The story quickly became known, and the Minister of the Interior ordered that the deportations must end (seven trainloads were actually recalled from the border). Despite the years of serious anti-Semitic agitation and the various anti-Jewish laws, Hungary was not yet ready to collaborate with the mass murder of the Jews by the Germans, even of alien Jews who had sought refuge within her borders.

Miklós Kállay succeeded Bárdossy as prime minister in March 1942, a post he retained until the German occupation in March 1944. Kállay was the least pro-Axis leader of all the wartime prime ministers, and during his premiership Hungary moved slowly away from the German orbit. The defeat of the Hungarian Second Army by the Russians in fighting at Voronezh on the Don in December 1942, where almost 40,000 Hungarian soldiers died and the rest were wounded or captured, came as a heavy blow to Hungarian pretensions. As it had been preceded by the German defeat of El Alamein in October–November 1942 and followed by the even larger German defeat at Stalingrad in January 1943, Hungary's adherence to the Axis seemed increasingly unwise. Kállay made a number of cautious approaches to the British and Americans during this period, and he encouraged the Smallholders and the Social Democratic Parties in parliament to be vocal in their demands for an 'independent foreign policy'. As István Deák wrote, 'By 1943 Hungary was, for all intents and purposes, a neutral country.'[50] There were publicly voiced demands for the withdrawal of Hungarian troops from the front, and in politically informed circles in Budapest the gossip was about Kállay's secret contacts with the Allies. It was also known that the prime minister rebuffed a number of concerted German efforts during 1942–1943 to agree to a resolution of the 'Jewish problem' along the lines of the Final Solution.[51]

Nevertheless, Kállay too had to pay his due to the anti-Semitic bloc in parliament. Within days of his appointment he announced that he would initiate a new round of anti-Jewish legislation. Unlike the previous laws, Kállay directed his attack to Jewish property rather than to the Jews as citizens. Specifically, Kállay (himself a land-owning member of the gentry) wanted to limit Jewish ownership of land. The previous legislation, which was designed to limit the role of the Jews in the economy, had included clauses that could compel Jewish landowners to surrender their property, but these clauses were not effective. Kállay now proposed legislation that would prevent Jews from owning agricultural land and would bring about the speedy expropriation of existing holdings. He justified his initiative by stressing the special significance of land ownership to the Hungarian national identity, and thus the need to exclude Jews from that avenue of assimilation and influence. He also pointed out that the legislation was directed at Jewish property rather than at the Jews *per se*, and was a necessary concession to popular feeling. The Jews themselves would be able to appreciate the significance of the distinction and the necessity of the step:

In view of the privileged position of Jews in Hungarian economic life, such measures could assume the character of economic adjustments and could be regarded by the fair-minded section of Hungarian Jewry as their contribution to the national war effort.[52]

The proposed law was debated in parliament in May and again in June, and was finally promulgated in September 1942. The Bill on the Agricultural and Horticultural Real Estate of Jews (Law XV, 1942) prohibited Jews from acquiring land, forced the transfer of existing holdings, and offered compensation in 3.5 per cent non-negotiable bonds due to redemption thirty years later.[53]

A surprisingly large number of Hungarian Jews were affected by this law, which was first directed against the smallest holdings. By November 1942 Allied intelligence monitoring developments in Hungary reported that 400,000 acres had been expropriated from 14,000 Jewish smallholders.[54] The largest estates (half of the Jewish-owned land was in the possession of fifty-four families) were seized in a second stage of expropriations under the law.

Historians do not agree on the significance of the legislation initiated by Kállay. Perhaps because of Kállay's remarkably positive contribution to the safety of Hungarian Jewry during the period 1942–1943, despite public attitudes on the 'Jewish question', Braham's encyclopedic study of the Jews in Hungary during the war uncharacteristically ignores Law XV, 1942, relegating it to a longer footnote.[55] Katzburg, on the other hand, considers the symbolic significance of the legislation: 'Hungarian Jews regarded the right to own real estate as a symbol of their civil equality. The ban on land ownership removed one of the last remnants of Jewish emancipation.'[56] A more recent study dismisses the policy of the Kállay government as 'irrelevant' because it did not undo the exclusionary anti-Semitic policies of the previous years. According to this analysis, in the long run it was not possible to save the Jews by adding to the anti-Jewish legislation of the previous outspokenly anti-Semitic governments.[57]

But the true significance of this last round of anti-Jewish legislation lies in the deal that was implicit in Kállay's policy. If the Jews would surrender their property as 'a contribution to the national war effort', they would be able to fend off the worst of the anti-Semitic attacks on their persons, and gain time. This was the basis of the arrangements which Kállay offered, and he certainly lived up to his side of it. He refused to cooperate with the Third Reich on the 'Jewish question', and he moved Hungary away from Germany's orbit. But the arrangement worked only as long as Kállay remained in power. Ultimately, the Germans were not willing to tolerate the independence of Hungarian policy, and they forced Kállay's overthrow in March 1944.

Tragically, the Jews of Hungary had learnt a lesson in 1942–1943 which the Germans and their Hungarian collaborators would eventually turn against them. Kállay had taught them that if they surrendered their property they might save their lives. This made the task of the despoiling of Hungarian Jewry that much easier for the invaders when the Germans occupied Hungary.

HOLOCAUST REACHES HUNGARY

During 1943 the war began to turn slowly against the Third Reich. By the end of the year Germany had lost Italy as its closest ally, and had suffered major defeats in the Soviet Union. The Red Army was poised to break into Romania, while in Hungary Kállay maintained contacts with the Western Allies. By the second year of Kállay's premiership

Hungary was behaving almost as a neutral country. Allied planes flew over Hungarian territory without opposition, Allied POWs and pilots were given refuge, restrictions were placed on the transportation of German troops (especially via Budapest), and Hungarian war production was increasingly withheld for local use. Italy left the Axis in August 1943, and Hungary recognized the Badoglio government that replaced Mussolini. In January 1944, a year after the decimation of his Second Army at Voronezh in the Ukraine, the Hungarian Chief of Staff Ferenc Szombathelyi suggested to the Germans that the remaining Hungarian forces should be withdrawn from the Russian front so that they could take up defensive positions in the Carpathians against a possible Soviet invasion of Hungary. Szombathelyi made this request at a meeting with Hitler and his German counterpart Field Marshal Wilhelm Keitel, Chief of Staff of the High Command of the Armed Forces (OKW), and it was repeated by Horthy and prime minister Kállay in separate communications during February.

The Hungarian communications enraged Hitler. The latter was aware that Kállay was not reliable as far as German interests were concerned, but now Horthy had openly sided with his prime minister. And that, in turn, gave credence to a series of German intelligence reports that Kállay and other members of the Hungarian leadership were in contact with British, American and even Soviet representatives via neutral countries. During 1943 the Germans knew that both the British Special Operations Executive (SOE) and the American Office of Strategic Services (OSS) were preparing to parachute agents into Hungary for the purpose of establishing contact with the Hungarian Regent and negotiating Hungary's abandonment of the Axis.[58] (On the night of 15–16 March 1944 one such mission moved beyond the planning stage. Three OSS agents were parachuted into Hungary and made contact with senior members of Hungarian Military Intelligence, with whom secret talks had been going on for some time. However, 'Operation Sparrow' came too late to make any impact on the course of events. The German troops destined to occupy Hungary a few days later had already massed on the border. The OSS team was arrested by the Germans within twenty-four hours of the occupation – a clear indication that the SD, Himmler's intelligence organization, knew about it all along.)[59]

Germany had concrete strategic reasons for ensuring that Hungary remained tied to the Reich, but it now appeared Hungary wanted to extricate itself from the war altogether. This would have deprived Germany of the depth it needed to protect its southern flank, as well as cutting the Reich off from Hungarian raw materials necessary for the war effort. Hitler did not intend that to happen, and began planning the forcible occupation of Hungary. The Jewish issue was not a reason by itself. Nevertheless, if Germany controlled Hungary it would have an opportunity of seizing the Jewish community there and overcoming the longstanding refusal of the Kállay government to cooperate with the Final Solution.

The only question which remained to be answered was the nature of the occupation. One possibility considered in Berlin was to invite the other members of the Axis (Romania, Slovakia and Croatia) to join with Germany in the total dismemberment of Hungary. This would reverse the territorial adjustments to Trianon that Germany had permitted during the period 1938 to 1941, and would have allowed Hungary's enemies to take their revenge. However, other voices advocated a moderate policy, one which would keep the hated Romanians out and maintain the façade of legality of the occupation, while forcing Horthy to accept a pro-German government consisting of politicians acceptable to Berlin. Wilhelm Höttl (the expert on Hungary and the officer responsible for the Balkan desk in the SD) was able to make a convincing case in favour of this latter approach. In a detailed study which reached Berlin eight days before the planned invasion, Höttl argued that if the Romanians and others joined the occupation, then all of Hungary would be united in fighting against Germany. The Regent would resign and it would be impossible to form a new government. In short, Hungary would become a burden to the Reich. But if the Germans occupied under a semblance of legality (citing war needs), they would be in a position to impose a Hungarian government of their liking and would be able to enforce compliance with Germany's wishes.[60]

2

Diamonds, Gold and Genocide

SS Sturmbahnführer Wilhelm Höttl had been working for years for this moment. Since he first became involved in Hungarian affairs in 1939 as the Balkans expert for the foreign intelligence department (Amt VI) of the Sicherheitsdienst,[1] a part of the SS, his office had been assiduously cultivating contacts with Hungarians who identified with the Third Reich and with the ideology of National Socialism. These were people who would not flinch from the most radical and ruthless steps to fight the Bolsheviks, to destroy the Jews and to give precedence to Germany's war effort over the interests of Hungary. Now that Germany was poised to occupy Hungary, Höttl would soon be in a position to ensure that the people he had made contact with over the years, whom he had supported and financed, would be installed in positions of power and influence. Höttl advocated that Germany should retain the façade of Hungarian political independence by maintaining Horthy as Regent. He was confident that he had enough collaborators to staff the genuinely important foci of power in the Hungarian political system and in the bureaucracy for Germany to be able to achieve its objectives without becoming embroiled in local affairs of no relevance to her war aims. Unfortunately for the Jewish community, their physical destruction had long been listed among Germany's major objectives in Hungary.

The foreign intelligence department of the German Sicherheitsdienst was part of the large SS empire that Heinrich Himmler controlled directly. The officers of the department were not restricted to gathering intelligence but were also actively involved in diplomacy and in local politics, often undermining the authority of the local German embassy.[2] In the course of 1944 Höttl's political activities in Hungary often ran counter to the policies pursued by the representatives of the German Foreign Office in Budapest. Höttl had never been enthusiastic about Ferenc Szálasi. The latter's 'Hungarism', his respect for constitutional procedure, his loyalty to the Regent, and a suspicion that when the crunch came he would not be sufficiently ruthless in 'solving the Jewish problem', all marked Szálasi as an unreliable ally in implementing Germany's plans. Ever since 1938, the SD had favoured the small coterie of politicians around Fidél Pálffy's Hungarian National Socialists and some members of Béla Imrédy's Party of Hungarian Life. Höttl especially cultivated László Endre, László Baky,[3] Andor Jaross and a few others as collaborators on whom Germany could rely when the time came.

Units of the Gestapo arrived together with the first German troops to reach Budapest at dawn on Sunday, 19 March 1944. Under the command of SS-Obergruppenführer Otto Winckelmann, the security police drove directly to the German Legation, where Winckelmann was met by László Baky. Baky had received advance notice of the German invasion,[4] and he organized a small force of Gendarmerie to act as guides for the Gestapo units. He also prepared lists of political opponents to be arrested. When Winckelmann arrived they went immediately into action. By 8 a.m. the first arrests were being made by the Germans, with Baky's men showing the way.[5] The potential loci of opposition to German control in Hungary were being eliminated even before the Kállay government resigned and was replaced. Höttl's philosophy of controlling events by placing sympathizers in a few key positions was now beginning to pay off.

The new German Minister to Hungary, SS-Brigadeführer Dr Edmund Veesenmayer, arrived in Budapest on the same day as the invading German troops. So did Himmler's deputy in the SS, Ernst Kaltenbrunner. For the next three days Veesenmayer, Kaltenbrunner (with his subordinate, Höttl, on the sidelines) and their leading Hungarian collaborators busied themselves with selecting a government that would be acceptable both in Berlin and in Budapest. The Germans were not united in their approach. Veesenmayer represented a more conservative line, and pressed for a government that would have the maximum degree of credibility and support in Hungarian opinion. His political objective was to ensure Hungary's full and active participation in Germany's war effort (both economic and military support) and an end to all flirtation with the Americans and the British. Any government that could guarantee those objectives, while at the same time enjoying the support of Hungarian public opinion, would save Germany the trouble of total control of the local administration. Kaltenbrunner, representing Himmler, and very much senior to Veesenmayer in the Nazi hierarchy, had an additional objective: the total destruction of Hungarian Jewry, both economically and physically. In order to guarantee the success of this task he needed to ensure that whoever controlled Hungary at the highest level (that is, as prime minister) would not obstruct the specialist force of 200 to 300 men of Adolf Eichmann's Sonderkommando that had entered Hungary with the occupying forces. Furthermore, he needed to ensure that some of the personalities that Höttl had been cultivating for years among the various 'National Socialist' circles in parliament, the press and politics would now be appointed to key administrative positions to assist the Sonderkommando.

As soon as the invasion began, but before anyone in Budapest realized what was happening, Höttl gathered his protégés, including Baky, and kept them available while the make-up of the government was being negotiated.[6] Their task was to identify, isolate, concentrate, intimidate and finally deport the 725,000 Jews (and as many as 100,000 converts) within Hungary's borders. Furthermore, this had to be completed as quickly as possible before the Allied advance could prevent the completion of the Final Solution in the largest remaining community of Jews in Europe. The Germans could not do this by themselves; they needed local Hungarian assistance, and Höttl wanted to make sure that the politicians he had supported for a long time would now be ready to fulfil their roles. At the other end of the deportation process, in Auschwitz, the railway lines, gas chambers and crematoria had all been expanded and prepared for their Hungarian victims, and were waiting.

The only candidate for prime minister on which all Hungarian factions and Berlin would agree was Lieut.-General Döme Sztójay, Hungary's ambassador in the German capital since 1935. Sztójay had lived in Berlin since 1925 and was well known there as an enthusiastic supporter of the Third Reich. The Sztójay government included four ministers from the previous government, giving it the appearance of continuity and legality, and was endorsed by Horthy. But two of these ministers were German informers (Reményi-Schneller and Jurcsek), while the key position for the implementation of the Final Solution – Minister of the Interior – was given to Andor Jaross, an extreme anti-Semite on whom Höttl and Eichmann would be able to rely.[7] And Jaross's assistant secretaries (deputy ministers) in the Ministry of the Interior were László Baky and László Endre. (It is important to note that the Gendarmerie, a rural police and paramilitary force which provided the armed enforcers of the policy of ghettoization and deportation, was under the direct control of the Ministry of the Interior.) Another of Höttl's coterie, Jenő Rátz, although also an Imrédist but nevertheless entirely loyal to Germany, was appointed deputy prime minister. No member of the largest parliamentary group of the radical right, the Arrow Cross, was given a position. There were no 'Hungarists' in the new government. This was a government streamlined to do exactly what Höttl and his superiors in Berlin had been planning for years.

The changes in the government were reflected by changes in personnel at the level of provincial administration as well. Jaross, as the new Minister of the Interior, was able to find positions for many of his party colleagues. Two-thirds of the mayors of the larger cities and towns were replaced, as well as many senior officials in the civil service. Across Hungary, thirty-nine of the forty-one district governors (főispán) were replaced by the beginning of May.[8] Over half of the new appointees were members of the MMP, Jaross's own party, while others were identified with the Hungarian National Socialist Party.[9] László Baky was able to obtain an appointment for one of his closest associates, too. The new főispán of the important Fejér district was the ex-Gendarmerie Colonel Árpád Toldi. Toldi, who was a friend of Baky,[10] plays a central role in the events that follow.

ÁRPÁD TOLDI,* COMMANDER OF
THE GOLD TRAIN

Árpád Toldi was an unknown figure at a national level until the German occupation of Hungary. He was a career officer in the Gendarmerie, which he joined in 1915, and served in Hajdúszoboszló and Debrecen in the 1920s and 1930s. In 1938 he was appointed deputy commander of a Gendarmerie training camp at Pestszenterzsébet, responsible for officer training courses,[11] and in 1940 he served in Szentes (southern Hungary), and then in Kolozsvár (Cluj, Romania).[12] Toldi was promoted to the rank of major in 1938 and lieut.-colonel in 1941. In September 1942 he was transferred to Department VIb of the Ministry of the Interior, the department responsible for the service affairs of the Gendarmerie. In 1943 he was promoted to full colonel, and became deputy director of the department when it was reorganized as Department XX of the Ministry of the Interior, following the German occupation.[13]

Toldi's career was undistinguished, and in the course of almost thirty years he acquired the long-service decorations and medals accorded to those whose climb through the ranks has been unspectacular but predictable. He published a number of articles in the official journal of the Gendarmerie, dealing with technical matters of police work and criminal investigation,[14] and also a textbook for the use of the Gendarmerie training school.[15] In September 1941, three months after the Hungarian army participated in the German invasion of the Soviet Union and Hungary was officially at war with the Communist

---

* Toldi was born in 1898 in Kiskőrös, a predominantly agricultural town that had enjoyed a level of prosperity ever since the introduction of vineyards in the 1880s. Jews had lived there since the 1780s, and were a fairly constant 4–5 per cent of the population (400–500 people) up till 1944. Local industry (mills, the distillery, the regional printing press, brickyards) was largely owned by the town's Jews, and they were also involved in some of the local agriculture. In all of these features, Kiskőrös was a typical Hungarian town of its size. The Kiskőrös Jews were completely Magyarized and the local handbook for 1910 described them as 'totally assimilated to the Hungarian nation (not mentioning some minor differences) and were wholehearted Hungarians and good patriots'. Toldi's anti-Jewish animus was not typical of the town of his birth.

state, Toldi published a lengthy description of the Gendarmerie's role in the war against Bolshevism. After recounting the difficulties of the war on the eastern front, Toldi turned to the other object of his venom – the Jews. One could not be anti-Bolshevik, he argued, without also being anti-Semitic. The terms were synonymous, and anti-Semitism was 'the patriotic responsibility of all loyal anti-Communist Hungarians'.[16] The article gave public voice to Toldi's personal politics, and established his credentials as a reliable member of the pro-German, anti-Soviet and anti-Semitic right wing. This was precisely the ideological position necessary for any officer keen to advance through the ranks.

During his service as an officer, Toldi befriended László Baky, then a senior officer (major-general) in the Gendarmerie until he resigned in 1938 to begin his political career. When Baky was appointed assistant secretary in the Ministry of the Interior in April 1944, he was put in charge of a number of departments, including Department XX, where Toldi was the deputy director – affording an opportunity for the two to renew their acquaintance. They shared the same world-view – a virulent anti-Semitism, a belief in Germany as Hungary's closest natural ally and friend, and an unrestrained admiration for the political system of the Third Reich.

The friendship with his brother officer Baky stood Toldi in good stead. He was appointed főispán of the Fejér district, with Székesfehérvár as the seat of local government, on 26 April 1944, the first day of the week-long wave of administrative appointments implemented by the Ministry of the Interior with German approval. Székesfehérvár was the traditional site of the coronation of the kings of Hungary. Furthermore, it is only sixty-four kilometres from the capital, Budapest. Toldi's appointment as governor of the important Fejér district and of the historic city of Székesfehérvár was thus a sign of favour.

The role of the district governor was to be the voice of the central government expressed at regional level, while the day-to-day management of local affairs was usually left to the governor's deputy (the alispán). The inauguration of a new district governor was always a ceremonial occasion, with the participation of representatives of the government from Budapest. Toldi's accession was no exception. The forces that ruled Hungary after the German occupation used the opportunity to demonstrate to the regional politicians the changed character and agenda of the new regime.

Toldi took the oath of office at a ceremony held on 11 May 1944, before the municipal council and representatives of the government. Baky introduced him to the gathering, commending his 'old brother-in-arms in the Gendarmerie' to the audience. The Minister of Industry in the Sztójay government, Béla Jurcsek, spoke (although his words were not reported in the local newspaper's account published the next day), and Kálmán Hubay, one of the leaders of the Hungarian National Socialist Party, was also present. Toldi's own speech was reported verbatim, and it affords a rare insight into the 'revolutionary' fervour of the new regime. The fact that he spoke in the presence of a government minister (Jurcsek), a deputy minister (Baky) and a party leader (Hubay) suggests that Toldi was articulating the ideology of the government.

Although Toldi was not an open member of Pálffy and Baky's Hungarian National Socialist Party (MNSZP),[17] he was an outspoken supporter.[18] His speech closely followed the MNSZP party line, and was warmly received. Toldi used all the clichés of radical right-wing rhetoric with which Hungarian listeners had become familiar:

I am proclaiming here the national and social state, having an end in itself, which above individuals and generations serves the universal national idea, and means the good of the community and the eternal existence of the Hungarians. This Hungarian idea of the state has to be present consciously and with a passion of blind faith in the widest strata of Hungarian society. This idea must unite the nation into a new body and one soul, so that, gaining strength from the proud consciousness and uplifting greatness of the thousand-year-old primordial force, it may serve the future into the new millennium.

The current war was not simply a battle over borders. It was a conflict of Armageddon proportions:

The battle that the Jewish plutocratic and Bolshevist world has forced upon our allies and upon us is enormous in its dimensions and effect. Two worlds are fighting their decisive battle, from which assuredly only the eternal divine idea and its new world can emerge victoriously. All contrary ideas are a complete misunderstanding of our situation. In general, if we want Europe, which means the basis of Christian civilization, to survive, it is our duty to fight for it. It is indisputable that the gigantic struggle of the Germans is one and the same as the fight for Europe.

As for the 'Jewish question', Toldi was very clear about his position:

The most important primary condition is the total separation of the Jews and keeping them away from the Hungarians. The final solution of this question is advancing quickly. This parasitic type with its alien mentality has wormed its way into the body of the Hungarian nation and has caused immeasurable damage to the nation. In only a few decades, it has intruded into every corner of Hungarian life, in order to make our nation, with all its mental and material values, a tool and a servant for its own purposes of power, by undermining the self-consciousness and the moral strength of the nation. It has ridiculed everything and stained everything that had been the supporting pillars of our unique Hungarian life. Nothing was sacred for this race.

Toldi offered his audience an explanation for the virulence of his Jew-hatred. Referring to the 'Hungarian Soviet Republic' of Béla Kun, the new district governor explained that he had personal accounts to settle:

It is characteristic of the limitless excesses of this race that it even tried to kill this nation by the reign of the Jewish Marxist terror. It is no thanks to them that we are nevertheless alive today! But we have not yet forgotten how the terror commandos of the Jewish executioners terrified this nation, in the sacred homeland of the Hungarians, and that by attacking the peaceful population, the Jewish hangmen put the rope round the neck of the best Hungarians with great pleasure. A long line of martyrs, among them the closest member of my family,* will be an eternal reminder of this terrible, outrageous deed.

The Jews, he pointed out, were responsible for the war ('It was the Jews who wanted, planned and caused this whole war with all its outrageous sadism'), and were directly responsible for the Allied bomb-

---

* By referring to his 'closest' relative, Toldi was implying that his father was a victim of the Red Terror of 1919–1920. However, the name Toldi/Toldy does not appear in a list of the 'Martyrs of the Red Terror' published in the 1930s. It appears that Toldi embellished his speech to gain sympathy.

ing (which followed the German occupation and the creation of the Sztójay government) by the 'American gangsters whom the Jews have bought with money and with deceit'.* Once the Jews are purged from Hungarian life, then 'Our life will finally be ours, the unique communal life of the Hungarian family, and the fruit of our labours will serve only our own good from now on.'

Toldi was more succinct when he came to discussing Jewish property. Part of the revitalization of 'Hungarian life' that the new regime promised was a redistribution of Jewish wealth:

All of those economic resources that the Jewish plutocracy because of its power has so far used for the nourishment of its racial and power interests will from now on profit, strengthen and enrich Hungarian life and Hungarian businesses only.

After victory had been won, the 'national socialist economic policy . . . will distribute the goods of abundance'.

All the above would have amused Berlin's political advisers specializing in Hungarian affairs. But Toldi's concluding comments would certainly have won approval:

We are grateful to the Providence-given Leader of the Third Reich: to Adolf Hitler, who by lifting up his people has also freed our nation from its shackles, and we know that in this battle we also can walk the same road for life and death . . . The essence of it all: creating a national socialist community of people forming a solid union with the total exclusion of Jews; uniting all moral, financial and mental powers for the war and for work; making social justice prevail; keeping discipline and order. The highest goal of all, encompassing everything else, is to finish this war victoriously.[19]

The personality of the new district governor, his radicalism and the fact that he was a stranger to the region were all causes for alarm among members of the municipal council. A senior official in the

---

* Most of the Allied raids were directed against the industrial areas of Hungary, which did not usually have a significant Jewish residential population. As a result, there were few Jews among the civilian casualties caused by the bombing, a fact which caused much resentment. Toldi's anti-American invective was not unusual in these months, neither was his linking of the 'American gangsters' with 'Jewish plutocracy'.

previous regional administration, who stayed on as Toldi's secretary, described him as 'an educated, intelligent person who held politically extremist views – fascist, Nyilas. He was a violent man, and made life impossible for anyone who stood in his way.'[20] The mayor of Székesfehérvár also described Toldi as very intelligent, as well as being 'sadistic and cruel'.[21] In the first meeting with the council, Toldi was reminded of the 'ancient traditions and rights' of the town. The alispán (deputy governor) referred to the autonomy and independence of the council. (While the district governor was appointed by the central government, the deputy governor was elected by the municipal assembly, and had a local power base.)

Nevertheless, Toldi immediately set about removing the local politicians and installing his own men in the county and city administration. He did the same in the local police administration. Very soon, most office-holders in the area were directly beholden to him. He next took over the local newspaper, the *Fejérmegyei Napló*, and converted it into an official publication of the new Hungarian National Socialist Party branch in the city.[22]

All the local citizens felt the impact of the new regime. But Toldi's most radical policies were directed against the small Jewish community of the region, with particular attention to the fate of their property. Immediately after his appointment was announced, Toldi personally instructed the local police to take much more stringent steps against Székesfehérvár's Jews, especially the wealthier ones. When the local police chief found that he himself was not able to enforce the new laws against some of the city's most respected citizens (many of whom he would have known personally), he took early retirement, and Toldi was able to appoint a replacement who would enforce the anti-Jewish policy with enthusiasm.[23] It was a pattern that was repeated in towns and cities across Hungary. Requests that the Jews be treated less violently were ignored. In the few cases where local Jews were legally exempt from the deportation decrees (because of past service to the state, or decorations for bravery in combat), Toldi instructed that the exemptions be disregarded even though they were signed by László Endre himself.[24]

APRIL 1944

Immediately after the creation of the new government, the Germans, together with their Hungarian collaborators, began to prepare the way for the deportation of Jews to Auschwitz. Identification, isolation, ghettoization, despoliation and eventual deportation were all stages in a process that had been perfected in 1942 and 1943 during the destruction of the Polish and other Jewish communities throughout Europe. But unlike elsewhere in Europe, Eichmann and his closest assistants (of whom SS Hauptsturmbahnführer Dieter Wisliceny and SS Obersturmbahnführer Hermann Krumey were the most important) enjoyed the enthusiastic assistance of members of the government. They could count on the ruthless enforcement of new anti-Jewish laws by the Gendarmerie and police. The radical nature of the German 'solution' to the 'Jewish question' in Hungary, and its finality, was exactly what the radical right had worked towards for over a decade. The Germans could also rely on the cooperation of the entire Hungarian civil administration, and the passive approval of the population. Sources of potential opposition to the German plans had all been neutralized within weeks of the occupation. Left-wing and liberal intellectuals, and some of the leading members of the aristocracy, had been arrested, while the Social Democratic and the Smallholders Parties, and the Hungarian Peasants' Union, were banned and their membership fragmentized. As a result, the elimination of the Jewish community was able to proceed with a relentlessness and speed that was unprecedented elsewhere in Europe.

The first stage was the isolation of the Jews.[25] On 19 March, within hours of the Germans' arrival in Budapest, Wisliceny and Krumey informed the Jewish Council – a body created at German insistence from the various Jewish community groups in the capital – that Jews would no longer be allowed to travel. At the same time, across Hungary Jews were arbitrarily arrested at railway stations. On 27 March the Sztójay government issued its first, formal anti-Jewish law: a ban on the use or ownership of telephones. Within days Jews were prohibited from employing non-Jews, were dismissed from the civil service, debarred from practising law or working in the media and the theatre, and required to declare any motor vehicles they owned. On 5 April Jews over the age of six years were compelled to wear a yellow star of at least ten-centimetre size, firmly sewn in a prominent place on outer garments. (Jewish groups outside Hungary were aware that the yellow star marking was a prelude to deportation. Requests to the Allies that a warning be broadcast to Hungarian Jews against wearing the distinctive marking were rejected.)[26]

Over 100 new anti-Jewish laws were issued during 1944, affecting every aspect of life. All were designed to isolate the Jews from the rest of the Hungarian population, to intimidate and terrorize them. Books by Jewish authors were burned, and a campaign organized to expunge the 'Jewish influence' from everyday culture. These were the necessary first steps prior to the expulsion of the Jews from the country, and were gazetted in April, at the same time as plans were drawn up for their physical isolation in ghettos, and timetables prepared for their deportation region by region.

Concurrently, additional steps were taken to continue the economic war against the Jewish community that began with the legislation of 1938. This time the objective was not to remove the Jews from the Hungarian economy but to seize their property. Previous legislation had the cumulative effect over years of pauperizing large sections of the Jewish community. Now the laws were more direct – despoiling the Jews of their possessions. Braham describes this phase as 'systematic state-directed plunder'.[27] The description is certainly accurate, but does not capture the full significance of what was happening in Hungary since the German invasion.

The destruction of European Jewry was not only racial warfare against the Jewish people, but was also a very profitable venture for the German state, for the bureaucracies within that state that were involved with the killing programme, and a lucrative opportunity for personal enrichment by thousands of officials, SS and soldiers. The Third Reich had become used to the idea that as the Final Solution was introduced into each occupied country in turn, new opportunities were opened up for individual looting and for the official seizure of Jewish property. Now that the installation of the Sztójay government ensured Hungarian cooperation with German plans for the largest remaining Jewish community in Europe, new possibilities of enrichment opened up for Germany. The SS and Wehrmacht officers who remained in Hungary (most of the occupation forces soon returned to the front) took immediate advantage of the situation. Apartments of affluent Jews in Budapest were sequestered for the use of Germans, and the occupants were instructed to leave furnishings, art works and other valuables intact when they moved out. Only two days after the occupation the SS demanded that the Jewish Council provide them with silverware, automobiles, paintings (as well as toiletries, lingerie and perfumes) according to detailed lists which the Germans prepared.[28] Individual SS officers (especially Wisliceny, who arrived in Budapest with a letter of introduction from the Jews of Slovakia from whom he had already accepted large bribes)[29] let it be known that they were open to payment in cash or diamonds in exchange for relief from the avalanche of restrictions that were soon placed on Jewish life. This was doubly beneficial for the Germans. Bribes not only enriched them but also encouraged the Jews to believe that they would be able to come to terms with the new situation, and might be able to avert the worst consequences of the new anti-Jewish policies. It also encouraged a growing psychological divide between the provincial (and poor) Jews of the countryside and the wealthier Jews of the capital. At least the wealthiest and most sophisticated Jews believed that they could buy security for themselves.

Indeed, the very wealthiest were able to buy their own freedom directly from the Germans, without the intervention of the Hungarian government. Manfred Weiss Industries, the largest industrial concern in Hungary, with interests in banking, mining, armament manufacture, textiles and other concerns, was owned by an interlinked group of families (Weiss, Chorin, Kornfeld and Mauthner). Individually they were highly assimilated and many family members had converted to Christianity or had married non-Jews. They were well connected with the establishment (some were on close personal terms with Horthy), and even represented in the upper house of parliament. The members of this group had largely avoided the consequences of the previous rounds of anti-Jewish legislation by passing control of their enterprises into the trusteeship of the non-Jewish members of their families and other trusted associates. Most members of the group were arrested on 19 March, but by 4 April SS officers had already begun negotiations with their leaders, offering safe passage to Portugal and Switzerland in exchange for control of the non-Jewish shares of the conglomerate (they had already seized the Jewish shares). The negotiations were conducted by SS Standartenführer Kurt Becher, who was occasionally assisted by Winckelmann himself.

The takeover of this huge industrial enterprise was an SS operation, directed by Himmler, with Hitler's approval. The assets which now came under SS control were so significant that the deal exposed the façade of Hungary's supposed continued sovereignty under German occupation, and the Sztójay government tried hard to block the agreement.* But the negotiations between directors of the group and the SS succeeded, and on 17 May they handed over control 'for twenty-five years' of Hungary's largest industrial and investment conglomerate in exchange for their lives and the lives of over forty family members.

The discussions over the Weiss-Chorin-Kornfeld-Mauthner assets were the largest of the ransom negotiations. The SS, and specifically Kurt Becher, negotiated other ransom deals with less wealthy Jews (through the intermediary services of Rezső Kasztner – cf. Appendix 1), and Eichmann attempted to ransom all Hungarian Jews for trucks and food supplies to be obtained from Jews outside of Hungary, but these were exceptions. The crude extortion used by the SS went against the spirit of the agreements between the German and Hungarian authorities on the 'Jewish question'. While it was understood that Jewish property could be requisitioned by the Wehrmacht on a temporary basis for its immediate logistical needs, the wealth of the Jews was

---

* Tensions between Germany and Hungary over the control of Hungarian Jewish assets were already apparent in the spring of 1943, a year before the SS takeover of Manfred Weiss Industries. Germany made persistent demands regarding the fate of Hungarian Jews living in Nazi-controlled countries outside Hungary. The main concern of the Hungarian Foreign Ministry was the fate of the assets that these Jews owned, should the Jews be deported to the East by the Germans. A special delegation sent to western Europe to study the problem reached the conclusion that these Jews would be willing to surrender their possessions in exchange for protection by Budapest as Hungarian citizens. The Foreign Ministry delegation suggested that a formal commission be sent to take control of the assets, in order to avoid their seizure by the Germans (MOL, XIX-J-1-k, 112.d, Report by Dr Andor Schedel Concerning Hungarian Jewish Assets in Western Occupied Territories, 22 March 1943).

supposed to accrue to the Hungarian state.[30] The assets of Hungarian Jewry were supposed to become the 'property of the nation' – as Toldi had informed his audience in Székesfehérvár in May, 'to strengthen and enrich Hungarian life and Hungarian businesses only'. At least formally the German share of the loot was restricted to the fee that the Germans extracted for the transportation, guarding and disposal of the Jews sent to Auschwitz or to labour camps – 5,000 Reich Marks per person. (In the months that followed, the Hungarian government paid 2.5 billion RM for the 'services rendered' by the Germans in the removal of the Jews.)[31] And, of course, the Third Reich kept for itself any valuables which the victims of the gas chambers succeeded in hiding among their few possessions or on their bodies (especially dental gold). But the bulk of the belongings of the vast majority of the Hungarian Jewish community soon became the focus of the government's particular attention and avarice. While most Hungarians studiously avoided informing themselves of the fate of their Jewish neighbours (everyone claimed total unawareness of the real meaning of 'deportation'), the fate of Jewish property excited great concern and interest. As Braham points out, almost all offices at every level of government – central, county, district and local – were directly involved in the despoliation. Five government ministries were involved, and all acts of expropriation and plunder bore official stamps of approval.[32] This was not spontaneous looting but a planned and orchestrated campaign of ethnic asset-stripping.

On the morning of 19 March, many Jews rushed to withdraw their savings from the banks. By the end of the first business day after the German occupation, the Minister of Finance issued orders banning Jews from withdrawing more than 1,000 pengő from their accounts, and ordering that all Jewish safe deposit boxes be sealed. On 6 April all police departments were instructed to take measures to prevent Jews hiding jewellery and valuables, or from selling or giving them to Christian friends for safekeeping. On the same day sweeping new restrictions on employment were published. Twenty-five per cent of Jewish employees were to be fired by 30 April, and a further 25 per cent by 30 May. The remainder were to be dismissed by 1 October. (Already one week previously all Jews had been dismissed from the civil service, municipal administration, public institutions and public works.)[33]

On 16 April the government published the most drastic legislation against Jewish property – Decree No. 1.600/1944 'Concerning the Declaration and Sequestration of the Wealth of the Jews'. The new regulation required all Jews to declare the value of their property by 30 April on official forms (which had to be purchased). All possessions beyond a basic 10,000 pengő ($2,500) for household items and clothing, plus a further 3,000 pengő for each family member, had to be listed.[34] Cash beyond 3,000 pengő and all gold, platinum, jewellery, precious stones, *objets d'art* and foreign currency had to be surrendered to the authorities. In order to avoid Jews handing their property to friends or neighbours rather than to the officially designated banks, all transfers of savings, securities, gold and jewellery from Jews to non-Jews after 22 March were considered invalid. Jewish-owned industrial or commercial businesses were closed forthwith and their inventories seized on 21 April – creating chaos in Budapest, where 18,000 Jewish-owned shops out of a total of 30,000 were forced to close.[35] Shortly afterwards the Jews were required to surrender their ration cards for sugar, fats and meat.

After only one month of the occupation, Hungarian Jews had been legally stripped of most of their possessions. To a large degree, they complied with the new regulations. Perhaps, it was felt, the Germans and the radically anti-Semitic members of the Sztójay government would be satisfied with the plunder of Jewish property. Eighteen months earlier the Kállay government had argued that by surrendering some of their assets the Jews were 'making a contribution to the national war effort' which would forestall the worst of the anti-Jewish measures that had been taken elsewhere in Europe. The Jews complied. This approach had worked, and the previous government had more than once been able to refuse German demands for the surrender of the Hungarian Jews to 'deportation' and 'resettlement' (i.e. to Auschwitz).

This time, however, it was a self-deception born of desperation, which Eichmann's team carefully cultivated and encouraged. Two years of experience in dealing with Jewish communities in other countries across Europe taught them how to lull the community into believing that by cooperating with the authorities they would be able to divert the harshest measures. The wealthiest and most prominent members of the community had saved themselves in this way, and hints by the leaders of the SS to members of the Jewish Council that they were open to bribes encouraged the leaders of the community to believe in the cruel deception. The message was intuitively understood throughout the country.

During April, long lines of Jews formed outside the offices of the Royal Hungarian Postal Savings Bank across the country, waiting to surrender their possessions. First they were required to surrender their bicycles and radios, and later their savings, jewellery, gold and other valuables. The latter items were placed in individually named envelopes and detailed receipts were issued, creating the reassuring illusion that one day they would regain their belongings. The deception was total. Each stage of the legalized plunder was designed to keep the flames of hope alive, and to cultivate the belief that by making yet another material sacrifice, by giving up more and more of their personal possessions following each new decree and official demand, they would be able to avoid the fate of other Jewish communities across Europe. The authorities understood this willingness to embrace self-delusion and made cynical use of it to the greatest effect. The same pattern was repeated across Hungary in each of the twelve administrative districts.[36]

The spoliation of the Jews took place at a time of general economic disruption. Heavy Allied bombing of industrial targets throughout Hungary caused losses and large-scale dislocation of civilians in the bigger urban centres (especially in Budapest), and the shortages caused by the war effort also disrupted normal economic life. The closure of Jewish shops and businesses, and the surrender of Jewish property, added significantly to the disorder. And in this chaos all notion of propriety vanished, both as regards ownership and correct behaviour.

GHETTOIZATION AND THE DEPORTATIONS

Parallel with these developments, Baky, Endre and other senior officials of the Ministry of the Interior prepared detailed plans for the concentration of Jews from small communities into larger towns, and the segregation of all Jews in these towns into separate ghettos. The plans were formulated at a number of high-level official meetings starting in early April. The main concern of the government planners was to identify the people subject to the measures, and to ensure that they were concentrated in the areas designated for the Jews until deportation could be effected. The fate of Jewish property was high on the official agenda while the logistics of the deportations were being planned. Homes that would be vacated, agricultural plots abandoned, household effects left behind, and especially any valuable items that might be transported, hidden or concealed on the persons of the Jews – all these were considered in the planning process and instructions issued for their seizure and safekeeping.

On 26 April the Sztójay government approved the ghettoization measures and a decree was published two days later. But many provincial authorities began the process on the basis of the draft instructions formulated by the Ministry of the Interior even before formal approval had been given. From mid-April until mid-May, hundreds of thousands of people across Hungary were forced out of their homes and into disused factories, brickyards, Jewish community buildings and synagogues. The Jewish communities of towns of less than 10,000 inhabitants were moved into the larger regional centres and ghettos established near the railways. In the bigger towns Jews were forced to leave their homes and move to the ghettos. Only the Jews of Budapest were spared full ghettoization at this stage, although their turn would come. (It was widely believed that the Allies would not bomb the Jews, therefore leaving them in the capital would give the city a degree of immunity.[37] Höttl explained the decision to leave the Budapest community till last in his memoirs, noting that it was feared that the Jews of the capital would flee to the countryside if they were the first to be targeted.)[38] Throughout the provinces the ghettoization process was accompanied by widespread looting. Although the government made plans to take control of abandoned Jewish property and distribute it according to its political needs, in fact it proved impossible for the officials of the Ministry of Finance, the police and the Gendarmerie to do more than seize the most valuable items, and the inventories of Jewish businesses. Household chattels were left for the public. Riotous scenes of celebrations and looting made the government's anti-Jewish policy even more popular. Even poor households were looted:

They looked for everything, from alcohol, flour, sugar, everything. They said that the Jews have full storerooms, which they don't have. No one had anything to eat, and we certainly didn't. But they said that the Jews have everything. They looked, but there was nothing to find.[39]

The government's real interest was in taking control of the personal gold, jewellery and other transportable items of value. Before the actual ghettoization process was begun in each town, local teachers and civil servants were trained to assist the police in the task of ferreting out hidden valuables from the homes of the Jews. As people were forced to leave their homes, these seekers of treasure moved in.[40] Items of value that were uncovered in this way were, in theory at least, deposited in local banks, as were the compulsory deposits made following the 16 April regulations.

A member of the Hungarian parliament from the city of Munkács, Aladár Vozáry witnessed the process in Ruthenia (north-eastern Hungary):

The gendarmes go from home to home, they give several minutes for gathering some clothes and food, then they drive the Jews into their temples. They rob them of their cash, valuables, and jewels. The abandoned houses are not locked, so the free plunder starts right away. Also the livestock from Jewish barns disappears . . . On the eighteenth of April the Jews of Mukacevo, that is, 13,000 people, are notified that by 6.00 p.m. the next evening they have to move into a part of the city designated as a ghetto. One may well imagine the havoc. The transfer is carried through, nevertheless. By night most of the abandoned Jewish apartments were broken into and the pillage goes on until there is nothing left to rob. When, after a month, the official inventory in the Jewish apartments is taken, they find in most places only empty walls . . . On 26 April, there is a secret conference at city hall. Professors, teachers, public servants are given short courses on how to carry out the search of Jews in the ghetto, both as far as their persons and their homes are concerned. Next day these trainees in groups of three enter the ghetto and gather everything of value. The result of these exploits is taken from the ghetto in wagon trains and much Jewish property is plundered. German soldiers are billeted in the empty Jewish homes. They empty the available property into boxcars and send it to Germany. Inscription on the boxcars: 'Gift of the Hungarian Nation to the Germans who suffered from the bombings.'[41]

The final act of despoiling the Jews came during the period between ghettoization and the forced embarkation on the trains to Auschwitz. By this stage the authorities had nothing to gain from the deception that the assets would eventually be returned to their legitimate owners. On the contrary, anything still hidden by the hapless people awaiting deportation was being held back 'illegally' under the decrees of 16 April.

In each town the wealthier and more prominent Jews were individually interrogated by the Gendarmerie in a very brutal fashion. People were tortured to reveal any gold or jewellery that they might have hidden in their homes or given to friends and neighbours for safekeeping. (The Gendarmes accompanied the wealthier Jews back to their homes and ensured that they revealed any hidden valuables.)[42] Midwives were brought in to conduct intimate body searches on the women, and both men and women were savagely beaten.* Survivors' eyewitness reports on the brutality of the Gendarmerie during these events show a consistent pattern of behaviour across Hungary. In Székesfehérvár, where Toldi was in charge, the wealthier members of the community were 'interrogated' in Eppinger House, on Kégl György Street, with fatal results:

In June 1944 I was taken by the Gendarmes to the so-called Eppinger House. Here the Jews were beaten before they were sent to Auschwitz. The commander of Eppinger House was Károly Hanti, who was in direct contact with Toldi. All the residents of Székesfehérvár knew what was happening in Eppinger House, the cries of people were heard in the street day and night . . .

---

* Judit Molnár's account of the process of ghettoization and deportation in Szeged, a city in south-eastern Hungary, shows the extent of the examinations and the humiliation inherent in them. The deputy mayor of the town proudly reported to the Ministry of the Interior: 'the necessary medical examination and the body search was carried out by two city doctors, ten midwives and ten office nurses, in the course of ten days, usually working from 5 a.m. until late in the evening. An additional city doctor worked for one day.' The Bishop of Csanád (Endre Hamvas) complained to his superior, Archbishop Justinián Serédi, that the searches 'per inspectionem vaginae' were conducted 'in the presence of men. What is this if not completely and pervertedly treading on the dignity and modesty of women?' (J. Molnár, *Zsidósors 1944-ben az V. (szegedi) csendőrkerületben*, Budapest, 1995, pp. 140–41).

[detailed description of torture deleted] Later, in Auschwitz, I heard that the people from Székesfehérvár were the ones that arrived in the worst condition, because of the brutal tortures they had gone through even before they were deported.[43]

Toldi's direct responsibility for the conduct of the Gendarmes in his district was specifically mentioned:

Some of the residents of Székesfehérvár, as well as the president of the [local] Jewish Council, tried to appeal to Toldi to stop these brutalities, but they still continued, until all the Jews were moved together in the brick factory. These tortures caused the death of many Jews, because they were in such a bad condition when they arrived at Auschwitz that they were sent straight to the gas chambers at the first selection. If Toldi had not been the District Governor, brutalities of such proportions would not have taken place.[44]

The Hungarian Gendarmerie were aware that this would be the last opportunity to seize the assets for the benefit of Hungary. Once the Jews were on board the trains to the gas chambers anything that they had concealed would become the property of the Germans. The Jews of Székesfehérvár were deported on 14 June 1944, together with the communities of six neighbouring towns, a total of either 2,743 or 3,625 people (the sources differ).[45] The process was repeated across Hungary. Between 15 May and 8 July, 437,000 Jews were deported to Auschwitz. Between 70 and 80 per cent of them were selected for the gas chambers immediately and the remainder sent to slave labour, of whom only 50 per cent survived until liberation.

It is almost impossible to estimate the value of the property taken in this process. The economic assault on Hungarian Jewry had begun in 1938 and continued through 1944. The anti-Jewish laws created widespread unemployment, with the result that those who retained their jobs had to meet the constantly growing demands of communal philanthropy. Even before the German occupation and the formation of the Sztójay government, the community as a whole had already lost much of its relative prosperity. But the bulk of the plunder took place in the brief period between the German occupation on 19 March and the end of the deportations in July 1944, a period of only four months. Contemporary American intelligence estimates (prepared in October

1944) reported that Jewish losses were approximately 20 billion pengő ($4 billion),[46] while Braham, citing Lévai, appraised Jewish wealth at 7 to 9 billion pengő. An estimate prepared in 1946 by the Jewish community in Budapest made the most cautious evaluation of all:

It seems impossible to give figures concerning the material ruin of the Jews, as for doing so an exact evaluation of pre-war Jewish wealth would be required. Still a fair idea of the tremendous value of the robbed properties can be formed when pointing out that the entire property of 525,000 persons was concerned. It should be taken into consideration that Hungarian Jewry consisted in majority of middle-class people and that motivation of the anti-Jewish laws pretended that they had a too big share in first instance in the country's commerce and industry, and that they possessed the national wealth to a limit going far beyond their number. Cautious economic experts estimated the property of Hungarian Jewry at the time of enactment of the first anti-Jewish law to 6–8 milliard [billion] Gold-Pengő, which sum was at that time equal to some $1.2–1.6 milliards. To the stolen property should be added the damage suffered in form of lost gain caused by restrictive measures concerning the possibilities of earning.[47]

A significant part of these assets had already been consumed in the six years prior to the events that followed March 1944. Another part was seized by the Germans, whose 'expropriations' for billeting of German soldiers and officers amounted to direct looting.[48] There are few detailed local histories, but one that exists for the Jász-Nagykun-Szolnok county shows that the German forces occupied 21 per cent of the Jewish flats in the area, and would not allow the local Hungarian officials from the Financial Directorate to make inventories of the contents. When the Germans eventually withdrew, the apartments had been emptied of their contents.[49] Senior SS officers were able to asset-strip the wealthier urban Jews by the more elegant means of selling safe passage out of Hungary to a neutral country, as they had successfully dealt with the Weiss family. Some 3,000 of Hungary's wealthiest Jews were able to save themselves in this way. Yet another part of the overall sum was lost to local looting by the Hungarian population, although this affected mainly household chattels. Housing and other property was distributed to victims of Allied bombing, or to those close to the authorities. Inventories of shops, workshops and factories were taken over by the government and distributed from central warehouses by the property control officers for the benefit of the army, the Hungarian Red Cross, the Nyilas Party and others who claimed to make a contribution to the war effort. (By the end of the year the government made no pretence of control over these stocks, and the orderly distribution of the inventories turned into wholesale looting.)[50] The material possessions of the poor, the middle class and the rich were dispersed across the provinces of Hungary.

Only the transportable items of supposedly high marketable value were collected and marshalled, guarded against theft by the population or by the Germans. These were items deposited in the banks after the law of 16 April, or taken from their hiding-places after homes had been vacated during ghettoization, or forcibly removed during pre-deportation interrogations. They included items of value such as jewellery and gold, silverware and watches. It also included much that was fancied by the despoilers but was of little marketable value. Occasionally, some of the pieces were genuinely valuable or expensive, but most were mundane. The most impressive fact about these assembled objects was not the worth of individual pieces. These were the ordinary possessions of 800,000 people, and only because of the huge quantities involved was it possible to conjure up illusions of fabulous wealth.

3

Collapse of the Reich and *Hungarizmus*

On 8 July the Regent Horthy ended his self-imposed isolation from the day-to-day affairs of government. Imposing his will on Sztójay, Horthy forced the government's hand and banned any more deportations to Auschwitz. His sudden intervention was the result of many factors. Influential conservative political circles in Budapest were alarmed at the treatment of the Jews, and in June the previous prime minister and long-time adviser to the Regent, Count Bethlen, sent Horthy a letter on Hungary's political path. He took the opportunity to express forcefully his moral objections to the deportations and the looting. Although Bethlen was in hiding from the Germans, he was fully aware of what was taking place across the country. The deportations had 'soiled the name of Hungary', while the plunder of Jewish property 'has become the source of the most atrocious corruption, robbery and theft in which, alas, very considerable portions of the Hungarian intelligentsia are also involved ... the whole Christian Hungarian society will soon be contaminated irreversibly'.[1]

Horthy was also subject to increasingly insistent international pressure to stop the deportations. The Allied governments, Sweden, the Holy See and the International Red Cross all protested at the continuing deportations, and there was a distinct possibility that the Hungarian leadership would have to account for its actions at the end of the war. Furthermore, on 2 July there had been a massive daylight air raid by Allied bombers over the city of Budapest, and Horthy feared the possibility of the carpet bombing of his capital.

The Regent's intervention did not go unopposed. László Baky ordered Gendarmerie units to the capital in a move which Horthy interpreted as an attempted coup. As a result Baky and Endre were removed from their official positions of influence on Jewish policy the same day. Béla Imrédy and Andor Jaross, who had also been deeply involved in the deportations programme, were removed from power on 7 August, one month later.

On 29 August Horthy appointed General Géza Lakatos as prime minister. These moves were a conscious attempt to undo the radical right policies of the Sztójay regime and to remove the people who came to power in the wave of local government reform which the latter had initiated. Árpád Toldi was forced to resign as főispán of the Fejér district two weeks after Lakatos became prime minister.[2] But even during the Lakatos era, despite the easing of anti-Jewish pressures, the official plundering of whatever Jewish property was left continued, although, according to Braham, 'in an environment of greater legality'.[3]

In the midst of Horthy's reforms and the apparent easing of anti-Jewish pressures, the despoiling of the surviving Jews actually gathered pace. On 21 July, Albert Túrvölgyi was appointed, as officially gazetted, the Government Commissioner for the Solution of Questions Relating to the Jews' Material and Property Rights (hereafter Jewish Property Commissioner), although archival evidence shows that he was active in this role as early as the beginning of June.[4] His bureau was part of the Ministry of Finance, although other ministries were also involved in the expropriation process and there was considerable administrative confusion in the implementation of the endless laws and regulations applying to Jewish property. Túrvölgyi set up offices in Szabadság Square in Budapest, in the centre of the city's financial district and next to the imposing headquarters of the National Bank of Hungary, as well as at other sites in the capital. Branch offices were opened in the provinces. During August he began issuing detailed instructions for the valuation of the merchandise and furnishings found in Jewish property. At the same time as Túrvölgyi was appointed, the director of the Hungarian Museum of the Fine Arts, Dénes Csánky, was appointed Government Commissioner for the Evaluation and Protection of Works of Art Sequestered from Jews.[5] A veneer of legality was maintained throughout, and extensive records were kept. Goods taken from homes, shops and warehouses were brought to central storage areas, and from time to time distributed to the public to make good the serious shortages caused by the war. Procedures were established for selling the stock of Jewish businesses, especially shops, and these sales were immensely popular. Across the country forty-two 'Financial Directorates' (regional tax offices) were given the task of managing the seizure, storage and sale of the goods. Official bodies such as the Red Cross, the army and the Nyilas Party (after 15 October) were entitled to present requests for supplies, which were delivered to them regularly.[6] The Ministry of the Interior, where both Endre and Baky had the status of deputy ministers, played a supervisory role in the early stages (March–October) of the despoliation process. They made sure that the police and Gendarmerie were available for the necessary enforcing tasks, and they also ensured that the most valuable, transportable items of loot were securely deposited in a local branch of the government savings bank.[7] The occupying German forces also pursued Jewish property, and often billeted themselves in the homes of the wealthy with an eye to seizing the carpets, paintings and tapestries to be found there. But the largest concentration of valuable transportable items was in the Postal Savings Bank, where the compulsory deposits of April 1944 were held.

Even though the enthusiastic pursuit of Jewish property continued throughout the summer months, following Horthy's July intervention against the deportations, Budapest had become a less secure place for the radical right anti-Semitic groups. Baky, Endre, Jaross and Toldi were now all without official position. Further away, the Russians were approaching from the east.

In August–September 1944 the German armies in south-eastern Europe began to withdraw in the face of a massive Soviet onslaught. The Romanian and Hungarian armies contributed little to the struggle, and were of doubtful loyalty to the German cause. On 23 August the situation on the Romanian front changed dramatically when the Romanian King Michael arrested the leaders of the Antonescu fascist regime and surrendered unconditionally to the Allies. Romanian troops first laid down their arms, and later, with the signing of an armistice on 12 September, they committed nineteen divisions to fighting against the Germans rather than with them.[8]

The Wehrmacht and the Honvéd (army) formed a combined defence of five German and eight Hungarian divisions against the Soviet armies led by Marshal Malinovskii. By the middle of September the Red Army began pushing into Transylvania (north-west Romania, occupied by the Hungarians in 1940), reaching the Hungarian frontier one week later.[9] In the early weeks of October fighting took place around Debrecen, approximately twenty-five kilometres inside Hungarian territory (Trianon borders). By 24 October the Debrecen operations were successfully concluded, and the approach to Budapest across plains stretching for 300 kilometres was now open to the Soviet forces.

As the Russians crossed the border into Hungary, the government began implementing in earnest a policy of scorched earth, leaving as little as possible for the oncoming invaders. Convoys of farming and industrial equipment, food stocks and raw materials, transportation equipment and public health facilities, in fact everything that could be dismantled and loaded on trucks, freight wagons or river barges, began to flow westward in vast convoys. On 17 October, one day after the Szálasi government took office (discussed below), the new Minister of Industry, Emil Szakváry, signed an agreement with the German plenipotentiary, Veesenmayer, relating to specific supplies (4,000 tons of aluminium and other important raw materials, and manufactured items) that would be evacuated to Germany for immediate use in the war effort. Other *matériel* was to be taken to Reich territory for safekeeping, while remaining the property of the Hungarian state.[10] The Wehrmacht joined in the spirit of things, and also took 'whatever they wanted and could carry'.[11] Between 31 October and 31 March 1945, 45,383 tons of bread grain, 11,203 tons of lubricating oil, 7,905 tons of sugar, 3,040 tons of medicines and chemicals, 189,753 tons of machinery and 100,000 head of livestock were transported out of Hungary on 2,050 trains and 314 barges. The means of transportation were themselves part of the assets transferred – approximately 50 per cent of Hungary's railway rolling stock and almost 100 per cent of the Danube river transport. Those items not transported were probably in the area no longer controlled by the Szálasi government when the agreement was signed.[12]

The large-scale evacuation of Hungarian economic resources and productive capacity to the Reich was not a sudden response to the advance of the Red Army. Ever since the Hungarian decision to join Germany in the invasion of the Soviet Union in 1941 the ties between German and Hungarian industry had been growing apace. Hungarian military industries were increasingly seen as part of the German war machine, and following the German occupation in March 1944 the Sztójay government agreed to triple Hungarian production of military aircraft and engines and to maximize the exploitation of raw materials for Germany. In June, the government gave in to a German demand to make the Hungarian economy subservient to the 'global planning' of the German economy necessary for the Axis war effort. Overall, in the period 1941 to 1944, Hungary was able to retain only 20 per cent of its vital aircraft production for itself. Under the guise of establishing German–Hungarian production cooperatives, major Hungarian factories were moved to the Reich between April and August 1944.[13] The scorched earth policy agreed in October was a logical continuation of a trend that had been developing for months.

On 5 October, five weeks after the formation of the Lakatos government, the most valuable items of Jewish gold and jewellery were evacuated from Budapest to a secret and well-concealed site near the town of Zirc.[14]

In the first full-scale account of the Holocaust in Hungary, published in 1948, Jenő Lévai mentions 'Óbánya, near Zirc' as one of the sites where Jewish assets were hidden.[15] A report prepared in 1946 by a Hungarian diplomat in Austria, based on interviews with participants in the events, mentions 'Obanya puszta [meaning 'desolate area'] near Zirc'.[16] Detailed evidence collected by the French occupation authorities in post-war Austria refer to 'Óbánya Castle'.[17] These conflicting accounts reflect the obscurity of the site chosen. There is a small town named Óbánya in southern Hungary, but that is not the place referred to: the latter is far in the south, in the opposite direction from the route into Austria, and Malinovskii's forces were on the verge of capturing it in October 1944. Neither is there an 'Óbánya Castle' on any map of Hungary. The green countryside and gently rolling hills of the Zirc area are scattered with small and not very prosperous farming villages with a significant local population of Swabians. One kilometre outside of the village of Lókút (or Rossbrunn to the local German-speakers), and only six kilometres from Zirc, hidden by a grove of trees, are the remains of a modest castle, today part of what was most recently an orphanage. One hundred years earlier, the family of the Hungarian nationalist leader Lajos Kossuth lived there, hidden from the political turmoil that Kossuth had set in motion in 1848–1849. This secluded and obscure building is Óbánya Castle.

The only thing that remains of the structure that denotes a castle, apart from a marble floor and fireplace, and a plaque marking the residence of the Kossuth family, are the stone cellars. During the war the building was surrounded by a military base, adding to the security. The most valuable items of gold and jewellery were delivered by lorries to the site in the first weeks of October 1944, and stored in the cellars. The valuables were safe there, at least for a while – but it is not clear from whom: the Germans, the Russians or the government of Lakatos. Officials of Túrvölgyi's agency stated that they were ordered to the site to continue the task of inventory.[18] They were all government-appointed officials and they generated paper. Receipts were kept for everything – except, ironically, for the most valuable of the gold and jewels. These officials (one of whom, István Mingovits, plays a more significant role later) reported subsequently that Jewish valuables were also stored in three other places at this stage – Kőszeg, Sopronkőhida, and Sopronkövesd – north-west of Budapest and very close to the border with Austria.[19]

The dispersal of the most precious items from Budapest to Óbánya and the other sites marks a significant stage in the saga. Although this was a logical development in view of the danger to the capital, it is significant that the plundered goods were not yet evacuated totally from Hungary to Austria or Germany, as was beginning to happen to so much of the infrastructure of the Hungarian economy. The gold and jewels were being isolated from the mass of household effects and other movable property, which made it much easier in the months that followed for the officials in charge of the assets to take personal control of the most valuable of the loot. It is also significant that the move out of Budapest to the obscure, hidden site of Óbánya Castle took place within days of a German demand to the Hungarian government that the National Bank transfer all Hungarian gold to Germany for safe-keeping. The Germans justified this demand by pointing to the fact that the Soviets had already crossed the border into Hungarian territory, and they promised that the gold assets of the Hungarian National Bank would remain under the control of the Hungarian government even while on deposit in the Reichsbank branch in Dresden.[20] This demand came at a time when Veesenmayer's messages from Budapest to Berlin were full of reports of a possible anti-German coup in the Hungarian capital, and by offering to 'protect' their gold Berlin was probably testing Hungary's loyalty. In any event, the guardians of the Jewish assets were reconfirmed in their belief that the loot had to be safeguarded not only from the Russians but also from the Germans. Transporting the goods to Óbánya was the best that could be done to meet both of these threats.

On 16 October, the internal political situation in Hungary was once again transformed. As the Red Army approached Budapest, Admiral Horthy sought ways of breaking with Germany and taking Hungary out of the war. He hoped to achieve what King Michael had done in Romania – change alliances, or at least call for an armistice. The Germans responded the same day that Horthy broadcast his announcement to the people. They deposed him as Regent and ousted the Lakatos government, putting in its place an Arrow Cross (Nyilas) government led by Ferenc Szálasi.[21]

Szálasi had been pushed aside during the events of March that year. Neither Horthy nor the Germans wanted the radical Hungarist Party in the government. Höttl, in fact, had been a forceful opponent of the Arrow Cross for years. He distrusted their Hungarian nationalism, which would stand in the way of any willingness to make sacrifices on Germany's behalf. He felt they were too radical and erratic, and that there were other groups within Hungarian politics more reliably loyal to Germany than the Arrow Cross.[22] Following the German occupation in March, Szálasi too had had reservations – about the Germans. The Arrow Cross movement had actually distributed leaflets against the massive German presence.[23] This act ironically cast the party in the role of the sole defenders of Hungarian sovereignty, and in the seven-month period between the German invasion in March and the deposition of the Lakatos government in October, the Arrow Cross membership reversed a trend that had existed since 1940 and began to grow significantly. By October 1944 it was the largest remaining independent political force in Hungary, and therefore the only political option left to the Germans. They had no choice but to overcome their doubts and embrace Szálasi.[24]

Under the violently anti-Semitic Nyilas, Jewish property was seized in an increasingly frenzied orgy of looting – albeit under the cover of 'legality'. Árpád Toldi, who had one month earlier been deposed by Lakatos as the district governor in Székesfehérvár, was now appointed to the new position of Commissioner for Jewish Affairs (*A zsidóügyek kormánybiztosa*), under the auspices of the Ministry of the Interior (i.e. Baky's old fief under the minister Gábor Vajna), while Túrvölgyi remained Commissioner for Jewish Property, under the auspices of the Ministry of Finance.[25] His bureau remained officially active until at least February 1945, but the last documents signed by him are from November, three or four months earlier.[26] In effect, Toldi took over Túrvölgyi's responsibility for the stolen Jewish property, as well as control of the gold and jewels hidden in the cellars of Óbánya Castle. Despite the fact that Toldi was an appointee of the Ministry of the Interior, he was able to impose his authority on officials of the finance directorates who staffed Túrvölgyi's office. (Subsequently, tensions between the colonel of the Gendarmerie, acting for one ministry, and the bureaucrats, who worked for a different ministry, were the cause of significant developments in this story.) Toldi was now in the most strategic position possible, allowing him to implement the transfer of wealth that he had so forcefully enunciated during his inaugural speech as főispán of the Fejér district in May.

He lost no time. On 4 November, just nineteen days after Szálasi came to power, a new draconian law (Decree 3.840/1944) was introduced confiscating *all* Jewish property of any kind, except two weeks' supply of food, fuel and light, a few items for personal use and a small amount of cash. The law authorized the Commissioner for Jewish Affairs (Toldi) to remove all other property from Jewish houses, to take over frozen bank accounts, and to distribute the assets that had been sequestered by previous governments.[27]

ENCIRCLEMENT OF BUDAPEST

By the time Horthy made his abortive move for an armistice, all that remained of the Hungarian army was an under-equipped force of 1,071,750 men. The battle at Debrecen had been lost to the Russians, the region east of the River Tisza was no longer tenable, and the plains between the Tisza and the Danube were quickly falling to the Red Army. The railway network and factories were largely destroyed by Allied bombings (although the evacuation of *matériel* continued), and there were almost no anti-aircraft defences.[28]

Horthy's broadcast to the nation, intended to explain his change in alliances, just added to the chaos. The Germans moved quickly to establish control in Budapest, even before the Szálasi government was installed. In effect, as the Hungarian army ceased to exist, the Wehrmacht began incorporating Hungarian units into the German army, and recruiting Hungarians directly into German units (including the formation of special Hungarian units of the Waffen-SS). To reinforce German control, all of Hungary was declared an operational war zone in which soldiers were compelled to obey German commands.

For both Hitler and Stalin, Budapest became a symbol of the Reich's ability to stabilize the military situation in south-eastern Europe. Both were prepared to invest major military resources to gain the city. Malinovskii controlled almost one-third of Hungary by the end of the Debrecen campaign. He now wished to regroup before beginning his move on the capital, but on 28 October the Soviet High Command ordered him to proceed at once. Shortly afterwards Stalin reinforced this order by a direct phone call to Malinovskii's headquarters. The latter recalled the conversation in his memoirs:

STALIN: We cannot consider postponing the offensive for five days. It is necessary to go over to the offensive for Budapest at once.

MALINOVSKII: If you give me, as of now, five days, five days as an absolute maximum, Budapest will be taken . . .

STALIN: You do not understand the political necessity of mounting an immediate attack on Budapest.

MALINOVSKII: I am asking five days . . .

STALIN: I categorically order you to go over to the offensive for Budapest tomorrow.[29]

Although he was not yet deployed at the strength he felt necessary, Malinovskii had no choice but to comply. On 29 October the first direct attack on the capital began. Within a week the first Soviet tanks reached the southern and eastern suburbs of Pest (the part of the capital on the eastern side of the Danube). But just as he feared, the

Soviet forces were not yet adequately deployed to sustain the sudden advance, and German units were able to hold the line. The second, and also unsuccessful, Soviet attack on the city began on 11 November, and lasted sixteen days. The residents of the capital began to face a Russian bombardment from outside, and a frenzy of killing, looting, murder and rape by the Nyilas troops of Szálasi from within.

On 2 December the final act of the Holocaust in Hungary began. Ever since 8 July, when Horthy blocked the deportations, the Germans and the radical right had been pressing for a resumption of the deportation policy. The Jews of the capital had not been touched in the earlier wave of deportations, but the Jewish communities in the outlying suburbs of the city had been seized and sent to Auschwitz in a last act of defiance by Eichmann and his Hungarian assistants (this actually happened ten days after Horthy's ban, but was a 'rogue' action). Some 70,000 Budapest Jews had been marched off to forced labour, building fortifications around Vienna.[30] But the Jews of the capital had avoided until now the final trip to the gas chambers. Veesenmayer and the German garrison forces were keen to have the Jews removed, fearing that they would be a dissident element in the anticipated siege of the city by the Red Army. The law of 2 December forced all Jews to abandon their apartments and move into two small defined areas which were then closed off; 103,000 were crammed into these two separate ghettos in the Erzsébetváros district, the old Jewish ghetto. This was the second transfer of the city's Jewish population. Five months earlier the Jewish population of some suburbs had been concentrated into 1,840 apartments – resulting in 19,000 apartments being vacated and the contents seized.[31] This second forced transfer provided yet another opportunity for looting the emptied apartments, and the Nyilas made full use of it.

Despite their initial failure to break through to the heart of Budapest, the Soviet forces kept gathering strength around the capital. The Russians gradually encircled the city until, on 26 December, it was under full siege. The violence outside Budapest was reflected in, and perhaps incited, the violence of the armed Nyilas against the Jews in the ghettos. They made a sport of hunting down victims, and over 7,000 died as a result.[32] The fate of the Jews of Budapest during this period is well documented, as is the continuing plunder.[33]

In November and December 1944, for reasons of security and to ease the supply problems in the capital, the major government ministries were evacuated to western Hungary, close to the Austrian border and safely behind German lines. Government offices were dispersed between Szombathely, Kőszeg and Sopron, with the latter as the provisional seat of government and of parliament.[34]

The evacuation of the government left Budapest even more completely under the control of the German military and the Nyilas units. It was a perfect cover for the work of the Commissioner for Jewish Affairs. Sometime during the last weeks of November and early December, the safety deposit boxes in the Magyar National Bank were emptied in an orderly and 'official' manner, presumably under Toldi's supervision, although it is safe to presume that there was also individual looting. The asset-stripping that had been such an important part of the Holocaust in Hungary was conducted as official government policy. Once the radical right became the government, they also gained control of the transportable assets that had accumulated. Toldi's position as Commissioner for Jewish Affairs gave him the official standing and legal authority for what was the next major step in the spoliation of Hungarian Jewry. Once the long-term civil servants had been evacuated from Budapest with their ministries, Toldi was free to make a major move. Sometime between 6 and 8 December, Túrvölgyi issued instructions that whatever the Hungarian Red Cross or the army (by now effectively non-existent) did not take would be passed over to the ownership of the Nyilas Party. From that moment on, the transportation and use of the property would be the responsibility of the party. On 7 December, the remaining non-Nyilas civil servants running the 'Jewish Property Office', László Avar and István Mingovits, were instructed to leave Budapest for Sopronkövesd, near the Austrian border, taking with them a quantity of cash, jewellery and gold watches.[35] The sorting and inventory of the valuables began in Sopronkövesd during the second week in December, in the same manner as it had been proceeding in Óbánya for the previous two months.

The obsession for the appearance of legality was ludicrous. The assets had been accumulated through a process of ghettoization, brutality, and deportation to the gas chambers or slave labour at Auschwitz. Yet the façade of due process and of the orderly conduct of affairs was maintained by a collection of laws, ordinances and official authorizations. The appearance of legality was maintained to the very end. Criminals had come to power, and looting was now government policy. But despite the appearance of legality, the reality of theft and murder was never far below the surface.

THE TRAIN LEAVES BUDAPEST

Sometime between 16 and 20 December (the exact date is uncertain and the evidence is contradictory), Toldi decided it was time to evacuate the rest of the transportable items of value from the city. The Russians were closing in, and soon all escape routes from Budapest by rail would be cut. Even more threatening to Toldi was a Russian thrust that was developing from the south, and would eventually push between Lake Balaton and the Danube. This would not only complete the encirclement of Budapest, it would endanger Székesfehérvár, Zirc and Óbánya Castle. Székesfehérvár, where Toldi first came to national prominence, was sixty-four kilometres west of Budapest. Nevertheless, the forces of Marshal F. I. Tolbukhin's Third Ukrainian Front got perilously close on 23 December, a full seven weeks before the capital fell. Whatever the fate of the capital was to be, Toldi had to evacuate the valuables hidden in the cellars of Óbánya Castle as soon as possible.

In mid-December, a train of forty-two freight wagons was prepared in Budapest. There are no inventories of what was loaded onto the train at this stage, as most of the genuinely valuable items were no longer in the capital. Thousands of Persian carpets, quantities of furniture, personal items of value (watches, stamp collections, cameras, binoculars, even sewing-machines) plus literally tons of Jewish religious silverware (Sabbath candlesticks, Kiddush cups, Torah crowns and breastplates, Hallah plates, and other items) were loaded onto the train. Supplies of food and fuel (almost more scarce than the looted Jewish valuables!) were also put on board. But the exact contents and the date of departure are not certain. There is even some uncertainty about the size of the train.[36] However, as the train that transported the goods from Budapest was not the same train (although it may have contained some of the same freight wagons) that crossed the border into Austria months later, the exact size is not of great importance. What is certain is that this transport was the last chance that the people responsible for the murder and plunder of Hungarian Jewry had to escape with their loot. They took whatever seemed to them to be most valuable from the goods that had accumulated in the Property Commission's warehouses in Budapest, collected *en route* the more precious items that were hidden in the countryside, and moved all these assets closer to the border.

For as long as the train remained in Hungary, and as long as Toldi had the authority to determine what was to become of the Jewish assets, there are almost no documentary records. Later, when the train or its contents were safely under American and French control, there is a plethora of information and documentation. But for the period from December 1944 to March 1945 there are only two sources of information about the train, Toldi and his accomplices: the evidence collected by the police in post-war Budapest and Székesfehérvár for the war crimes trials, and reports of the post-war French occupation forces in Austria. Neither is very clear on this period.

However, one document survives which illuminates the handling of goods that were being stored in Budapest. It is a protocol of a meeting held on 5 December 1944 to estimate the jewellery and silver objects being held by the 'Liaison Office of the Financial Department'. The meeting was held to discuss the handling of a small quantity of goods presumably looted from Jewish apartments in Budapest that had been vacated during the forced move into the ghetto the day before. It appears that these were the pickings of one day of looting in the capital. It says nothing about the valuable items that were in safekeeping in Óbánya Castle at the time; nevertheless, it does reflect the sort of objects that filled the Gold Train. The committee recorded the following:

300 dollars in assorted banknotes
22 pieces of assorted gold jewellery
20 pieces of assorted gold jewellery with precious stones
1 silver cigar box
28 pieces of assorted silver trays
12 assorted silver dishes

13 assorted silver teapots
9 silver sugar-basins
4 silver candlesticks
8 silver vases
1 goblet
20 small silver plates
12 liqueur glasses with one plate
21 assorted small silver objects
1 silver cigarette box
1 leather wallet
2 bronze statues
11 small glass objects
1 velvet lady's handbag
[and so on, listing another 100 small items of bric-à-brac]

The tone of the committee's deliberations is reflected in the meticulous notes kept of the meeting:

Brother István Végh declares in front of the committee that there are no more valuables being held by the Finance Department, and adds that among the clothes that arrived on the 4th and 5th of December there are more valuables, but he has not seen those yet . . . The committee decided to give the $300 and the twenty pieces of jewellery with precious stones and one silver cigar box to the President of the National Bank, Brother László Temesváry, in order for him to deposit them in the National Bank, while the rest of the silver goods will be transported to the cellar of the National Bank in three boxes and one basket. The deposit receipt will be guarded by Brother Richárd Arnold. [Signed by Temesváry, a party secretary and two others.][37]

This lone document is characteristic of later records. The formality of address, 'Brother' ('Testvér', the Hungarist version of 'comrade'), the official protocol signed by four participants, the involvement of the president of the National Bank – all for a very ordinary collection of low-value items. It was as if the formality of the proceedings gave it legality.

In addition to the looted household effects and personal property, and a large quantity of supplies, the train also carried 25 uniformed police, various Customs officers and officials from the Ministry of

Finance, over 60 armed Gendarmerie and assorted Arrow Cross party officials and family members. According to some sources, over 130 people were on board when the train left Budapest. (In the months that followed, this number grew to over 200.)

Leaving Budapest, the train headed directly west to Székesfehérvár, reaching the city just before the Russians. As the village of Lókút/ Rossbrunn is not near any railway line, Toldi obtained lorries from a local army base there in order to retrieve the valuables at Óbánya Castle,[38] while the train waited in Zirc (six kilometres away). On 20 December the fully loaded train crossed the western half of Hungary towards Sopron, the final destination being Brennbergbánya, a small Hungarian mining settlement on the border with Austria. Had this been just another train in the endless stream of freight trains passing into Austria, there would have been no reason for any further delay. But this train stayed hidden within Hungarian territory for another three months.

OPERATION FRÜHLINGSERWACHEN ('SPRING WATCH')

An atmosphere of unreality, irrationality and a powerful streak of self-delusion underlie the last strategic moves of the Third Reich in the final months of the war. Hitler himself made the key decisions, but he had many willing accomplices who believed that some master stroke of military genius, or the imminent unveiling of a secret weapon, or the sudden break-up of the grand alliances between Stalin, Roosevelt and Churchill, would save the National Socialist revolution. To the millions of ordinary Germans, Austrians and Hungarians who watched their armies retreat before the Allied forces under Eisenhower in the west and the Red Army from the east, the delusion of a victory snatched in the face of defeat must have sounded as hollow and as meaningless as Toldi's constant use of the Arrow Cross greeting (last heard two days before the Russians finally occupied all of Hungary), 'Persevere! Victory is at hand!'[39]

To the surprise of his generals, Hitler decided to reinforce the German troops in Budapest and to defend the area west of the Danube, between the Hungarian capital and Vienna. This could only be done by diverting troops from the defence of Berlin against the Soviet troops moving through Poland. But it was a risk that Hitler believed he had to take. Hungarian oil and aluminium had to be defended if Germany was ever to make a comeback.

The loss of the Ploesti oilfields in Romania (in August 1944) and the extensive American bombing of the German synthetic oil industry which began before D-Day and continued throughout 1944 had deprived Germany of almost all its fuel resources. (Ploesti was one of the most heavily defended targets in all of Axis Europe. Only Berlin, Vienna and the Ruhr industrial area were allocated more anti-aircraft resources. The Americans alone lost over 300 aircraft in the effort to cut off Germany's oil from the Romanian field.)[40] After the loss of Ploesti 80 per cent of Germany's oil came from the Hungarian fields at Nagykanizsa, which produced 70,000 tons of oil monthly in 1944,[41] and a small Austrian field at Zistersdorf.[42] Allied bombing had destroyed almost all of Hungary's refining capacity; in February the Nazi Minister of War Production, Albert Speer, visited the fuel-rich areas to ensure that no scorched earth policy was being implemented for the small amount of refining that was still possible, as this would have deprived Germany of some of its last fuel resources.[43]

But oil alone does not explain Hitler's strategy. As the German war industry began to collapse under Allied bombing in the early months of 1945, the supply of raw material became a meaningless consideration. The Hungarian front, the constant attempts to relieve the siege of Budapest, and the anti-tank defences being built around Vienna (largely by Jewish slave labour taken from Budapest) absorbed resources out of all proportion, given the very real threats facing the regime in Berlin.

Perhaps Hitler believed that it would be easier to stop Malinovskii's forces in the Hungarian theatre than it was to stop the massive Soviet thrust on the Warsaw–Berlin axis. A success – any success – might have had the effect of galvanizing the German people for one last mighty effort. Whatever Hitler's reasoning, he overrode the objections of his generals and devoted to the Hungarian front seven of the eighteen Panzer divisions available in the east.[44] In January 1945 the elite Sixth SS Panzer Army of Sepp Dietrich was withdrawn from the Ardennes and sent to Hungary, with the objective of relieving the garrison in Budapest. Other experienced Wehrmacht and Waffen SS were also diverted to the Hungarian theatre. This disproportionate and inexplicable allocation of resources by the Germans did manage to slow down the Soviet advance in that sector. Neither Malinovskii nor the other leader of the Red Army forces in Hungary, Tolbukhin, used all the resources available to them, deploying only twelve divisions for offensive purposes out of the thirty-six Soviet and Romanian divisions available.[45] Only in mid-March did the Russian thrust move in the direction of north-western Hungary. Soviet forces entered Székesfehérvár as late as 19 March 1945, by which time Győr, further to the north-west, had already fallen.[46]

By the end of March the oilfields at Nagykanizsa were completely encircled. Sopron, seat of many of the ministries of Szálasi's government after it had evacuated Budapest in November, fell on 1 April. The Soviet forces had come within seven kilometres of Brennbergbánya and the Austrian border. By 4–5 April they had occupied the whole of Hungary, and the fighting there ceased. The relatively slow advance of the Soviet forces across western Hungary, and the fierce opposition they faced from the Germans under Hitler's personal supervision, had, coincidentally, gained valuable time for Toldi and the Gold Train.

4

Brennbergbánya

Rablóból lesz a legjobb pandúr ('A thief makes the best policeman')   – Old Hungarian proverb

The German decision to make a stand west of the Danube, and the commitment to hold the line against the Russians, were fortuitous for Toldi. It provided the extra time necessary to complete the work of 'processing' the Jewish assets. The train proceeded to Zirc, 120 kilometres from the capital, and the closest railway embarkation point for Obanya. While the train waited, Toldi was able to commandeer several lorries from a nearby Hungarian army base, which were then used to collect the Jewish gold and jewels stored in Óbánya Castle.[1] These goods were loaded on board the train, which then continued to Sopron, in the north-western corner of Hungary, very close to the Austrian border. The train proceeded from Zirc to Sopron with caution. German military transportation moving east towards the front along the Danube had top priority and crowded the railway network. The general evacuation of people (especially the Swabian ethnic Germans in western Hungary) and of goods to the relative safety of the territory of the Reich in the west created additional congestion on the railway network. Months of Allied bombing, the lack of rolling stock and poor maintenance after years of war, made progress difficult. This was especially true of Toldi's train, which travelled as inconspicuously as possible. State authority was in disarray at this stage of the war, and a trainload of gold and jewels would be a target for armed German and Hungarian soldiers out for private gain, as well as, ironically, the armed, violent and undisciplined units of the Nyilas that were not under Toldi's direct command.

Sopron was now one of the main seats of the Szálasi government, and whatever happened there was constantly in the public eye. Furthermore, it was a major transfer point for German troops operating in Hungary, and the Germans were even more of a threat to Toldi's plans than the presence of journalists and politicians in the town. So Toldi ordered that the train should proceed a further eleven kilometres out of Sopron, to the coal-mining settlement of Brennbergbánya.

As Toldi himself has left no account of his actions, it is impossible to know if this choice was the result of planning or was simply a happy coincidence. Brennbergbánya had been a coal-mining settlement since 1753, set in deeply forested hills on the Austria–Hungary border. Today local residents, retired miners, tell visitors the (probably allegorical) story of a shepherd who lit a fire one evening to cook his food and was later unable to extinguish it. Shallow deposits of coal began burning, giving the place its name – 'the town of the burning mountain'. The good-quality coal deposits were exploited from the eighteenth century, and a small mining town of perhaps fifty company homes grew up. By the twentieth century the Brennbergbánya mine shafts were the deepest in Hungary, and during the Second World War it became the most important source of coal in the country, with over 1,000 miners working three separate shafts. Production reached a peak in 1943.[2]

One of the largest buildings in the town in 1945 was the central bathhouse, and today a photograph of it as it looked fifty years ago has pride of place in the town museum. (The town's pub was also reputed to have been large and impressive too, but the German SS troops billeted there burnt it in an act of spite when they were ordered to retreat.) Although half demolished today, and now a private residence, the bathhouse in 1945 provided an essential service for a coal-mining town. Coal mining is hard and dirty work, and by the end of the day the dust and grime of the pit left the miners looking as dark as the coal they brought to the surface. At that time, houses did not have private bathrooms and heated water, and the communal bathhouse was a necessity rather than a luxury. It was also part of the daily shared experience of a small and close-knit community. If the bathhouse was not available (as happened when Toldi took it over for three months from late December 1944), all the families in the town were seriously inconvenienced. It was an event that would not be quickly forgotten. The miners were forced to use the more distant bathhouse at the Szent István shaft, five kilometres distant (which they had to walk, there and back).

In addition to its isolation, the limited access roads, and the great depth of its oldest mine shafts, Brennbergbánya had another very interesting feature of which Toldi must have been aware. The mine shafts in the area knew no borders. They crisscrossed the line between Hungary and Austria underground. It was possible to enter a mine in Hungary and emerge some distance from the border inside Austria. Anything hidden in the mines would be accessible from a number of different directions, and the long shafts were a convenient crossing-point for anyone who wished to avoid the border guards above ground (which was why the mines were dynamited and finally closed in 1952 by the Communist government of Rákosi).

Elsewhere in Europe, miners were identified with left-wing politics, and mining communities were usually a bastion of socialist and unionist radicalism. But Hungary lacked an organized workers' movement, and the miners had shown that they were closer to the radical right wing. In 1940 the Arrow Cross Party began to organize the miners as a first step in becoming a political party with a mass base of supporters. During October of that year the Arrow Cross organized a strike for wage increases in one mine (in Salgótarján) and then effectively spread the agitation to mines across Hungary. By the middle of the month almost 40,000 miners were on strike. It was the single most successful industrial action since the mid-1930s, and was not to be repeated for many years after.[3] The Germans eventually became alarmed at the disruption of Hungarian war production, and pressured the Arrow Cross to abandon the strike, which they did. Nevertheless, the strike demonstrated widespread support for the Hungarian radical fascists, which must have made Toldi and his Nyilas supporters feel particularly safe in the midst of a mining community, even four years later.

Toldi attempted to create an aura of 'state secrecy' around the train and around the final disposition of the Jewish assets. Although there were many rumours about the train, no one – not even the highest officials of the Szálasi government – seemed to know what was really going on.[4] The stealth, the risk of allied bombing, and the congestion on the tracks, all contributed to the delay. The train eventually reached Brennbergbanya on 27 December, a week after it left Zirc.[5] It was shunted to a siding in the town, next to the electrical sub-station, a distance of two to three kilometres from the bathhouse, where it stayed for the next three months, heavily protected by armed guards. There were also German troops in Brennbergbánya, but they were kept at a safe distance by the Hungarians. (Details of the events in Brennberg- bánya have been taken from a number of participant accounts.)[6]

When he became Commissioner for Jewish Affairs, Toldi acquired command over the government officials who worked for the Jewish Property Office. These included not only armed guards, but also accountants, jewellers and assessors. In October and November, Toldi instructed these officials to leave Budapest for Óbánya, so that a start could be made on sorting the Jewish loot into various categories, and separating out the most valuable items for special treatment. When the Gold Train evacuated the loot from Óbánya, many of these officials travelled with the train to Brennbergbánya. Others went by lorry in the same direction, but stopped at Kőszeg and Sopronkövesd where more hoards of Jewish property had been stockpiled. Loot from additional regional depots (Nagylózs, near Sopronkövesd, thirty-five kilometres away, and Sopronkőhida, sixteen kilometres distant) was trucked directly to Brennbergbánya in the weeks that followed.[7] The towns where the looted goods had been collected and warehoused were border towns, next to Austria. It would appear that the collection of Jewish property was planned with the possibility of quick evacuation in mind.

The archival record for the six months of the Szálasi government is scant. Despite frequent Nyilas insistence that victory for their cause was near, in reality the Soviet forces were making rapid progress across Hungary. By the time the train started its odyssey, the Russians controlled almost all of Hungary east of the Danube. Even the most loyal and fanatic Nyilas must have seen that the Szálasi government would not survive. The ministries had dispersed themselves in towns along Hungary's western border with Austria and maintained a façade of conducting the affairs of state from there, even though they no longer controlled much territory. The records they generated were either intentionally destroyed (to cover up their most criminal activities, including much of the documentation relating to the Holocaust), or evacuated to Austria (where they were captured by American and Russian forces in the months that followed),[8] or abandoned. These records are full of quixotic plans for agrarian reform, the redistribution of wealth and the revival of a Hungarian rural folk culture, but contain little concerning the day-to-day administration of the country. Szálasi himself withdrew almost entirely from the regular conduct of state affairs, devoting his time to writing his memoirs. (Ironically, he too found refuge in Brennbergbánya.) The tensions between the Ministries of the Interior and Finance over control of Jewish property were resolved by an order of 15 January 1945, giving the latter precedence.[9] But the Gold Train is never mentioned – either because it was considered a 'top secret affair of state'[10] or because of the criminality of the whole episode. The appearance of official business and of legality was maintained throughout, and the civil servants who gathered, listed, sorted and packed the stolen Jewish loot were acting on official instructions from Toldi. Formally, at least, they were convinced that they had done nothing wrong, and after the war when they were interrogated they gave detailed accounts of the events in which they participated. The interrogations were undertaken at different times by the American and French occupation forces in Austria, and far more extensively by the Hungarian police on behalf of the war crimes prosecutors in Budapest after the war. Some of the participants spoke from memory, others had kept notes of events as they happened and relied on these notes during questioning. At various times during the saga of the train they had even held formal meetings with written protocols, duly signed and witnessed. These protocols survived. The account which follows is based on evidence given by the custom officers, finance ministry officials, guards and drivers who were at Brennbergbánya and accompanied the stolen goods afterwards.

Once the train reached its destination the sorting and processing resumed, at a safe distance (for the time being) from the advancing Soviet troops. One by one, the contents of each wagon were unloaded onto lorries and delivered to the bathhouse, where the sorting process began. It was slow work. The items that came from the enforced deposits in the Postal Savings Banks (following the decree of 16 April) were still in the individual envelopes marked with the owners' names. Hundreds of thousands of envelopes were opened and the receipts showing ownership discarded before the items were sorted. The sorting was not done by expert assessors but by people close to Toldi, including three army officers.[11] Nine categories for sorting were established:

- precious stones and jewellery with precious stones
- gold objects without precious stones
- gold jewellery with semi-precious stones
- gold coins
- gold watches
- silver objects
- silver and metal watches
- textiles [carpets]
- furs

According to the account of one participant, it took ten days to 'process' the contents of one wagon.[12] (If this testimony is correct, the assessors and other officials must have worked in parallel teams. The train was in Brennbergbánya for ninety-two days, and there were over forty wagons to sort.) While the work continued, more transports arrived from other sites (Sopronkövesd, Kőszeg, Sopronkőhida, and presumably additional locations). The Gold Train in Brennbergbánya had become the centre for the processing of 'legally' looted assets on a large scale, and the scene left an indelible impact. As one resident of the town remembered it over half a century later:

The bathhouse was a two-storey house and it also had a big pool in it, and that was completely full with the gold and the table-sets, and all the Persian carpets, they were all stored there. The gold itself was in the Borbála shaft . . . The gold was everywhere – in the bathhouse and also in the shaft. I once went with a brigade to Köszeg and the people there told me that there was a cellar and even in that they had gold and jewellery from the government.[13]

The less valuable items were returned to the train for storage, while those of higher value were stored in crates specially manufactured for the purpose. Much of the jewellery was broken up and the resulting gold, diamonds, pearls and precious stones were sorted separately.[14] All evidence of provenance of individual items was thereby destroyed.

As the crates accumulated, they were moved for safekeeping to the central work area of the Borbála mine shaft (the deepest mine shaft in Brennbergbánya). One hundred and fifty metres underground, the crates were safe from any unwanted attention of German or Hungarian soldiers. Cash was deposited in the local branch of the Postal Savings Bank.[15]

Toldi supervised the work closely. He visited the outlying sites at Sopronkövesd and Kőszeg every three or four weeks, and the officials working there visited Brennbergbánya twice a month. Throughout the Brennbergbánya phase of the events (and even more so subsequently), the officials of the Ministries of the Interior and Finance repeated a consistent mantra: these goods were the property of the Hungarian nation, and the work of sorting, inventory and packing safeguarded the goods for Hungary by keeping them away from the Russians. This motive was repeated frequently in the post-war testimony of the participants. While it obviously contains a large degree of self-justification after the event, nevertheless it should not be dismissed entirely. By hiding the most valuable items, as they were sorted out from the mass of cargo on the train, in specially reinforced crates inside the deepest mine shaft in the country, Toldi encouraged the officials to believe that the goods would never leave Hungarian soil. The plan, they believed, was to detonate the entrance to the mine and bury the goods until, in some future time and under different political circumstances, Hungary would be free of the Soviet Red Army.

Preserving the nation's estate from the looting and raping Russian forces was seen as a noble task, but in fact it covered a basic moral inversion. These were stolen goods, which the Hungarian state had looted from its own (Jewish) citizens, and was now trying to hide from the army that was fighting to liberate Hungary from its fascist government and German occupiers. In the mad world of genocide, it was possible to disguise greed, theft and murder behind the sophistry of 'national interest'. The whole process was criminal on a massive scale, and small but obviously illegal individual acts of theft were easily overlooked.

While the officials were purportedly safeguarding the national domain, Toldi was sorting out the most valuable of the looted goods and storing them separately. Two or three times a day his personal assistant at Brennbergbánya, János Zajácz, conveyed closed packages of varying size from the bathhouse to Toldi's residence. Late at night (so the transactions would not be observed), Zajácz returned all the parcels, or what remained of them, to the bathhouse. In his post-war testimony, Zajácz maintained that he never saw the contents of the packages. But his wife was more forthcoming:

In some parcels she saw clothes, large pieces of cloth, and heavy little bags. She also saw gold watches and jewellery on the table. On one occasion Toldi showed his wife a shiny object taken out of a little bag. While dealing with the packages they would lock the doors. Mrs Toldi told her daughters on several occasions: 'Come, choose something.'[16]

From time to time Toldi authorized the sale on credit, at very low prices, of clothes, especially fur coats, and watches to the officials and the guards of the train. They were allowed to resell the goods to civilians in exchange for food. Payment for the items designated for bartering was to be deducted from future salaries, and detailed lists were kept. For Christmas, he gave the guards a few watches from the tens of thousands that were among the goods on board.[17]

As the Russians advanced, Brennbergbánya's isolation and proximity to Austria made it appear increasingly attractive. Hungary's foremost national relic, the thousand-year-old crown of St Stephen, with its elite guard, found refuge in the town for a short period. And the prime minister Ferenc Szálasi, together with his girlfriend, hid out there too.*

* The townsfolk only saw him when there was an air raid. Then his Nyilas guard (ten to thirty strong) would close the streets to clear a path for him to the air-raid shelter (these details from the Kromp interview). Höttl, in the expanded autobiography which he published in 1997, gave the following account of Szálasi's leadership in the last days of the regime: 'Szálasi showed a boundless incapability as experts had predicted. This man, who had already seen "visions" in jail and purported to have been prophesied in his future office as leader of Hungary directly by the Mother of Christ, did not think of practical measures in these days when the wave of Bolshevism swept over his country. He moved to a castle [sic. In fact, he lodged in the local doctor's residence – RWZ] near the Austrian–Hungarian border in order to write his memoirs, similar to Hitler's *Mein Kampf*, far from the world. In March 1945, he finished the first part. At that time, only a few square kilometres of Hungarian soil were still unoccupied by the Soviet army. In this last remainder of Szálasi's Hungary, there was not a single working publishing house;

The work of sorting and repacking the Jewish goods continued until late March, and was still under way when the Soviet forces occupied Győr and the surrounding area. By 27 March the officials who were working on the sorting of Jewish property stored in Sopronkövesd began to panic and decided to abandon their post. Unable to find any vehicles for transport, they walked the thirty-one kilometres to Brennbergbánya, arriving the next day to a scene of great chaos. Despite earlier plans to bury the Jewish valuables in the mine shaft where they had been stored, Toldi suddenly announced that the bulkier items (carpets, furs, silverware, household goods) were to be loaded onto the train. The more valuable jewellery and diamonds and the most expensive of the watches were to be divided between the train and a convoy of lorries and cars which were to accompany the train into Austria. (There are contradictory accounts of the size of the motorized convoy, but it seems that there were at least six and possibly eight vehicles, two lorries and between four and six large cars.)[18]

The reason Toldi gave for dividing the goods was that the train was too conspicuous a target for Allied aircraft, and these 'national assets' should be dispersed to avoid total loss in case of bombing. Only later did it become clear to the officials who accompanied the train to its final destination that the distribution of goods between the train and the convoy was not random. The most valuable items, which Toldi and his closest associates had been quietly separating from the rest of the goods, were loaded onto the lorries and cars. The train carried the bulky items and the detritus of the months of sorting and dismantling the jewellery. Five months after the event, two of these officials, István Mingovits and Vilmos Biró, gave a graphic account:

---

he therefore asked for German help to have his work printed in Vienna. His fantasies were so far-reaching, and he was so trapped in his illusionary world, that he ordered his book – similar to Hitler's – to be given to every couple on their wedding day, and decreed that no officer or clerk could be promoted without passing a test on its contents. Szálasi was not able and did not even attempt to give the country some last strength; the regime rapidly declined and finally collapsed altogether.' (W. Höttl, *Einsatz für das Reich* (Koblenz, 1997), pp. 271–2.) When Szálasi was interrogated by his American captors, his interrogator, Marton Himler (OSS), began by formally asking the prisoner to identify himself. Szálasi replied, 'Leader of the Nation.' (This anecdote from Marton Himler's nephew, Charles Fenyvesi.)

Loading the train back again was similarly chaotic, undertaken without much consideration for the value of the cargo. The boxes were just thrown about, objects became damaged. Cars carrying carpets went unchecked as of letting water through and neither the parcels' place of origin, nor their contents were documented. The same thing could be said about the carpets as neither their place of origin, nor their type received documentation (oriental or not, hand- or machine-made, etc.). Likewise, it went unrecorded how much of the gold, of the precious stones and the jewelry Toldi had taken apart. We warned Toldi that the load should be kept safe from burglary and he promised to take action. Nothing happened, however . . . The train was ready to leave. Some more boxes with silver and some carpets were added to the cargo which were previously in the storehouse. The gold left over from the lorries was put inside boxes and these placed in the covered cars of the train.[19]

As the preparations for departure proceeded, more and more people wanted to get on board the train. The officials of the Property Directorate had their families with them, as did some of the armed guards. Miners who had ferried the boxes in and out of the Borbála shaft and their families, sundry Nyilas officials and others with some claim to official status were all keen to ride out of Hungary on this train.

As loading continued, and food and fuel supplies were scrounged for the journey ahead, fear of the Russian advance began to take hold in the mining town. People who had departed by car towards the west soon returned, reporting that Soviet troops had already reached the road to Vienna. The Nyilas troops in the town became increasingly unruly, and the mine workers also began to prepare arms (although against whom is not clear). A doomsday atmosphere prevailed, and drunken Nyilas troops attempted to coerce the train's guards into handing over some of the contents. At 11 a.m. on 29 March some of the train's officials managed (through bribes of gold watches) to obtain two more carriages, which were set aside for miners and their families, and for a party from the Ministry of War Production. Because pressure for places on the train threatened to disrupt its orderly departure, Toldi ordered the unloading of crates of china to make more room for refugees. Many carpets and other valuables were also left behind. (The townsfolk who remained were able to make good use of them. A short time after the end of hostilities, some of the surviving Jews from Budapest visited Brennbergbánya on a regular basis in order to buy back household goods from the locals.[20] It is doubtful if anyone identified their own possessions, but it does demonstrate that despite the secrecy which originally shrouded the Gold Train, by the spring of 1945 its existence was well known.)

While the loading, unloading and rearranging of the train proceeded, Toldi gathered the senior officials of the Property Office and his closest collaborators – László Avar (previously mayor of Zenta and Toldi's deputy since January, in charge of the operations at Sopronkövesd), Ernő Z. Kiss, Béla Zsolnay, and Sándor Ercse. Taking the cash that had been found among the looted Jewish goods, he divided it up equally between them. Each received US$14,950, SFr17,460, £29, CAN$22, SwKr10, Palestine£6 and 5 Reichsmark. (In today's values the total amount of cash of different currencies that was divided would be worth circa 1 million dollars.)[21] The Hungarian 260,484 pengő earned from the sale of items during the months of processing were not distributed, but instead kept in a safe on the train.[22]

When the loading of the precious cargo was completed, Toldi ordered that the freight wagons be locked with official customs seals, creating the impression that the contents were of immense value. But no inventories were available to the officials on the train, and only Toldi's closest associates knew of the relative difference in value of what had been loaded onto the train and what had been diverted to the lorries. As Toldi frequently lectured the officials that worked under his command, they were 'saving part of the national estate of the Hungarian nation', and the seals on the freight wagons gave an extra aura of solemnity to the events. In fact, as became clear to Avar and his colleague, the customs seals were just another prop in the fraud that Toldi was perpetrating.

One matter remained to be finalized before the train could depart. According to the terms of the German–Hungarian agreement of October 1944, goods and supplies evacuated to the territory of the Reich remained the property of the Hungarian government. Diplomatically the Gold Train would have been protected under that agreement. But in the last days of war, when retreating German troops had priority on the railway network, Austrian railway officials began (miraculously) to rediscover their Austrian national identity as opposed to being part of the Third Reich, and marauding troops of all sorts paid scant attention to the property rights even of friendly countries, Toldi had to protect the train with whatever official documents and transport authorizations he could arrange. Just before the train was ready to leave, he was able to produce a document (*Vereinbarung* – an Agreement) of dubious authenticity, but nevertheless satisfactory to the bureaucratically-minded officials on the train. Signed in Sopron on 28 March by Dr Boden, head of the German Economic Mission to Hungary in the German Embassy, and by Toldi, the document offered asylum in the Reich to the Hungarians on the train, and recognized that the contents of the train ('*etwa 50 Eisenbahnwaggons*') were Hungarian state property and therefore they eventually would be returned to Hungary ('without customs duties being imposed').[23]

In view of the desperate circumstances in the weeks immediately before the end of the war, there is little point in examining too closely the official standing of this document. The Reich was collapsing, and no German government document had any real value. The purpose of the 'Agreement' was to assuage the consciences of the officials of the Property Office that these valuables would eventually be returned to Hungary and therefore need not be buried in the mine shaft on Hungarian territory, as they had originally attempted to argue.

With the document in hand, the train was loaded and finally ready to depart as soon as a locomotive arrived. Twenty-four carriages of loot, up to fifteen additional carriages for gendarme and army officers and soldiers, customs guards, officials of the Ministry of Finance and the Jewish Property Directorate together with their families, plus food, coal, diesel fuel, luggage, and up to seven carriages of miners and Ministry of War Production personnel – a total of forty-six freight wagons[24] – were ready to move. (A list of the 213 passengers on the train and motorized convoy, their position or rank, date of birth and town of origin is in Appendix 2.) There was last-minute panic when those in charge of the train were informed of plans for an armed attack on the cargo by Nyilas soldiers, but the attackers were bought off with gifts of alcohol and watches.[25] Late on Thursday, 29 March, both the convoy of lorries (with the most valuable of the gold and jewels), the cars (with Toldi, his wife, son and two stepdaughters, and his closest associates) and the train were ready to leave. Suddenly Toldi announced that he personally would accompany the lorries, and appointed László Avar as commander of the train.

After supervising the loading and arranging documentation to ensure, as far as possible, that the train and its contents were recognized as Hungarian property, Toldi and his immediate entourage vanished. During the night of 29–30 March, the lorries and cars carrying the most valuable of the gold, diamonds and assorted jewellery drove off into Austria, heading west. In a detailed letter which he left behind, Toldi instructed Avar to take the train to Hallein, on the other side of Austria, south of Salzburg, and the closest access by rail to the Alps on the German–Austrian border. He assured Avar that he was going ahead in order to make the necessary arrangements for the reception of the train and its passengers at the destination, and he instructed him on how to handle any German official obstructions to the train on its journey.[26]

The decision to take the valuables out of Hungary surprised the officials who had been handling these goods for the past months, and Toldi's departure with the most valuable items must have raised additional doubts. However, with the Soviets so close and the Arrow Cross regime in ruins, the possibility of refuge within the remaining territory of the Third Reich would have encouraged them to repress any doubts. In the previous months they had accepted many illusions about the course of the war and the ultimate victory of National Socialism. Now, with the Red Army units only ten kilometres away[27] and their heavy guns clearly audible, this was not the time to debate whether or not the Jewish loot should be buried in the mine shafts of Brennbergbánya. As realists, they knew they had no other option but to follow Toldi. Only weeks later did Avar and the other Property Directorate officials who were left behind on the train raise any doubts about the suddenness of Toldi's departure, and his motives.

But the train could not move until the promised locomotive turned up. It finally arrived just before noon, and after the freight wagons were attached, Avar gave the order and the train left Brennbergbánya at 5.20 p.m. on 30 March, heading towards Hallein as Toldi had instructed.[28]

5

Into Austria

TOLDI AND HÖTTL

SS Sturmbahnführer Wilhelm Höttl has already appeared in this account. As the RSHA expert on Hungary, Höttl had spent years cultivating contacts with pro-German factions of the ultra-right-wing politicians there. The link between Höttl and Toldi's patron, László Baky, was public knowledge and was well documented after the war, and the Germans had a direct role in the administrative appointments of April–May 1944 that brought Toldi to prominence as district governor of the Fejér district and of Székesfehérvár.[1] When the Szálasi regime withdrew from Budapest in October–November, Höttl relocated to the Sopron area, and he was close at hand when the Gold Train reached Brennbergbánya in December.[2]

The evidence of a direct Höttl–Toldi link *in Hungary* is circumstantial, with the possible exception of the testimony of Mrs Zajácz, cited above. This sharp-eyed woman, who had observed Toldi and his wife take jewels for themselves during the months that the loot was being processed, added the following comment in her report to the post-war Hungarian police: 'In the last days [at Brennbergbánya] SS officers came to see the Toldis with a small, dark man who wasn't wearing a uniform.'[3] The appearance of the travel authorization for the train and the determination of Hallein as the destination shortly after this meeting, together with the subsequent meetings of Höttl and Toldi *in Austria* four weeks later, suggest that Höttl, either on behalf of Himmler's RSHA or else for his own private purposes, was seriously involved in the saga of the Gold Train. Toldi's choice of Hallein as the destination links the train story – already bizarre –

to one of the most unusual episodes at the end of the Second World War.

During the last months of the war various members of the Nazi regime considered the possibility of establishing an *Alpenfestung*, or Alpine Redoubt, in the mountains of the southern rim of the Bavarian plateau.[4] The political and military leadership would withdraw there, protected by 100,000 elite troops and underground military factories that could produce the means of defending the mountains against any Allied incursion. The idea was modelled on the military plans of the Swiss army, and was discussed with various degrees of seriousness. However, while there is some evidence that preparations were made to begin building fortifications,[5] the idea was never formally adopted by Hitler nor were real steps taken to create the Redoubt.[6] Nevertheless, the topography of the area favoured defensive positions, and the idea of a Redoubt was plausible. The Allies would not risk very heavy casualties in an assault on an Alpine fortress, so the Nazis would gain time, allowing one of the favourite scenarios of Nazi foreign policy to mature – that the grand alliance of America, Britain and the Soviet Union would crumble once hostilities ended in Europe. Eventually the Anglo-Saxon powers would have to contain Stalin, and when that happened they would need the Germans as their allies. The Nazis' problem was to survive politically until that scenario could come about, and the Alpine fortress offered hope of the necessary margin of time. Even if no real steps were taken to prepare a Nazi retreat into the Alps, the logic of the idea was appealing at a time when the German army was being pushed back on all fronts. And it was appealing not only to the Germans.

As an intelligence officer, Höttl was adept in making use of the developing situation. When Germany's military position deteriorated, it was Höttl's job to prevent the Hungarian Arrow Cross government from wavering in its support for the Third Reich. The promise to include the Hungarian political and military leadership, and elite Honvéd units, in the Alpine fortress was an effective means of strengthening their resolve to fight on. As Höttl recalled in his memoirs, the fact that many European governments-in-exile had found refuge in Britain following the occupation of their countries (by Germany) at the start of the war was a convincing precedent, and similar refuge in a Redoubt organized by Germany might save the necks of her own allies at the end of the war.[7] Many of the leading figures of the Szálasi regime – politicians and generals – did in fact make their way to the Salzburg–Alt Aussee area, which was part of the territory that Höttl defined as the Redoubt.[8]

Hallein was certainly within the defined area, and that was where Toldi had directed the train. Instead of ordering Avar to bring the train to the Swiss or Liechtenstein borders of western Austria (the logical route for anyone attempting to escape with looted assets), Toldi directed him to the mountains, where so many of the senior members of the regime he served were also to be found. (There is no documentary evidence to support this explanation for Toldi's actions at this stage as he did not share his reasons with any of his assistants, but there is ample documentation of a Toldi–Höttl link at the next stage in the story of the train.)

The illusion of the Alpine fortress also served Höttl and some of his superiors in the RSHA in an additional, but very different, way. As the end of the Third Reich approached, some of the most senior SS officers of Austrian origin attempted to form alliances with non-Nazi conservative circles in Austria, with whom they had common cause in avoiding a Russian occupation. Between February and April 1945, Höttl established contact with the Bern station of the American intelligence organization, the Office of Strategic Services (OSS). His objective was to facilitate the Anglo-American occupation of Austria before the Red Army crossed the border from the east, and as a bait he offered to sabotage the establishment of the Alpine Redoubt. The idea certainly attracted the attention of Allen Dulles, the OSS chief in Bern who was responsible for contacts with German factions that wanted to hasten the end of the war. Dulles authorized his agents to meet Höttl a number of times between February and April, and at each meeting Höttl tried to entice the Americans into making political concessions regarding the nature of the Allied occupation in Austria.[9] At the meeting of 29 April with Dulles's representative, Edgeworth Murray Leslie, Höttl went so far as to present a crudely drawn map of the purported borders of the Redoubt, and, as an additional incentive, drew the American's attention to the presence of the Hungarian Gold Train, which by then was well within the area of the Alpine fortress. The OSS listened to

Höttl, and Dulles's reports to Washington about his talks with the emissary of the SS were even positive. (The OSS station in Bern was one of the main conduits for intelligence information about the Redoubt. Höttl was only one of many 'well-placed' sources that Dulles attracted.)[10] By the crucial last month of the war, all Allied intelligence units believed that the retreat of the Nazi leadership into an Alpine fortress was a possibility. For the Allies, that was a matter of real concern. For the Hungarian fascist leadership, it was a last hope.

Dulles allowed the talks with Höttl to proceed during the period February to April solely for the purpose of gaining information. The demands of Höttl's Austrian clique were totally unrealistic in the context of agreed Allied strategy for the occupation of Austria, and Washington was not prepared to make any concessions to an Austrian 'opposition' group at the expense of the Soviets. All Höttl achieved was to establish his bona fides with the new political overlords of southern Austria, the Americans – something which served him in good stead in the months ahead. But the threat of the Redoubt, Höttl's only card in a desperate gambit, was a bluff, to the relief of the Allies but to the great disappointment of the Hungarian politicians, generals and army units who had concentrated in the area only to discover that the fortress did not exist.

TRAIN JOURNEY TO NOWHERE

The trip across Austria to the train's destination of Hallein, on the border with Germany, is a distance of 350 kilometres. Today it can be comfortably driven in a few hours. But in April 1945, during the last weeks of the war, this remaining area of the Third Reich was one of the most chaotic in Europe. Hundreds of thousands of Wehrmacht and SS troops withdrew to southern Austria – some units fleeing the Allies in total disorder while others regrouped to block the Allied advance into the mountainous region. There was no longer any functional central control from Berlin, and land communications throughout the Reich were subject to continuous Allied bombing. The only effective authority was that of the local Nazi Gauleiters, in particular the powerful personality of Franz Hofer, Gauleiter of the Tyrol–

Vorarlberg region. As the day of reckoning for the Nazi regime approached, many local politicians in towns and cities across the Tyrol and Vorarlberg areas of southern Austria suddenly revived their regional loyalties. Self-interest dictated that they were Tyrolians and Vorarlbergers before they were Austrian, and certainly they were 'never' Nazis. Their future well-being depended on persuading the Allies, when they arrived, to share this convenient view of the preceding years, despite the fact that the region was one of the first in Austria to vote Nazi (even before 1933) and to support the union between Germany and Austria in 1938. Other local residents remained loyal to the Nazi regime to the end, and there were armed clashes between SS units and local residents.[11] To add to the chaos, tens of thousands of Hungarian soldiers and civilians[12] (including the entire Arrow Cross government, stray Hungarian soldiers and 8,000 members of the Hungarian SS division)[13] sought refuge in the area. As late as the summer of 1945 considerable concentrations of SS troops had still not been disarmed, and sporadic anti-Allied activity (including occasional sabotage) continued in the Salzburg and Tyrolian Alps.[14] It was into this chaos that the Gold Train had to travel and, not surprisingly, its progress was slow.

Through this confusion, and along the route that the train was to take through Austria, the final phase of the Holocaust of Hungarian Jewry was taking place. In October and November 1944 the Germans demanded Jewish slave labourers from among the surviving community in Budapest. Seventy thousand people, including whole families, were marched across western Hungary and into Austria. For months these people were forced to dig anti-tank trenches along the Austrian–Hungarian border, and around Vienna. Others were sent to armament factories and still others to clear bomb damage in the city. In April 1945, as the Soviet Red Army approached, the Germans began to move the surviving Jews westward, deeper into Austria, towards the concentration camp of Mauthausen and its satellite camps of Gusen, Gunskirchen and Ebensee. Starved and poorly dressed, they were marched through a broad swathe of Austrian villages and towns in groups that spread over almost 200 kilometres. Many thousands died of exhaustion. Those who straggled or slowed down the progress of this forlorn column were ruthlessly shot and their bodies discarded by the wayside. Previously the Austrian population had been able to insulate itself from the violence of the Nazi system; these things took place inside the closed camps. But now, in its last days, the Nazi regime was flaunting the brutal realities for the Austrian population to see. For the civilians who witnessed these death marches, it was a last opportunity to extend humanitarian aid to the passing columns (by offering food or water), or to participate in the killing and cruelty, and both responses are on record.[15] It was one of the cruel ironies of the period that as they trudged through the towns of Wiener Neustadt, Wilhelmsburg and Amstetten, their property passed by them on the Gold Train.

The first stage of the train's route, Brennbergbánya to Ágfalva, and then on to the Sopron–Wiener Neustadt line via Laipersbach, was not used by military transport because the tracks were weak, with bad roadbeds,[16] and so there was no congestion on the line. But a few kilometres out of Brennbergbánya the train met its first mishap. The poorly maintained track between the mining town and Ágfalva is very steep, and the first ten carriages became separated from the rest of the train. Although the train driver slowed down, there was minor damage when the separated carriages crashed into the back of the train on the downhill slope.[17] They managed to reach Wiener Neustadt, across the border, before the anticipated evening air raid. Another carriage (of unknown origin) was attached to the train at this point, but in the process a coupling hook was broken and the train delayed till 4 a.m. the next morning before it could continue. (This carriage was taken as far as the next stop, where it was left.)[18] On the afternoon of 1 April the train reached Wilhelmsburg, south-west of Vienna, having travelled 207 kilometres in the first twenty-four hours after leaving Brennbergbánya.

At this point it appeared that the train might not be able to proceed at all. The locomotive that pulled the train came with a German operator and four German soldiers under the command of a Captain Kleckner. The Hungarians had taken care to ply them with food, drink and gifts (from the train's ample supply), and they had been very cooperative. Kleckner was particularly effective in warding off curious officials and rowdy, marauding soldiers. But the soldiers were replaced at Wilhelmsburg, and when the Austrian railway officials discovered the nature of the train's contents they attempted to prevent its departure. There was a delay while Avar, Kleckner and the Austrians were arguing, and the locomotive, together with its operator, was sent elsewhere.

During the days spent waiting for a new engine, the neighbouring town of St Pölten, just twelve kilometres from Wilhelmsburg, was bombed in an air raid. The general disorder grew. As Mingovits, Avar's second-in-command, observed, 'the area was swarming with fleeing, penniless Hungarians'. The only hope for obtaining a new locomotive was through the intervention of higher railway authorities. Once again it was necessary to distribute some of the looted goods, and only after they had been bribed with alcohol and watches did the station officials direct Avar and Kleckner to the residence of the regional railway director. On the morning of 6 April, after visiting this official at his home, a new locomotive became available, and at 11 a.m. the train was able to leave. The Hungarians were required to agree to keep off the main rail line and follow a circuitous route on secondary tracks in order to avoid any obstruction to scheduled traffic. The train reached nearby Wieselburg[19] at 6 p.m. that evening. After wasting five days at Wilhelmsburg, the train was now travelling at only five kilometres an hour.

The next morning the train was able to return to the main line, but progress was still slow. Somewhere between Wieselburg and Linz, German soldiers tried to force Avar and his party to surrender some of the cargo. (The testimony of the passengers on the train routinely refers to armed German soldiers as 'SS', which makes the attribution doubtful. But at that stage in the hostilities all armed German units could have presented an equal danger to the Gold Train.) The Hungarians were also armed, and they managed to contain the Germans in the brake compartment of the train, finally forcing them to get off when the train passed through Linz.

The passage to Salzburg was uneventful, and they arrived towards the end of the day. However, at Salzburg they were informed that the train would not be allowed to proceed to Hallein, and nor could it stay where it was. The German military transport authorities in the region did not want a ramshackle Hungarian train loaded with loot and refugees anywhere near the lines of rail communication in such a vital area for military traffic, and the train was sent on its way. Travelling south-west, it passed through the foothills of the mountains of the Bavarian Alps, with Hitler's mountain-top sanctuary at Berchtesgaden only a few miles away. These towering peaks had been their only hope of protection from the oncoming Allied forces, but they remained unreachable as the train continued its journey. As for asylum in an Alpine fortress, it now became clear that there was no such thing.

The train eventually found refuge in the mountain village of Hopfgarten in Nordtirol on the morning of 8 April. It had travelled 500 kilometres from its starting-point in Brennbergbánya in ten days. Under other circumstances, Hopfgarten would be a good place for seclusion and some mountain air. But in the last weeks of the war it was the worst place possible. A few kilometres down the road, at the entrance to Brixen im Thale, stood Schloss Itter, a prisoner-of-war camp for prominent French military and political figures since 1940[20] and now also the headquarters of the Southern Command of the Luftwaffe – the only functioning command centre that remained for the German air force. There were also very large numbers of retreating Wehrmacht and SS units in the area.

TOLDI'S JOURNEY

Far less is known about the journey of the lorries and cars after they left Brennbergbánya than is known about the train's. While the group travelling with the train eventually returned to Hungary and gave evidence, Toldi's party could not risk appearing before any tribunal. Toldi was accompanied by his wife,[21] their twelve-year-old son, and his two stepdaughters. Ernő Z. Kiss, an official of the Property Directorate and active in the special work of sorting out the most valuable items at Brennbergbánya, was also in Toldi's party, together with his family. There were also a number of guards and drivers.

Shortly after the convoy abruptly left Brennbergbánya during the night of 29–30 March, it was caught up in an Allied air raid. The cars and lorries scattered, and the passengers took refuge in the forest. When the air raid was over, the Z. Kiss family discovered that the vehicles were nowhere to be found. They had been abandoned, and had no choice but to return on foot to Hungary.[22] Toldi had managed to shake off one of the most important of the Property Directorate officials, and now travelled with his own family, the drivers and some guards. Despite the chaos on the roads and the risk of armed attack, he managed to get the convoy to Hallein, ahead of the train.

Once the train had reached Hopfgarten, Toldi tried to reimpose his authority on Avar and the others. The refusal of the German army transportation officers to allow the train to stop at Hallein was a blow to Toldi's image as a man of standing with the German authorities, and he tried to brush it off as a mistake. In a letter sent to Avar the day the train arrived at Hopfgarten, Toldi said that 'as there are no marshalling yards here [Hallein] at all, I arranged for the train not to be sent back [to Hallein] but to have it proceed towards Innsbruck'. After instructing Avar 'to keep good order', he said he would join him in Hopfgarten soon.[23] Two days later Toldi wrote again – this time ordering Avar to have the civil servants (the finance and customs officials), and all the employees of the Ministry of War Production, leave the train. Only the armed guards should be allowed to remain. The officials who had worked with the property should be paid a last salary of 1,000 Reichsmarks. (Toldi also asked Avar, who had the keys to the cash box, to prepare Toldi's own salary for March, April and May.)[24]

Three days later, on 13 April, Toldi turned up at Hopfgarten together with his family and the lorries and made a preposterous demand: he instructed Avar to hand over to him another six boxes of gold from the loot on board the train.[25] Previously, in his capacity as Commissioner for Jewish Affairs for the Szálasi regime, Toldi had the full authority of government behind him and his authority was credible. But the Russians had occupied all of Hungary by 4 April, and continued their push west. The Red Army was fighting on the outskirts of Vienna when Avar's train passed through Salzburg, and on 13 April, the day Toldi attempted to take over control of the rest of the Jewish valuables, Vienna fell to the Soviets. Avar might well have asked himself whose authority Toldi now represented. In any event, Avar refused the order.

While Toldi and Avar debated the control of the assets, another two lorries turned up at Hopfgarten, carrying expensive furs that had been stockpiled at the repository in Sopronkőhida. Toldi sold one of these coats for 3,000 Reichsmarks and took a further three for his family, as well as offloading from the train some of his personal luggage.[26] Two days later he departed, taking the lorries and their most valuable contents with him in the direction of Innsbruck and the Vorarlberg region. He announced that he would try to find a suitable refuge for the train, and would be in contact again soon.[27]

The incident seems to have raised doubts in the minds of the officials on the train. For the first time a strong note of suspicion of Toldi enters into their testimonies. He was known to be carrying a number of fake identities with him, and Avar openly expressed concern about his real motives. Until their suspicions took hold, Avar and his colleagues were satisfied in the belief that while they did not have any inventories of the goods on the train or on the lorries, Toldi, as the senior officer responsible, did have a detailed record. However, once Toldi's motives were questioned, the officials charged with the care of the confiscated Jewish assets suddenly realized they had no accurate record of the contents of either the train or the lorries. Avar searched for inventories among the boxes stored on the train, but without success.[28] They had no choice but to begin to compile a new inventory, based on notes which some of them had kept privately, and on memory.

THE INVENTORY

Inventories do exist for the contents of both the train and the lorries, although none of them were compiled in Brennbergbánya prior to departure. Toldi intentionally did not allow a full record of the goods to be made while they were stored in the mine shaft, although he was careful to ensure that the contents of each box were clearly identified. As the myths about the Gold Train spread, the supposed value of the loot was constantly inflated. The records of the Foreign Ministry in Budapest contain two separate inventories from Hungarian sources, one prepared by Avar while he was waiting in a displaced persons camp for repatriation to Hungary (presumably based on the notes and memories of the Property Directorate officials on the train in Hopfgarten), and the second of unknown provenance. The report of the Hungarian Consul in Salzburg, Andor Gellért, to the Hungarian Foreign Ministry (see n. 16, Chapter 3) cited the information given to him by Avar in August, and itemized the contents of the train. But Avar's subsequent report of October 1945 was far more detailed. These reconstructed lists became the basis for all subsequent demands by the Hungarian government and the Jewish community of Budapest for the return of the assets. After the war, the Allied occupation authorities were able to prepare detailed inventories based on a direct count of the items under their control.

AVAR INVENTORY, OCTOBER 1945[29]

10 boxes of gold, average weight 45 kilograms

1 box of gold money, average weight 100 kilograms

18 boxes of gold jewellery, average weight 35 kilograms

32 boxes of gold watches, average weight between 30 and 60 kilograms

In a sealed suitcase $44,639; SFr52,360; Palestinian pounds 840; CAN$66; SKr5; Reichsmarks 15; 260,484 pengő, and in this suitcase there was a separately sealed package of diamonds

1,560 boxes of silver items, varying weight

1 box of silver bullion

Approx. 3,000 Hungarian and Persian carpets (not all hand-made)

'I can't tell the number of boxes, which contained clothes, valuable fur coats, stamp collections, lace collections, cameras, gramophones, silver jewellery, porcelain, watches and pocket-watches (approx. 8–10,000 pieces) . . . there were also two unselected wagons, which contained all kinds of mixed items of value.'

The following valuables were taken from Bremberg to St Anton (located in Vorarlberg) by Lieut.-Colonel Árpád Toldi:

31 boxes of gold

2 boxes of gold money

3 boxes of gold watches

8 boxes of diamonds

2 iron caskets which contained diamonds and real pearls

UNIDENTIFIED INVENTORY, OCTOBER 1945[30]

Type of box	No. of pieces	Average weight	Note
Gold	41	45 kg	Plain gold objects, bracelets, cigarette holders, pocket-cases, chains
Gold watches	35	—	Male and female pocket and hand watches
Gold jewellery	18	35 kg	Jewellery with precious and semi-pr. stones
Diamonds	8	38 kg	Jewellery with diamonds, real pearls
Gold money	3	100 kg	Mixed money and gold bars
Total		105 boxes and 2 iron caskets with selected diamonds and real pearls decorated jewellery	

Taken to St Anton by Dr Toldi,* commissioner, or by his order by Dr Balogh, Gendarme captain:

Gold signed boxes	31 pieces
Gold money boxes	2 pieces
Gold watches boxes	3 pieces
Diamond boxes	8 pieces
Total	44 pieces, plus 2 iron caskets of selected diamonds

The American authorities had brought from Werfen:

Gold signed boxes	10
Gold money	1
Gold jewellery	18
Gold watches	32
Total	61 boxes

Summary:

Dr Toldi took 44 boxes

The Americans took 61 boxes

Total: 105 boxes, plus 2 iron caskets

* It should be noted that the title 'Dr' in this case implies the holder is a graduate in law of a central European university. None of the main protagonists in this story was a doctor of medicine, or holder of a Ph.D. – R.W.Z.

When Toldi left the train this second time, two of the officers of the guard unit left with him. One of them, Captain János Balogh, a Gendarme officer, was closely associated with Toldi when the latter was in Székesfehérvár as főispán.[31] Toldi appointed two of the army officers in their place as commanders of the guard unit on the train. Lieut.-Colonel Count Markovits and Lieut. Csillagi only joined the train at the last moment in Brennbergbánya, and Avar's colleagues among the civil servants resented their presence: 'They called us communist renegades and said that Avar was a working-class agitator, and threatened to turn us over to the Gestapo.'[32]

Toldi had advised Avar to take the train on to Innsbruck, seventy kilometres away (and closer to the Swiss border), where he would await them. Markovits and Csillagi's intimidation and threats were effective, and on 17 April the train was made ready to move on.[33] But before a locomotive became available, the rail bridge at Brixlegg (south of Hopfgarten), the only crossing over the river Inn on the main east–west railway line through the Inn valley west of Wörgl, was destroyed in a massive Allied raid on 19 April, and the way to Innsbruck was blocked.[34] There was nothing to be done but protect the cargo and 'await the authorities'. This was the safest course for civil servants – their problem was that they were no longer sure who those 'authorities' were going to be in the changing military and political situation of the final days of the war.

Food supplies for the guardians of the treasure and their families now began to run low. The miners and officials of the Ministry of War Production (who had joined the train at Brennbergbánya and had not yet dispersed) seem to have had an ample supply, and were doing a brisk trade on the black market with the local residents. Another Hungarian train, carrying Nyilas officials and large supplies of food, was somewhere nearby (between Hopfgarten and Kirchberg, fifteen kilometres away), but the local Austrian authorities seized those supplies for the local population. So food reserves became a growing concern for Avar's group.

While the train was stranded, it began to attract unwanted attention. On 20 April one of the carriages was broken into through the roof. Witnesses reported seeing a German soldier, a railwayman and a civilian with an axe on the carriage. When Avar broke open the customs seals on the doors and inspected the contents of the carriage, there were signs of pilfering.[35] A suitcase containing fountain pens and another containing 'gold and silver valuables in envelopes' were found open. An indignant Avar reported the burglary to 'the authorities', asking them 'to start the criminal procedure'.[36]

In the broader scheme this was a trivial event, although pilfering was to become increasingly problematic as the days passed. But it is very revealing. The contents of the train were the property of Hungarian Jews whom the Hungarian state had despoiled and then sent to their deaths or to forced labour. Yet the guardians of the loot had convinced themselves that they were the conscientious guardians of state property, and they carefully documented their own involvement at every stage of the processing and transportation of the treasure, believing that they would be applauded for their diligence. Only Toldi understood the indefensibility of what they were doing; as he instructed Avar before the train left Brennbergbánya, 'do not mention my name or anyone's name. Everyone should remain unknown.'[37]

On 22 April, a lorry appeared unexpectedly. The driver, Gyula Galambos, announced that he had brought an additional shipment of Jewish goods and that he had travelled with a second lorry which had run out of fuel not far from Hopfgarten. (This lorry was retrieved the next day when Avar provided fuel from the supplies carried on the train.) Galambos had left Hungary by way of one of the other sites where Jewish property was collected, driving through the German lines with a cargo of diamonds, gold, alcohol and clothing. Toldi had instructed him, as he had instructed Avar, to take his cargo to Hallein. Galambos had survived aerial bombardment, accusations by the Germans that he was a Russian spy, attacks by retreating German soldiers, and, finally, running out of fuel. In the course of his adventures he had passed through Vienna, where the Quartermaster-General of the Hungarian army, Major-General István Olchárvy, provided him with documentation authorizing him to deliver the goods to Hallein.[38] Galambos had also met on the way with minister Hellebronth and the former German plenipotentiary to Budapest, Veesenmayer. Hellebronth told him that he thought Toldi was in Hallein, but Veesenmayer, who was apparently well informed of Toldi's whereabouts, told Galambos that Toldi was either in Hopfgarten or Landeck, 110 kilometres further west than Hopfgarten, in the Arlberg area. Galambos had only enough fuel for the closer possibility, and thus turned up in Hopfgarten.

The next day, 23 April, Captain Balogh returned to the train, carrying a letter from Toldi to Avar and Ercse. The letter was a reprimand, accusing Avar of lax discipline. Toldi demanded to know why the train had not gone to Innsbruck as he had instructed and why Avar had not submitted written reports on the departure from Brennbergbánya and the journey as far as Hopfgarten. The letter concluded with an order that 100 litres of alcohol on the train be handed over to Balogh, together with changes of clothing and under-wear for three men and five women.[39]

Balogh's visit to the train for supplies came at an opportune moment, and he demanded the valuables from the lorries that had just arrived, for delivery to Toldi. An argument developed between Balogh and Avar, who did not want to give up any more of the treasure to Toldi's care. A compromise was reached, with some of the newly-arrived gold and jewels going with Balogh and the rest staying on the train.[40] Distressed by the initiative he had taken, and in search of a 'superior authority' to endorse his actions, the next day Avar went to Kitzbühel to consult with the senior Hungarian officials and politicians who had found refuge there.

Balogh reappeared three days later in Hopfgarten. This time he carried another letter from Toldi, full of censure for Avar and worded much more strongly than the previous one. Blaming Avar for allegations against himself (presumably made during Avar's meetings in Kitzbühel), Toldi berated the commander of the train for weakness in these 'deadly serious times', for lack of discipline and resolve, and threatened punishment. Then, in an abrupt change of tone, Toldi reminded Avar that the purpose was to avoid 'the enemy' taking control of the valuables, and to save them for 'the new Hungarian life'. The German authorities supported this goal fully, Toldi wrote, and Avar should prove himself worthy of it, too.[41] Besides conveying this letter, Balogh had come to claim the rest of the gold and diamonds transported on the Galambos convoy. The bluster of the letter was clearly designed to soften Avar's opposition to handing them over. But it had the opposite effect. Avar and his party now resolved to obstruct

Toldi. Balogh demanded the crate of diamonds, and was given instead a sealed box of office equipment as a ruse. When he also demanded a large (200lb) box of gold coins, he was refused.

The train, and the differences between Toldi and Avar, were becoming a *cause célèbre* in Hungarian refugee circles. Politicians and senior Hungarian officers visited Hopfgarten, and Avar and his colleagues lobbied for support in Kitzbühel. On 30 April they met Béla Imrédy (the previous prime minister) there, but he refused to intervene.[42] (The Kitzbühel visits at least produced some cash relief. Hungarian treasury officials handed over 10,000 Reichsmarks to Avar's men to enable them to buy food. It was distributed equally among all the passengers on the train.) The next day the Hungarian Consul-General in Vienna (of the Szálasi regime and earlier), Ferenc Vajta, turned up in Hopfgarten and attempted to take control of the assets on the train. When Avar refused, Vajta asked Gábor Vajna (Minister of the Interior in Szálasi's government), who was also in Kitzbühel, to intervene, but Vajna refused to be involved, just as Imrédy had.[43] As Vajna had worked closely with Toldi during the Brennbergbánya period, and was the source of his authority as Commissioner for Jewish Affairs, the fact that he now washed his hands of the whole matter was a clear sign to Avar. Avar informed Ferenc Vajta that he would defend the train with armed resistance, and prevent him from taking control.[44] Other emissaries from the pro-Szálasi community also tried to persuade Avar to hand over the treasure, but they too had no success.[45]

Toldi made a final attempt to win back Avar's loyalty. In a letter sent on 27 April, one day after his last missive, he issued a series of orders about personnel changes among the guard on the train, about the fate of his personal luggage, and most importantly, he insisted that the three crates of precious stones on the train be sent to him at once ('instead of the box [of office equipment] that was sent to him by mistake'). He tried to reassure Avar that he had made 'arrangements' with the German authorities, and that 'matters will be dealt with when the need arises'. They were in a foreign country, he reminded Avar, and should stick together as Hungarians. The treasure would be 'saved for the future' if he could be assured of 'disciplined and honest help'. Perhaps as a sign of his earnestness, or as a bribe, Toldi added that the chickens he had had transported with his luggage were 'hereby given to Avar for free'. The letter was signed 'with brotherly Hungarian love'.[46]

A more serious threat to the train appeared from ragged, marauding SS soldiers. On 3 May the train's passengers watched as the Germans took up positions on the surrounding slopes (the Hopfgarten railway station is in a valley with steep mountains on either side), preparing to attack the train. There were approximately 150 Hungarians still on the train, but that number included women and children, and the guard was only lightly armed. Avar was able to defuse the situation by offering the SS soldiers 500 watches, clothes, and some rum. The next day there were reports of two more groups preparing to attack the train, and once again Avar used his negotiating skills to avoid greater loss by offering the various groups food, carpets, more watches, and alcohol. In each case he insisted that the SS should sign receipts for the goods they had received [47]

The unwanted attention the train was attracting began to alarm the town's authorities. Even worse, the internal Hungarian conflicts over control of the treasure made its status as state property of a friendly country now appear questionable. Perhaps they were just looted goods? The Allies would soon occupy the region (the American forces were already very close to Hopfgarten and the French had already occupied the Vorarlberg zone to the west) and the train might prove an embarrassment with the new authorities. So on 4 May the Kitzbühel Regional Council decided that the train would have to leave. Locomotives would be found to pull the carriages to Böckstein, a safer and more isolated town in the Gasteiner valley, 122 kilometres away. (Böckstein is at the end of the road that passes through the better-known resort of Bad Gastein.) Not only was Böckstein more isolated, but it stood near the entrance of the Tauern railway tunnel. The train could be hidden there until the Allies were in firm control of the region.

Preparations for the journey began at once. Five members of Avar's party and their families decided to leave the train at this point (including Sándor Ercse, the only senior Property Directorate official to have left after Z. Kiss had been abandoned by Toldi). But before the locomotives arrived, officers from the SS unit turned up once again, and demanded more food, fuel, the lorries (presumably those of the Galambos convoy) and more loot from the train. The SS were desperate, and they kept returning to the train during the course of the afternoon. Before the locomotives turned up and the train could leave, the SS had to be bought off once again. When the train did finally depart Hopfgarten, at 7.45 p.m. on 4 May, the remaining Hungarians on board shared a genuine sense of relief.[48]

BÖCKSTEIN

The train arrived at Böckstein station during the night of 4–5 May, to a chaotic scene. 'There were soldiers everywhere, and the railway workers were so distracted that they paid us no attention. The stationmaster was given a present [of alcohol], which persuaded him to offer the necessary assistance.'[49] The next day the locomotive took the twenty-four carriages with cargo to the Tauern tunnel (a few kilometres away) while the carriages with the refugee passengers remained at Böckstein station.

On the same day, more Property Directorate personnel abandoned the train with their families and some of the guards deserted, disappearing into the stream of displaced persons and refugees. Those who remained awaited the arrival of the Americans. Either because he still felt the need for the protective embrace of some form of authority, or perhaps just needed to reinsure his own position, Avar began to look for anyone in the vicinity who had been in an official position in the wartime Hungarian government. At Bad Gastein he met the secretary of the Hungarian National Opera, Jászai, but he was not senior enough. Jászai told him that members of the staff of the Szálasi government's Embassy in Vienna were staying at a hotel in the town, and Avar immediately went to ask them to extend their 'protection' over the train.[50] At the same time, he sought out the assistance of the Swiss consulate and the office of the International Committee of the Red Cross in Bad Gastein, asking them to notify the US forces that the train was awaiting their arrival.[51] Avar prepared white flags and armbands, and the watch for the US army began.

Avar was anxious that the train might come under attack from armed looters. His fears were justified. At noon on 10 May, a group of twenty to thirty German soldiers attempted to break into one of the freight wagons, but they were forced to leave by the armed Hungarian guard.[52] This attack came after the formal end of hostilities, and is indicative of the lawlessness of the interim period until the Allied forces took full charge of their zones.

Three weeks before these events, on 15 April, General Eisenhower had directed that the US 3rd Army and 6th Army Group, fighting their way across southern Germany, turn south and south-east into Austria. General Patton's 3rd Army was to seize Salzburg and progress eastward till he met up with the Soviets on the Danube, while General Devers was to take control of the Alpine area south of Salzburg, to capture the Alpine passes and routes into Italy.[53] The first American troops crossed the border between Germany and Austria on 28 April, at approximately the same time that the French 1st Army, led by General Delattre de Tassigny, crossed into Austria from the west at Bregenz. For reasons of prestige and in order to gain topographical advantages for the zones each of the Allies would occupy in the post-war period, Devers and Delattre raced each other for control of the Arlberg passes and the town of Landeck. At the end of April, snow blocked the road passage over the top of the Arlberg and on 5 May SS units blocked the tunnel under the Arlberg mountain in order to stop Allied progress from the west. But German resistance was crumbling, and by the beginning of May the Allies were hindered more by the weather and the huge number of surrendering Axis soldiers (including a Hungarian unit of 8,000 men, the Hunyadi SS Division)[54] than by any real armed opposition. As the official US army historian described the last days of the war in Austria, 'It was not even pursuit warfare any more; it was more a motor march under tactical conditions.'[55] On 4 May the Americans reached Brixen im Thale, just a few kilometres away from Hopfgarten. Had the burghers of that town not lost patience with the train, Avar would have met up with the new 'superior authority', to whom he could hand over charge of the treasure, on 5 May. But the train left Hopfgarten that night for its journey southeast. The hostilities in Europe ended formally on 8 May, before the Allies had occupied the whole of Austria, and during the first week of the post-war period the Americans fanned out, occupying the rest of the zone allotted to them without having to overcome any opposition.

TOLDI'S TREASURE

Avar and his colleagues were civil servants, bureaucrats. Believing they had done nothing wrong as the plunder was sanctioned by the state, they had kept records, and gave repeated detailed testimony regarding their roles in the seizure and processing of Jewish assets from the summer of 1944 to the summer of 1945. Toldi, who had previously been a senior Gendarme officer (i.e. a policeman), a teacher of the techniques of criminal investigation at the Gendarme training school, and a district governor, had a much clearer understanding of the criminality of what they were doing. So while Avar made great efforts to document events, Toldi went out of his way to cover his tracks. But he was only partly successful. Over the next few years, as French, Hungarian and American government agencies began investigating the fate of the looted cargo, it became possible slowly to piece together the story.

For the first two months after the end of the war, the demarcation line between the US and French armies was the regional border between Vorarlberg and the Tyrol, a line running north and south from the Arlberg pass. Innsbruck, Landeck and St Anton were east of the pass, in the area liberated by the US forces, and Feldkirch and Bregenz lay to the west, liberated by the French. But these were not the lines of post-war occupation that the Allies had agreed on before they entered Austria, and on 6 July the American forces withdrew east of Innsbruck to the Salzburger–Tyrol regional border, handing over to French control the areas that the US armies had liberated in May. From that date the French controlled both Vorarlberg and the Tyrol. Neither the American nor the French occupation authorities were aware that throughout both of these areas Toldi and his few associates had carefully hidden dozens of crates of gold, diamonds, jewellery and cash.

When Toldi left Avar and the train at Hopfgarten on 15 April, his party consisted of his family, János Balogh, Balogh's wife and two-year-old son, Miklós Dobai (a Finance Directorate official, acting as a driver), and as many as fifteen guards.[56] In St Anton Toldi informed his two stepdaughters that they could no longer travel with them, and would have to fend for themselves.[57] His family group now included only his wife and their twelve-year-old son. The Toldi family, Balogh, and a small group of guards and drivers travelled west, trying to get as close to the Swiss border as possible. But progress must have been very difficult because of the congestion resulting from retreating Wehrmacht forces through the Brenner and Resia passes from northern Italy, moving in the opposite direction to Toldi and his group. SS troops patrolled the roads, summarily executing anyone they suspected of being deserters. And the weather conditions were difficult. The Arlberg tunnel was blocked, and the mountain route to the Swiss border was closed by a heavy snowfall on 29 April. Fuel supplies could not have been easy to obtain (although, with the amount of jewellery that Toldi could use as barter, it was presumably still available to him). Not surprisingly, the group decided to wait in the Tyrol until conditions were easier and they could pass over to Vorarlberg and the border area with Switzerland.

Between 18 and 28 April, the group hid half the treasure at various points in the town of Landeck, the village of St Anton, and smaller villages in between. Five cases were hidden with a local mountain guide of known Nazi sympathies, Funder, at the Tannenhof Hotel in St Anton. Another nine cases were hidden with a retired Austrian railway employee, who buried them in his stable. Eight or nine more cases were buried near the small village of Pettneu, two kilometres outside St Anton.[58] The cases were of a standard size, approximately 45cms × 30cms × 20 or 30cms (the sources are not consistent), and weighed between forty and fifty kilograms each.

In addition to the goods that Toldi brought in the lorries and cars from Brennbergbanya, it appears that additional quantities of Jewish property were transported by lorries from other sites directly to Toldi in Austria. Gyula Galambos was looking for Toldi when he arrived on 24 April in Hopfgarten, and there were rumours that two lorryloads of fur coats were brought to Toldi at St Anton from Sopronkőhida in Hungary.[59] From subsequent information collected by the French police, some of the buried boxes contained wedding rings and gold teeth with human blood on them.[60] It is doubtful that such incriminating evidence would have remained on valuables processed at Brennbergbánya, so the possibility exists of additional points of origin. With almost half the cargo of looted goods apparently safely hidden,

Toldi's party then made its way further west to Feldkirch, a few kilometres from the border with Liechtenstein and Switzerland.

After the war, Toldi told the French military authorities that his intention was to bring the valuables to the Hungarian Legation in Bern, Switzerland, 'to save it being pillaged by the *Germans* [emphasis added]'.[61] As it was usually the Russians whose pillaging had been used as an excuse, this was a creative twist to the story of the loot, appropriate to the circumstances. But when he attempted to enter Switzerland, the Swiss border police did not believe it, and as they wanted to have nothing to do with Toldi's cargo he was turned back at the frontier. A few days later, either out of genuine concern for the fate of other Hungarian assets in Austria, or as a means of establishing some sort of credibility as a loyal Hungarian, or in order to create a diversion from his own hoard of loot, Toldi phoned from Austria to the Hungarian Legation in Bern, and told them that the gold of the Hungarian National Bank, the crown of St Stephen, and other important national assets were in southern Austria. He neglected to tell them of the Jewish loot that he had with him or of the items still in Avar's care on the train. The Hungarian Legation informed the OSS, who passed the information back to Washington.[62] But the information was already well known, and Toldi gained no credit for it.

There is an additional version of Toldi's actions, which casts a different light on what transpired at the Swiss frontier. In the post-war Hungarian war crimes trial of Vajna, the ex-Minister of the Interior and Toldi's immediate superior, the government prosecutor recalled Toldi's contacts with the Swiss, and said that he offered them gold 'in exchange for the rescue of a small group'.[63] If this is correct, then it appears that Toldi replaced the failed Alpine Redoubt with Switzerland, and he remained loyal to the original intent of using Jewish gold to buy refuge for the Hungarian fascist leadership. His next move was entirely appropriate to this plan.

Returning to Feldkirch on 29 April, after his unsuccessful attempt to enter Switzerland, Toldi met with SS Sturmbahnführer Wilhelm Höttl.[64] Höttl's account of this meeting, in a sworn testimony to the French police in 1949, suggests that the meeting was fortuitous, but the SS intelligence officer was adept at straining the truth.[65] He would not have wanted the French occupation authorities to know how deeply involved he had been in Hungarian fascist affairs or of his close association with the Hungarian National Socialists, the party Toldi supported. Four years after the end of the war, when Höttl gave his testimony, he had good reason to believe that the world had moved on, and that as the French authorities would not be particularly interested in the minutiae of the German role in Hungary he could blur some of the embarrassing aspects of his past.

Höttl and Toldi quickly worked out a deal. Even in the two weeks before the end of the war, Höttl remained an intelligence officer and was able to move around freely across borders. He had the authority, and a car and driver at his disposal. In exchange for 10 per cent of the goods, Höttl would transport all the boxes to Switzerland, and would provide Toldi and his family with German passports under a different name[66] and with valid exit permits. The fact that Höttl and Toldi happened to meet, that the Hungarian was willing to entrust Höttl with 10 per cent of the valuables even before anything had been delivered to Switzerland, and the fact that Höttl was able to produce new passports in such a short period, at such a far-flung spot and during such a chaotic period (three or four days before the French forces reached Feldkirch), suggests that the meeting was not just fortuitous. (There is another possible twist to this story. Toldi found Höttl in Feldkirch after he had established telephone contact with the Hungarian Legation in Bern. The Military Attaché's office at the Hungarian Legation had been infiltrated by German intelligence (the SD) one year earlier, and since October 1944 the wireless communications of the attaché's office were controlled directly by Höttl.[67] It is not unreasonable to conclude that when Toldi contacted the Hungarian Legation, he was told where he would find Höttl, who in turn would have been able to get the valuables across the border.)

Höttl travelled with an associate, Friedrich Westen. Westen was an Austrian with business interests in Poland,[68] Romania, Italy and Yugoslavia (i.e. wherever Jewish property had been aryanized and the German army was present – prerequisites for large-scale looting), and in Switzerland and Liechtenstein. He had been associated with Höttl since 1938, when Höttl began his career in the Sicherheitsdienst.[69] In February 1945, when Höttl first made contact with the OSS in Bern, Westen acted as the original go-between until the American intelligence agency was willing to meet Höttl directly.[70] After the war there were rumours that Höttl and Westen had been involved together in extensive looting in Yugoslavia and that Höttl had provided Westen with the necessary political protection for a convoy of goods, jewellery and carpets which the latter had taken out of Yugoslavia before the German army withdrew.[71] It appears that the Höttl–Westen association was a serious partnership for disposing of Jewish property. Westen's ability to move goods around German-occupied Europe, and into Switzerland, together with the cover and authority that Höttl could provide as a senior intelligence officer in the SS, was a perfect complement of talent.[72] As Toldi had just failed to get the loot in his possession into Switzerland, he now turned to Höttl for expert assistance.

Both Westen and Höttl gave identical accounts of their actions to the French investigators (a fact that caused the investigating officers to believe that they had been rehearsed). According to both their accounts, when Toldi received his false passports (and new identity), he turned up at Höttl's hotel with the four crates that Höttl–Westen were to receive as their commission, and another two crates which Toldi claimed for himself. He asked Höttl to take these additional crates to Switzerland as well, so that he (Toldi) would be able to maintain his family and entourage there.[73]

This much of the account given by Höttl and Westen was confirmed in separate testimony given to the Hungarian authorities in November 1946 by Miklós Dobai, a member of Toldi's party:

We arrived in Feldkirch on the 29th of April between 8.00–9.00 p.m. We stopped in front of the Post Hotel where Toldi was already expected by two German officers. Rooms had been reserved for Toldi and his family on the first floor. Toldi went to talk with the German officers in a separate room. I do not know what they discussed. About 2 a.m. Toldi came and found me in the lorry and ordered me to bring six cases of valuables to the hotel room. Toldi took one case, I took another one and the porter of the hotel the third one. The three other cases were then brought by myself and the porter. The porter was involved in the story, because the next day he twice helped taking cases from the hotel to a car [Höttl's two-seater BMW].[74]

(The subsequent fate of these boxes, and the diplomatic problems they caused the French occupation authorities, is related in Chapter 10.)

From the hotel, Toldi, Westen and some others drove to a brick factory on the outskirts of Feldkirch, where they buried the eighteen boxes remaining on the lorry. Dobai specifically mentions that Westen was present, but Westen neglected to mention the episode of the additional eighteen boxes in his detailed testimony in 1949. Dobai also mentioned the presence that evening of Ferdinand Nigg ('German officer called Nick'), the deputy chief administrative officer of Liechtenstein, who was involved in hiding the loot.[75] The border with the principality of Liechtenstein was only a few hundred metres away from the brick factory, and that was Höttl's preferred route for taking the valuables into Switzerland.

There is another and very different eyewitness account of what transpired at the brick factory. In addition to Dobai's testimony, there is a report from an unwilling participant who managed to survive the war. In the summer of 1945, two or three months after the burial detail at the brick factory, Károly Oláh walked into the Hungarian consulate in Bratislava with an unusual story. Oláh was a Czech (probably also Jewish) and had been sent to the Reich to work as a slave labourer. He was assigned to the brick factory in Tisis, a suburb of Feldkirch. He told the Hungarian diplomats that in the spring of 1945 a party of Hungarians arrived 'in a big Mateos car'. He named Dobai as a member of the party, and remembered that Dobai identified himself as an official of the Hungarian Ministry of Finance. According to Oláh's account, the Hungarians divided some valuables among themselves, and then ordered him to conceal eighteen crates in the chimney of the brick factory.[76]

The French forces occupied Feldkirch on 3 May, four days after these events, and the war in Europe ended another five days later. The treasure on the train was at Böckstein, hidden in the Tauern tunnel, while Avar awaited the arrival of the US army to take charge of the property. The treasure that Toldi had taken was now buried at a number of different sites across the Tyrol and in Feldkirch. The share taken by Höttl and Westen vanished.

6

In Allied Hands

As the Allied forces completed the occupation of Germany and pushed into Austria, US army units began to report the discovery of more and more hidden hoards of loot. By the beginning of May the list of individual finds was five pages long.[1] From the evidence being uncovered, it was clear that Wehrmacht and Waffen SS soldiers had looted widely across occupied Europe, on an individual basis as well as on behalf of the Reich. Many of the stolen valuables were hidden during the chaotic German retreat, for retrieval later[2] – and it was these goods that the Allied forces were now uncovering. The most spectacular, and most famous, cache was hidden in the Kaiseroda potassium mine at Merkers in Thuringia, Germany, which troops of the US 3rd Army found on 8 April 1945.[3] A preliminary inventory found that the gold bullion, gold coins and currency in the mine were worth $517 million (in 1945 values).[4] Most of the Merkers deposit had been stolen by the German government from central banks across Europe. But there were also over 200 sacks, suitcases and boxes of gold, silver, diamonds and jewellery whose origin was clearly from the extermination and concentration camps: 'Evidence indicates that this part of the treasure represents loot taken from individuals who have been murdered, as it includes thousands of gold and silver dental crowns, bridges and plates and some personal items.'[5] They were indeed victim assets from the camps, representing the SS loot delivered to the Reichsbank in the last months of the war, for which there had been insufficient time to dispose of discreetly by melting down. The victim loot uncovered at Merkers represented thirty-five deliveries from the camps. Another forty-three deliveries had been made earlier and 'processed', with the proceeds deposited into special SS bank accounts.

After Merkers, no one in Washington was excited by the frequent reports of much smaller discoveries of gold stolen by the Nazis or their allies, and in the enthusiastic reportage of the Allied victory in Europe subsequent finds were cast in the same mould as Merkers – larger and more important than they eventually proved to be.

When the Allies pushed into Austria, the uncovering of Nazi plunder continued, but this time much of the recovered loot was Hungarian. The gold of the National Bank of Hungary (633 cases of gold bullion and coins, worth $32 million, paper currency and other valuables) was found in early May on a train in the village of Spital am Pyhrn in southern Austria, guarded by armed Nyilas troops and bank officials.[6] Shortly afterwards, the crown of St Stephen, one of Hungary's most important treasures, was uncovered in the village of Mattsee, near Salzburg. The coronation robe, sceptre, orb, coronation cross and the mummified right hand of St Stephen, Hungary's holiest relic, were uncovered in early June in the same area.[7] The *New York Times* reported most of these finds enthusiastically, and was caught up in the spirit of the discoveries elsewhere when it wrote that the value of the National Bank gold was $800 million (a twenty-fold exaggeration).[8] It appeared as if the Nazi loot had created an El Dorado in Central Europe, and it was in this heady atmosphere that American troops stumbled on the trainload of confiscated Hungarian Jewish property, concealed in the Tauern tunnel.

On 11 May, three days after the end of the war, an American military intelligence unit made contact with the train. The Hungarian officials on the train were relieved to have the protection of the army of occupation. Now that the war was over, the threat of armed SS or Wehrmacht attack on the train had passed, only to be replaced by treasure-seeking local Austrian civilians. Attempts were made almost daily to break into the freight wagons, despite the Hungarian armed guard and the fact that the train was parked in a tunnel. Avar and his men frequently found items of jewellery or carpets discarded on the ground around the train, and protecting the goods was becoming a burden.[9] As his second-in-command, Mingovits, noted, 'We awaited the arrival of US troops every day.'[10] But the US occupation authorities chose not to deal with the train at this stage. They opened a few of the sealed carriages for a perfunctory inspection of the contents,[11] and also reported that there were fifty-two remaining armed Hungarian guards, and eighty-four civilians.[12] They decided to leave the train under Hungarian guard, but as Böckstein and the Tauern tunnel were difficult to reach, the army ordered that the train should be moved to a town twenty-five kilometres south of Salzburg. On 15 or 16 May the train and its passengers arrived in Werfen, where they waited for another four weeks of enforced idleness. Avar had found new patrons, but they were not particularly interested. Although news of the find appeared in the *New York Times*,[13] the report made no mention of the fact that the train carried 'persecutee' loot, nor was it accurate in any of the other details. ('Persecutee' was official shorthand for the formal designation 'victims of Nazi racial or political persecution'. Eventually it applied only to racial victims, and was a polite term for Jew/Jewish.)

For the next two weeks the train was almost forgotten, as details of the discovery slowly filtered their way up the army's 'Civil Administration' bureaucracy.[14] On 29 May, army intelligence officers returned and prepared a more orderly listing of the freight wagons, noting whether they were still sealed or not. They interviewed Avar and began to piece together an early version of the story of the train.[15] As the train was still protected by the Hungarian guards, and as the American occupation authorities had not yet organized facilities for storing the train's valuable cargo, there was no apparent reason to take over the goods.

The situation changed ten days later when General Levushkin, a Soviet member of the Allied Control Commission in Budapest, demanded to know why so many valuable Hungarian assets were still under the control of armed Hungarian fascist soldiers. Speaking on behalf of the new Russian-sponsored National Provisional government of Hungary, Levushkin pointed out that one month after the end of the war the Americans had not yet taken control of the gold of the National Bank of Hungary or of the 'fifty wagons transported from Hungary to Austria and which, according to reports by the *New York Times* and Reuters, were taken into custody by American troops in the surroundings of Salzburg'. Levushkin also pointed out that twelve kilometres from Spital (where the National Bank gold was kept) a fugitive battalion of Hungarian soldiers was guarding a pool of 100 automobiles. The Russians wanted these soldiers and the guards disarmed, and demanded that the gold be returned to Hungary. And they wanted the cars back, too.[16]

Soon after the Red Army carried the war over into Hungarian territory, the Soviets sponsored the formation of a new Hungarian government in Debrecen (in November 1944) representing all the anti-fascist forces in the country – the Smallholders, the Peasants, the Social Democrats, and of course the Communists. The National Provisional government, formed with active Russian backing, faced the daunting task of repairing the damage of war fought on Hungarian territory, and the self-inflicted damage caused by the policies of the Sztójay and Szálasi regimes in their alliance with the Third Reich. Hungary was specially affected by the massive evacuations of its productive capacity. Much of the asset base of the Hungarian economy was now in Germany and Austria, and production in Hungary itself in 1945 was only a fraction of the pre-war average. The economic disruption was total, and the Hungarian population faced very real hardships and severe shortages.[17] The effort to return to Hungary those assets evacuated by the wartime governments dominated Hungary's relations with the Allies after the war. But because Hungary had been an ally of Nazi Germany during the war, her right to claim back property afterwards was by no means self-evident. The trainload of Jewish loot soon proved to be among the hardest of all the many restitution issues that Hungary faced. The Soviet attempt to ensure the return of the most valuable gold assets was the first step in a four-year struggle to ensure restitution of all Hungarian property. Ten days after the Soviets demanded that the Americans take steps to safeguard Hungarian gold in Austria, the recently reconstituted Hungarian Foreign Ministry made an almost identical demand.[18]

The Soviet and Hungarian demands sparked a flurry of activity. The State Department in Washington was embarrassed by the Soviet reference to the groups of right-wing Hungarian military units in the US zone of occupation in Austria that had still not been disarmed. At the same time, the army began to investigate all the various Hungarian assets dispersed throughout western Austria.

The first to be investigated was the National Bank gold (and other assets) in Spital am Pyhrn. The army had had the gold bullion and coins removed from the National Bank train two weeks earlier, taking it to SHAEF's Financial Division repository in Frankfurt. Only the Hungarian paper currency (9.1 billion pengős[19] – already worth relatively little owing to post-war inflation in Hungary, and soon to be almost totally worthless)[20] and the bank records were left in Spital. Now, in early June, officers of SHAEF's Financial Division visited the village to investigate the history of this transport. They reported that the remaining assets were protected by twenty-five armed Hungarian guards. There were also 230 civilians – members of the bank's staff and their families. The National Bank train had arrived in Spital in January 1945, under the leadership of the director of the bank, László Temesváry, a Szálasi appointee. Temesváry had been deposed by his own subordinates in May, when the Americans arrived to remove the gold. Since then, the bankers had kept themselves busy 'by re-counting the pengős in the Bank's possession, and planning to move to Switzerland'. They hoped to use the National Bank assets to establish a Hungarian bank in Zurich. Overlooking the fact that Hungary had been an enemy of the Allies, the bank's officials expected the Americans to endorse their efforts to save Hungarian state assets from the Soviets. But instead of encouraging them in their fantasies, the American officers decided to end the farce, take over all the remaining assets and records and disperse the bank's officials.[21] The assets of the National Bank of Hungary remained in American custody until the Allies could resolve the question of how much, if anything at all, Hungary, as an ex-enemy state, was entitled to get back.

In mid-July the turn came of the looted Jewish assets on the train, waiting for the last two months in the marshalling yards of Werfen railway station. Lack of provisions became a serious problem. As ex-enemy nationals, the Hungarians were not entitled to any official assistance unless they were in a displaced persons camp, and food was so short that Avar's assistant Mingovits began to suffer from malnutrition. Eventually, the US military arranged for them to get regular supplies.*

---

* This account is based on the testimony of Mingovits and Biró, although the idea that these dedicated guardians of 'Hungarian national assets' were prepared to starve themselves rather than engage in a little black market trading of their highly marketable cargo does require a willingness to suspend disbelief.

On 10 July the Hungarians were interrogated by the 'Hungarian Unit' of the 430th Detachment of the Counter Intelligence Corps based in Salzburg. Marton Himler, the officer responsible for the arrest, interrogation and eventual forced repatriation of the Hungarian wartime political and military leadership, almost all of whom were arrested in western Austria,[22] led the investigation of the train.[23] The involvement of the CIC, with its links to American military intelligence (G-2) and to the civilian OSS (forerunner of the CIA), ensured that a search would begin for the rest of the Hungarian Jewish gold in Austria, including – as Toldi would soon discover – even the French zone of occupation.

With the sudden international interest in the Gold Train (now officially called the 'Werfen train' by the US army) a warehouse was found in Salzburg for the contents of the twenty-four wagons of loot, and on 19 July the train finally came under full American control. The freight wagons were separated from the rest of the train carrying the Hungarian guards, officials, families, miners, and assorted others. Personal luggage was removed from the wagons containing the valuable freight, the remaining food supplies were distributed, and a search conducted among the civilians and guards for any 'misplaced state-owned property' (i.e. items stolen from the cargo of Jewish loot). The guards' ammunition was handed over to the US army unit handling the transfer, and Avar gave Captain John F. Back (of 'Target Force', US Forces, Austria) the suitcase of the most valuable diamonds, pearls and small jewellery, and the remaining cash (distributed by Toldi at Brennbergbánya). This was the suitcase that Toldi tried unsuccessfully to retrieve from Avar at Hopfgarten. The thirteen carriages of Hungarian civilians were then attached to a repatriation train going back to Hungary, while the senior Property Directorate and Finance Ministry officials remained behind and were transferred to a displaced persons camp.[24]

The disarmed Hungarian guards travelled with the train to Salzburg to help the American soldiers unload the wagons.[25] There were at least 1,500 crates of watches, jewellery and silverware, 5,250 Persian and other carpets, and large amounts of fur coats, stamp collections, cameras, china, and even furniture, to be off-loaded.[26] The goods were to be stored on the ground floor of a military warehouse at the north-western edge of Salzburg, on Klesheimer Allee. The storage area was already partly filled with looted art and other goods when the Hungarian shipment arrived, and next door was a chemical warfare munitions collection point.[27]

Fifteen months after Jewish personal property had suddenly become Hungarian 'state property', and three-and-a-half months after leaving Brennbergbánya, the organizers of the Gold Train were finally relieved of their onerous responsibility. But then came the painful realization that all their efforts had been in vain: 'It was here that we understood that something had gone terribly wrong, since all we had received were promises and verbal encouragement.'[28] The Americans had taken over the assets without making any written commitment that they would ever be returned to Hungary. In the weeks that followed, Avar, Mingovits, Biró, Dr Tibor Touttenni and others from the group of officials who had been on the train made the rounds of the offices of the American military administration pleading the case for a 'receipt', or at least a document recognizing that the goods were the property of the Hungarian state, but to no avail. From the very outset the occupation authorities considered the train's cargo to be 'persecutee property' and 'looted goods' rather than Hungarian state property.

TOLDI IN VORARLBERG

Toldi spent the next weeks between Feldkirch (where Höttl's partner, Westen, had buried the eighteen boxes of gold) and the Swiss border. He chose to stay as inconspicuously as possible in the town of Dornbirn, presumably living under an assumed name.[29] His position was hardly secure. The Swiss authorities did not want to know him and the Hungarian Legation in Bern refused to help. He had received no word from Höttl about smuggling the treasure into Switzerland (for which he had paid in advance a commission of 10 per cent), and, as the weeks went by after the end of the war, Toldi must have realized that regardless of whatever influence and contacts the SS intelligence officer had in the past, Höttl was now either a prisoner-of-war or was hiding from the Allies just as Toldi himself was.

In fact, two weeks after Höttl had taken the 10 per cent commission, he turned himself in to the US 3rd Army CIC unit at Kirchdorf (not far from Hopfgarten and Kitzbühel), together with six men under his command. As an American prisoner he was safely out of reach of irate Hungarians, and he immediately began trading on his OSS connections and the fact that he controlled a network of Nazi agents throughout the Balkans, which he offered to transfer to the Americans.[30] The six crates of jewels and gold he had received from Toldi in Feldkirch were well hidden, and never recovered. Meanwhile, Toldi's own position in these immediate post-war weeks was about to become very dangerous indeed.

When the Americans took over the train, and Avar and the others were interrogated by the CIC, those counter-intelligence officers responsible for blocking the escape of leading Hungarian war criminals would certainly have listened carefully to Avar's grievances against Toldi. The possibility that the ex-Commissioner of Jewish Affairs was in Austria, with enough gold to help the most wanted war criminals to escape, would have focused their attention. And a few days after the CIC became involved in the story of the train, Avar's account of how he 'heroically saved' this Hungarian treasure 'from the SS and from the avarice of Colonel Toldi' was published in the Budapest communist daily newspaper *Szabadság*. Avar regretted, he told the newspaper, that he could not stop Toldi from disappearing with some of the most valuable items of the treasure.[31] (This was the first of a series of articles on the Gold Train. Over the next months the Hungarian press returned to the subject many times.)[32] The CIC's Marton Himler, like other officers in the 'Hungarian Unit', were naturalized Americans who spoke Hungarian as their mother tongue. These articles would have been brought to their attention.

Coincidentally, and very much more seriously for Toldi, on 9 August 1945 the OSS distributed the second in a series of lists of wanted Hungarian war criminals. Based on detailed information from the former head of the political department of the Hungarian Foreign Ministry, the list provided details of the roles of leading politicians and generals in Hungary's alliance with Germany and in the destruction of Hungarian Jewry.[33] Twenty-five names appeared on the second list, and Toldi was in fifth place after Vajna, Baky, Endre and Ferenczy (the officer responsible for coordinating the Gendarmerie's role in the ghettoization and deportation process). These four names were well known to Himler's unit, and all of them were eventually caught, returned to Hungary and, in 1946, tried and executed. Toldi's prominent position on the list would have made him a major target of the war crimes unit. Whether because of Avar's frequent testimony, or the newspaper report, or the secret OSS information, Toldi had lost his anonymity. He very quickly found out that far from being unknown, he was now the subject of great interest for American intelligence units.

On the night of 4–5 August the French occupation authorities in St Anton intercepted a Czech lorry[34] that was involved in a search for the Hungarian treasure. In all probability this was a probe by the Hungarian consulate in Bratislava, resulting from the testimony a few weeks earlier by Károly Oláh, the slave labourer who had buried the gold in Feldkirch.[35] For the first time the French occupation authorities became aware of the existence of considerable quantities of looted Hungarian Jewish valuables hidden in their zone, and very quickly afterwards they began to uncover the various hoards in St Anton and Feldkirch.

Colonel Henri Jung, head of the French 'Control Detachment' (responsible for civil administration) in Vorarlberg, has left three different accounts of the next, dramatic, development. Years after the events, Colonel Jung recounts how, at 2 a.m. on the night of 11 August, he was woken by one of his officers who said that a 'Hungarian colonel' wished to speak to him urgently. Jung refused to meet anyone at that late hour, but 'the colonel' (Toldi) said that his life was in danger if he could not speak to the most senior French officer in Vorarlberg within the hour. Jung agreed to have Toldi brought to his residence at Schloss Wolfurt, four kilometres from the city centre of Bregenz:

Twenty minutes later, a tall man, of military bearing and with a grave face, entered my office which was situated on the first floor, built against the tower of the medieval castle. He presented himself as a Hungarian colonel in the active Hungarian army, who was ordered by his government, before it collapsed under the Russians, to fulfil an important mission. According to him, he was to deliver to the Western Powers an important treasure, which comprised several cases of gold ingots and coin, and two cases of jewellery. For over a month he had tried to hide the treasure, but various Allied intelligence services which had become aware of the treasure were trying to outwit each other to gain possession of it. The cases of gold had already been taken by agents of one of the services (he did not specify which) which happened to be near St Anton. He only had possession of the jewellery, which he wanted to get rid of, as he was afraid he would be imprisoned and tortured to reveal where the rest of the treasure was hidden. Effectively, the Hungarian officer gave the impression of being terrorized and pursued.[36]

Jung gave the order that Toldi should lead French officers that night to the buried treasure, which was hidden in a farm near the town of Schruns in the Montafon valley (off the main road, near St Anton). In the morning, Jung recounts, 'the famous cases which were agitating all the Allied Secret Services' were in his office. When they were opened, Jung found 'a considerable quantity of jewels of every kind, of which some were of extreme beauty, solitaires, emeralds, *rivières* of diamonds, bracelets set with brilliants . . .'. Toldi was asked to make a sworn statement as to the provenance of the jewels, which he did by explaining his patriotic efforts to save this small part of the Hungarian national estate from the Soviets and the Germans. He revealed the sites of all the caches in St Anton, Pettneu and Feldkirch, and concluded: 'I hereby demand to put myself, my wife and my son under your protection, to relieve me of my duty to Hungary.'[37]

Jung's other versions of these events differ only in the time of day when he met Toldi (3 p.m.),[38] and whether Toldi came forward voluntarily or was detained following the arrest of the Czech lorry and the subsequent uncovering of the first boxes of valuables. But the important facts are clear: by August 1945 the French occupation forces controlled forty cases and two smaller boxes of gold and jewels, weighing approximately 1,600kg. Further quantities of treasure were uncovered in 1946 (discussed in Chapter 10). Toldi did not tell the French of his deal with Höttl and Westen, nor did he mention that there was a considerable amount of gold unaccounted for. They discovered this for themselves in the years that followed.

The following inventory was prepared by Jung's assistants, in his presence, two days after the surrender of the boxes.[39] It was clear that this was victim loot, and Toldi was arrested. He remained in French custody, safe from his American pursuers, until he was released without charge three months later, in early November 1945.[40]

TOLDI'S TWO BOXES

First Container

1 large ring

9 rings of great value containing brilliants

132 pairs of earrings

355 rings

81 bracelets and one bracelet of pearls

1 pair of combs in brilliants

24 watches with platinum straps

5 pins

129 brooches

9 large earrings

4 clips

5 pearl and diamond necklaces and 1 baroque style pearl necklace

2 chain bracelets

9 chain necklaces

27 pendants with and without chains

3 diadems of which 1 in baroque pearls

1 set of ruby and brilliant jewellery

2 men's watches

1 brilliant diadem in bad state

1 set of jewellery in box (watch and earrings)

1 piece of bracelet in ruby and brilliants

1 piece of bracelet in platinum with brilliants

1 piece of bracelet or necklace in platinum with brilliants

19 earrings, dismantled or incomplete

14 medium-sized brilliants

8 very small brilliants

1 small pearl

1 diamond set in platinum

TOLDI'S TWO BOXES

Second Container

Banknotes:

2	notes of	1000	Pengös
77	,,	100	,,
5	,,	50	,,
60	,,	20	,,
51	,,	10	,,

1 note of 50 French Francs
1 Yen
2 gold men's watches
550 Pengős in coins (roll)
1 coin bag
2 sealed envelopes
5 gold wedding rings
1 disassembled earring

Toldi's arrest led to a series of additional discoveries. French police searched the homes of all Toldi's associates (including his wife and stepdaughter), János Balogh and others in the Hungarian exile community, and uncovered a further 21kg of gold and jewels. Balogh had dug up four or more of the crates buried near St Anton with the assistance of another Hungarian exile living in Feldkirch, Karl Farkas, who was known to the police as a black marketeer. When Farkas's home was raided in August 1945 the authorities uncovered a further 44kg of gold and 15kg of jewellery which was identified as having come from the Gold Train.[41] There were additional discoveries in the months that followed, as more hoards of Hungarian Jewish gold and jewels began to surface in the French zone. By November, the French authorities had seized between 2,100 and 2,215kg of gold and jewels from Toldi's associates and from local Austrians who had helped them.[42] It appears that Toldi and his associates had to pay heavily for the logistic support they needed to transport the crates, to find lodging for themselves, and to buy the silence of those who helped them. More gold was to turn up during the following year.

The French occupation authorities now became the guardians of the real treasure taken from Brennbergbánya. This provided Paris with a major card in its relations with post-war Hungary, and became a significant point of tension in its relations with Washington.

7

The Survivors

The defeat of the Third Reich was accompanied by the total, and unexpected, collapse of the German civil administration. The occupation of Germany and Austria left the victorious armies of America, the Soviet Union, Britain and France responsible for the civilian populations of the ex-enemy countries. They were also responsible for looking after a huge number of displaced persons and refugees. These groups were made up of Germans and Austrians who had been scattered because of heavy fighting and aerial bombardment; millions of voluntary foreign workers; and millions of slave labourers, freed prisoners-of-war, and liberated concentration camp inmates. SHAEF, the Allied headquarters, pursued an active policy of repatriating these people as soon as possible, using every means at their disposal. During the summer of 1945 over 8 million people were sent to their homes under the army repatriation programme. But 1 million remained, refusing to return to the countries of their birth either because they had fought alongside the Nazis and were afraid of punishment, or because they had survived Nazi racial persecution and felt they no longer had homes to which they could return. This latter group, the surviving remnants of European Jewish communities, made up between 5 and 10 per cent of the displaced persons problem in the American and British zones of occupation in Germany and Austria by the end of 1945.

The Allies had, to a degree, anticipated this problem in their wartime planning for the post-war period. It was clear that massive efforts would have to be made to allow Europe to recover from the destruction of war, and to undo the concerted economic exploitation and plunder of the resources and wealth of all the countries occupied by the Nazis.

American and British planners recognized that resources would also have to be found for the rehabilitation of the victims of Nazi racial and political persecution, and various ideas were put forward to allow the surviving victims to rebuild their lives.[1] The civil administration planning for Europe after the liberation began two years before the end of the war, and continued until the end of hostilities. The planning was detailed but it was conducted in a vacuum, distant from the full extent of the horror of what had happened, and was still happening, in Europe. Although the Soviets liberated extermination and slave labour camps in July 1944, and Auschwitz was liberated in January 1945, the terrible scenes discovered at these places did not enter western consciousness until the US and British forces crossed over into German territory in March 1945 and began freeing camp after camp during March and April. By spring, the papers were full of detailed descriptions of what had happened in these camps, and the horrors of the Holocaust became familiar to everyone.

The Germans had murdered 6 million Jews (and many non-Jewish civilians, too). Entire communities and families disappeared, leaving their homes, schools, synagogues, hospitals, and so on, without heirs. Normally, the property of people who die without heirs and without wills (i.e. intestate) reverts to the state in which they lived. But in the case of the Jews of the Reich, that would mean rewarding the German state for killing its Jews so effectively, which was unacceptable. The civil administration planners solved this problem by adopting an idea originally proposed by Jewish welfare groups – that heirless individual assets and Jewish community property be used to provide funds for the relief and rehabilitation of the Jewish survivors of the Holocaust.[2] But such a plan, which eventually came into effect in 1948, was too complex and too fraught with legal and political difficulties to be a solution to the immediate problems of the surviving concentration camp inmates. Something had to be done far more quickly or else these people would become a long-term burden on the budgets of the Allied occupation authorities.

During the meeting of the Allied leaders at Potsdam in July 1945, the question of reparations from Germany for all the Allies was one of the main issues on the agenda. The American delegation suggested that the Jewish people should also be considered a legitimate claimant of reparations from Germany, and that 2 per cent of the overall reparations payments be set aside for the rehabilitation and resettlement of Holocaust survivors.[3] The idea was rejected following British opposition to the special legal status that any Jewish reparations claim against Germany would give the Jewish people, and a compromise formula was found. As the intention was to provide immediate liquid funds for the benefit of the victims of Nazi persecution, it was agreed that all non-monetary gold found in Germany be set aside for their benefit, as well as all heirless victim assets in neutral countries (primarily Switzerland) and a charge of $25 million against German assets in neutral countries. This policy was endorsed by the Allies at the Paris Conference on Reparations, and became Article 8 of Part One of the Final Act on Reparations. The Intergovernmental Committee on Refugees (IGCR) was given the task of supervising the allocation of these funds, but the question of which organizations would actually receive the money derived from Article 8 was still left open.[4]

Article 8 became the basis of all subsequent dealings between the Jewish world and the Allies concerning the fate of Nazi loot. The Article clearly differentiated between monetary gold, belonging to the central reserve banks of the countries occupied by the Nazis and destined to be returned to those governments through what became known as the 'gold pot', and non-monetary gold which derived from looting the homes, possessions and even the bodies of the victims of Nazism.[5] The gold jewellery, rings, dental gold, currency and securities which were uncovered in numerous sites across Germany would not be used to compensate the governments of the countries which the Germans had occupied (i.e. they would not become part of the 'gold pot') but would be used instead for the benefit of the survivors, many of whom were officially stateless.

The Jewish organizations saw Article 8 as a major breakthrough in the development of a coherent policy of restitution and rehabilitation for the survivors, and looked to it as a source of meaningful funds for rebuilding Jewish life after the Holocaust.[6] Although it would only represent a very small part of the overall material loot taken by the Nazis and their allies (estimated in 1945–1946 to total $8 billion for the years 1933–1945),[7] Article 8 established the important principle that the Jewish welfare organizations would be able to use these heirless or unidentifiable victim assets for the benefit of the survivors of Nazi persecution, regardless of where they came from. The State Department in Washington quickly pointed out that not all non-monetary gold would be allocated for rehabilitation purposes, as the Nazis had also looted Catholic churches and many non-Jewish ceremonial items had been found among the recovered gold.[8] Common sense prevailed, and the American government now took an active role in making sure that the Jewish organizations received the victim-derived loot as quickly as possible.

JEWISH ORGANIZATIONS

Jewish life is decentralized, and every Jewish community is an independent, autonomous entity. There is no centralized authority in the Jewish world, but there are a number of social welfare organizations and political groups that function globally, and are frequently at odds. As they are voluntary organizations, they depend on fund-raising to finance their programmes, and fund-raising requires that they should be prominent and often in the limelight. After the end of the war in Europe, two issues dominated Jewish public life: the well-being of the survivors/displaced persons, and the struggle for a Jewish state in the British Mandate of Palestine. The Jewish community in Palestine was governed by the Jewish Agency for Palestine, and this semi-governmental body was also the conduit for diaspora support for the Jewish community there. Furthermore, although officially the Jewish Agency was only involved in legal political activity and in the flow of legal migrants to Palestine, in reality the leadership which ran the Agency also dominated the secret underground organizations that controlled the armed forces of the Jewish community (the Haganah and the Palmach), the Bricha, which brought Jews out of eastern Europe to the displaced persons camps of the American zones of occupation during 1946–1948, and the Ha'apala, the illegal immigration of Jews from Europe to Palestine. In the strongly pro-Zionist atmosphere of the Jewish world after the war, the Agency had a unique standing in Jewish public life.

The American Jewish Joint Distribution Committee was an American Jewish welfare organization active since 1914. The 'Joint', as it was popularly known, was a highly professional welfare agency with excellent ties to the American government. By the summer of 1945 both the Jewish Agency and the Joint had acquired official status as 'operating agencies' which were allowed to assist the US army in the management of the Jewish displaced persons camps. No other Jewish organizations were granted this privilege. Fortunately, the Joint and the Agency cooperated closely at all levels – in the legal, official programmes, and at the unofficial level of the Bricha and the Ha'apala. They also cooperated in combined fund-raising in the United States. The ideological differences between the Zionist, nationalist Jewish Agency and the non-Zionist, philanthropic Joint Distribution Committee were irrelevant in the immediate post-war Jewish world.

The third organization, the World Jewish Congress, was outside this magic circle. Created in the mid-1930s in order to protect Jewish political rights in an increasingly anti-Semitic and fascist Europe, the World Jewish Congress was also active in refugee affairs before and during the war. Each of the organizations – the Congress, the Agency and the Joint – had been active during the war to save Jews from the Nazi onslaught by all means possible. After the war, however, the American military occupation authorities did not want to recognize a political organization as an operating agency in the displaced persons camps. That privilege was reserved for the genuine welfare agencies, which had the ability and the experience to assist the survivors materially and professionally. As a result, the Congress was increasingly pushed to the sidelines in Jewish public affairs.

While Article 8 established the principle of using heirless assets for the benefit of the Holocaust survivors, it did not establish the mechanism for administering the funds. This was to be discussed at an additional conference of five countries (America, Britain, France, Yugoslavia and Czechoslovakia) who were to supervise the implementation of Article 8. Washington was keen to get this programme under way. But the British government understood that if non-monetary gold was transferred to the Jewish organizations the money would be spent on illegal immigration to Palestine and on underground arms purchases for the Jewish community there.[9] Not surprisingly, London tried everything to prevent the conference convening, and six months were wasted in diplomatic exchanges between the two governments.[10] Eventually, Washington lost patience and threatened to implement Article 8 as it saw fit if the British continued to obstruct allocations to the surviving victims. As the State Department pointed out to the American delegation to the Five Power Conference on Reparations for Non-Repatriable Victims of German Action, 'This Government considers it a moral obligation of the first order to secure these funds as expeditiously as possible so that work of reconstruction can begin as quickly as possible.'[11]

Behind this fine sense of 'moral obligation' was the reality that most of the displaced persons were congregating in the American zones of occupation in Germany and Austria, and as long as the displaced persons were not resettled and rehabilitated, they would remain a burden on the American taxpayer, and on the manpower resources of the US army. A secret report prepared for the War Department in Washington in June 1946 stated that 3,000 officers and enlisted men were fully engaged in administrating the displaced persons camps (Jewish and non-Jewish), 74,000 soldiers spent 10 per cent of their time in logistical support, and the direct cost of food, clothing and shelter for the displaced persons cost almost $8,000,000 a month.[12] In the early summer of 1946, Jews represented approximately 10 per cent of the overall displaced persons problem, but that percentage would grow dramatically during the year.

As almost all the non-monetary gold had been uncovered in the American zones in Germany and Austria, the Americans could act independently if the British persisted in their obstructionism. To make the point perfectly clear to the Foreign Office in London, the State Department appointed Dr Eli Ginzberg, a prominent American Zionist, to head the American delegation.[13]

The Five Power Conference met in Paris from 11 to 14 June. In the end, the British decided to avoid a conflict with the US on refugee policy (there were more important issues to argue about), and it was agreed that the funds deriving from Article 8 would all be paid to the IGCR, which would in turn transfer 90 per cent of the funds to the Jewish Agency and the Joint Distribution Committee, for the benefit of Jewish survivors.[14] (The remaining 10 per cent was reserved for non-Jewish survivors of Nazi racial and religious persecution, but most of these funds were never claimed.) From that point on, the Joint and the Agency had a direct interest in the recovered victim loot, including that of the Gold Train. Furthermore, as the only Jewish organizations accorded a privileged role in the allocation of the funds deriving from reparations and restitution for the victims of Nazi persecution, they acquired a pre-eminence in Jewish public affairs that was unprecedented. Other Jewish organizations, and in particular the World Jewish Congress, understood that they had lost a battle and could not aspire any more to be as important or as effective as the Joint and the Agency. Article 8 and the Five Power Agreement gave these two organizations access to heirless asset funds and also gave them a standing in international affairs (including effective access to the State Department) that no other Jewish organization could hope to attain. Senior officials of the World Jewish Congress recognized this as soon as Article 8 was formally adopted,[15] although the full implications of these developments only became clear in the course of time.

While Ginzberg was in Paris negotiating the Five Power Agreement on the fate of the heirless assets, a member of his team travelled to the headquarters of the US occupation forces in Germany and in Austria to try and establish an estimate of the amount of money that would be realized from the sale of the recovered loot. On the basis of early estimates, it appeared that the amounts were considerable. The Frankfurt repository, under the control of OMGUS, had received seventy-eight shipments of loot seized or uncovered by US troops. As most of this was from Merkers, and as most of the Merkers gold was monetary gold destined for the 'gold pot', it was not relevant to the Article 8 funds. But at least twenty shipments to the Frankfurt repository were of non-monetary gold, and these could potentially be used for the benefit of the victims.[16] The report of the US military government in Austria was also promising. There were many small deposits of recovered loot, and there was the huge amount of property taken off the Gold Train: 'None of the individual items seems to be of great value but the total value of seizure may be considerably more than those at Frankfurt.'[17]

It had taken thirteen months since the end of the war for the Allies to agree on how these goods could be used for the benefit of the survivors, and for a preliminary estimate of the quantity of recovered loot to be made. The decisions of principle had been settled. But it would take another two years of diplomatic wrangling and a detailed inventory before any of the displaced persons could benefit from Washington's genuinely felt 'moral obligation of the first order'.

HUNGARIAN JEWRY AFTER LIBERATION

As the Soviet forces moved westwards across Romania and Hungary, Jewish communities were progressively liberated in their wake. The Transylvanian Jews of Greater Hungary were liberated in September 1944, but the last of the provincial Hungarian Jews west of the Danube were only freed in April 1945, when the Red Army took control of the whole of Hungary. Other Hungarian Jews were liberated from concentration camps throughout the Reich. These communities had been devastated; 80 per cent of the Jews living outside the capital had died in the labour battalions of the Hungarian army, in the gas chambers of Auschwitz or in the slave labour deportations to Austria.[18] By the end of 1945, with the return of the surviving labour battalion members, concentration camp inmates and slave labourers, provincial Jewish communities across Hungary numbered 46,000. The Budapest Jewish community did not fare much better, even though it avoided the deportations to Auschwitz. At the beginning of the war there had been 185,000 Jews in the capital, and an additional 62,350 'Christian converts of Jewish origins'. Their number had been depleted by conscription to the labour battalions, Nyilas killings after 15 October, widespread starvation and the mass deportations for slave labour during October and November 1944. When the Red Army liberated Pest on 18 January and Buda on 13 February, there were only 119,000 still alive in the capital. In the year that followed, 25,000 returned from the Hungarian army labour battalions or from slave labour in the Reich, and the number of Jews in Budapest (including converts to Christianity) grew to 144,000 by the end of 1945.[19]

The whole city was severely damaged in the prolonged battle for control during the Soviet siege, and when the Jewish community could finally emerge from the ghetto and the protection of the Swedish and Swiss 'safe houses', their own distress (50 per cent loss of population and the loss of all their property after the German occupation) was submerged in the general misery. The Soviet authorities had been generous to the surviving Jews they had liberated in Poland, because Poland had been an Allied occupied country. But Hungary had fought against Russia and was treated as an ex-enemy, and the Russians did not make any distinction between non-Jewish Hungarians and persecutees.[20] The Jews had to fend for themselves. This once large, assimilated, prosperous and dynamic community was now destitute, and entirely dependent on material assistance from international Jewish organizations.

The first trainload of supplies provided by the Joint for the community arrived from Romania in February 1945, almost immediately after the liberation of the city,[21] and a few weeks later the Joint re-established its offices in Budapest. The Jewish Agency was able to reopen its offices with the assistance of local Zionists and representatives from Palestine, and soon it was able to offer aid through its welfare organization 'Ezra', as well as through the usual Zionist political and youth movements.[22] The local Hungarian branch of the World Jewish Congress reconvened in June, and concerned itself with a large-scale documentation project designed to record the experiences of the survivors.[23] Within months of the liberation, the Jews of Budapest organized a 'National Relief Committee for Deportees' (Deportáltakat Gondozó Országos Bizottság, but known by the acronym DEGOB), which became the umbrella organization for most of the relief activities. DEGOB sent lorries into Poland, Germany and Austria to find surviving deportees and bring them home. Family-tracing departments were established, as well as hospitals and clinics for the returnees (who continued to arrive until late 1946).[24] Soup kitchens fed 90,000 people daily in 278 communities, and additional cash relief was provided to over 35,000 people in Budapest alone.[25] Relief work expanded to such an extent that it became a major source of employment for the community.[26] The Budapest community had the resilience to look after its own affairs, and the real role of the international organizations was to provide funds to pay for the extensive relief work being done. This financial dependence continued for a long time, and for five years after the war up to half of Hungarian Jewry were kept alive by the large-scale relief programmes financed with the help of foreign Jewish aid.[27]

Their wartime experiences severely affected the relationship of Hungarian Jews to the society of which they had once been proud and deeply loyal members, and tensions between Jews and part of the non-Jewish population continued after the war. The ethnic antipathies of central and eastern Europe had not vanished with the liberation. In March 1945 the National Provisional government declared all the previous discriminatory confiscations of property null and void, and the desire of the returning Jews to get back their homes simply added fuel to the prevailing anti-Semitism – sentiments which were exploited by local political interests.[28] There was a full-scale pogrom in Kunmadaras in May 1946, and mass demonstrations against Jews took place in Diósgyőr-Miskolc in July.

In February 1946 all sectors of the community (Orthodox, Neolog, Status Quo, as well as representatives of the World Jewish Congress, the Zionists and anti-Zionist groups) collaborated in the preparation of a detailed study under the heading 'The Position of the Jews in Hungary and their Endeavours to Emigrate'.[29] The report concluded that, of the 140,000 members of the Jewish community in Hungary at that time, 63,500 wanted to emigrate to Palestine, 45,000 to other countries, and only 31,500 wished to remain.[30] The study was prepared for the Anglo-American Committee of Inquiry on Palestine (November 1945–April 1946), and its conclusions were very probably framed so as to influence the recommendations of that committee on the need to open the gates of Palestine to free Jewish immigration. Nevertheless, even if the emigration figures were exaggerated, they do reflect the deep mood of despair and alienation of the surviving Jews. It was reasonable to expect that this state of mind would lead to significant emigration in the months and years that followed, even if it was less than the 70 per cent suggested by the memorandum.[31] The anticipation of future emigration only increased the influence of the international Jewish organizations within the Hungarian community, as the Jewish Agency controlled the legal and illegal routes to Palestine, and the Joint would look after the migrants if they chose to go elsewhere.

RUMOURS OF GOLD

The population of Jewish survivors in the displaced persons camps in Germany and Austria stabilized towards the autumn of 1945. The concentration camp inmates who had been fatally weakened by their internment died in the weeks following their liberation (as many as a fifth of those liberated), while others gained strength and recovered. Many of them returned to their former homes or went off in search of surviving family members. In the autumn of 1945 there were 50–60,000 Jewish survivors in camps throughout the zones of occupation. But soon afterwards the numbers of Jewish displaced persons began to grow dramatically. Many Jewish partisans who had fought against the Nazis in the forests of Poland and the Baltic states decided to quit Europe as a place too dangerous for Jews. They began to trickle into the American zones of occupation, from where they believed they would be able to find their way to Palestine, either legally or illegally. And in the spring of 1946, Polish Jews who had found refuge within the Soviet Union during the war joined this general stream. The growing communist influence in eastern Europe, and a wave of pogroms when the Jews returned to their homes, encouraged these people, too, to pack their bags and try to migrate to America, Palestine or elsewhere. By the spring of 1947 the number of Jewish displaced persons in Germany and Austria had quadrupled, eventually reaching a peak of 225,000 people. Many of them wanted to go to Palestine as their first preference, and most of them were willing to try their luck there if no other possibilities emerged. However, the world was largely closed to displaced persons (especially Jews), and very few opportunities for migration were available. The Jewish displaced persons problem was a constant thorn in the side of the American and British military occupation authorities.

The British government was responsible not only for its zones of occupation in Europe, but also for the League of Nations Mandate in Palestine, where tensions between Jews and Arabs verged on open warfare. In order to appease Arab opinion, the British limited Jewish migration there to 1,500 per month, and conducted an aggressive battle against the organizers of illegal immigration. As many as 40,000 of the Jews from the displaced persons camps in Germany and Austria attempted to run the British blockade and reach Palestine.[32] While the British attempted to stop this flow, the American military authorities quietly encouraged it, attempting to balance the infiltration of displaced Jews into their zones of occupation in Germany and Austria with the 'exfiltration'[33] of Jews to Palestine.

The Jewish Agency and the Joint cooperated at every level in the movement and care of the Jewish displaced persons, although both organizations attempted to maintain a façade of legality. The Agency maintained its appearance of respectability by delegating the organization of the illegal movement of people from Poland to the American zones of occupation in Germany and Austria to underground operatives who belonged to a different organization (Bricha), and the shiploads of illegal immigrants to Palestine to yet another organization (Mossad Le'Aliya Bet). The Joint also maintained the appearance of propriety by ensuring that its involvement in these expertly planned and implemented operations was the concern of the Joint's officials in Europe and not of the organization's executive in New York. Nevertheless, this large-scale population transfer from eastern to central Europe, and from there to the coast of Italy or France where people secretly boarded boats for Palestine (including the famous case of the 'Exodus' in the summer of 1947), was regulated and directed by the Joint and the Jewish Agency – exactly as the British government insisted was the case.

Austria was an important crossroads for this traffic, and there were a number of Jewish displaced persons camps in Austria. But more significantly, it lay on the route of Jews coming from Poland through Czechoslovakia to Germany, and on the route of those passing from Germany to the Mediterranean ports of Italy.[34] Not surprisingly, Vienna was one of a number of centres for official and unofficial operatives of Jewish organizations involved in the affairs of the Holocaust survivors. In this colourful community of young Palestinian Jews busy with Zionist affairs, activists from among the displaced persons, and Jewish soldiers in the American forces, rumours of looted victim assets hidden by the Nazis ran rife. Like all rumours, they were larger than life and were embellished as they passed from hand to hand. One such story caught the attention of a member of the Political Department of the Jewish Agency, Gideon Rafael:[35]

I believe it was at the end of December 1945 when I first heard the rumour about the fabulous gold train. Groups of Palestinian Jews and friends from the Allied occupation armies used those bleak days in Vienna to meet every evening in a little apartment . . . The place was the clearing house for rumour and information – and a sort of headquarters for our rescue work. People spoke different languages and sometimes discussed different matters at the same time. It was not always easy to follow the conversations. Perhaps this was the reason why I did not pay much attention to the story. Lieut. Sam Kaplan (US Forces) was talking . . . I heard something about boxes full of gold and diamonds, silverware and watches which had been captured some time ago by the American army in a train which had originated from Budapest. A day or two later, however, the matter came back to my mind, when a refugee from Hungary told us his tribulations during the war. How in 1944 the Jews were driven into ghettos, how they had to surrender their gold and jewellery, silverware and other valuables to the Hungarian National Bank in Budapest before they were carted away in freight trains to the death camps in Auschwitz and Mauthausen . . . We had heard so many stories like this that somehow our senses had become dull. But when that refugee from Budapest reached in his story the point where he described his lining up in front of the special counter of the bank meekly delivering his family jewellery which was sorted by the receiving officials and put into different boxes neatly and appropriately labelled, Sam Kaplan's story of the gold train suddenly flashed back through my mind.[36]

Official Hungarian sources confirmed the rumour, and told Rafael that they estimated the looted goods on the Gold Train were worth around $300 million. Because of the deliberations taking place in Paris at the same time (December 1945) on the Final Act on Reparations and the decision on Article 8, the Gold Train was of great interest to the Jewish Agency and the Joint. Given the needs of the Holocaust survivors, and in view of the struggle of the Jewish community in Palestine for survival and for statehood, Jewish communities in America and throughout the world were being called on to donate large amounts of money to meet the challenges at this juncture in history. Jewish philanthropy was stretched to the limit. $300 million-worth of non-monetary gold and silver (over $3 billion in today's currency) would have solved the chronic shortage of cash and would have transformed the ability of the Agency and the Joint to care for the displaced persons and to resettle them in Palestine.

The fact of the train's discovery by the Americans and its transfer to Salzburg had already been published in the Hungarian press, and while Rafael was investigating the story the leaders of the Budapest Jewish communities (Lajos Stöckler and Ernő Munkácsi)* were taking the first steps towards claiming the looted goods. They met with Hungarian Foreign Minister János Gyöngyösi to obtain the assistance of the Hungarian government,[37] and on the same day they petitioned the American ambassador in Budapest, Arthur Schoenfeld, for the return of the train. In what was the first of many subsequent appeals to the American embassy, Stöckler and Munkácsi explained the history of the legalized despoiling of Hungarian Jewry and offered to supervise the return of the items on the train to their individual owners. Where this was not possible, the items would be used for general Jewish welfare purposes in Hungary.[38]

The Hungarian government had been pressing the United States authorities since June to allow official Hungarian repatriation commissions to trace general Hungarian property in the US zones of Germany and Austria, but without success. The Americans consistently replied that the 'disposition of Hungarian properties is a matter for inter-Allied determination', and that until an Allied policy towards Hungary as an ex-enemy state had been established, they would not entertain any Hungarian requests for the return of property.[39] This principle applied to the request by Stöckler and Munkácsi. When they approached the US Embassy again, two months later, asking that at the very least the army should provide an inventory of the Hungarian Jewish loot it was holding, they were told that the Hun-

---

* Lajos Stöckler came to prominence in the Jewish community during the Nazi occupation. Although a junior member of the Jewish Council during that period, he regularly risked his life in welfare activities in the ghetto. He was the only member of the wartime Jewish leadership who was not rejected by the community after the war. On the contrary, in March 1945 a small coterie of communal activists elected him head of the Jewish community of Budapest. Stöckler remained the most prominent figure in the community until his arrest by the Communist government in 1953. Ernő Munkácsi was the vice-president of the community's central organization from 1945.

garian Foreign Ministry would have to make an official request to the Allied Control Commission – in other words, they were turned down.[40]

The Hungarian government was more helpful. A few weeks after Stöckler and Munkácsi asked for the Foreign Minister's assistance, Gyöngyösi convened an inter-departmental committee on 15 January, together with representatives of the Jewish community, to coordinate steps to get the train back to Hungary. Two weeks later, the government authorized the Jewish community to take charge of the negotiations on the Jewish Gold Train, and the government itself withdrew its hand. The inter-departmental committee was disbanded at the end of the month.[41] This sudden change of policy was at the specific request of the Jewish community, which was acting in accordance with an agreement reached with the Jewish Agency during those two weeks.

Gideon Rafael travelled to Budapest towards the end of January to discuss the Gold Train (and other matters) with the communal leaders. Rafael wanted the community to give the Agency a power of attorney to negotiate with the French and Americans over the victim assets. He also asked the community to obtain the agreement of the Hungarian authorities that the train's cargo was persecutee property and that the Hungarian state had no claim to it. According to an account prepared by the Budapest community's representative in Vienna (Viktor Schwartz), an agreement was worked out whereby the $120–300 million value of the seized goods would be used for the benefit of Jews remaining in Hungary, Jews wanting to emigrate, Jews in the ex-Hungarian areas (Transylvania and Slovakia), and Jewish communities elsewhere in need of support. The funds would be administered by a committee representing all sections of the religious community (Orthodox, Neolog and Status Quo), the Zionists, and also Christians of Jewish origin.[42] Rafael's own account of this agreement was subtly different. According to the report he sent to the Jerusalem headquarters of the Agency, the Hungarian Jewish leaders agreed that the funds would be 'put at the disposal of a general Jewish reconstruction and resettlement fund and that only a minor part of this property should be returned to the remaining Jews in Hungary'.[43]

In view of the diplomatic circumstances, Rafael's approach to the fate of the looted assets was practical, although it was later perceived as paternalistic. The Jewish leadership was aware that the majority of

Jews had stated they wanted to leave Hungary. Further, the American authorities had made it clear that they would not return to Hungary any Hungarian property in their zones of occupation for a while, if ever. And at the Paris Conference on Reparations, whose results had been published on 14 January, only a few weeks before Rafael's visit to Budapest, the Allies stated in Article 8 that non-monetary gold would be used for the benefit of the victims of Nazi persecution everywhere. The only possibility that the Hungarian community might retrieve anything from the train was by agreeing to give the Agency the power of attorney Rafael requested, and accepting that the community would only be one among a number of beneficiaries of the valuables once they were returned to the Jewish world. But first it would be necessary to obtain the agreement of the Hungarian government that the Jewish community should be allowed to pursue the return of the looted victim gold, and that the government would not pursue it in its own official restitution claims for the victim assets.[44] This agreement was apparently forthcoming, because the government's interdepartmental committee on the issue was dissolved two weeks after it was established. The community received the official approval for its own attempts to retrieve the goods.

Rafael left Budapest at the end of January and travelled to Munich to meet David Ben-Gurion, chairman of the Jewish Agency and leader of the Jewish community in Palestine. Ben-Gurion had come to Germany on the second of a number of visits to the Jewish displaced persons and to conduct talks with the US army concerning conditions in the camps. From December 1945, teams of social workers and educators sent by the Agency were working with the survivors, and the Agency was also responsible for the allocation of the available legal immigration certificates to Palestine. Ben-Gurion also used the opportunity to meet Zionist activists from the liberated countries, and to survey the degree of political support for Zionism in each community. His diary (which often ran to a number of pages of text for each day) is a mournful stocktaking of the 10 or 20 per cent of the pre-war communities across Europe that had managed to survive the Holocaust.

Rafael accompanied him for three days of his visit, in Munich and Frankfurt, and reported on the state of the Jewish community in

Hungary.[45] He told Ben-Gurion about the Gold Train, pointing out that estimates of its value ranged from $120 to $300 million, and that following the agreement with leaders of the Jewish communities in Budapest this huge resource could become available for the work of the Jewish Agency and the Joint. Rafael argued (and this soon became the official position of these organizations) that unless the Hungarian Jewish community gave up its claim for these goods and agreed that they should be handed over to the international Jewish organizations, the goods would be lost to the Jewish world.[46] Ben-Gurion gave his approval to Rafael's activities and the appropriation of the Gold Train became Jewish Agency policy.[47]

Rafael's next step was to find out what he could about the train from the US forces headquarters in Austria, and here he met the chief of the Finance Division, Lieut.-Colonel Arthur Marget (whom Rafael described as 'an excellent Jew'). Marget estimated the value of the train at between $50 and $120 million, and advised Rafael that 'if the American government were to receive sufficient guarantees that the funds will not be returned to Hungary where they might be confiscated by the government or even seized by the Russians as reparations', Washington would be willing to hand over the valuables to 'an international Jewish body for the purposes of relief and resettlement'.[48] The best possible 'guarantee' would be an official Hungarian government renunciation of any claims on the train – which was a significant step beyond the agreement between the government and the community in January to leave the negotiations for the return of the train in the care of the community. Marget's advice was that if the Agency and the Joint wished to benefit from the train, they had to persuade the Hungarian government to waive unequivocally all claims it might have on the victim loot. Rafael returned to Budapest at the end of March or in early April with the intention of obtaining this waiver, in writing.

Since the first post-war elections in November 1945, Hungary was ruled by a coalition government led by the Smallholders Party together with the Social Democrats and Communists. Although the Communists had received only 17 per cent of the vote, and the prime minister, Ferenc Nagy, came from the Smallholders, the real power was held by the deputy prime minister and leader of the Communist Party, Mátyás Rákosi. Rákosi was a loyal Stalinist and the effective instrument of

Soviet control. In 1948, when Hungary was officially transformed into a 'people's republic', he became prime minister. But for almost three years after the liberation, the government of Hungary was shared between a number of centre and left-wing parties, while the Soviet occupation forces encouraged the gradual communist takeover of all institutions and organizations.

The Jewish community, and especially the Zionists, had no effective lines of communication with the Smallholders Party; but this was not the case in their dealings with the communists and with the Soviet occupying forces. The ability of the Joint to send relief supplies to the community in Budapest immediately after the liberation of the city was useful to the Russians, as 5 per cent of the food, clothing and cash sent by the Joint were allocated to the non-Jewish population.[49] Hungary was also on the route of many Polish Jews on their way to the American zones of occupation in Germany and Austria. As this movement increased the size of the displaced persons problem in the American zones and ultimately complicated the position of the British in Palestine, the Soviets were willing to allow the traffic to continue. But the most important consideration was that the American dollars which the Joint sent to finance its activities in Budapest (and the work of DEGOB, the community's welfare organization) represented the largest single source of foreign hard currency available to the Hungarian economy in 1945–1946.[50] For all these reasons, and other minor ones,[51] the foreign Jewish organizations and the Zionists were able to deal with the communists and their Soviet backers directly.[52]

As a result, Rafael and Shimshon Nathan, director of the Jewish Agency offices in Budapest, were able to bypass prime minister Ferenc Nagy and approach Rákosi directly. Both Rafael and Nathan later provided graphic accounts of the interview with the communist deputy prime minister.[53] In view of the obstacles to the return of Hungarian assets created by the Americans, Rákosi was interested in proving Hungary's good faith and gaining the support of 'world Jewry'. He was particularly interested in having American Jewish support for the return to Hungary of the gold of the Hungarian National Bank. Hungary was destitute, and the $32–35 million worth of National Bank gold would have allowed the country to institute a reform of her domestic currency and end the terrible inflation. Rafael promised the full support of the Jewish Agency and its friends in Washington, and a deal was quickly struck. Rafael and Nathan were still in the room when Rákosi telephoned the prime minister and instructed Nagy to prepare a letter waiving any Hungarian claim to the persecutee gold held by the Allies.[54]

The letter was the Hungarian 'Balfour Declaration' on heirless victim assets: 'The Government of the Hungarian Republic wants to do everything in its power to render possible the rehabilitation and financial restitution of Jews who suffered to such a great extent under fascist persecution.' Nagy stated that the government recognized the Jewish Agency as the appropriate body to pursue the restitution of these Hungarian assets 'so that these assets may serve the purpose of the social and financial restitution of Jews who fell victim to the above persecutions'.[55] There was no obligation to return the assets to Hungary, or even to use them for the exclusive benefit of Hungarian Jews.

It was as if Rafael and Nathan had drafted the letter themselves – which, in fact, Nathan's version of these events claims they did. According to the latter's account, after their success with Rákosi, Rafael and Nathan decided to go directly to the prime minister's office to complete the transaction. On their way, they stopped at the offices of the Jewish Agency to type up a draft of the letter of authorization they hoped Nagy would sign, in English and Hungarian. Nagy did, and the letter was quickly prepared on the letterhead of the prime minister's department.[56] Shortly after Rafael's meetings in Budapest, the US government agreed to return the National Bank gold to Hungary. Rákosi was a member of the delegation that travelled to Washington to negotiate the return. On his way back to Hungary, after the success of the talks in Washington, Rákosi phoned Rafael (then in London) to thank him for the assistance of the Jewish Agency.[57] The Jewish Agency had no sway whatsoever in Washington in this matter, but the myth of 'Jewish influence' was very useful.

Throughout this period there was no reliable estimate of the value of the train's freight. The first, superficial, army evaluation was set at $120 million. Marget's '$50 to $120 million' was the most sober estimate so far. But Hungarian Jewish sources consistently referred to $300 million or more. Ernest Marton, the representative of the World

Jewish Congress in Romania and the man responsible for organizing most of the earliest relief supplies sent to the community in Budapest, visited Vienna in March 1946. There he met officials of the Hungarian Jewish community who were also on the trail of the Gold Train. In a detailed letter sent to the leadership of the Congress, he recounted that the value of the train was reported to be '$300–350 million', an estimate established by 'jewelers from Milan' who were brought in (presumably by the American authorities) to assess the value of the goods in the Salzburg warehouse.[58]

The 'Italian experts' are often referred to in Hungarian documents relating to the train, to give credence to the high estimate of its value. However, American records of the supervision of the warehouse make no mention of any Italian assessors. Furthermore, when an inventory was finally made (in 1947) it took a team of assessors over six months to complete. In view of the huge quantity of goods involved, no casual estimate of value could have been accurate. Nevertheless, the inflated figure of $300 million caught everyone's imagination and became the standard Hungarian estimate of the value of the train. American estimates of the value of the victim loot decreased rapidly during the period 1946–1947 as they familiarized themselves with the goods. Hungarian estimates, however, were calculated on the basis of Jewish community losses during 1944, and they constantly increased as the full extent of the Holocaust of Hungarian Jewry became clear. The Gold Train began to assume mythical proportions as the cargo of the train that left Brennbergbánya in March 1945 came to symbolize all the looted property of Hungarian Jewry.

8

Gold and Politics in Washington

Under the terms of the armistice signed between the Allies and Hungary on 20 January 1945, the Hungarian state undertook to pay reparations (in 1938 values) of $200 million to the Soviet Union, $70 million to Yugoslavia and $30 million to Czechoslovakia, all within six years. This was a heavy burden in view of the extent of the war damage and the massive evacuations to Austria and southern Germany. Practically the entire gold reserve of Hungary, railway rolling stock, motorized transport, the most valuable industrial equipment, pedigree cattle, horses, and huge stocks of raw material and food were now in zones controlled by the Americans. According to official published Hungarian estimates, which were adopted by the Soviets, the value of Hungarian property in American control was approximately $3 billion (1945 values). As the Soviets pointed out, this was ten times the total amount of reparations that the Hungarians owed Russia, Yugoslavia and Czechoslovakia together,[1] and which the Hungarian economy was unable to pay according to schedule.[2]*

American analysts rejected these estimates, believing that they were grossly inflated for political reasons, and argued that Soviet looting of Hungary, rather than any American delay in restoring to Hungary property from Austria and Germany, was to blame for the dire state

---

* In 1946 the Soviets agreed to extend the deadline from six years to eight years, stipulating only a small increase in the amount to be paid. Two-thirds of the debt to the Soviet Union ($134.3 million) was paid within the first three years. But once the Communist regime was established in Hungary in 1948, the Soviet Union cancelled the remaining debt of $65.7 million as a gesture. Note in this connection the Soviet appropriation of Hungarian non-monetary gold in the summer of 1948, discussed in Chapter 11, below.

of the Hungarian economy.[3] A detailed US intelligence report on the state of that economy, based on unpublished Hungarian official data, stated that while 16 per cent of the damage to Hungarian manufacturing capacity was caused by German removals and a further 5 per cent by Nyilas removals, the greatest damage was due to Russian removals, which were almost twice as large (36 per cent) – data which the Soviets and Hungarians wished to suppress.[4] Ironically, the economic distress caused by Soviet depredations in Hungary was driving that country to even greater dependence on the Soviet Union. American analysts recognized that shortages of food, manufactured goods and housing, combined with raging inflation, had created a situation in which Hungary was rapidly falling under complete Soviet control. By 1946, the value of the Hungarian pengő had been so undermined by inflation that when the director of the Joint's welfare offices in Budapest, Frigyes Görög, wrote a cheque in pengő worth $5,000 it contained 32 digits.[5] The cash reserves of the Hungarian National Bank (9.1 billion pengő), which had been seized together with the bank's gold reserves one year earlier at Spital am Pyhrn, were now worth $45.

This created a dilemma for the policy-makers in the State Department. On the one hand, the Americans wished to win the battle for Hungarian public opinion, and the best way to do that was by allowing the return of property that had been evacuated to Germany and Austria. On the other hand, restituted property, if it was of any economic significance, would probably be seized by the Soviets as part of Hungary's reparations payment to her liberators/occupiers. Local sources in Budapest told the Americans confidentially that 'Hungarians would welcome a blunt refusal by the US to return anything owed by Hungary or Hungarians until after the peace treaties are signed' (which would have regulated the Soviet expropriations).[6] But this approach, too, played into Soviet hands. There was a concerted campaign in the communist press to convince the Hungarian public that their difficulties were caused by the American failure to return displaced Hungarian property:

While we hunger and starve, while the sick perish in the hospitals for lack of medicines, while our infants die in the public nurseries and our working

1 Propaganda photo in Hungarian Fascist newspaper *Harc* (June 1944) showing confiscated Jewish valuables (*Hungarian National Library*)

2 Jews waiting to hand in their radios to the authorities, Budapest, May 1944 (*Bundesarchiv*)

3 Jew arrested outside the Budapest ghetto (December, 1944) by plain clothes and uniformed Arrow Cross agents. An arrow cross insignia can be seen hanging in the background (*Yad Vashem Photo Archives*)

4 (*above*) Árpád Toldi, taken from a 1944
Hungarian gendarmerie publication
(*author's collection*)

5 (*above right*) Wilhelm Höttl, 1946 at
Nuremberg. (*NARA, Washington, DC*)

6 (*right*) Kurt Becher in 1944 (*Spiegel
Archiv*)

7 (*above left*) Jewish authored books collected for destruction at a Budapest papermill, June 1944 (*US Holocaust Memorial Museum Photo Archives*)

8 (*above right*) Looting by villagers of Jewish property after removal of Jews to ghettos, April–May 1944 (*US Holocaust Memorial Museum Photo Archives*)

9 Official removal of household effects from formerly Jewish homes, April–May 1944 (*US Holocaust Memorial Museum Photo Archives*)

10 The Szálasi government, photo taken one day after the Arrow Cross seizure of power, 16 October 1944. Count Fidél Pálffy (Minister of Agriculture), standing second from the left; Gábor Vajna (Minister of the Interior), standing third from the left; Baron Gábor Kemény (Minister of Foreign Affairs), sitting second from left; Ferenc Szálasi (Prime Minister and Acting Head of State), sitting centre

Holder GIDEON RUFFER
Address 27. ALFASI ST.

Occupation OFFICIAL
Employer JEWISH AGENCY
*Area of Validity Jem.

*Valid only from Residence
                                    (place)
To EMPLOYMENT
                                    (place)
*Via
*Valid only from A-C (hours)
          to Hours (hours)

*Cross out where inapplicable

ISSUED UNDER THE AUTHORITY
OF THE MILITARY COMMANDER

THIS PASS MAY BE WITHDRAWN AT
ANY TIME WITHOUT ANY REASON

ANY   WILL
        RENDER IT INVALID
LOSS OF PASS TO BE REPORTED
AT ONCE TO ISSUING AUTHORITY

11 Gideon Rafael (Ruffer), 1947 Palestinian Mandate pass (*Mrs Nurit Rafael*)

12 Óbánya Castle cellars, where the initial sorting of the loot was carried out (September–December 1944) (*author's photo*)

13 Brennbergbánya, pre-World War II photo showing both the bath-house where the loot was sorted and the Borbála mine-shaft where the loot was stored (*County Museum Sopron*)

14 Eisenhower and Patton (among others) examining the Merkers loot (*NARA*)

15 (*below*) Colonel Bernhard Bernstein with some of the Merkers loot (*NARA*)

16 The Merkers mine, Thuringia, April 1945 with part of the SS loot discovered by US troops (*NARA*)

17 The Gold Train under American command being moved from Werfen to Salzburg, July 1945 (*NARA*)

18 Another photo of the Gold Train (*NARA*)

19 Miklós Nyárádi, Hungarian Deputy Minister of Finance, signing for the Hungarian National Bank gold, returned by US forces in Austria, August 1946 (*NARA*)

```
Se  SS SS       204   298      LONDON      45   15   1746     VIAIMP =
Instructions
Handed in at ................  .......ـ في نمسر ـ     Orig. No.
On ................            التاريخ ביום         Words
Time ................          الوقت הוזن|          Recd from
Received at ........  /600    وصلت في نتقبد ـ        By

    To        NLT JEWAGENCY JERUSALEM  =

        UNDERSTAND    GIDEON  RUFFER    KNOWS     NAME    GERMAN

    COLONE' INNSTRUC K      REPORTED   POSSESS     LARGE

    Q UANTITIES   UNCUT    DIAMONDS  ORIGINALLY —

    BELONGING    HUNGARIAN       GOLD  TRAIN AND  TAKEN     FROM

HUNGARIAN   JEWS    STOP    TRAIN    NOW IN  FRENCH  ZONE  AUSTRIA

    STOP PLEASE        ASK      RUFFER  CABLE ME  DETAILS  ABOUT

THIS   COLONEL  INNSBRUCK GOLDMAN  =

                                   32998—900000—31.12.44—G.C.P.
```

20 Nahum Goldmann's telegram referring to 'large quantities of uncut diamonds' (*Central Zionist Archives, Jerusalem*)

21 Part of the Toldi loot discovered at Schnann by farmers and later confiscated by the French authorities (*Archives du ministère des Affaires étrangères, Colmar*)

22 The Toldi loot (*Colmar Archives*)

23 The Toldi loot (*Colmar Archives*)

24 The Salzburg loot: boxes of costume jewellery (*Abba Schwartz Papers, Central Zionist Archives, Jerusalem*)

25 The Salzburg loot: watches (*Abba Schwartz Papers*)

26 (*above*) The Salzburg loot: counting up watches and clocks under guard (*Abba Schwartz Papers*)

27 (*below*) The Salzburg loot: crates ready for shipment to auction (*Abba Schwartz Papers*)

28–30 The Salzburg loot: gold dentures; miscellaneous ornaments (note the Mickey Mouse); forks (*Abba Schwartz Papers*)

31 (*left*) Abba Schwartz leaving the Salzburg warehouse (*Abba Schwartz Papers*)

32 (*right*) The Salzburg loot: smelting gold fragments (*Abba Schwartz Papers*)

33 The Salzburg loot: purses (*Abba Schwartz Papers*)

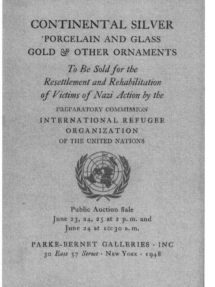

CONTINENTAL SILVER
'PORCELAIN AND GLASS
GOLD & OTHER ORNAMENTS

To Be Sold for the
Resettlement and Rehabilitation
of Victims of Nazi Action by the
PREPARATORY COMMISSION
INTERNATIONAL REFUGEE
ORGANIZATION
OF THE UNITED NATIONS

Public Auction Sale
June 23, 24, 25 at 2 p. m. and
June 24 at 10:30 a. m.

PARKE-BERNET GALLERIES · INC
30 East 57 Street · NEW YORK · 1948

ORIENTAL & MACHINE-WOVEN
RUGS AND CARPETS

To be Sold for the Resettlement and
Rehabilitation of Victims of Nazi Action
BY THE
MERCHANDISING ADVISORY COMMITTEE OF THE
INTERNATIONAL REFUGEE
ORGANIZATION
OF THE UNITED NATIONS

Public Auction Sale
October 20 at 1:30 p. m.
AND
Exhibition October 18 and 19
AT
SOFIA BROTHERS WAREHOUSE
61st Street and Columbus Avenue
New York

Under Management of
PARKE-BERNET GALLERIES · INC
NEW YORK 22 · 1948

34–5 New York auction catalogues, 1948 (*Abba Schwartz Papers*) classes become ragged, many billions of dollars in goods, carried away by the Germans, are lying idle in Austria and Germany.[7]

As Arthur Schoenfeld, the American ambassador, laconically pointed out, the press campaign distracted attention from the 'far greater losses of Hungarian national assets through Russian looting'.

In November 1945, six months after the end of the war in Europe, the American Joint Chiefs of Staff authorized the start of a broad programme of restitution to Allied nations, returning to the rightful owners the industrial, commercial and other property that had been found in the US zones of Germany and Austria.[8] However, the ex-enemy nations (Italy, Hungary, Romania and Finland) were not included. For almost a year the American authorities had refused to concede to Hungarian demands that their property be returned, and they even refused to allow a Hungarian 'repatriation commission' to inspect and inventory Hungarian assets that had been uncovered in Austria and Germany.[9] Instead, the Hungarians were told to submit lists of missing goods, an almost impossible task which took them nearly fifteen months to complete. This was understandable, given the chaotic internal situation in the last months of the war during which the goods were transported out of Hungary, and the destruction of records by the Szálasi regime.[10]

Eventually, the Americans relented. The results of parliamentary elections in November 1945, in which the Communists won only 17 per cent and the Smallholders and Peasant Parties won 57 per cent, encouraged Washington to reconsider its chances of influencing developments there. In February 1946, the State–War–Navy Coordinating Committee (the highest policy-making body for the American zones of occupation in Germany and Austria) recommended that the policy of the restitution of goods to Allied nations should now be extended to ex-enemy nations as well. The new policy tried to distinguish between voluntary Hungarian evacuations after 15 October, and the forced German evacuations from Hungary after 20 January 1945, when the armistice was signed between the Hungarian National Provisional government and the Allies.[11] At first only the latter would be returned, but soon afterwards Washington liberalized its ruling once again and extended the period back to the coming to power of the

Arrow Cross regime, 15 October.[12] The policy shift evoked a storm of protest from General Joseph McNarney in Germany (USFET) and General Mark Clark in Austria (USFA). They believed that the new policy would deprive their zones of occupation of important economic resources and make the task of reconstruction much more difficult.[13] John Erhardt, the US Political Representative in Vienna, also argued that American interests would be best served by using Hungarian property for the benefit of the Austrian economy.[14]

Washington's sudden generosity towards Hungary and the other ex-enemy states was not unqualified. In view of the intelligence information that certain Hungarian circles would be happy if vital assets were not returned as long as Hungary remained under Soviet military occupation, the State–War–Navy Coordinating Committee modified its policy shortly after it had been released and decided that the 281 Hungarian Danubian barges (*circa* 60 per cent of Hungary's river transportation capacity) captured by US forces would not be returned, so as to prevent the Soviets seizing them.[15] But this was not enough for Erhardt, McNarney and Clark, the senior American officials on the spot, and during April and May 1946 the State Department re-evaluated its policies as it sought to answer their objections.

The reply was finally forthcoming in mid-June, when Washington informed the American occupation authorities in Europe that the decision to restore property to the ex-enemy states would stand because it was consistent with American foreign policy objectives. Non-restitution was harming the standing of the United States in the public opinion of these countries, especially in Hungary, where the Communist Party was using the situation to further its own position. Moreover, from the beginning US policy was designed to return those goods looted by Germany and not the goods willingly handed over by the ex-enemy countries.[16] The one amendment to its previous statement of policy which the Coordinating Committee in Washington was prepared to make was to distinguish between victim property and general Hungarian assets, and to leave the door open that the former might not be restored. For a brief time, the Property Control officer in charge of the Salzburg warehouse understood the new policy to mean that the Jewish goods would not be going back to Hungary. So he permitted US army officers, billeted for the foreseeable future in Austrian homes that had usually been stripped bare by their owners prior to army personnel moving in, to requisition household goods for their accommodation from the holdings in the warehouse.[17] The permission was retracted three months later and an order issued that 'the materials [already distributed] shall be carefully protected'.[18]*

Events now began to move quickly. The Hungarian government was invited to send official commissions to make an inventory of Hungarian property and prepare it for transportation back home,[19] and Washington instructed that preparations be made for returning the gold of the Hungarian National Bank to Budapest.[20] This was the gold that had been discovered at Spital am Pyhrn in April 1945, and had been at the top of the list of all Hungarian demands for the return of their property. Once it had been decided to allow restitution of Hungarian property, the National Bank gold was the first item to be shipped back. The Hungarian Commissioner for the Repatriation of Looted Property and Under-Secretary of Finance, Miklós Nyárádi, travelled to Berlin and Frankfurt to hold talks with the US occupation authorities and to supervise the loading and certification procedures of the bank's gold.[21]

The Americans wanted to achieve the maximum impact possible when the National Bank gold arrived back in Budapest, and the return was planned with a surprise gimmick – the train included Hitler's personal dining-car, which was guaranteed to attract comment. Thirty tons of gold (in 1,222 sacks) and five tons of silver were loaded in Frankfurt on 5 August 1946, and the train travelled to Vienna with

---

* Lieut. Treece simply formalized a practice that had become commonplace since September 1945, when army officers took household items from the train's cargo. The Property Control office kept a detailed record, but the goods were rarely returned. As the quantities borrowed were a very small fraction of the overall cargo, these losses were not significant. Nevertheless, in its 1999 Interim Report the Presidential Advisory Commission on Holocaust Assets in the United States accused the US army of large-scale larceny, an accusation that made front-page news in the *Washington Post* and the *New York Times* on 15 October 1999. There is no evidence to support these charges; in fact the opposite is true. The Property Control Division of USFA went to great lengths to protect the cargo against theft. The charges by the Presidential Commission were not repeated in the Commission's Final Report in 2001.

an impressive American armed guard, a representative of the State Department, members of the Hungarian and American press, and a small contingent of Soviet officers to ensure smooth passage across the border. The American legation in Budapest organized a reception at Budapest railway station for the arrival on 7 August, and monitored the reactions of the local press very closely.[22]

Before the train left Frankfurt, however, Nyárádi was required to sign a receipt on behalf of his government 'waiving all claims which it may have for losses arising out of looting or otherwise wrongful removal of monetary gold from Hungary during the war'. It is not clear if any one troubled to instruct the visiting Commissioner for the Repatriation of Looted Property on the significance of the American definitions of 'monetary' and 'non-monetary' gold, but Nyárádi refused to sign the waiver until he received assurances that the waiver did not apply to 'Jewish monetary gold'. He was assured that it did not.[23] Either the American officials he talked to were uninformed of Washington's plans for the Gold Train of victim loot, or else they played on the fact that the victim loot was non-monetary gold and that there was never any 'Jewish monetary gold' by definition (because there was no such thing as a 'Jewish currency' produced by a Jewish central bank which was backed by its own monetary gold). The Hungarians received their own monetary gold back, and Nyárádi believed he had received an indication of the American intention to return the Toldi train, too. The American military authorities in Germany and Austria, however, believed that the Finance Minister had just signed away any Hungarian claims on the victim gold.

At this point, the Departments of State and of War in Washington were not yet seriously interested in the Gold Train. The Jewish community in Budapest, the international Jewish organizations, Ginzberg's team at the Five Power Conference in Paris in June, the government of Hungary and the American occupation officials in Europe were all occupied with the fate of the victim loot on the Toldi train, but in Washington there were more urgent problems to deal with. Only when Nagy's letter to Rafael (authorizing the Jewish Agency to take control of the assets) reached the State Department, and showed how it was possible to resolve the fate of the looted assets in a way that was entirely consistent with American policy objectives in favour of refugees and against sending too many assets back to Soviet control, did Washington begin to show an active interest in the story of the train.

In late May 1946, the War Department requested detailed information about the train from the army,[24] and received a reply one week later. Despite the enthusiastic reports from Jewish sources, and contrary to the excited rumours of hoards of loot which were common currency of the weeks immediately after the end of the war, this report was sober and almost disappointing:

Property is of unknown origin and ownership . . . General inventory consisting of approx. 800 cases assorted silverware; 440 cases assorted porcelain and china; 152 cases assorted furs; 300 cases assorted table silverware; 140 cases assorted linens and clothing; 100 cases assorted watches and jewelry; 80 cases miscellaneous items; bales of assorted rugs. No evaluation made.[25]

No mention was made of the gold or the currency that had also been taken into custody, and the general image conveyed was of a large collection of household goods.

In mid-June, Nahum Goldmann, who headed the Jewish Agency's Washington office, and Maurice Boukstein, the Agency's legal representative, met State Department officials a number of times to discuss the future of the train. The State Department did not consider that Nagy's letter to Rafael was sufficient by itself to justify the handing over of the Gold Train to the Agency and the Joint, as the letter was not addressed to the American government. The Department felt that the two Jewish organizations should obtain the formal consent of the Hungarian Jewish community, and that they should also undertake to restore to living owners any property that could be identified as theirs.[26] Washington was eager to hand over the train, but they did not want to expose the Administration to any potential criticism.

While these talks were going on, Ferenc Nagy made an official visit to the United States. As the Hungarian prime minister wished to meet Jewish groups in America,[27] Goldmann considered approaching him and asking for an additional letter, drafted to meet the conditions of the State Department. However, as the American government had already agreed to return the Hungarian National Bank gold, the Hungarians no longer needed the support of the Jewish organizations, and inviting Nagy to revise the letter would give him an opportunity to revoke it altogether. As Goldmann later explained, 'there are some arguments in favor of not having seen [the prime minister] as we can now interpret the letter to Ruffer [Rafael] with a clear conscience as a release renunciation of this property by the Hungarian Government'.[28] Rather than approach the prime minister again, the Agency and the Joint decided instead to concentrate on obtaining a suitable statement of the wishes of the Hungarian Jewish community. On 14 June Rafael sent the following cable to Lajos Stöckler in Budapest, reminding him of what had been agreed with the community in January and asking for his written concurrence:

Negotiations between Jewish Agency and United States authorities for release of Salzburg property far advanced. At present stage [of the] negotiations [it is] imperative we obtain declaration from Hungarian Jewish representative body that assets be made available for Jewish victims of fascist persecution on similar terms as prime minister's letter to Jewish Agency . . .[29]

Circumstances had already changed in Hungary since Rafael's first visit there in January, and his telegram was received with great ambivalence. The Jewish communal institutions in Budapest were now functioning, and a local leadership had emerged that was able to speak on behalf of all sections of the community. Furthermore, as the Americans had announced their general willingness to begin the restitution of Hungarian property, the Jewish Agency's argument that the only hope for the return of the train's assets to the Jewish world was by allowing the international Jewish organizations to take control was no longer self-evidently true. Nevertheless, the community remained dependent on the financial support of the Joint, and the Agency and the Zionist movement controlled the possibilities of migration to Palestine, which many members of the community hoped to use. Both considerations were a very real leverage in the organizations' conflict with the local Jewish community.

No doubt with this in mind, a reply was sent in July which clearly indicated that a difficult compromise had been reached within the community. It was signed by six communal leaders representing all major sections of the community. The carefully worded text repeated the language of the May letter of the Hungarian prime minister, authorizing the use of the train's assets for the benefit of all Jewish victims of fascist persecution, but added a new condition: 'The way in which the valuables to be released shall be used will be decided by the competent organizations of the Hungarian Jews.'[30] This message was reinforced in August, one month later, by a communication from Schoenfeld, the US ambassador in Budapest, to the State Department, pointing out that the Jewish community was cooperating closely with the Hungarian government, and had formed a special joint committee to supervise the return of the train assets, and to decide how much would be allocated for the benefit of Jewish survivors outside Hungary and how much would be used for the benefit of the community. Schoenfeld added that Nyárádi planned to visit the United States to discuss the matter with the government and with the Jewish organizations.[31]

The reply of the Budapest Jewish community indicated that they intended to take control of their own affairs, and would not accept the paternalistic oversight of the international organizations. But nothing is ever that simple or direct in Jewish public affairs. Despite the multiple signatures there was no real consensus, and formulation of the reply led to a serious split in the internal management of the community between Zionist and non-Zionist factions.[32] In the light of the lessons of the immediate wartime past, the community was torn between different visions of the future. The Zionists believed that Jewry had no future in Hungary, and that their main task was to prepare the young people for life in Palestine, while others, especially the pro-Soviet factions, argued that the Jews had a role in the construction of socialism in the country of their birth. The controversy over who would control the assets on the Gold Train was an expression of this deep ideological split.

Lajos Stöckler was accepted as the first among the various factional leaders of the community, and he was highly efficient as an intermediary with the government. In the complex political situation in Hungary under Russian occupation and creeping communist control, the fact that Stöckler was formally a communist served the community well, as it increased his effectiveness in relations with the authorities.[33] In 1946–1947, Stöckler and the Zionists parted ways because of the dispute over the Gold Train and related matters, and the Zionists attempted to unseat him by calling for long-overdue communal elections. Stöckler and his government supporters managed to have the elections delayed until May 1948, by which time Hungary was firmly under communist control. Not surprisingly, Stöckler won election, as he had been declared the sole legal candidate.[34] In the events that followed the community's ambivalent response to Rafael's request for a clear power of attorney, Stöckler led the campaign for the return of the train to Hungary.

Another reason for the shift in opinion within the community was the fact that important progress had been achieved in talks between the Hungarian government and the community on the question of the restitution of local heirless Jewish property in Hungary. The surviving Jews had already benefited from the restoration of their property under the March 1945 legislation, but the fate of the property of the majority of the Hungarian Jewish community who had perished without heirs remained problematic. Throughout 1946 the Hungarian government negotiated a Peace Treaty with the Allied governments. At the insistence of the US State Department, which in turn was responding to pressure from American Jewish organizations,[35] the Peace Treaty specifically mentioned the restoration of the property rights of racial and political persecutees of fascist actions, including heirless property. Article 27, paragraph 2, of the Treaty stated that such property 'shall be transferred by the Hungarian Government to organizations in Hungary representative [of persecutees]. The property transferred shall be used by such organizations for purposes of relief and rehabilitation of surviving members of such groups, organizations and communities in Hungary.'[36]

In anticipation of the signing of the Treaty, the Hungarian government introduced legislation to create a National Jewish Rehabilitation Fund which would take control of all heirless Jewish property and use it for the rehabilitation of surviving Jews, both at an individual and communal level. The legislation was passed on 3 October 1946 and the fund was established six weeks later,[37] but it only began to function in March 1947 after the government and the communal leadership agreed on the composition of the 36-member executive board. (It is interesting to note that Greece and Hungary were the first two countries in Europe to create formal bodies for the restitution of heirless Jewish property, but ultimately they were the two countries with the worst record of actual restitution.) Ironically, the establishment of the fund was delayed because of a conflict between the provincial Jewish communities, who had lost the most people in the deportations and therefore had the highest percentage of heirless property, and the Budapest community, who wished to dominate the board administering the fund.[38] It was almost a mirror image of the evolving conflict between the international Jewish organizations and the Central Board of Hungarian Jews, with the same paternalistic attitude to the use of heirless property.

The situation had now become immensely complicated. The July response of the Hungarian Jewish community was an obstacle to the most convenient solution for disposing of the Gold Train, and the State Department was very willing to listen to informal reports that it did not really reflect the wishes of the community. Information soon reached Washington that regardless of what they had stated publicly in their response, most of the leaders of Budapest Jewry did not want the assets returned to Hungary.[39] Hungary was going communist, and the State Department understood that the leaders of the Jewish community there found it politic to take public positions (on the fate of the Gold Train) that they did not actually support. The Department was also willing to accept the argument of the Joint and the Jewish Agency that most of the goods on the Gold Train were looted or confiscated from the provincial Jewish communities of wartime 'Greater Hungary', which was no longer part of the territory of post-war Hungary. As these communities had been deported to Auschwitz and very few had returned, the valuables were effectively heirless. Given all these considerations, the Hungarian Jewish community could only claim a proprietary interest in approximately 27 per cent of the valuables, whereas the Jewish world as a whole, as heirs to those who had perished, had a claim on the rest.[40]

But the State Department did not have to get too deeply involved in the conflict between the international Jewish organizations and the Hungarian community in order to find grounds not to send the Gold Train back to Hungary. It had an excellent reason that had nothing to do with Jewish politics. Article 8 and the Five Power Conference had determined that non-monetary gold and victim loot was potentially a major source of funding for the refugee resettlement programmes of the Intergovernmental Committee on Refugees. As the original budget of the IGCR for 1946 was only $8 million,[41] the promise of additional funds through Article 8 ($25 million, plus perhaps as much as $50–100 million in non-monetary gold) was a very significant development. If the Gold Train assets were released through the IGCR to the Jewish operating agencies instead of being returned to Hungary, then the post-Second World War Jewish refugee problem would be much closer to being solved without becoming a continual burden on the American taxpayer. This line of thinking acquired added force in the summer of 1946, when American expectations of progress in the resettlement of displaced persons, and the resulting continuing decline in the numbers of displaced persons in the US zones of occupation, were suddenly reversed.

For some months the US occupation authorities in charge of displaced persons affairs had been aware of a worrying trend of infiltration of Jews from eastern Europe into the American zones in Germany and Austria. In June 1946, while Ginzberg was negotiating the Five Power Agreement on non-monetary gold and Rafael was seeking the cooperation of the Hungarian Jewish community concerning the Gold Train, the US army noticed a significant increase in the number of Jewish displaced persons. By the end of June, alarming reports were reaching Washington. In addition to the 90,000 Jewish displaced persons already in the US zones, General Clark in Vienna reported that 'between 350,000 and 750,000 Jewish refugees may be expected to move into western countries this year, with the majority migrating to the US occupied territory in Austria and Germany'.[42] Clark's estimate was greatly exaggerated, but he identified the trend correctly. And coincidentally, one week after his cable reached Washington, the most serious post-war anti-Jewish pogrom took place in Kielce, Poland, and another, much smaller one, in Miskolc, Hungary – events which only increased the pressure on the Jewish minorities in those countries to leave. Similar anti-Jewish sentiment was also felt in Romania (where a serious drought had led to unrest in rural areas), and thousands of Romanian Jews joined the general flight into the American zones of occupation in Austria. British policy would not allow them into Palestine, it was not possible to close the borders of Germany and Austria to prevent their infiltration, US immigration law blocked their entry into the United States, and no other resettlement prospects were feasible.[43] Instead of being able gradually to close displaced persons camps as the refugees dispersed, it looked as if this was a problem that would not go away. The responsible officials in the State Department and in the occupation zones in Europe were grateful for the assistance of the Joint and the Jewish Agency, and for the prospect of a refugee resettlement programme that would become possible with the flow of non-monetary gold into the coffers of the relief agencies.

In early July the State Department took a number of steps towards utilizing the potential of the Gold Train in the general effort to manage the displaced persons problem. First, it was necessary to make absolutely certain that the victim loot would not be sent back to Hungary by mistake, in the wake of the general restitution of Hungarian assets that was now beginning.[44] As the non-monetary gold would be channelled through the IGCR, the Department obtained British agreement that the mandate of the IGCR should be broadened to include resettlement activities,[45] and engineered the appointment of an American lawyer (Joel Fisher),[46] who had close ties to the Jewish organizations, as an assistant to the British head of the IGCR, Sir Herbert Emerson.[47] But these were secondary issues. The real obstacle to utilizing the Gold Train assets was the fact that Article 8 referred to non-monetary gold in Germany, while the looted Hungarian Jewish assets under American control were in Austria and were largely not gold at all.

In August the State Department began the task of redefining Article 8 so that the original allocation to the IGCR of 'non-monetary gold found in Germany' would be extended to all victim assets (not only gold) found anywhere in the European theatre, including Austria. American occupation officials with experience of these assets agreed that it would be impossible to organize restitution to individual owners, because the dental gold and other goods that came from the Nazi camps were clearly heirless and any evidence of individual ownership of the Gold Train loot had been methodically erased by the wartime Hungarian authorities. Although exceptional items of jewellery might be identifiable, in general it was felt that there was no point in making a serious effort at tracing individual owners, most of whom had presumably been killed at Auschwitz. The directive prepared by the State Department applied to all victim assets under American control, including the victim gold found at Merkers in Germany, the Becher Deposit in Austria (see Appendix 1), and the Gold Train, which represented by far the largest quantity of victim assets in American safekeeping, certainly by volume and perhaps also by worth. The new policy was designed to prepare the ground for the early release of all these assets to the IGCR, with the exception of books and some cultural objects which were to be treated differently.

The draft of the new policy was issued for comment to the US occupation authorities in Germany and Austria on 23 August,[48] and interested groups in Washington soon became aware that a turning-point had been reached. In addition to the unilateral redefinition of Article 8, the State Department's new approach reopened the dispute over the real wishes of the Hungarian Jewish community. The Hungarian deputy Finance Minister, Nyárádi, announced plans to come to the United States in September to meet the Jewish organizations and convince them that they should allow the Hungarian Jewish community to apportion the contents of the Gold Train between local and international Jewish needs.[49] But at the same time, Arthur Marget, chief of the Financial Division of the US forces in Austria, reinforced the view that the *real* intentions of the Hungarian Jewish community were very different from those they were stating publicly:

Representative members of Budapest Jewish Community are reported to have indicated strong view that US authorities should not repeat not accede to Nyárádi demand since Hungarian Jewish Community will not receive full benefit of the loot. Hungarian Jews prefer transfer of loot to such Refugee Fund which is expected to aid emigration of Hungarian Jews.[50]

The new policy directive renewed a debate of unexpected intensity, and the State Department decided to suspend all discussion until the visit of the deputy minister. Nyárádi's planned visit to Washington would give the Department an opportunity to broker a compromise arrangement between his government and the Jewish organizations, based on vague hints of 'the desire of the United States to assist Hungary's reconstruction' if the Hungarian government would give up its problematic claim to the Gold Train.[51]

The Gold Train was only one issue in the whole gamut of United

States policy considerations in Hungary, and within the State Department the officials responsible for political relations with Hungary did not have the same agenda as those officials responsible for refugees and displaced persons. The Hungarian specialists would have preferred to continue the generous policy of returning all Hungarian assets, including the Gold Train, just as they had returned the National Bank gold in early August. They wanted Washington to demonstrate a positive interest in Hungarian economic reconstruction, and during July and August the American Legation in Budapest asked the Hungarian government for economic data as a prelude to formulating economic aid measures.[52] However, the Soviets bristled at the American intrusion into their sphere of influence, and instructed the Hungarian government not to provide the requested information. At the same time, steps were taken to harass the British and American missions to the Allied Control Council (including reducing their food supplies).[53] The Soviets made it perfectly clear that they would not allow the United States to gain any political advantage from the return of the National Bank gold. The dispute was very public, and the increasingly vituperative diplomatic exchanges between the Soviets and the Americans were published verbatim in the *New York Times* almost as soon as they were despatched.[54] In this situation of deteriorating relations with the Soviets in Budapest, the voice of those officials who opposed returning the Gold Train to Hungary was able to prevail. The general programme of restitution of Hungarian assets from Germany and Austria continued for the time being, but an exception was made of the Jewish loot.

The State and War Departments dealt frequently with the Jewish lobby during the summer months of 1946 because of the crisis caused by the large-scale infiltration of Jewish refugees into the American zones of occupation in Germany and Austria. The Administration looked to the Jewish organizations as an important means of regulating this population movement, although the fragmented, disorganized character of the Jewish lobby made the task of negotiating policy and agreeing on responses to the events in Europe unnecessarily difficult.

Accordingly, in anticipation of Nyárádi's visit to Washington, the State Department asked major American Jewish organizations to present a united front in the talks with the Hungarian deputy minister.[55] But at the most sensitive moment in these discussions, the World Jewish Congress threatened to undermine any possible deal with the Hungarian government by siding with the Budapest community against the other international Jewish organizations. The appointment of the Jewish Agency and the JDC as the 'operating agencies' which would receive the reparations payments via the IGCR had left the World Jewish Congress out in the cold without any prospect of participating in the potential bonanza of victim assets. Furthermore, at the same time as the fate of the Gold Train was under discussion, the Jewish organizations were formulating policies on the claim for Jewish heirless assets in Germany. This promised to be a much larger source of income for the voluntary agencies' relief budgets than the Gold Train, and the World Jewish Congress was determined not to be left out as a beneficiary on this issue as it had on the non-monetary gold in Germany (and Austria).[56]

The intra-Jewish differences were resolved in a series of meetings between all the leading Jewish organizations, and by mid-September a broad-based unity had been established. The Gold Train was only one of a number of pressing issues on the agenda of the organizations (displaced persons, restitution in Germany and the Palestine issue were all more substantial), but it was the catalyst for the creation of a high-level consultative body.[57] Nyárádi's anticipated visit was only the immediate occasion for this unity, as there were many other issues on the Jewish public agenda during the late summer of 1946. Nevertheless, it was the clear threat of creating disruptive mischief over the Gold Train that gave the World Jewish Congress the necessary leverage to force the Joint and the Jewish Agency to cooperate with a new umbrella organization representing all five of the leading American Jewish organizations (the American Jewish Conference and the American Jewish Committee together with the Joint, the Agency and the Congress). Both the State and War Departments were now assured of a united Jewish lobby in Washington – an unprecedented development in Jewish public affairs, and one which made life easier for all parties concerned. The 'Five Organizations' appointed David Wahl, the Washington representative of the American Jewish Conference, as their intermediary with the State and War Departments. It was a very effective arrangement and went far to facilitate the dialogue between the Administration and the Jewish lobby.[58]*

Just as Nyárádi's expected visit to Washington had brought the differences between the various Jewish organizations to a head, it did much the same for the State Department. Differences in policy approaches had been aired and resolved, and a broad consensus reached on American Jewish and American government policy towards the Gold Train. So when Nyárádi cancelled his planned visit in late October (presumably because of Soviet pressure), the State Department was immediately able to present its policy recommendations to the State–War–Navy Coordinating Committee, and the Joint Chiefs of Staff, advocating that Article 8 be applied to *all* looted victim assets (not just non-monetary gold) throughout the American zones of occupation in Europe (not just in Germany):

US policy should favor the broadest possible interpretation of the obligation assumed by the signatories under Article 8 of the Paris Reparations Agreement . . . To the extent that assets can be realized from this source, the burden upon the Government of the United States in connection with the financing of rehabilitation and resettlement problems will be diminished.[59]

Approval was quickly given, and the occupation authorities were instructed to prepare the goods for transfer to the IGCR.

One-and-a-half years after the end of the war, another milestone had been reached in the saga of the Gold Train. The decision had finally been taken not to return the goods to Hungary, regardless of

---

* Herbert Fierst, deputy to Assistant Secretary of State for Occupied Areas, General John Hilldring, and the State Department official who worked constantly on Jewish refugee affairs, credits Wahl with the efficient management of this dialogue on the whole gamut of American policy as it affected the Holocaust survivors. Fierst and Wahl were in frequent contact, sometimes as often as two or three times a day. Two weeks after the 'Five Organizations' reached agreement on a united approach to the government departments, Assistant Secretary of War Peterson was able to report a 'noticeable improvement' in the working relations with the Jewish lobby. Ironically, however, the unanimity soon collapsed on the very issue for which it was created – the Gold Train. At the last moment, the World Jewish Congress changed its mind and decided not to support the non-return of the Hungarian Jewish assets, but they agreed not to oppose publicly the position of the other organizations.

whatever the real wishes of the Jewish community there might have been. But there were other hurdles which still had to be overcome. An inventory had to be prepared of the huge quantity of goods in the Salzburg warehouse, and the State Department had to convince the British and French governments of the propriety of the unilateral American redefinition of Article 8. Washington was determined to proceed, regardless of any possible objections by its allies.

9

Between Paris and Budapest

In late 1946, after the US authorities finally resolved not to send any of the victim assets back to Hungary, it was already clear that the most valuable part of the Gold Train was not under American control. The French and British were initially evasive about non-monetary gold in their zones of occupation in Germany and Austria.[1] When it became known that the only victim assets uncovered by the British were small quantities of gold and other items found at Bergen Belsen and Neuengamme concentration camps, the focus shifted to the French. Unofficial reports that the most valuable victim loot from Hungary had been uncovered by the French in the Vorarlberg area of western Austria were widely circulated within weeks of the discoveries, together with reports of Toldi's dramatic 'surrender' to the French military authorities.[2] However, there was no official French confirmation of these reports. Gold was a sensitive subject and information was not freely exchanged between the Allies.

The earliest rumours alleged that some of the freight wagons of the original train had made their way to the French zone, and these rumours proved very persistent[3] despite the testimony of all the Hungarians on the train that Toldi had transported the most valuable items by lorry. Representatives of the post-war Hungarian government were fully aware of the loot uncovered in the French zone, and of the fact that Toldi was hiding out there.[4] When Nyárádi visited the American zones of Germany and Austria in June 1946, the French authorities gave him permission to travel to Innsbruck, in the French zone, to conduct talks about the return of general Hungarian assets and specifically about the Jewish victim loot.[5]

Although the facts concerning the victim gold in French hands were of great relevance to the Americans, the only information they could obtain after Nyárádi's visit was based on rumour and informers. From 'secret sources' they learnt that

Hungarian Nazi officials now at liberty in French zone, who conducted looting and burying operations, officially admitted the removal of 54 cases of gold and 2 cases of diamonds, although it is believed that this amount constitutes only a part of the real cache. As yet only 45 cases of gold were recovered and 36 are now subject to restitution. These 36 cases ... contain only 1,700kg gold at present although they contained over 3,600kg when they were taken off the train.[6]

The 'sources' were confused about the quantity of Gold Train loot actually in French custody (54 plus two cases, or 45, or 36), but the State Department representative in Vienna was able to report

an unusually persistent rumor ... of a sharp deal having taken place between French Zone officials and Hungarian Restitution Delegation to protect the former from consequences of disappearance of major part of treasure in return for French token restitution strengthening Hungarian position in controversy regarding fate of Gold Train.

The 'secret sources' were no doubt Hungarian and probably part of the same Hungarian Jewish rumour mill which had fuelled so much misinformation about the train. It was widely accepted in American circles that official Hungarian estimates of all their restitutable property in Austria and Germany were grossly exaggerated, and in fact were frequently ridiculed in internal correspondence. But the image of the fabulous wealth of the train was very persistent, and as the goods in the Salzburg warehouse did not approach the fabled $300 million, or even $100 million, and if the French were only admitting to a limited amount of gold and diamonds, then it was assumed that they were hiding the rest. In this atmosphere, 'secret sources' were accepted as not only believable but even reliable.

From the moment the Americans decided to use the Gold Train assets for refugee resettlement and rehabilitation (through the IGCR, the Joint and the Jewish Agency), any information concerning the Toldi loot in the French zone became relevant to Washington. In particular, the State Department was anxious that both Britain and

France should endorse the unilateral American extension of the definition of non-monetary gold to include all victim assets in all zones, not only gold uncovered in Germany. But as the Americans soon discovered, the French Foreign Ministry had a different agenda. The French zones of occupation in both Germany and Austria were significantly smaller than the American zones. There were no UNRRA-run Jewish displaced persons camps in the French zone of Austria at all,[7] and very few Jewish displaced persons in either French zone. In short, France had nothing to gain by surrendering the Jewish victim assets to the IGCR.

Even more significantly, none of the short-lived governments in Paris during the post-war years shared Washington's hostility to the Soviet Union. The French Communist Party was a coalition partner in some of these governments, and together with the French labour movement it did not support American policy against the Sovietization of eastern Europe. Furthermore, the French bristled when any attempt was made by America to impose a common policy on European affairs, and did not agree to the American stand on selective restitution to Hungary. The fate of the Gold Train assets was only one of many disputed issues over which French–American relations were to become strained.

France was not a member of the Allied Control Commission in Hungary, and was able to cultivate its relations with the post-war Hungarian government without undue concern for the constant wrangling with the Soviet Union within the Commission. A French diplomatic presence was re-established in Budapest as early as June 1945.[8] One year later, a commodities bartering agreement was negotiated by the two governments, and French–Hungarian economic relations improved rapidly over the next three years (from FFr100 million to FFr3 billion).[9] From the outset, the French government saw the return of the Jewish victim loot under its control as a legitimate means of cultivating its growing ties with post-war Hungary.[10]

Both the French and British governments were informed of the new instructions on non-monetary gold sent to the American zone commanders in Germany and Austria,[11] but there had been no attempt at inter-Allied consultation beforehand. The British had initially adopted a very restricted definition of non-monetary gold – 'unidentifiable gold looted from the bodies of people killed by the Nazis in concentration camps'.[12] In effect, this meant only dental gold, but the amount of victim assets in British control was insignificant (less than $1 million), and London had already conceded to American pressure in June, during the Five Power Conference on Article 8, on the payment of reparations to victims of Nazi persecution.

It was the French position that was now decisive, both because the French had formally chaired the Five Power Conference and were responsible for the implementation of the agreements reached there, and also, more practically, because they had the valuable part of the Jewish victims' assets from Hungary. Long before the American decision to include victim assets in Austria, the Quai d'Orsay had already decided that Article 8 of the Five Power Conference did *not* apply to Austria, and France considered that it was free to return Hungarian Jewish assets in exchange for reciprocal commitments regarding French assets in Hungary.[13] In fact, in early October 1946 the *New York Times* printed an article stating that France was about to return the Gold Train assets to Budapest. Under the heading 'Hungarians Hope to Get Treasures', the paper stated that 'Hungary is beginning to have hopes that a considerable fortune in gold, diamonds, and other valuables will pour into her famished economy.' Significantly, the article pointed out that while Hungarian sources estimated the Gold Train's value at $300 million, American sources believed it to be closer to $35 million. This was the first public expression of the reduced estimates of the value of the victim loot. As guardians of the train loot became more familiar with the actual contents of the Salzburg warehouse, the myth of fabulous wealth began to deflate.[14]

During the winter months of 1946–1947, Washington attempted to convince London and Paris of the need to redefine, for the sake of the displaced persons, what constituted non-monetary gold, but neither government was willing to follow the American lead automatically. The State Department specifically referred to the Gold Train assets, and defended the case for not returning them to Hungary by repeating the arguments made by the Jewish Agency: '. . . large majority [of the] original owners [are] now deceased or [have] migrated and approximately 3/7th of the surviving Jewish population are located in territory now no longer Hungarian due to border adjustments'.[15] The issue was placed on the agenda of the fourth Council of Foreign Ministers meeting held in Moscow during March–April 1947, where the French delegation tentatively agreed to hand over the Gold Train assets to the International Refugee Organization (IRO, the successor to the IGCR)* on condition that 'the Hungarian government has no objection'.[16] However, in the months that followed the Foreign Ministers meeting, it became clear that the French and the Americans had very different understandings of what actually had been agreed. The fate of the Gold Train loot was the subject of prolonged, unpleasant correspondence between the two governments, and became a textbook example of all the tensions inherent in the relations between the two wartime allies.[17]

The term 'non-monetary gold' was a euphemism that conveniently hid the unpleasant realities of dental gold and personal possessions looted from concentration camp victims. But it was a dry and neutral term, and increasingly the State Department used the more accurate phrase 'assets which belonged to victims of Nazi aggression' to remind the French, and everyone else, that these goods should be used for refugee rehabilitation, as the Americans wanted, rather than as a tool of (French) foreign policy. The United States was paying for the maintenance of most of the displaced persons, and also for the largest part of the budget of the Preparatory Commission of the International Refugee Organization (PCIRO). Not surprisingly, Washington believed that the French were taking unreasonable advantage of the fortunes of war that had left the most valuable Hungarian Jewish assets in the French zone of occupation.

The French had different, but equally serious, issues to consider in formulating their policy on victim assets. Non-monetary gold was only a small part of the overall gold problem after the Second World War. The Germans had taken to themselves the monetary gold and the transportable financial reserves of every country they occupied during

---

* The IRO was formally created in February 1946 in place of UNRRA, but conflicts with the eastern bloc delayed its full operation until August 1948. In the interim, the Preparatory Commission of the International Refugee Organization (PCIRO) was created in July 1947 and took over the tasks of the IGCR as well.

the war, and the task of returning the gold reserves to their rightful owners was one of the major challenges of post-war economic diplomacy. The monetary gold, as opposed to the victim-derived gold uncovered in the territory of the Reich (Germany and Austria), was known as the 'gold pot', from which allocations were made according to the amount of gold each country had lost to German seizures. The problem was that less than two-thirds of the gold seized had been recovered, and the 'gold pot' was not large enough to meet all the legitimate claims against it. Accordingly there was considerable pressure to define as many assets as possible as 'monetary gold', which would then increase the size of the 'gold pot'. Some victim gold fell into this category – the forty-three or forty-five shipments of SS loot from concentration camps that had not been recovered at the Merkers mine in April 1945 because they had already been integrated into the German banking system – and it was decided not to diminish the 'gold pot' by defining this vanished victim gold as payable to the IGCR or the PCIRO under Article 8.[18] There were a number of questionable collections of gold, usually gold coins, for which the definition 'monetary' or 'non-monetary' was arbitrary. If these collections of gold were defined as 'monetary', then the 'gold pot' would be increased by the amount concerned and all claimant countries (France included) would benefit proportionally to their recognized claims. One such case was a collection of gold coins discovered in Salzburg after the war, worth $4.7 million. The Austrian government claimed that these coins had been part of Austria's gold reserve before the Anschluss with the Reich in 1938, and therefore was not looted gold. The American government, wishing to strengthen the Austrian government politically and financially, accepted the Austrian case, despite the fact that in internal correspondence they recognized that the evidence for the Austrian claim was weak.[19] The French, on the other hand, strongly opposed returning this gold to the Austrians. The case of the 'Salzburg monetary gold' was, they argued, very similar to the Hungarian non-monetary victim gold. If the Americans would agree to enlarge the 'gold pot' by defining the Salzburg coins as monetary gold and turning them over to the 'gold pot' rather than to the Austrian government, the French would agree to turning over the non-monetary victim gold and other assets for refugee rehabilitation rather than to the Hungarian government.[20] As the senior French Foreign Office official in charge of reparations and restitution, Henri Chargueraud, stated: 'We will only agree to include Austria in Germany on the issue of non-monetary gold if the same is done for monetary gold. We are still waiting for an American answer on this issue.'[21]

The Quai d'Orsay was in no hurry to concede to American pressure on the victim assets, and it was quietly encouraged in its attitude by the British. Although His Majesty's government wanted to be seen as supporting American policy on general refugee policy, the British Foreign Office made sure that its counterpart in Paris understood that London would welcome a French refusal to channel the victim assets to the Joint and the Jewish Agency via the IGCR/PCIRO: 'The British Embassy has, on this issue, transmitted the desire of the Foreign Office not to ally itself to a decision which would, in its opinion, benefit an American Jewish Organization, essentially charged with furnishing men and matériel to the Jewish terrorist formations in Palestine.'[22] During late 1947 and early 1948 the British suggested repeatedly to Paris that any non-monetary gold found in Austria should be given to the IRO but not passed on to the Joint and the Agency. Although they did not suggest the idea to the American government, London hoped that the French would undo the Five Power Agreement of June 1946, and keep the victim assets away from the Jewish struggle in Palestine.[23]

The State Department was well aware of the real reasons behind British obstruction to a generous pro-refugee policy on non-monetary gold, even if the Foreign Office in London had not formally opposed American policy in the international forums where it was discussed. In informal meetings, senior officials in London had explained to their American counterparts that His Majesty's government considered that the Joint (and obviously the Jewish Agency, which was so far beyond the pale that it was not necessary to mention it) was 'involved in political Zionist activities as well as illegal immigration to Palestine . . . While British soldiers were being shot down in Palestine the Foreign Office could not possibly aid the authors of these deeds by enabling them to gain possession of more funds.'[24] The British position was understood, if not shared, in Washington. But the State Department did not realize that the British were actively encouraging the French government to oppose what the American administration understood to be a joint Anglo-American policy on non-monetary gold.

The French position was further strengthened when the Jewish community in Budapest twice petitioned the French Embassy during 1947 not to follow the American precedent but instead to agree to return the French-controlled part of the Toldi treasure to them. Perhaps as a last ploy, in the belief that they were about to lose their claim, in his second appeal to the Quai d'Orsay in August Stöckler raised the possibility that the assets might not be returned to Hungary but kept overseas under the control of the Hungarian Jewish community, rather than be passed on to the Joint and the Jewish Agency.[25]

IN THE FRENCH ZONE

Independently from the diplomatic wrangling over victim assets, the Hungarian Jewish loot was a real burden to the French military administrators in the Tyrol and Vorarlberg regions. After the initial flurry of activity in August 1945 when the loot was first uncovered, the assets were put into storage and forgotten, until, in July 1946, the Quai d'Orsay began to make inquiries about them.[26] This created some embarrassment, because for at least three months the occupation officials could not find them. No one was sure whether the crates had been shipped directly to Paris in 1945 or were still in storage in Innsbruck.[27] They were administratively lost until September, when they were rediscovered in the vaults of the Österreichische Nationalbank in Innsbruck, where they had been deposited by the military authorities.[28]

But there was more to the story of the Hungarian loot yet to come. The crates of high-value loot that had been uncovered in August 1945, together with those turned over voluntarily by Toldi, were only part of the original Toldi convoy. An additional quantity of gold, diamonds and jewellery were seized by the French occupation authorities in June–July 1946 from a number of local families in the tiny farming village of Schnann, next to Flirsch and only twelve kilometres from St Anton. The 'Gold of Schnann', now a local legend in the Tyrol, introduced an element of farce into the events. Thanks to the eventual trial of twenty-two local residents, their friends and business partners further afield, the story of the Schnann gold has been documented in detail.[29]

Toldi's men were either very careless in their efforts to conceal the loot which they buried in April 1945, or they were in a great hurry. They did not make a serious effort to hide the crates in the forests or mountains, but buried them where they could be easily retrieved later. Nine of the original crates were buried opposite the church in Schnann, at the very centre of the village. The freshly dug earth was noticed by Franz Schmid, a local villager, almost immediately. As the loot had been covered with only ten centimetres of soil, Schmid quickly discovered the boxes and their contents. But the village was swarming with retreating SS troops, and the last thing Schmid wanted was to attract their attention. So he covered the treasure and waited till the SS were diverted. At 6 p.m., while the German troops fell in for roll call elsewhere in the village, Schmid returned with his brother Bruno and together they hurriedly removed the unusually heavy boxes to a nearby barn, where they concealed them beneath hay in the loft. Life in this small Tyrolean village was about to be dramatically transformed.

With the loot safely out of view of the SS, and hidden where the Hungarians would not find it when they returned, the Schmid brothers pondered their good fortune. The goods were obviously stolen, and probably victim loot. The gold dentures, the large number of wedding rings, and the Hungarian inscriptions on some of the jewellery and cigarette boxes clearly indicated that the hoard was not the result of local theft. Possession of gold and jewellery in such large quantities was seriously dangerous in the chaotic last days of the war. The only legally constituted authority in the area was the Waffen SS, and they would have seized the loot for themselves. In April–May 1945 there was no way of disposing of it legally or any possibility of selling it illegally. Bruno Schmid decided to consult his father-in-law, Albert Schwenninger. As an older man, Schwenninger's advice was sage. Using his copy of the civil penal code, which he happened to have at home, he managed to persuade Schmid that the finders of abandoned property were entitled to one-third of the excavated goods when they handed them over to the authorities. Schwenninger recommended that they bide their time until a post-war government was formed and local authorities, who could be relied on to respect the law, began to operate once again.

Schwenninger was a poor and invalid farmer, with five cows and twelve acres. But he had a large family, including twelve sons, and was shrewd. Schwenninger realized that if the Schmids received the reward, he would be cut out. So shortly after he had advised his son-in-law Bruno not to act precipitately over the treasure, he had three of his sons remove five of the nine crates to another site, safer than the barn and out of reach of the Schmid brothers. He intended to obtain a reward himself for surrendering the bulk of the treasure to the police, just as he had advised the Schmids. But the boxes were from the Toldi loot, which was the most valuable of the Hungarian victim assets, and the gold and diamonds they contained represented an impossible temptation for the small village. Gradually, other members of the Schwenninger family learned of the buried treasure. The three sons who had helped in the first reburial had taken souvenirs, which family members spotted. One by one all the members of the family were inducted into the secret of the incredible windfall. Prompted by their wives, these sons soon reached the same conclusion that the elder Schwenninger had reached earlier. If they didn't look after their own interests, they would be cut out. Alliances were formed within the family as small groups of brothers, brothers-in-law and their friends each stole from the original hoard and re-hid the loot they had taken. Some took whole boxes, others only a few dozen kilograms of jewellery. Within a few months, the treasure had been dispersed and reburied in hiding-places in the forests and mountains that surrounded the village.

By August 1945, a serious local trade in Hungarian Jewish valuables was developing in that part of the Tyrol. Friends and accomplices received gifts of rings, jewellery, cigarette boxes. The nearest jeweller was employed to remove inscriptions in Hungarian and replace them with endearments in German to the wives and girlfriends of the Schwenninger boys. But none of them was able to match the extravagance of August Jenny, a new member of the family who had married Schwenninger's daughter Frieda one year previously. Jenny mobilized villagers from outside the family, and made a number of raids on the treasure. These villagers also received a share, which they began to spend. Jenny took the largest share (claiming that he had to pay off fictional guards who, he said, had looked after the treasure). Very soon his largesse was the subject of gossip throughout the region. He ordered suits from the local tailor, and tipped him with handfuls of jewels to speed the work. He had three sets of living-room furniture made by the local carpenter, and later another two sets.

Jenny managed to convert the loot into cash by selling jewellery and small gold ingots just across the border in Italy, to members of the Allied forces in the area and to known fences of stolen property. He had an additional stroke of good luck when the local jeweller announced that his wife owned a jewellery shop in nearby Switzerland. Much of the loot was sold there. Schwenninger's sons also began to sell parts of the hoard and to share it with friends. Franz Schwenninger, who had since joined the Austrian Gendarmerie, bought a car which had been stolen from the German army, refurbished and, with forged papers, was once again usable.

This spending spree would have raised eyebrows at any time in this small farming community. But in the circumstances of post-war shortages and hardship, it was particularly conspicuous. By June 1946, the French occupation authorities began to take notice. Their attention was immediately attracted to August Jenny, and he became their chief informant concerning the origins of this seemingly limitless wealth. Very soon, Jenny's father-in-law Albert, five of his twelve brothers-in-law, the Schmids and everyone else involved were arrested for theft, fencing stolen goods, dealing in gold, and other serious charges.

In September 1946, twenty-two defendants found themselves in the dock of a French court in Innsbruck, facing criminal charges. The trial took eight months as the judges ordered additional investigations to clarify the provenance of the loot. The fact that it contained gold dentures, and that some of the rings bore signs of human blood, gave the episode a particularly ominous character. There were suggestions that some of the loot might have come from the camps in Poland, like the Melmer gold. The court ordered that this possibility be investigated, and the trial was suspended while the origin of the loot was clarified. But there was no confirmation that the valuables came from any other source but the Toldi loot when the trial resumed in April 1947.

Most of the defendants pleaded guilty, and received stiff fines. They had been detained for months during the proceedings, and the court did not think that additional prison sentences were called for. Those who were not farmers were employed as railway workers, customs officials, or with the Austrian police force, and the criminal charges to which they pleaded guilty meant they could no longer be Austrian civil servants.

The French authorities retrieved just over 100kg of gold, diamonds and other jewellery – perhaps a third of the original hoard, although the proportion might be significantly higher. Except for a few selected items, the valuables had been fenced for ludicrously small sums. The loot entered the local barter economy of the post-war black market, and was traded for small amounts of cash in various currencies, for cigarettes, clothing and other tradeable goods. As far as can be established from the existing records, the gold changed hands for less than $2–3 per ounce, 5 to 10 per cent of the official price of gold ($35 per ounce). The fate of the Schnann gold was characteristic of the destruction of value inherent in the whole process of despoiling the possessions of Hungarian Jewry. The crates the police were able to recover were added to the rest of the Hungarian victim assets, which were by then in the eye of a diplomatic storm.

In mid-January 1947 the forty crates and packages that remained of the Toldi convoy were labelled 'Archives' (so as to avoid attracting the attention of the Americans or British)[30] and, with an armed guard of eight French gendarmes, transported by train to Paris.[31] Most of the boxes were of a standard size – 45 × 30 × 28cms – and the total weight of the shipment was precisely 1,597.24kg. The boxes, sealed with steel bands, were loaded into a separate freight wagon for the trip to Paris. At all times there were at least two armed gendarmes with the freight. The cargo was the total of the goods uncovered at Feldkirch, St Anton, and Pettneu, plus the two boxes handed over by Toldi, and the unspent remainder of the boxes uncovered by the farmers of Schnann. The only part of the treasure that was missing were the six boxes which Toldi had handed over to Höttl and Westen, and two additional gold seizures made by the French authorities in 1945 which had been briefly overlooked.

Once the goods arrived in Paris they were stored in safe room 115 of the Banque de France, but were now clearly under the control of the French Foreign Ministry. In the months that followed, a detailed inventory was prepared by two separate firms of assessors, Laboratoires P. Dubois et Fils and the Boudet Laboratoire. The French inventory and assessment of value was conducted during the spring and summer of 1947, at the same time as the parallel inventory and evaluation was being made of the victim assets in American safekeeping. For the first time, the full consequences of the destructive sorting and 'processing' of the valuables at Brennbergbánya during January–March 1945 under Toldi's direction became apparent. The 'metallic waste' and 'yellow metal' listed in the official inventory was the detritus of the breaking-up of jewellery. Whatever the cost of these items had been when purchased, or their value when confiscated by the state during March–June 1944, many of the more precious pieces had been reduced to debris.

These facts were not widely known in early 1947, and rumours of the fabulous wealth of the Gold Train were still current. In fact they grew with time, and as the realities of the low value of the goods in the Salzburg warehouse became known, the focus shifted to the French holdings. Once the State Department had committed itself to handing over the victim assets in Salzburg to the PCIRO,[32] as a conduit to the Jewish Agency and the Joint, the Agency directed its lobbying efforts to Paris in an attempt to mobilize support for the adoption of a similar policy by the French government. The leading role in the pursuit of the Gold Train assets had passed from the Agency's political operative (Gideon Rafael) to its legal representative in the United States, Maurice Boukstein. As the shipment of the French part of the treasure reached Paris from Innsbruck, Boukstein wrote to political contacts in Paris recounting the story of the Gold Train. But by this stage, two years after the war and three years after the despoiling of the Hungarian Jews, the myths about the train bore less and less resemblance to reality. Boukstein suggested that the French-controlled portion of the loot included 'two and a half tons of uncut diamonds'.[33] This wishful thinking was the cause of significant misunderstandings about the victims' assets in the years that followed.

INVENTORY OF THE HUNGARIAN ASSETS IN
SAFE ROOM 115, BANQUE DE FRANCE

Lots 1–5, 7, 8, 10, 14, 17–23, 27–29, 32: Assorted valuable objects

Lots 6, 9, 15: Various watches and assorted valuable objects

Lots 7–8: Assorted valuable objects

Lots 11, 24: Assorted valuable objects and ingots and metallic waste

Lots 12, 25: Assorted valuable objects with stones, pearl necklaces real and
false

Lot 13: Assorted valuable objects and metallic plates

Lot 16: Various coins and money

Lot 26: Watches contained in bags, some with name

Lot 30: (suitcase) Assorted valuable objects and, also contained in labelled
boxes, a gun, various documents and banknotes

Lot 31: Assorted valuable objects, metallic ingots, gold coins, metallic
waste

Lot 33: Assorted valuable objects and documents

Lot 34: Various precious objects, in different bags with inventory

Lot 35: Assorted valuable objects contained in a package, with an affidavit
signed by Alois Schwenninger[34]

Lots 36–37: Various packages containing precious objects

Lots 38–39: Containing various precious objects

Lot 40: Two lots of various precious objects

Lots 44–45: Precious objects with stones or real and false pearls

The watches with movements are in case 9

In cases 31 and 41 there are unidentifiable objects

Coins, banknotes, currencies, ingots and metallic waste are in lots 11, 16,
42 and 43

Non-valuable objects: Lots 33 and 46

The cases, bags, suitcases, . . . had their contents returned to them, and
were sealed except for some documents . . .

[Signed by a representative of each laboratory,]

Laboratoires P. Dubois et Fils and the Boudet Laboratoire

For most of 1947 the French government avoided a decision on the Hungarian loot. The slow pace of the compiling of an inventory in the vaults of the Banque de France allowed it to delay making a choice between the open and vocal demands of the Americans and the discreet supplications of the British. The repeated requests of the Jewish community in Budapest did not impress the Quai d'Orsay sufficiently to make a decision. But in late November the Hungarian Embassy in Paris presented a detailed claim for the Gold Train assets, demanding that they be returned to Hungary.[35] The Hungarians explained the history of the despoiling of Hungarian Jewry during the war, and recounted all that was known of the work of Toldi and the history of the Gold Train. As France claimed the restitution of French property in Hungary, it could not afford to ignore the official request of the Hungarian government for the return of Jewish victim assets.

The Hungarian *démarche* arrived at the height of yet another French–Anglo/American crisis over restitution – this time, ironically, over railway rolling stock. Although it is difficult to appreciate today the critical importance of railway systems to European post-war reconstruction, the restoration of the railways was considered the single most important step towards French economic recovery.[36] The German occupation had wreaked havoc with the railway network, and French rolling stock had either been destroyed in the fighting (including Allied bombing) or scattered across all the countries of Europe. (The same was true for every country occupied during the war.) The French government claimed German rolling stock as part of the reparations due to France, while at the same time refusing to return the German freight wagons left in French territory at the end of the hostilities. An inter-Allied attempt to coordinate policy on the use of railway resources, and to allocate American production of freight wagons, foundered on France's unwillingness to cooperate.[37] The importance of this issue, which came to a head while Paris was deciding how to answer Hungary's official claim for the Gold Train assets, lay in the fact that there were 3,000 more French freight wagons in Hungary at the end of the war than there was Hungarian rolling stock in France. It was estimated that 10 per cent of the available rolling stock in Hungary was in fact French property.[38] France wanted its rolling stock back, and the Gold Train assets were a useful bargaining chip.

During the second half of January a high-level Hungarian del-egation[39] visited Paris to negotiate a comprehensive settlement of all outstanding economic issues between the two governments – including the question of rolling stock and the non-monetary gold from the Gold Train and the Toldi convoy. France was not a signatory to the Peace Treaty signed by the other Allies with Hungary in August 1947 because France had never declared war on Hungary. As a result, there had been no formal settlement of French claims for restitution of property in Hungary, or protection of French commercial interests there. The talks in Paris between 19 and 31 January 1948 were designed to resolve all outstanding issues between the two countries. The French–Hungarian Agreement (signed on 19 February) included a long list of steps to be taken by the Hungarian government to protect French interests in that country and to encourage commercial relations between them.[40] At the heart of the agreement, however, lay a simple deal: France would return to Hungary the victim assets and Hungary would return to France 3,000 freight wagons and various pieces of machinery.[41] The Hungarian government undertook to restore the victim assets to the original owners, if they could be found, or use them on behalf of the Jewish community in Hungary where neither owners nor heirs could be traced.

The agreement brought to an end months of inter-Allied unpleasant-ness over victim assets, Article 8 and other difficult points in dispute. But at the heart of the disagreements on concrete issues lay a French determination to pursue its own interests even at the expense of inter-Allied policy coordination and shared goals. The large areas of foreign policy agreement between the United States and Britain did not neces-sarily include France. In fact, considerable resentment had built up in American official circles concerning French diplomatic behaviour on all matters relating to restitution and 'Safehaven' work.[42] By returning the Jewish victim assets to the Hungarian government in exchange for economic benefits instead of handing them over to the International Refugee Organization for the benefit of Holocaust survivors, the French government increased American resentment of France's inde-pendence in matters of policy. The fact that the goods were actually returned to Budapest at the start of the Berlin crisis only highlighted France's detachment from Anglo-American positions.

News of the agreement quickly began to leak,[43] and *Le Monde* published a brief notice of the fact that the agreement had been signed by the two governments 'in an atmosphere of understanding and cordiality'.[44] But the Americans and the British were only told formally of the terms of the French–Hungarian negotiations after the agreement had been signed.[45] The government in Budapest moved quickly to implement its obligations under the agreement, and the Quai d'Orsay soon informed the Hungarian Legation in Paris that the forty crates of non-monetary gold were ready for delivery.[46] Miklós Nyárádi, now the Hungarian Minister of Finance, immediately announced that he would come to Paris personally to collect the valuables.[47] They were repacked into twenty-nine crates (weighing 1,750kg – the additional weight presumably due to sturdier crating for shipment) and finally returned to Hungary on 24 April 1948.

For over a year, the victim assets had been held in the Banque de France in Paris while the French Foreign Ministry negotiated their fate. The French occupation authorities in Austria were, for a short time, able to close the file on this troublesome affair.

However, as the Hungarian–French agreement was being signed in February 1948, the French Property Control Office in Innsbruck unexpectedly discovered a further eleven bags of jewellery and one bag of stocks and bonds in its safe. The bags had been seized in August and in November 1945 from Toldi's wife and daughter, from Toldi's associate János Balogh, and from two other Hungarians. They contained specially selected items from the hoard, and weighed 20.9kg.[48] Inventories of the contents of the bags were quickly made in Innsbruck (see below), and sent to Paris, from where they were restored to the Hungarian government at the end of June.[49] (There was an unexplained difference between the weight of the valuables before inventory and the weight of the goods when returned to Budapest (13.629kg).)

LOOT SEIZED FROM MRS TOLDI AND JÁNOS BALOGH

Inventory of 7 bags of valuables and one bag of securities, Seizure No. 19, 12 August 1945

Bag 1: 1 gold bar, 3 necklaces of yellow metal,* 39 watch chains of yellow metal, 115 yellow metal wedding bands, 25 rings without stones, 13 bracelets, 35 women's chains (3 worthless), 2 watches, 3 pendants, 2 pins, 48 pieces of gold debris, 1 eyeglass frame in yellow metal, 1 earring, 1 cufflink.

Bag 2: 25 yellow metal wedding bands, 11 large rings, 11 ring debris, 1 round piece of yellow metal, 11 yellow metal chains, 4 chains with medal, 11 watch chains, 4 bracelets, 1 cufflink.

Bag 3: 30 yellow metal wedding bands, 24 chains of various yellow metal, 4 rings, 1 watch in white metal, 1 very damaged watch in yellow metal, 1 chain with two medals, 18 bracelets in yellow metal, 2 cufflinks, 3 brooches, 1 pendant, 1 yellow metal remainder, 1 medal of remainder yellow metal, assorted gilded metals (of which 17 very small pieces), 1 box of yellow metal.

Bag 4: 1 mark, 1 schilling, 4 groschens, 3 pairs of earrings, 7 yellow metal chains, 1 large necklace of yellow metal with white pearls, 5 brooches, 1 pendant with pearls, 1 necklace with pearls and rubies, 1 watch of yellow metal, 4 bracelets, 11 tie pins, 1 lady's watch, 4 men's pendants, 68 wedding bands, 1 large ring, 1 brilliant wedding band, 1 lady's watch, 9 pairs of earrings, 9 earrings, 2 breloques, 1 cross, 7 cufflinks, 1 earring setting, 3 debris.

Bag 5: 24 pieces of gold coin French francs, 6 pieces of 20 Hungarian kor., 1 coin of 10 Hungarian kor., 1 coin of 20 Italian lire, 13 silver coins, 1 gold medal, 61 gold wedding bands, 2 yellow metal watches, 2 yellow metal bracelets, 9 divers rings, 3 breloques, 1 pair of earrings, 1 earring, 3 gourmet bracelets, 1 pendant, 1 large diamond with chain, 10 yellow metal chains, 1 heavy watch chain, 1 watch bracelet, 3 chains for men, 8 yellow metal rounds.

* 'Yellow metal' was presumably gold of unknown purity.

Bag 6: 85 wedding bands, 5 rings without stone, 12 men's watch chains in yellow metal, 5 yellow metal necklaces, 1 round yellow metal piece, 17 yellow metal debris, 5 gold dental plates, 3 women's bracelets in yellow metal, 12 necklaces, 7 yellow metal gold chains, 2 brooches, 3 cufflinks, 2 men's pendants for watches, 4 women's pendants, 5 earrings, 1 yellow metal heart, 2 bracelets.

Bag 7: Hungarian bonds.

Bag 8: 10 gold coins: 5 French, 5 Hungarian, 20 Swiss centimes, 6 bracelets, 1 lady's watch bracelet, 11 men's watch chains, 1 cigarette case in white metal, 2 watches, 2 men's pendants, 7 round pieces of gold, 2 chains for men's watches, 14 wedding bands, 4 large rings, 5 rings with brilliants, 1 silver goblet.

Inventory of 4 bags, Seizure No. 21, 26 November 1945

Bag 1: 4 yellow metal necklaces, 4 ladies' chains, 1 man's watch chain, 3 bracelets, 4 pens, 1 swastika.

Bag 2: 2 yellow metal cigarette cases, 1 little box in white metal, 1 man's watch, 1 woman's watch, 5 men's pendants, 2 men's watch chains, 1 pair of cufflinks, 1 pair of earrings, 2 ladies' bracelets, 1 pendant with medal, 4 wedding bands, 5 large rings, 2 fantasy rings, 1 earring.

Bag 3: 2 cigarette cases, one white metal, one yellow metal, 3 bracelets, 4 wedding bands, 3 rings, 1 necklace of white pearls with pendant, 1 fine pearl necklace, 2 light yellow ladies' chains.

Bag 4: 3 cigarette cases, one white, two yellow, 1 cigarette case without cover, 7 wedding bands, 2 rings with large diamonds, 2 necklaces of fine pearls, 1 chain with cross, 6 bracelets, 1 lady's watch with bracelet, 1 silver powderbox.

BUDAPEST

When the assets arrived in Budapest in April 1948, a new inventory was made by the Hungarian National Bank. Fifty bank employees worked for six weeks counting and evaluating the loot, which included 40,000 wedding rings and some jewellery.[50] For three years the Jewish community in the capital had called for the return of the Gold Train assets to Hungary. Now that the most valuable of the assets were in Budapest, the community looked to its own government for the rapid return of the valuables. Although the identification of ownership of individual items was impossible, the community expected that the Jewish Restoration Fund, which the government itself had established almost two years earlier as a trustee fund for heirless property, would be the logical beneficiary.

However, it soon became clear that the government had other plans. Six weeks after he returned from Paris with the valuables, Nyárádi gave a lengthy interview to the communist daily newspaper *Szabadság* in which he discussed the fate of the Gold Train. While he acknowledged that the French authorities had recently returned items of non-monetary gold, this was not necessarily of Jewish origin. In fact, Nyárádi argued, the Nyilas and the Germans had looted indiscriminately. On the other hand, everyone knew that 'the Jewish assets' were on the infamous Gold Train which had been seized by the Americans. Furthermore, much of the Jewish loot had not been found by any government and was still missing.[51] Other members of the Hungarian government made similar public statements during 1948, shifting the focus of public interest in the Gold Train to the American holdings, and dismissing the assets returned by the French as irrelevant.[52] Gradually, the Hungarian authorities linked the looted Jewish assets to the non-monetary gold which had passed into American control and had not been returned to Hungary, in an attempt to 'de-judaize' the assets repatriated by France. (As discussed in the final chapter, this position was repeated by official Hungarian spokesmen in the 1960s and again more recently.)

By mid-June the Jewish community began to understand that the government was developing its own designs on the returned victim assets. A representative of the community met with Nyárádi to discuss the return of the assets, only to be told that the government and the National Bank were still busy making inventories of the material. When the community asked to participate in the inventory process, Nyárádi refused.[53] In all the public references to the restitution of non-monetary gold, Nyárádi repeated that some (or at least one item of) jewellery with Nazi or Nyilas insignia had been found among the material returned from France. Given that it was impossible to identify ownership of the bulk of the gold and jewels in any positive manner, the Hungarian government stated that it was no longer certain that the assets were in fact victim assets.

In December 1948, Nyárádi, together with some senior officials from the Finance Ministry, defected to the West. Once in Switzerland Nyárádi was willing to be more frank about the treatment of the Jewish assets. In an interview with a representative of the American Jewish Committee sent from New York especially to discuss the question, Nyárádi stated that the Hungarian government had appointed a special commission of three leading communists to handle the property, and that they had decided not to return the assets to the Jewish community.[54] The officials who defected with Nyárádi were even more forthcoming. In a three-page memorandum they prepared at the request of the Joint, they confirmed Nyárádi's report that a special government committee had resolved not to return the assets to the Jewish community or the Jewish Restoration Fund. The Hungarian ex-senior officials (one of whom was identified as Dr László Kokas, Head of the Foreign Currency Department of the Ministry of Finance, the department dealing with the repatriated treasure)[55] added the following insight into the thinking of the current Communist government:

It would be rather unpopular for the Hungarian government as well as for the Jews to get compensation for their fortunes lost during fascism which they would have lost later by war events, Russians, etc. – at least this is the opinion of the non-Jewish population which deplores anyhow the renewed increase in the social and economic wealth of Jews.[56]

POSTSCRIPT

The course of events was exactly as the international Jewish organizations had anticipated, as the State Department had expected, and as some (unidentified) members of the community leadership in Budapest had quietly warned: the Hungarian government took the assets and the Jewish community did not benefit. At some stage in these events the government did agree to restore to their rightful owners a small collection of jewellery that was still in the original named envelopes. These 200 envelopes had apparently been overlooked during the 'processing' at Brennbergbánya at the beginning of 1945. By anyone's definition, these were identifiable looted assets which could be restored to their original owners. As one concession to the community, the government agreed to return these items in 1949. (They came from two towns – Tata-Tóváros and Nagykőrös according to one account,[57] or Tata and Felsőgalla according to another version.)[58] The only problem was that in all these provincial towns the Jewish communities had been devastated during the deportations to Auschwitz, and only 10–15 per cent of the members of the original communities remained alive. Furthermore, as many as one third of these survivors had left Hungary since the end of the war. So on the basis of simple statistics it seems that fifteen to twenty people had their possessions returned, out of a total wartime Jewish community of 800,000.

IO

New York City

The redefinition of 'non-monetary gold' by the American government cleared the way for the final distribution of the Gold Train assets held in the warehouse in Salzburg, as well as the other victim assets held in Frankfurt by OMGUS. A special position was created in the IGCR to supervise their receipt and sale, converting them into cash which the IGCR could then use for refugee resettlement. Since the end of the Second World War, the IGCR, headed by Sir Herbert Emerson from the UK, had functionally been divided into two separate elements. The largest was headed by Emerson's senior assistant director, Dr Gustav Kullman, and was responsible for the resettlement of non-Jewish refugees who could not be repatriated to their home countries; many had been Nazi collaborators. The other dealt with Jewish displaced persons, most of whom had been victims of the Nazis in one way or another. The head of the section dealing with the Jews was traditionally appointed on the recommendation of the Jewish refugee aid organizations, and they maintained close working relations with the Joint, which was the largest non-Zionist organization dealing with Jewish resettlement and rehabilitation. For most of the period under discussion here, the IGCR assistant director responsible for Jewish affairs was Joel Fisher.[1]* The relations

---

* Moses Beckelman was assistant director of the IGCR from 1944 to 1946, after which he returned to the Joint, where he was a senior official. When Joel Fisher left the IGCR/PCIRO in 1947 he became the legal counsel of the Joint in Europe. Fisher, unlike Beckelman, maintained close unofficial ties with the State Department. Fisher wrote periodic lengthy, confidential letters to Herbert Fierst informing him of the internal affairs of the IGCR. Fisher's insider accounts of the IGCR were shared with the Joint and the World Jewish Congress, and many of his letters can be found in their respective archives.

between Kullman and Fisher were never cordial, and there was a lot of mutual suspicion within the refugee organization.[2]*

As a result of the policies adopted in Article 8 and at the Five Power Conference in June 1946, the IGCR hoped to receive large amounts of money derived from looted victim assets. Ninety per cent of these funds were to be allocated to the Joint and the Jewish Agency, and 10 per cent set aside for the benefit of non-Jewish refugees. Perhaps not surprisingly, the Jewish organizations believed that as these funds were almost entirely derived from Jewish victim loot, the supervision by the IGCR of the resettlement programmes planned by the Joint and the Jewish Agency should be only a formality. Further, Article 8 specified that the 10 per cent set aside for non-Jewish refugees should be spent for the benefit of victims of Nazi persecution. The intention was to aid those non-Jewish German and Austrian left-wing exiles who had been hounded out of the Third Reich. But in the changed political circumstances of post-1945 Germany and Austria, these people were looked upon as heroes and were hardly languishing in refugee camps. As a result, Emerson and Kullman wanted to spend the 10 per cent of the funds derived from victim assets for the benefit of the non-Jewish displaced persons who were still in the displaced persons camps – including Ukrainians and Balts, many of whom had fought alongside the Nazis and had been actively involved in atrocities.[3] These policy differences between Fisher and the Jewish organizations, on the one hand, and Emerson and Kullman on the other, meant that non-monetary gold and victim assets were a cause of tension and discord within the international refugee-assistance official community.

Abba Schwartz, a young American lawyer, was appointed to the IGCR as Reparations Officer to organize the taking over of the victim assets and their sale. Within three weeks of the official American decision to expand the definition of non-monetary gold and give all of the victim assets to the IGCR, Schwartz went to Berlin, Frankfurt and

---

* Fisher considered that the IGCR senior staff were apathetic, anti-Zionist and at times even anti-Semitic. Emerson considered that Fisher 'was not a harmonizing element' in the IGCR, and refused to recommend him for a post in the successor organization, the IRO, because Kullman refused to continue working with him. Fisher was also upbraided for leaking stories about the IGCR to the State Department and the *New York Times*.

Salzburg to work out procedures for IGCR–army cooperation and to organize the handover. It immediately became apparent that the acquisition, inventory and eventual sale of the victim assets would be a complicated and time-consuming process. The army insisted that all items be listed and appraised before anything was turned over, but only six army appraisers were available in Frankfurt and another three in Salzburg. As the State Department required that the IGCR provide an additional team of appraisers of its own to work in tandem with the army appraisers and check their work, it looked as if the whole process would take many months.[4]

Four collections of non-monetary gold in Frankfurt were destined for the IGCR. By the time Schwartz arrived there, the 'Auschwitz loot' found in 207 sacks and suitcases at the Merkers mine had already been inventoried, appraised and repacked into 140 boxes. These boxes represented only a part of the total amount of gold and other items of value which had been taken from the victims of the gas chambers at Auschwitz and Maidanek. (Details of the provenance of the 'Auschwitz loot' only became known later in 1947, when the SS officer responsible for the collection of gold from the camps and its deposit in the Reichsbank in Berlin, Colonel Melmer, was found and interrogated.)[5] Forty-three earlier shipments from these camps had been processed by the Germans into gold bullion, and had disappeared into the Reich's banking system. The original 207 sacks found at Merkers represented the last ghoulish shipments from the extermination camps, which the Germans had not had time to process. This was the most distressing of all the victim loot. The army avoided public discussion of its nature and the fact that it included 560kg of 'scrap gold', the army's euphemism for dental gold and wedding rings.[6] When eventually smelted and purified, the 'Auschwitz loot' yielded approximately 300kg of very pure gold.

By the time Schwartz arrived at the OMGUS headquarters in Frankfurt, the appraisers were working on the 'Buchenwald loot', victim assets found hidden in caves near the concentration camp when it was liberated by the US army. The third large collection was the 'Dachau loot' – 2,826 named envelopes containing valuables from the Natzweiler and Dachau concentration camps. Because the envelopes recorded the owners' names there was a chance that this loot could be returned to its original owners, if they were still alive, and legally this was the most difficult of all the collections. When the Dachau envelopes were eventually processed one year later, over half of them were returned to the countries of origin of their former owners. The remainder came from German nationals of all faiths, and contained cheap watches, fountain pens, personal pictures and papers and small amounts of currency. Because of the low value, the IRO declined to accept them and they were given to the German Red Cross.[7] In his report to Emerson, Schwartz mentioned that part of these three collections included valuable jewellery, and that leading Paris jewellers had approached him with offers to purchase. An alternative avenue for converting the jewels into cash for the IGCR was to market them through leading New York department stores; Gimbels and Macy's were mentioned.

The fourth category of 'non-monetary gold' that Schwartz hoped to take over on behalf of the IGCR were the gold coins, currencies and securities that had been uncovered. For a long time it was not certain if these would be considered 'non-monetary gold' and passed over to the IGCR, or would be combined with the 'gold pot' for allocation among the allies. Ultimately it was decided that only coin collections of numismatic value would be considered as victim assets,[8] while much of the paper currency was discovered to be counterfeit and was destroyed.

Schwartz's next stop was Salzburg, where he was to examine the Gold Train goods in the warehouse. As he quickly discovered, the army had not yet prepared an inventory of the vast bulk of these goods. The only listing that existed was a very incomplete record of the boxes and crates made when they were offloaded from the train and moved to the warehouse. During almost three years since 1944 when they had been seized from their original owners, many of the fur coats and some carpets had begun to deteriorate and had to be discarded. Some of the other goods had been re-boxed, probably as a result of the requisitioning of household goods by US army personnel during 1945–1946. As a result, the army's preliminary lists had become useless. But lack of an accurate inventory was not the only reason that Schwartz was disappointed. As he reported to Emerson:

Since this property consists largely of bulky silver items, rugs, fur coats, cameras, all of doubtful value, and a relatively small quantity of valuable personal jewelry, I do not believe that we will net from the Hungarian Gold Train property nearly as much as I anticipated before I viewed it.[9]

The striking fact about the goods on the Gold Train was not the great value of each item, but their huge quantity. The amount of silver tableware and religious items ('Judaica' in the catalogues of the auction houses) was so large that the only practical way of appraising the goods was to weigh them in bulk and ascribe a nominal value to each item based on the market value of the silver. Similar solutions were found for the valuation of the 5,250 rugs and carpets, and for the huge number of watches, clocks, and so on. Called 'overall inventory and appraisal', this wholesale approach to making an inventory and appraisal was the only way that the goods could be brought to market in a reasonably short time. The process would otherwise have been delayed for years and the refugees in the displaced persons camps would have long since dispersed.

Schwartz summed up the results of his talks with the US army and OMGUS officials responsible for looking after the victim assets by saying that the very valuable items held in Frankfurt were being carefully listed and stored, while the bulky but much less valuable items in Salzburg from the Gold Train were not yet listed, there were no accurate records, and the goods were deteriorating rapidly. He recommended that they should be shipped to the United States as quickly as possible, to relieve the army of the responsibility of looking after them and to realize whatever value could be derived for the benefit of the survivors.

Among the goods taken off the train was the collection of the City Museum in Győr, near Sopron. This collection consisted of approximately a hundred paintings, which had been carefully crated by the curators of the museum and placed on the train at the last moment in March 1945 to avoid capture by the advancing Red Army. Although these paintings were stored in the same Salzburg warehouse, they were not victim assets, so they were not handed over to the IGCR. Instead, they were returned to the Varosi Museum in accordance with American policy on the restitution of cultural objects.[10]

A large part of the religious silverware in the Gold Train collection had been looted from synagogues and other communal institutions across Hungary rather than from private homes. There were 487 Torah breast plates, 960 Torah crowns (used in pairs) and 520 scroll pointers, 836 Hanuka menorahs, 1,115 assorted candelabra, 203 Kiddush cups, 58 charity boxes and 9 Esrog boxes. There were also boxes of metal prayer-shawl fringes that had been torn off the shawls.[11] These items were distributed to Jewish communities outside of Hungary, and damaged religious silverware was sent to displaced persons camps to be repaired in the occupational training courses for silversmiths, and then given to Jewish communities in Germany.[12]

The jewellery and items of special value from the Gold Train were stored separately from the rest of the goods. The most valuable individual items of jewellery (forty-four pieces) were kept in a special safe, and were appraised piece by piece. There were another sixty to eighty crates of gold and silver rings, bracelets, necklaces, cigarette cases, watches and 'scrap metal, apparently gold' – an almost identical listing to the victim assets being inventoried at the same time in the vaults of the Banque de France. In addition, there were cameras, binoculars, china, figurines, ivory pieces, lace and embroidery. Valuable stamp collections filled sixteen crates.[13] Despite the large quantity of apparently valuable loot, the amount of money that the IGCR, or anyone else, could hope to realize from a well-managed sale would be very low. In view of the widespread illusions about the value of the Gold Train, the marketable reality was dispiriting. Schwartz reported all this to his superiors in the IGCR, concluding: 'The proceeds upon liquidation of the Hungarian Gold Train property are not likely to be as substantial as was anticipated.' Instead of a bonanza of looted gold in the mode of the Merkers mine, the warehouse in Salzburg contained the debris of the Holocaust in Hungary. In planning the inventory and appraisal work that would be carried out in the next few months, Schwartz wrote in a note of resigned disappointment that 'it is clear that our operation at the Salzburg warehouse is one which will require more of the services of hands to move the property and pack it than the service of experts [appraisers]'.[14]

Schwartz's detailed reports on the goods in Salzburg deflated even the most moderate expectations concerning the Gold Train. The revised estimate of the value of the Hungarian victim assets under American control soon became known to the State Department, the Jewish Agency and the Joint. Moses Leavitt, one of the most important officials in the world of voluntary refugee aid organizations by virtue of his role as executive vice-chairman of the Joint, visited the warehouse in May 1947, and he quickly understood that Schwartz's preliminary estimate was correct.[15] In the two years since the end of the war the estimates of the value of the Gold Train goods in Salzburg had dropped from $300–350 million to $4–5 million.

The State Department, the IGCR/PCIRO and the Jewish organizations now shifted their focus to the loot that Toldi had transported to the Tyrol and Vorarlberg areas, and to the French occupation authorities there. As the plundered great wealth of Hungarian Jewry was not in American hands, then it was assumed that the French had it. During 1947 increasing diplomatic pressure was exerted on France to cooperate with the American decision to hand the treasure over to the IGCR/PCIRO. At the same time, the Budapest Jewish community began lobbying the French government to do the opposite and to return the assets to Hungary.[16] But the French authorities remained secretive about the Toldi goods in their control, and their unwillingness to share information only added to speculation about the extent of their holdings.

The inventory and appraisal of the Gold Train goods in Salzburg finally began in May 1947, when Schwartz gathered an IGCR/PCIRO team of four appraisers and an additional expert who specialized in jewellery. This appraiser spent ten days examining the boxes of especially valuable items, while the other four were instructed to use the 'bulk appraisal' approach which had previously been agreed with the army's Property Control officers. The wisdom of this approach had been confirmed by a representative of the US department store chain Gimbels, who had inspected the goods at Schwartz's request and concluded that 'it would take [their] complete staff from the US several years to examine, itemize and appraise the bulk silverware'.[17] The 500 crates of silver vessels (bowls, dishes, vases, etc.) were valued at $7.50 per pound, a sum intentionally set at a low rate in order to take into account plated and non-silver items. Otherwise it would have been necessary to sort all the items individually, which would have delayed the transfer of the assets for months. Between 200 and 300 complete and incomplete sets of silver tableware were valued on a per item basis, between 25 cents and $1 per piece. The twenty-eight crates of furs were reduced to four larger crates (valued at $200 per crate). Many furs were discarded because they had deteriorated or were out of fashion and considered unsaleable.[18]

The practical approach of bulk inventory and appraisal applied to all the other categories of goods as well – figurines, stamps, china and glassware, rugs and paintings, of which there were approximately 200 left in the warehouse after the paintings of the City Museum at Győr had been returned.

As the work proceeded, the army's Property Control Division attempted to retrieve those household items (tableware, furniture, carpets) that had been requisitioned by army officers for their billets in the past two years. Detailed lists were produced of the household items that had been 'borrowed' from the warehouse.[19] Not surprisingly, almost none of these items were retrievable. The army units that had borrowed them had been demobilized, the officers who had signed for them were untraceable, or the goods had suffered the wear and tear that bored soldiers stationed in places they do not want to be are capable of inflicting on their surroundings. In view of the utilitarian nature of the goods lost to military requisitioning, however, it is very doubtful if the loss of these items from the Gold Train collection had any meaningful impact on the value of the goods finally passed on to the IGCR/PCIRO for sale.

Rumours were rife that US army personnel had taken much more than the requisitioned household goods. The senior Jewish Agency political representative in Austria, Yehuda Golan (Gaulan), informed Gideon Rafael that the IGCR team of appraisers had uncovered eighteen separate cases of pilfering from the warehouse, and that 'he himself had witnessed strong boxes being broken open and robbed of their contents'.[20] Rafael received an even more graphic account of army theft from Arthur Marget, the Chief Finance Officer of the US forces in Austria:

M. said it is a well-known fact to him that many officers and among them top level people had 'taken over' privately very valuable things not only from the

Gold Train but had looted also other property in Austria. It was known, for example, that a very important general who recently left Austria had carried with him a whole train load of 'private property'.[21]

Beyond these wild rumours, incidents of small-scale theft were also recorded. The process of making inventories exposed the warehouse contents to many more people than had been the case in the preceding two years, including many Austrian civilian workers. Six weeks after the work began, one of the US officers had cause to examine a pile of dust and rubbish that had been swept together for disposal. Hidden in the pile he discovered a small sack of gold and silver filings and fragments which had come from the victim assets. Although the pile of sweepings was placed under observation in the hope of catching the shrewd thief, the next day the sack had mysteriously disappeared.[22]

There had been a series of break-ins at the warehouse in the summer of 1946, and a number of American soldiers stationed in Salzburg were arrested for stealing gold rings, watches, brooches, necklaces and other items. The jewellery began to appear around the army base next to the warehouse, and clearly a lively trade was going on. Enterprising young women from Salzburg were seen wearing extravagant amounts of jewellery. Captain Mackenzie, the Property Control officer responsible for the warehouse, called in the Military Police when he noticed that boxes had been broken into, and within a few weeks twelve soldiers and seven civilians were arrested and tried. Five of the soldiers were subsequently sentenced to prison terms of four to ten years with hard labour, sentences that were subsequently reduced but nevertheless remained harsh lessons for anyone else with access to the victim loot.[23]

Each of the organizations that stood to benefit from the Gold Train loot – the IGCR/PCIRO, the Joint and the Jewish Agency – were quite aware of the details of the 'requisitioning' and of the minor thefts from the warehouse. However, and unlike their counterparts today, they decided not to draw public attention to these facts. There were many reasons to be discreet about the possible mismanagement of the storage and protection of the goods. First of all, the amounts missing were not, it seems, significant. The requisitioning of household goods by the army was considered reasonable, given the fact that the officers of the army that defeated Hitler had to arrange their own furnishings in billets they were allotted in a situation of general post-war scarcity. Given the speed with which the authorities had arrested the soldiers accused of theft from the warehouse and the serious investigations and military trials that followed (the protocol of the trial proceedings runs to over 500 pages),[24] there was no real reason to doubt the army's integrity as guardian of the loot.

Furthermore, the US army in Austria was a sympathetic onlooker at the activities of the Jewish Agency and the Joint concerning the displaced persons. Austria was an important staging post in the influx of Jewish refugees from eastern Europe and in the flow of illegal immigrants to Palestine. Despite the constant pleading of the British, the US forces in Austria did not intervene in what was technically an illegal traffic. The American military command in Land Salzburg (the American zone of occupation in western Austria) considered the large displaced person population in its zone to be one of the major problems it had to deal with, and balancing the unstoppable influx of refugees across Austria's borders with their 'efflux' to other countries was in the interest of the US military authorities. Excellent relations developed between the army and the Joint, the Jewish Agency and the 'Jewish underground' that operated the illegal traffic in and out of the American zone.[25] For most of the period under discussion here, Major-General Harry Collins was the commanding general of Land Salzburg. One of Collins's senior officers, and the man responsible for displaced persons affairs in the US zone, was Captain Stanley Nowinski. Nowinski, an American of Polish Catholic background, developed such close ties with the Bricha and the Mossad Le'Aliya Bet that he was informed in advance of their operations.[26] Between November 1945 and November 1947, 121,500 Jewish displaced persons entered the US zone of Austria; 45,000 of them were transferred to displaced persons camps in Bavaria, over 65,000 departed 'illegally', many of them destined for Palestine, and a small number settled elsewhere.[27] This large-scale operation would not have been possible without the connivance of the American military authorities.[28] Under these circumstances, it is not surprising that no Jewish organization active in refugee affairs wanted to make a public issue of Major-General Collins's requisition of a small quantity of carpets and tableware from the Hungarian Jewish loot. Almost 10 per cent of the Jews passing through the American zone came from Hungary, so it might well have been considered that this tiny fraction of the looted assets of their community had been well used.

In addition, it was felt that any accusations of impropriety on the part of the army would result in the suspension of the compilation of the inventory and a lengthy delay in the processing of the assets. Any delay was undesirable, but especially so as the IGCR/PCIRO was about to be replaced by the IRO, an organization in which the influence of the State Department would be greatly diluted. As British opposition to giving the assets to the Joint and the Jewish Agency continued beneath the surface, it was felt that unnecessary delay would disrupt the whole agreement on the use of non-monetary gold.[29]

The final consideration was intangible, but nevertheless self-evident to the Jewish organizations at the time. During the war General Collins had been the commanding officer of the 42nd 'Rainbow' Division, the leading unit in the liberation of Dachau. To suggest that Collins or his officers were guilty of misconduct would not only be unpolitic but would also be wrong. The Jewish world owed a debt of gratitude to these soldiers.

The Hungarian government followed the activities in Salzburg from a distance, and was informed of the ongoing appraisal of the market value of the goods in the warehouse. Hungarian official circles also sought to account for the huge discrepancy between the expectation of great wealth and the realities of the depreciated worth of the victim assets. There was no shortage of rumours of American wrongdoing. One very original approach was passed on by an informant to the Hungarian Embassy in Switzerland, and from there to the Foreign Ministry in Budapest. According to this account, Abba Schwartz engineered the low valuation and was organizing the shipment of the goods to America where they could be sold to a consortium at a fraction of the real value. Schwartz, the Agency and the Joint were behind this consortium. They planned to resell the goods discreetly at their real value which was ten times higher than the appraised value, and to split the profits between them. The Embassy in Bern passed on this account in a very sceptical tone, pointing out that the informant was 'young and energetic' and probably not reliable.[30] Nevertheless, this rumour of fraud and the more general rumours of grand larceny have proved to be remarkably resilient. They answer a need to explain the discrepancy between the fantasies of fabulous wealth and the sad reality of the limited marketability of the victim loot.

The making of the inventory continued until January 1948, eight months after it began. The goods were sorted, listed, weighed and appraised, and then packaged for shipment. On 5 September 1947, the US army made the first formal transfer of inventoried goods to the PCIRO, and soon afterwards forward shipment to America began. The one crate of diamonds from the victim loot was flown to the United States in November. The first bulk shipment, in November 1947, travelled via Frankfurt, where the other four categories of non-monetary gold (the Auschwitz, Buchenwald and Dachau deposits and the coin collections) were added to the most valuable parts of the Gold Train loot. The crates were loaded onto freight wagons which were attached to a demobilization train taking American troops and their dependants back home. Once again, the personal property of the Hungarian Jews was travelling by train.

BREMERHAVEN

The train then travelled to the north German port of Bremerhaven where it waited for available shipping space to the United States. This first bulk transport consisted of ten freight wagons containing almost 850 crates of silverware, carpets, jewellery and stamp collections.[31] The wagons were shunted to the Columbus Bahnhof dock area and kept under unusually strict guard for three weeks.

The mysterious train with its heavy guard immediately became the focus of anti-American gossip in the port city. It was quickly dubbed the 'Gold Train' by the German population and rumours spread that the Americans had seized *German* gold and works of art and were removing them to the United States. The port workers included many communists and, ironically, ex-Nazi officials who had failed the de-Nazification security checks and had been removed from their previous comfortable jobs. The only employment open to them was manual labour in the docks, and their anti-American animus coexisted comfortably with the same sentiments of the communists. The port of

Bremerhaven was fertile ground for stories of American wrongdoing. The final proof of the fact that the Americans were stripping Germany of its national assets came at the same time as the assumed German gold, actually Hungarian Jewish gold, was being loaded on board the USAT 'General Sturgis' (one of three ships operated by the US War Department on behalf of the PCIRO to transport displaced persons to countries of settlement). Another American cargo ship arrived, the SS 'American Farmer', carrying 184 tons of 'printed matter'. As the city's inhabitants quickly learnt, this printed matter was the new German currency (destined to be put into circulation seven months later, during the German currency reform). It was now perfectly clear to everyone in the city that the ten heavily guarded wagons contained the gold that the Americans had seized in exchange for the 184 tons of new Deutschmark.

The whole incident was considered to be a public relations fiasco for the United States, and generated lengthy correspondence between the American consul in Bremerhaven, the US political adviser in Berlin and the State Department.[32] The secrecy that surrounded the Gold Train had once again fuelled outlandish fantasies.

EPILOGUE TO SALZBURG

The last shipment left Salzburg on 16 February 1948. During the months of inventory and appraisal, the experts employed by the IRO began preparing the goods for sale. The 'processing' begun by Toldi's men at Brennbergbánya and the other sites nearby, in which the diamonds and precious stones were separated from the gold, silver and platinum, continued at Salzburg and Frankfurt. Gold wedding rings, bags of gold teeth, gold and silver plate jewellery, scraps of precious metal, and much of the silver tableware, were refined into gold and silver bullion. The smelting was done locally in Frankfurt by Degussa AG, the same precious metal specialists who had converted the extermination camp gold for the Nazis. But Degussa's assay was no longer accepted by gold merchants, and the gold, silver and platinum smelted by the German firm had to be refined again by gold merchants in Britain. The private banking firm of Samuel Montagu & Co. in

London and Métaux Précieux in Switzerland sold the bullion on behalf of the IRO. There were minor discrepancies between the weights of metal sent for smelting and the assayed bullion sold by Samuel Montagu. The differences were explained by normal losses in the smelting and refining process, and by the inaccuracy of the scales used by the IRO appraisers in Salzburg – the only ones available to them were bathroom scales. Only the Reichsbank office of the Restitution and Reparations Division of OMGUS in Frankfurt was properly equipped to measure and weigh the diamonds and other especially valuable items. When the precious metals were sold, a sum of $884,914 was netted (after expenses) from the sale of gold and £41,888 from the sale of silver.[33]

The largest diamonds ('brilliants') had been separated from the mass of jewellery by Toldi's assistants before the loot left Hungary. The task was completed by the IRO expert appraisers, who separated the small remaining stones. A total of 6,000 carats of diamonds, mainly of less than one carat each, were set aside and sold separately by tender to jewellers in New York.[34] Three tons of Jewish liturgical silverware, occupying 450 cubic feet, fell into the category of 'cultural and religious items' and were not included in the victim assets passed on to the IGCR.[35] Subsequently, 1,450 kilograms of these religious items were distributed in displaced persons camps for repair and use in synagogues in Germany and Austria, under the trusteeship of the Joint.[36] (It is not clear what happened to the balance, or if any of it was repairable.)

Most of the goods inventoried and appraised were considered of such low value that they could not be marketed. Items of no value were either destroyed or, if they could still be used, were distributed in the displaced persons camps. There was a total of nine shipments from the Salzburg warehouse with items from the Gold Train, containing 1,544 crates.[37] It appears that eight of these shipments were in fact sent directly to the camps.[38] Only items that had a reasonable chance of being sold at auction were shipped to the United States.

INCIDENT AT HEGYESHALOM

During the seven months of inventory-making in Salzburg, the Hungarian Jewish community continued to petition the American Legation in Budapest, demanding that the goods be sent back to Hungary. The Hungarian Foreign Ministry, and the Hungarian Legation in Washington, also took up the issue, and in January 1948 diplomats from the Legation visited the State Department to press the demand that the goods be given to Hungary and not to the PCIRO.[39] But the goods had already been transferred, and it was too late. Moreover, totally unrelated events on the Austrian–Hungarian border led to a major deterioration in American relations with the newly-elected communist government in Budapest, and within a short time all restitution programmes to Hungary were suspended by the American authorities.

On 23 January 1948, a scheduled repatriation train from the US zone of occupation in Germany, carrying 488 Hungarian displaced persons, crossed the border at Hegyeshalom in north-west Hungary. It was a routine repatriation transport, and there was nothing exceptional about the Hungarian border police demand that the two US officers and eleven enlisted men accompanying the train should deposit their weapons at the border before proceeding to their destination sixty kilometres inside Hungary. The Americans complied. The Hungarian police then announced that while the train could proceed, the American soldiers would not be allowed further into Hungarian territory. The Americans refused to leave the train, and stated that they would take the train and its Hungarian passengers back to Germany. When the Hungarian police did not allow the train to depart, a diplomatic incident developed. The American officers were arrested, and the enlisted men harassed. The Americans accused Soviet troops of pilfering items from the train, and the Hungarians accused the Americans of drunkenness and selling cigarettes, chocolate and bedding in the local black market. The accusations escalated during the two days that the train was held up, and the Americans believed that they had been intentionally humiliated.

Whether or not the incident was used as a pretext, the US occupation authorities in Germany and Austria expelled the Hungarian Restitution Commission, suspended all restitution shipments to Hungary and demanded that Nyárádi, as the minister responsible for the restitution programme, deliver an abject apology in person on behalf of the Hungarian government. For most of 1948, the 'Hegyeshalom incident' and the suspension of the restitution programme overshadowed Hungarian–American relations.[40] The incident was characteristic of East–West relations as they evolved during 1948. The confrontation in Berlin a few months later was far more ominous. But in this emerging Cold War atmosphere the State Department did not entertain for a moment the possibility of reversing its decision on the victim loot. Nothing would be returned to Hungary, everything would go to the PCIRO/IRO for the cause of refugee rehabilitation.

ON SALE IN NEW YORK

Towards the end of 1947, as the work in Salzburg and Frankfurt was coming to an end, the IRO appointed a Merchandizing Advisory Committee made up of public figures in New York interested in refugee affairs,[41] to advise on the sale of the gems, carpets, silverware, china and stamps. The most valuable items were sent to auction at the prestigious Parke-Bernet Galleries in New York City, and the carpets were auctioned at the Sofia Brothers warehouse (under Parke-Bernet supervision). The auctions began in June 1948 and continued at intervals until December. Many tons of silverware that were not sent to London for smelting but were not valuable enough for sale by auction were sold by the Merchandizing Committee to bulk dealers. The most difficult items to sell were the 100,000 watches. The gold and enamel watches were eventually sold in bulk ($2 for each men's gold watch, $1 for each gold lady's watch, $5 for each enamel watch), and 20,000 nickel watches were sold for 25 cents each. The remaining 25,000 silver watches and a similar number of nickel watches remained unsold and were broken up for precious metal content.[42]

The entire process of inventory, appraisal and marketing the goods was closely audited by the accounting firm Price Waterhouse & Co.[43] The amount of money raised by the sales in America was

$1,636,688.97,[44] which was actually more than the total value estimated by the appraisers in Salzburg ($1,151,000). Additional sums became available from the sale of the gold, silver and a small amount of platinum, including the dental gold. By 1 April 1949 the total sales of 'non-monetary gold', broadly defined to include all non-restitutable victim assets from the Hungarian Gold Train and the other smaller deposits held in Frankfurt, produced a total of $2,171,874.[45] The overhead expenses of the IRO ($220,000) and the US customs fees for the importation of the Gold Train items ($125,000) were deducted from this total.[46] A first payment – $1,716,874 – was divided in instalments during 1948–1949 between the Joint, the Jewish Agency and the World Church Services. In accordance with the Final Act on Reparations: Reparations for the Non-Repatriable Victims of Nazi Persecution, 10 per cent of the Article 8 funds were allocated to non-Jewish agencies. The International Rescue and Relief Committee, Committee for Placement of Intellectual Refugees, Selfhelp, Unitarian Service Committee and Aide aux Émigrés, together with the World Church Services, received a share of the funds paid by Sweden and Switzerland. The latter organization also received a small part of the non-monetary gold funds.

But the sums paid were not significant to the budgets of any of these charitable organizations. The Joint's share of the Gold Train and other victim loot, $618,000, was 1.2 per cent of its budget in 1949 – enough to cover its refugee aid programme for four days. The share received by the Jewish Agency was even less significant in its overall refugee rehabilitation budget. Small additional sums became available during 1950 and 1951, which brought the total funds for refugee resettlement derived from 'non-monetary gold', the movable assets of the victims of Nazism and Hungarian fascism, to $3,500,000.[47] Most of this sum, but not all of it, derived from the Gold Train. This was a tiny fraction of the actual material losses, and an equally small percentage of the costs of the rehabilitation and resettlement of the survivors of Nazi persecution. Nevertheless, no matter how meagre the results of the massive effort to convert victim loot into usable resources, it was symbolic of the struggle to undo the madness of genocide.

I I

Aftermath of War

Shortly after the French returned their part of the assets to Budapest, the Hungarian government realized that there was very much less Jewish gold and jewellery than they had expected.[1] At the same time, the Hungarian police traced Miklós Dobai, who was able to give a detailed account of the events in Feldkirch when part of the Toldi loot was buried and a portion of it paid to Höttl as commission.[2] Dobai's testimony was only submitted to the French authorities in October 1948, three-and-a-half years after the events he described. He named both Höttl and Westen, and the Hungarian government now asked the French authorities to interrogate them.[3] Neither lived in the French zone, but Westen travelled frequently and was held for questioning when he crossed the border at Bregenz. The French authorities immediately asked about the missing six crates, and Westen agreed to persuade Höttl to return with him to the French zone in Innsbruck, where they would be able to give a detailed account of what had happened in their dealings with Toldi. Both were eager to demonstrate that they were loyal to the western Allies and were keen to avoid a closer probe of their Nazi past. Höttl (who had received a promise that he would not be arrested) denied having received anything from Toldi, but Westen admitted that he had received some boxes 'for safekeeping'. He claimed that only one of the parcels was still in his possession, which he was willing to hand over to the French authorities.[4] Westen also had a sum in cash from Toldi ($12,600) but that was in the safe of a factory he owned in Bassano del Grappa, Italy, and was not immediately retrievable. In December 1949, Westen surrendered a sealed package containing 16kg 750g of low-grade gold jewellery, dental gold, and other items that clearly identified it as part of the Gold Train loot.

This package was retained by the French authorities pending further investigations. The urgency had gone out of the matter, and by 1950 there was no further correspondence on the part of the Hungarian authorities.

Although the Americans suspected that Paris had done a deal with the Hungarians allowing France to keep up to half the victim assets, the frequency of Hungary's demands that the French continue the search for Toldi's loot does not support the American suspicion. On the contrary, the French occupation authorities continued to try to make sense of the Gold Train and of the Toldi loot for another six years. The documents were examined again and again as they tried to explain the discrepancies in the non-monetary gold claimed by Hungary and the amount that they had returned. The head of the Sûreté office in Vorarlberg, Commissioner Émile Dabonville, was appointed specifically to investigate Dobai's evidence concerning the six missing boxes, especially because of the rumours in Hungarian and American circles that 'the disappearance of these crates had been orchestrated by French officials'.[5]

In his testimony, Dobai had mentioned a 'German officer called Nick'. Although the post-war Hungarian authorities seemed to have no idea who this was, the French police in Vorarlberg recognized that the reference was to Ferdinand Nigg, who was by then the chief officer (*Regierungschefstellvertreter*) of the neighbouring Liechtenstein government. But as Commissioner Dabonville was well aware, all the evidence pointing to Nigg's involvement in the disappearance of the missing victim loot had come from shady, unreliable sources (Höttl, Westen, Dobai) and could not be considered reasonable grounds for casting suspicions that would lead to a diplomatic incident between France and the government of Liechtenstein. In fact, Dabonville believed that the testimonies of Westen and Höttl were designed to throw the French off the lead, and that Nigg's name had conceivably been mentioned with that purpose in mind. Other possible witnesses were unavailable, as Toldi was nowhere to be found and János Balogh had emigrated to Argentina. Dabonville's frustration was palpable, and it is possible to sympathize with the French police commissioner in Vorarlberg when he observed that 'the Hungarian Treasure affair is full of contradictions, errors, muddle – as if all the people concerned had only one idea in their heads: confuse the issues!!!'. Although Nigg's name had first been introduced by Dobai, not Westen, it appears that the French preferred not to request permission to interrogate the head of a friendly government.*

In June 1951, Westen died following a drunken incident. While drinking at a bar in the Innsbruck railway station, he argued that every Austrian policeman was open to a bribe. In order to prove his claim, he planned to slap in the face the first policeman he came across, and then offer a cash payment to soothe the affront to police authority. When Westen struck a policeman he met in the street, the latter replied with a punch that knocked him to the ground. Westen lost consciousness and died soon after. (Höttl was reported to have had a nervous breakdown following the unexpected death – probably because his accomplice had hidden the loot they had jointly taken.)[6] Having lost their main lead, the French were now forced to give up any further pursuit of the Hungarian loot.[7] The copious files on the missing six boxes were closed (the paper trail ends in 1954), without any final conclusions as to the fate of the missing treasure.

As a Nazi Sicherheitsdienst intelligence officer, Wilhelm Höttl had played a crucial role in Hungarian affairs during 1944, and was almost certainly responsible for Toldi's rise to prominence. He was involved in the evacuation of the Jewish assets from Brennbergbánya into Austria, and in Toldi's failed attempt to get the goods into Switzerland. After the war, Höttl managed to ingratiate himself with the American occupying forces, and attempted to trade his experience as an anti-communist intelligence expert with agent contacts in Hungary and Romania to the OSS and later the CIA. By 1949 the Americans suspected him of trying to sell the same information to almost every other interested intelligence agency in Europe. Höttl maintained links with his former wartime intelligence colleagues, hoping to offer intelligence services to the highest bidder. Eventually the Americans noticed

---

* Ironically, in 1942 Nazi intelligence had suspected Nigg of being too hospitable to Jewish refugees in Liechtenstein and therefore a negative influence on his government's policies. (Carl Horst, 'Liechtenstein und das Dritte Reich. Krise und Selbstbehauptung des Kleinstaates', in Volker Press and Dietmar Willoweit (eds.), *Liechtenstein – Fürstliches Haus und staatliche Ordnung*, Munich, 1988, p. 444, n. 69.)

that Höttl was living at a standard well beyond any visible means of support, and they began to suspect he had access to looted Nazi gold. Internal CIA files suggested that he had taken control of the assets hidden by Ernst Kaltenbrunner, Heinrich Himmler's deputy in the SS. Kaltenbrunner, who was eventually executed at Nuremberg as one of the leading war criminals, was, like Höttl, an Austrian, and he had been Höttl's patron within the SD (which was under Himmler's command). The CIA believed that Kaltenbrunner entrusted his protégé with information on the whereabouts of the assets he had hidden. Kaltenbrunner's widow believed the same, and turned to Höttl for assistance. But he denied any knowledge of Nazi loot. In 1952 he was arrested briefly as a possible communist agent, but was released. The CIA files show no awareness of Höttl's ties with Toldi or of his involvement in the Gold Train.[8] Höttl published a number of amazingly tendentious memoirs of his life as a Nazi intelligence officer, and became the respected headmaster of an exclusive boarding school for boys in Altaussee. He died in comfortable affluence in 1999.

The major protagonist of this account, Árpád Toldi, has proved to be the hardest to research. Toldi was an expert in criminal investigative methods, the subject he had taught at the Gendarmerie training school. He was well aware of the criminality of his actions, and went to great lengths to hide his involvement in the events described here. He constantly reminded his subordinates not to mention his name, and tried to buy a new identity from Höttl when they met in Feldkirch days before the end of the war. Perhaps it is not surprising that today his personal files are missing in the archives of the Hungarian Ministry of Defence, or at least are not available for research.[9] The French security authorities kept track of him until 1947, when he was last reported to be living in Innsbruck. From March 1946, and repeatedly after that date, the Hungarian government requested that Toldi be extradited to Hungary as a war criminal. Toldi was charged with the deportation of 4,000 people from the ghetto in Székesfehérvár when he was District Governor, and for the misappropriation of assets under his control when he was Commissioner for Jewish Affairs.[10] It is not clear why this extradition request was never enforced. Immediately after it was received from Hungary, the French took steps to implement it through the Allied Control Commission in Vienna.[11] However, the extradition was delayed due to technicalities, and when the occupation authorities planned to extradite him during 1947 they could not find him. They believed that he had either joined the Foreign Legion (as had many other Hungarian fascist refugees) or else had migrated to one of France's colonies in North Africa.[12]

Jewish circles in Austria entertained a number of theories about Toldi's fate, all based on refugee gossip, including the possibility that he was protected by the French authorities because his stepdaughter had reportedly married a high-ranking French official in Innsbruck.[13] A more likely explanation is that Toldi, like many other war criminals of lesser prominence, benefited from a growing disinclination of the western Allies to enforce any extradition request from east European countries under Soviet control. In October 1945, the Americans extradited 390 fascist political and military leaders to Hungary, but after this single effort no other war criminals were extradited from Austria.[14] After the war, Toldi and his family simply vanished from the records.

Toldi enters this story as a supporter of the radical right wing, and in particular of the pro-German branch of the Hungarian right. The despoiling of Hungarian Jewry and the transfer of their wealth to the Hungarian state formed an integral part of his ideology. The extent to which Hungary would make its resources available to the Third Reich in the historic war against Bolshevism was one issue that divided the Hungarian extreme right. From the limited evidence available today, it appears that Toldi identified with the Hungarian National Socialists of Fidél Pálffy and was prepared to commit Hungary to major sacrifices in the interests of a German victory in the war. The general policy of the Szálasi regime after October 1944 to evacuate Hungarian resources into the territory of the Reich – raw materials such as oil and aluminium, industrial plant, manpower (including Jews delivered for slave labour), and military units – was consistent with the more radical policies of the most extreme pro-German political groups. By insisting that the Gold Train and the convoy of lorries should take the Jewish loot into Austria rather than arranging to have it buried in the deep mine shafts at Brennbergbánya, Toldi may have surprised the officials of the Finance Directorate and the Commission for Jewish Property, but he was being consistent with the policies of his government and the ideology of his party.

That said, it must be recognized that in the *Götterdämmerung* of the last days of the war and the collapse of Hitler's regime, it is doubtful that anyone could have maintained a serious ideological commitment to the long-term goals of National Socialism or *Hungarizmus*. Whatever Toldi's motives were in the six months leading up to the sudden chaotic departure from Brennbergbánya, during March–April 1945 Höttl's promise of refuge in the Alpine Redoubt for the leaders of Hungary's Arrow Cross government must have been appealing, if only because there were no other promising options. When they reached Hallein, this fantasy, too, proved empty. The only alternative was to try to bring the goods to Switzerland and use the assets to sustain the Arrow Cross movement in exile. There is evidence, albeit scant, to support this possibility. In addition to the evidence given at his war crimes trial by Gábor Vajna, Minister of the Interior in the Szálasi government and Toldi's immediate superior,[15] the post-war Hungarian government was aware that Szálasi's regime had taken steps to finance their future exile by opening accounts and lines of credit in Sweden, Switzerland, Denmark, Turkey and Portugal. According to information in the files of the Hungarian Foreign Ministry, the lines of credit were backed by the gold of the Hungarian National Bank and by looted Jewish assets. A Hungarian agent in Switzerland was reported to be managing a deposit of approximately 1 million Swiss francs derived from the looted goods.[16] Whatever truth there was in these reports, it is reasonable to assume that some of the missing Jewish assets were successfully channelled into funding the exiled communities of Hungarian fascists, first in Austria and then as they dispersed around the world. None of these possibilities, as they emerged in the chaos of the last days of war and first months of peace, exclude the additional fact that Toldi, his family and closest associates all appropriated significant amounts of the valuables for themselves. The French occupation authorities uncovered a lot of this loot, but they were never able to establish if they had uncovered it all.

The unresolved story of the Gold Train has continued to attract headlines. During 1964–1967 the Hungarian government entered into negotiations with the United States for a settlement of all outstanding claims resulting from the war, the nationalization of American assets by the post-war Communist government and Soviet action against a United

States air force cargo plane forced down over Hungarian territory in 1951. The total American claim against Hungary was $130 million. The Hungarian government could make only one counter-claim against the United States – for the missing Jewish loot from the Gold Train. The facts supporting each of these claims were discussed in the course of twenty-five bilateral meetings of junior diplomats in the course of two years. This was one whole generation after the events, and the negotiators tried hard to reconstruct the details from the documents available to them.[17] But neither side was very familiar with the facts, and the archives of the State Department and the Hungarian Foreign Ministry could not provide enough information to illuminate what had really happened. The negotiations reached a dead end in 1967, and both governments decided to allow bilateral relations to develop without reaching a final claims settlement between them.[18]

Arguments over the fate of the Gold Train assets divided the Jewish community in Budapest in the immediate post-war years. The potential restitution of the property to Hungary compelled the community to confront directly the options available to it following the destruction caused by the Holocaust and the ruin of 150 years of Magyar–Jewish symbiosis. At an individual level, as in most other countries freed from Nazi or fascist rule, many Jews decided to speed the process of assimilation and to lose their communal identity. For those who wished to retain their Jewish identity, the options were either to rebuild or emigrate. The community was split over a range of options, with the deepest lines of division expressing themselves in the conflict between the Zionists and non-Zionists. The latter openly accused the Jewish Agency (i.e. the Zionists) of taking control of the last remnants of the looted assets of the pre-war community.[19] Although the Agency and the Joint had spent much larger sums in their subventions to Hungarian Jewry in the post-war years than they had received from the IRO sale of the Gold Train assets, until they were both expelled from Hungary by the Communist government in 1949, the sense of injustice was not appeased. (The Joint in America was able to send financial support to the community in Budapest until January 1953.) Resentment at the paternalistic attitude of the international organizations remains a live issue in contemporary Hungarian Jewish affairs even as this book is being written.[20]

The community was dispossessed a second time by a Hungarian government when the communist authorities refused to return to them the assets restituted by France, exactly as the international Jewish organizations had predicted would happen. Ironically, Lajos Stöckler, the communal leader who led the battle against the Jewish Agency to have all the victim assets returned to Hungary, was arrested by the authorities in 1952 and imprisoned for three years under the charge of being part of a 'Zionist conspiracy'. He emigrated to Australia in the early 1960s.

A partial account of the Gold Train story appeared in the Hungarian press in 1992, three years after the collapse of the communist regime. The new political atmosphere made possible a greater degree of honesty than before, and for the first time public reference was made to the fact that France had returned to Hungary the most valuable part of the Jewish loot shortly after the war. An article published in *Népszabadság* in August 1992 added new information. that in 1949 the Hungarian Ministry of Finance had scoured the banks in which, in 1944, the Jews had been compelled to deposit their valuables, in order to uncover any items that the local banks had not turned over to the central government during the war.[21] The article stated that the valuables returned by the French in 1948, together with those uncovered in the regional banks in 1949, were all sorted, and items of low value or which were broken were sent for repair and sale to the Budapest Horology and Jewellery Cooperative.

But what of the fate of the most valuable items, and the large amount of gold? All accounts of the period, including the defector accounts cited earlier, reported that the gold and valuable jewellery disappeared into the vaults of the government's National Bank of Hungary. The paper trail ends at this point, except for one tantalizing piece of information. In June 1948, two months after the repatriation by the French authorities of the victim assets, informants of the American Legation in Budapest reported that the Soviets were pressuring the Hungarian authorities to hand over gold deposits of the National Bank. Presumably this would be in part payment of Hungary's reparations debt to the Soviet Union. The first transfer was to be 200kg, to be taken to Switzerland and deposited to the credit of a Soviet trading firm there. More shipments were to follow. At the same time, the

Soviet authorities had asked for special landing rights for flights direct from Budapest to Zurich, which the American diplomats assumed were for the transportation of this gold.[22] Perhaps the loot that Toldi tried so hard to get to Switzerland arrived there after all.

12

Conclusion: Fantasies of Wealth

The Gold Train has come to symbolize the vanished wealth of a community that suffered terrible destruction during the war. The facts of the Hungarian Holocaust are well known and are not in dispute here. The same holds for the question of the economic standing of the different Jewish communities that came under the control of the government in Budapest by 1944, when the direct expropriation of Jewish property began in earnest. Other historians have examined this issue at length, and have reached the conclusion that there were rich Jews and poor Jews (that is, there were significant inequalities within the community), and that the economic standing of the Jews in eastern and south-eastern Europe was closely correlated to their degree of urbanization and education.[1] The Jewish elites in Hungary did play a prominent role in commerce, finance and industry. They were also highly assimilated and many of them totally divorced from the Jewish community by more than one generation. And except for the Yiddish-speaking Jewish population which was annexed to Hungary during the war, even the Hungarian Jews who did not convert to Christianity nevertheless saw themselves as entirely Hungarian in their national identity. In this situation, the boundaries between Jewish and non-Jewish wealth are not very meaningful.

What is far more important are the *fantasies* about Jewish wealth that were commonplace in Hungarian anti-Semitic circles. The anti-Jewish policies of the Sztójay and Szálasi governments were designed to place the Jews outside the Hungarian national community while seizing their possessions and 'returning' their wealth to the Hungarian nation. Toldi openly articulated this platform when he was inaugurated as főispán of Székesfehérvár in May 1944. But fantasies of Jewish wealth confused two separate issues – the material possessions of the Jews, which could be seized and redistributed, and their prosperity and economic well-being, which was based on intangibles such as education, expectations, motivation, professional standing, and experience, as much as it was based on the ownership of property. These are cultural attributes which cannot be seized and redistributed. They can only be destroyed, together with the society that created them and gave them meaning. Whatever prosperity was enjoyed by the Jews in Hungary could not have found its way to the Gold Train.

This approach to the 'fantasy of wealth' addresses the problem of the vanished prosperity of Hungarian Jewry. But it does not answer the simpler question: where did all the diamonds and gold disappear to? Why was the overall value of the material possessions retrieved after the war so low? The sensationalist accounts of the Gold Train start with the assumption that the looted valuables of 800,000 Hungarian Jews made up the cargo of the train, and as so little was eventually returned, then it must have been stolen by the Allied armies in Austria, just as it had been expropriated one year earlier by the fascist governments in Hungary.

But there are many other explanations for the missing wealth. Hungarian Jewry had been subjected to anti-Semitic legislation of increasing severity ever since 1938. While these laws were designed to reduce the Jewish role in Hungarian economic life, as opposed to the laws of 1944 which were designed to seize their property, the cumulative impact of the legislation was to create serious unemployment in the Jewish community and a drop in the standard of living. Even before 1944, many Jews were supported by community welfare, and economic distress was widespread. The Jews were also affected by the general economic shortages caused by the war effort. Following the German occupation in 1944 there was also German looting of Jewish property by German army units and officers, in direct competition with the official Hungarian seizures of Jewish assets. This local looting was compounded by the takeover of the Manfred Weiss industrial conglomerate by the SS. The Germans were also able to enrich themselves by demanding payment of ransom from the various community leaders. In Budapest, ransom payments reached significant proportions and were the cause of an additional conflict over restitution, concerning the Becher Deposit, between the Hungarian Jewish community and the international Jewish organizations after the war (see Appendix 1). By the time the Hungarian government began its own legalized expropriation of Jewish bank accounts and valuables, many Jews had already lost most of their savings and possessions.

The legislation of April 1944 obliged the Jews to deposit their valuables in local branches of the government Postal Savings Bank. A proportion of their possessions would have been hidden by the victims, or given to Christian friends and neighbours for safekeeping. The ghettoization and deportations that came soon afterwards were accompanied by widespread local looting of Jewish property. The official attempts to search for and take control of the more valuable assets, together with the brutal interrogations by the Gendarmerie of the more prosperous Jews in each community, was an opportunity for theft by local officials. Only in June 1944, two months after the expropriations began, did the Hungarian government attempt to impose some order into the system by the appointment of a Commissioner for Jewish Property (Túrvölgyi). It is not clear what percentage of the movable assets owned by Jews was actually handed over to the central government, and what remained 'unofficially' in the hands of the local police and Financial Directorate officials.

When the remaining victim loot was eventually sent in from the provincial depots, beginning in September 1944, it was sorted and processed in Óbánya and Budapest, and then later in Brennbergbánya and other depots closer to the Austrian border. There was a lot of pilfering at this stage, too. Many of the Financial Directorate officials and guards pocketed gold watches, coins and items of jewellery,[2] just as Toldi did. The processing of the jewellery – breaking it up into its component parts so that the gold could be smelted into bullion and the precious and semi-precious stones sold separately – also caused a serious loss in value.

In addition, account has to be made of the commission taken by Höttl and Westen, the discoveries and spending of the Schnann farmers, the pilfering by American soldiers, and, one can confidently assume, the loot not surrendered to the French authorities by Toldi and his associates. Together with the deterioration of the furs and carpets in the warehouse, and the losses caused in the process of smelting silver items and gold fragments during the IRO inventory and appraisal, the combined value of the victim assets sold in New York and elsewhere by the IRO and the value of the non-monetary gold returned to the Hungarian government by France in 1948 was much less than the value of the cargo when the Gold Train began its journey. And the cargo itself was worth only a fraction of the original conjectured value of goods before they were taken from their legitimate owners.

All the participants in this story were influenced by fantasies of fabulous wealth. The reality was the opposite – of value, wealth and prosperity destroyed and dispersed in the process of ethnic cleansing and despoliation. Only very few artefacts of exceptional workmanship and rarity have a value that remains constant outside the social context in which they were obtained, used and cherished. It was the people who used them who gave real value to the items on the Gold Train; the value was not inherent in the objects themselves.

There are various ways of ascribing monetary worth to objects of value. They have a purchase price, a sale price, an insurable value and a sentimental value. While there are significant differences in the amounts of these 'values', they are all much larger than the sale price of the raw materials used in making the jewellery, religious silverware and tableware, coin and stamp collections, which constituted the bulk of the victim loot. The real value of these items was not the market price but the value given to them by the original owners. However, the sentimental value of a wedding ring, or of Sabbath candlesticks passed from mother to daughter for generations, would be reduced to very little when the owners were deported to Auschwitz. There was not a large market for Judaica in Europe when the war ended. And the impure gold of the wedding rings or dentures fetched very little after the costs of storage, safekeeping, smelting, transportation and sale were factored in.

The assets of the Hungarian Gold Train may well have been worth $120 million or even $300–350 million in the circumstances of 1938, or even of those of 1944, when the owners of the items of value were still alive. By 1945, after the items had been vandalized and broken up, and the original owners could no longer be traced, the expropriated goods were worth very much less. It was a fantasy to believe that the prosperity of a community could be seized and redistributed, or transferred to the Reich.

The destruction of European Jewry during the Holocaust took place over a wide geographic area and time span, beginning in Germany with the rise of the Nazis to power in January 1933 and ending with the Allied victory in Europe in May 1945. The motives of the perpetrators included genocide, the exploitation of forced labour, and economic spoliation. Ultimately, however, these objectives were contradictory. Some degree of wealth could be transferred from one population to another by organized plunder, especially where that wealth was concentrated in a few hands. But the roots of popular wealth and prosperity are social, and they were destroyed when the societies that sustained them and gave them value were laid waste. This was the madness of genocide. Although justice demanded that the material damage of the Holocaust be undone, the real damage was in the individual lives lost and the devastation of a vibrant community, and that could not be made good again.

Appendix 1   The Becher Deposit

When Gideon Rafael, the senior representative in Europe of the Jewish Agency's Political Department, stumbled across the saga of the Gold Train in late 1945, he was actually pursuing an entirely different hoard of victim assets – the 'Becher Deposit'. Although the Gold Train quickly overshadowed all other discoveries of victim loot, the Becher Deposit, at one time rumoured to be worth over 8 million Swiss francs, was the first of the plundered Jewish assets to attract the attention of the Jewish Agency. While the Gold Train originated from the expropriation of Jewish assets by the Hungarian authorities, the Becher Deposit was an entirely German affair.

SS Standartenführer (Colonel) Kurt Becher arrived in Hungary in March 1944 as the requisitions officer of the SS. Although ostensibly in charge of acquiring military supplies for the German forces, Becher's real role was to acquire as many choice Jewish assets as possible on behalf of the head of the SS, Himmler. His greatest success was the takeover of the Manfred Weiss industrial concern, referred to in Chapter 2. Nazi policy towards Hungarian Jewry was divided between those, like Adolf Eichmann, who raced against time to deport as many people as possible to the gas chambers, and others, like Becher, who used the threat of deportation and death as a means of extorting ransom and bribes from the remaining Jews.

When the deportations from the Hungarian countryside were suspended in early July 1944, Budapest contained the largest surviving community of Jews in Europe. Eichmann repeatedly attempted to have the deportations renewed so that he could send these Jews to Auschwitz and so complete the work of genocide. Until the Red Army encircled the capital in late December 1944, this threat might have been realized at any moment, and the safety of the remaining Jews was tenuous. In this situation, Becher presented himself to the Jewish community as a representative of the other side of German policy. In the last year of the war, the Jews of Budapest represented one final opportunity of enrichment for the economic specialists of the SS. In exchange for large payments of cash, precious metals and jewellery, Becher offered to use his influence with Himmler to deflect the risk of deportation.

Becher had already successfully arranged the flight to safety of the owners of the Manfred Weiss enterprises, which was the single most profitable deal so far concluded by the SS. Six weeks later, in July 1944, he negotiated the safe passage of a trainload of 1,685 Hungarian Jews to Switzerland. (The train was first sent to Bergen-Belsen, but eventually reached Switzerland in December.) Passengers were selected for the train by various groups in the Jewish community. Approximately 10 per cent of the places were sold to those who had hidden part of their assets from the Hungarian authorities, and were still able to help raise the funds to make up the necessary bribe to the SS.

In organizing the train, Becher dealt mainly with Rezső Kasztner, a journalist and Zionist functionary who had participated in the creation of an *ad hoc* Aid and Rescue Committee in early 1943. Kasztner was not the formal head of the committee, but he was the effective leader. The committee, which consisted largely of local Zionists, operated outside of the formal institutions of the Jewish community, and was dominated by a daring and activist ethos that was entirely different from that of the established communal leadership. In the course of the committee's work, Kasztner learnt that the Germans could be bribed and their genocidal policies temporarily deflected. Originally, Kasztner's committee organized refuge for non-Hungarian Jews who had crossed the border into Hungary, and arranged the escape of Hungarian Jewish youth through Yugoslavia and Romania. By mid-1944, with the Germans in full control of the massive deportations from Hungary to Auschwitz, the committee's experience of dealing with the Nazis offered a possible avenue for saving many lives.

The train (which was widely known as the 'Kasztner train') was the first significant success in Hungarian rescue work, and Kasztner and Becher began to develop more plans – the former to save Jewish lives and the latter to receive payment of ever larger bribes. In August 1944,

Becher offered his services to Kasztner to block Eichmann's attempts to have the deportations to Auschwitz resumed. Kasztner in turn introduced Becher to Saly Mayer, the representative of the Joint in Switzerland, as a means of tapping the financial resources of American Jewry. From then until almost the end of the war, a series of talks was held on Swiss territory, just across the border from the Reich.

As all the participants in these talks realized at the time, the possibility of very large bribes was only one inducement to the SS. Becher and his associates were also attempting to create alibis and gain credit which might save them in the coming months when Germany would inevitably lose the war and they would be called to account for war crimes. The possibility that Becher was genuinely representing Himmler, who was motivated by a desire to avoid the gallows, to gain cash assets for a possible escape, and perhaps also to find a way of contacting the Allies, gave the talks in Switzerland a credibility enjoyed by no previous attempt to negotiate an end of the Holocaust. The American diplomatic and intelligence officials in Switzerland were fully informed of the various meetings held there by Becher and other top SS officials, and allowed them to proceed. In order to facilitate the negotiations, large sums of money were placed in closed Swiss bank accounts on behalf of Becher and others, for their use after the war. The history of Becher's role in these talks and of Himmler's attempts to negotiate the end of the Holocaust have been recounted elsewhere, and need not be repeated here.[1]

When the gas chambers and crematoria in Auschwitz were destroyed by the Germans at the end of October 1944 (to hide the evidence of genocide, before the advancing Red Army liberated the area), the focus of the talks with the SS in Switzerland (and later in Stockholm as well) shifted to finding ways of improving the treatment of surviving Jews in the concentration camp system. In the last six months of the war, 700,000 were thought to be still alive, and it was generally feared that Hitler or Himmler would order their murder before they could be liberated by the Allies.[2] In March and April 1945, as the Allies advanced into the Third Reich from every direction and orderly German administration began to collapse, Becher and Kasztner worked out plans whereby the SS colonel (who outranked most concentration camp commanders) would tour the largest camps still under

German control, to prevent a last-minute massacre of the Jewish internees and to ensure the orderly transfer of the camps to the British and American forces. Kasztner appears to have believed in Becher's ability to influence developments, and in exchange for the latter's intervention to save the surviving internees, Kasztner promised to testify on Becher's behalf before the Allies, a promise which he honoured.[3] American officials in Switzerland, who were fully informed of Becher's proposal to intervene in the camps, thought the idea was fanciful. They doubted both Becher's sincerity and his ability to have any impact on events: 'Daily changing military situation has rendered successful rescue action of this nature conducted by Becher most unlikely.' But they, like Kasztner, encouraged him. He would be a useful contact if the rumoured Alpine Redoubt were to materialize and if the Nazis took concentration camp internees there as hostages.[4]

Becher first went to Mauthausen, where he ordered the release of one of Kasztner's close associates, Nicholas (Moshe) Schweiger. Schweiger had been arrested and sent to the concentration camp when the Germans entered Budapest in March 1944. Kasztner specifically asked for his release, and Becher complied, keeping Schweiger both as hostage and witness for the events that followed. (After the war, Schweiger reported that Becher had been instrumental in the peaceful surrender to the Allies of Bergen-Belsen, Neuengamme, Mauthausen and Theresienstadt – a major achievement if true, but there is no other evidence to confirm Becher's role.) On 20 April 1945 Becher had Schweiger transferred to a section of the camp for privileged prisoners, where he was fed and could recuperate. Two weeks later, on 4 May, Becher escorted him out of the camp. Mauthausen was liberated by the US army the next day. Schweiger was taken to a hunting lodge in Weissenbach, near Bad Ischl, 120 kilometres away, together with two other Jewish hostages in Becher's care. They spent a week at this location (which Schweiger described as a 'castle') until Becher was finally arrested by the US army Counter Intelligence Corps on 12 May.

Becher travelled with six boxes of valuables. The boxes were part of the various ransom payments made in Budapest by Kasztner and others, which Becher had not managed to transfer out of Hungary or otherwise hide. The ransom for the 'Kasztner train' alone was estimated by the Jewish community to be worth 8,600,000 Swiss francs

APPENDIX I THE BECHER DEPOSIT

(but only 3,000,000 according to Becher's estimate) in 1944. It was paid in cash, jewellery and precious metals. Becher had also received other sums. Just before his arrest, Becher handed the boxes to Schweiger, asking him to return them to 'the Jewish Agency and the Joint'. This was the Becher Deposit.

Possession of these assets exposed Schweiger to real danger. The post-war Austrian authorities announced a death penalty for anyone hiding Nazi loot, and there was always the risk of theft. Schweiger had no means of contacting representatives of either the Joint or the Jewish Agency, so he concluded that he had no choice but to surrender the property to the US army. The 215th Detachment of the Counter Intelligence Corps took control of the loot on 24 May, twelve days after Becher's arrest. Although no inventory was made on the spot, Schweiger was given a detailed receipt for the goods a few days later.[5]

In July, a full two months after the end of the war, Schweiger was finally able to establish contact with the outside Jewish world. He informed the leaders of the Jewish Brigade (Palestinian Jewish units of the British army) about the Becher Deposit when he met them in Salzburg, and he informed an American representative of the Joint in August.

Schweiger left Austria in October and travelled to Geneva, where he was reunited with Kasztner. The two prepared a detailed report of their relations with Becher, and of the story of the Becher loot, which they estimated to be worth 8,750,000 Swiss francs.[6] Both men were active Zionists and considered that their first loyalty was to the Jewish Agency in Jerusalem. The report was sent to the Agency with a suggestion that the Agency should act by itself, without involving the Joint, to retrieve the Becher Deposit from the Americans. Two weeks later, Kasztner wrote another account of his dealings with Becher, in which he estimated the value of the bribes paid to be between 10 and 15 million Swiss francs.[7]

The Kasztner–Schweiger report was prepared *before* Article 8 of the Final Act on Reparations (Paris, December 1945–January 1946) set aside non-monetary gold for the victims of Nazi persecution, and they could not have known the future intentions of the Allies on this question. In their report, prepared in late October 1945, they were concerned that the Becher Deposit might be considered as war booty, and lost for ever to the Jewish world. Accordingly, they recommended that the Jewish Agency send a senior official to Europe as soon as possible, with the authority to deal directly with the American occupation forces and secure the return of the boxes that Schweiger had surrendered to them for safekeeping. Their recommendation was endorsed by the Agency's headquarters in Jerusalem,[8] and shortly afterwards Gideon Rafael was instructed to attempt to retrieve these, and other Jewish assets, uncovered by the Allied forces.

Although Rafael's attention was drawn to the Gold Train almost immediately, the Becher Deposit involved a unique set of issues. The American authorities tried hard to check the provenance of the loot before they would concede to the Agency's claim that the assets were the property of the Jewish organizations. Kasztner and Schweiger were unknown sources for the Americans, and their testimony was not considered sufficient. However, the Joint's representative in Switzerland, Saly Mayer, had worked closely with American representatives throughout the war years, and had been a central figure in the ransom negotiations conducted with Becher. Although Mayer was a Swiss national, he was the accredited representative of the Joint, an American organization, and he enjoyed a close working relationship with a number of American official representatives during the war. His opinion had great weight with them. But when Mayer was interviewed by American intelligence officers preparing the war crimes case against Becher (then under arrest awaiting trial), he had nothing good to say about Kasztner.[9] Mayer suspected Kasztner of financial improprieties and was not prepared to endorse any statements made by the latter concerning the negotiations with Becher.[10] As both Kasztner and Mayer had played central roles in the attempts to rescue Hungarian Jewry during the war years, the tensions between them were an embarrassment to the Jewish organizations in the immediate post-war years. The question of whether everything possible had been done in 1944 to prevent the deportations led to painful recriminations within the Jewish world after the war, and a verbal conflict between two of the leading figures in the rescue efforts only exacerbated the situation.

Without Mayer's confirmation, corroboration of Kasztner and Schweiger's account of the origins of the Deposit now depended on Becher himself. While Becher's hopes of avoiding serious punishment at his forthcoming war crimes trial depended on the evidence Kasztner would give on his behalf, Kasztner's ability to retrieve the Deposit for the benefit of the Jewish Agency (his future employers) depended on the former SS colonel. In July 1946, Becher gave detailed testimony to his American captors in which he focused on his role in the various rescue negotiations, and also confirmed the history of the Becher Deposit as recounted by Kasztner and Schweiger.[11] For his part, Kasztner gave evidence at the trials of Becher and two of his associates, as well as providing a number of written statements on his behalf.[12]

The details of what had actually transpired in Budapest during 1944 between the Rescue Committee and the SS were important after the war to all the parties concerned for an additional reason. Kasztner's rescue work in Budapest, and the activities there of other groups involved in relief and rescue for the community, were financed by 'donations' from wealthier local Jews. In some cases, as Kasztner argued after the war, these were genuine philanthropic donations for charitable or Zionist work and there could be no expectation of repayment. But other funds were collected with the specific promise of repayment by the Joint or the Jewish Agency after the war. By 1946, both of these organizations faced a number of demands for repayment by surviving family members. After investigating the facts in each case, these commitments were eventually honoured.[13] Neither the Joint nor the Agency had the budgets available to meet all their commitments in 1946 or 1947, and they agreed that if the Deposit could be retrieved from the Americans, then it would provide a source to meet the post-war Hungarian Jewish claims.[14] Increasingly, the return of the Becher Deposit was seen as a panacea to the budgetary problems of the two Jewish relief organizations – just as the Gold Train had been. But they were to be disappointed, ironically at the same time as the first reports reached them of the diminished worth of the Gold Train.

In January 1947 the State Department finally decided to release the Becher Deposit to the Jewish Agency and the Joint, while simultaneously deciding to release the Gold Train to the IGCR/IRO.[15] Fortunately, the transfer of the Becher Deposit was a much simpler matter than the inventory and shipment of the Gold Train's contents. Perhaps because this was the first collection of victim assets to be handed over, the treasurer of the Jewish Agency in Jerusalem, Eliezer

Kaplan, sent a personal representative to Austria to accept the assets. Dagobert Arian arrived in Salzburg in mid-February, and spent the next month dealing with the bureaucracy of the army's Property Control Office. A representative of the Joint appeared briefly on the scene, but allowed Arian to see the matter through by himself. The original twenty-nine bags which Schweiger had received from Becher in Weissenbach in May 1945 had been deposited in two separate banks in Salzburg. Arian, together with an accountant from the Jewish Agency's Paris office, and in the company of US army officers, was allowed to make a preliminary examination of the goods in late February. A complete inventory of the contents of all the bags was made between 7 and 10 March, before Arian took final receipt of them.

It was immediately apparent that the items were not worth anything like the sums anticipated. Instead of the expected SFr8,600,000 or more (over $2,000,000) which Becher had been paid in Budapest and with the other bribes he had received, the goods handed over by the Property Control Office were estimated to be worth only $65,000. However, the inventory drawn up by Arian in 1947 was identical to that prepared by the Counter Intelligence Corps shortly after they took over the assets from Schweiger in May and June 1945. Schweiger had accepted the first inventory as an accurate receipt for the goods he had handed over, and that inventory matched the 1947 inventory. Whatever was missing had not disappeared while it was under American control.

Arian offered one explanation for the disappointing results: Schweiger had been intentionally misled into believing that he was receiving a great treasure, whereas in fact Becher had already hidden the larger part of his Budapest profits before he was captured in May 1945.[16] He may well have transferred them to Germany long before he left Budapest. Nevertheless, Becher had a real interest in convincing Schweiger, and through him Kasztner, that he had returned all the bribes he had received and in encouraging them to believe that the Deposit was extremely valuable. Becher may well have considered that Kasztner's testimony on his behalf depended on it. Becher need not have been anxious on this account. When Kasztner was asked for his views on the discrepancy between the rumoured SFr8,600,000 and the retrieved $65,000, he made excuses for the SS colonel: 'Becher was certainly not obliged to return even a part of the valuables he received from our Committee in Budapest. What he has delivered to us is net profit. Whatever happened to the balance might merit an investigation, but only for the sake of the historical account.'[17]

An additional explanation of the discrepancy derives from the huge loss of value when precious personal possessions are lumped together *en masse* as victim loot. The same loss of value was experienced concerning the contents of the Gold Train. Furthermore, among the assets handed over to Arian was an amount of Hungarian paper currency. While the pengö had a value in Budapest in 1944, by 1947 these notes were totally worthless because of inflation and the Hungarian currency reform.

Arian took the jewellery and other items in two suitcases to Switzerland, where they were deposited in a bonded warehouse of the Swiss customs. They were eventually sold and a sum of $55,000 was raised. In late July 1947, the Joint's legal department questioned the Jewish Agency on the huge difference between the anticipated value and the final results. Kaplan replied that the Joint's own officials had been involved in every stage of the handling of the Becher Deposit, and that Arian's handling of the matter had been scrupulous. Ironically, Kaplan suggested that if the Joint's lawyers had doubts about the army's guardianship of the assets or the Agency's role, perhaps they should check the facts with Kurt Becher, who had recently been released from detention.[18]

The Becher Deposit, and its disappointing outcome, was yet another example of the inability to restore the material *status quo ante* after the war. The possessions handed to the SS in Budapest in the desperate attempt to save some lives were most valuable when their original owners were alive and the world in which they lived still existed. When this world was laid waste, Becher's loot was worth only the market value of the raw materials they contained, with a little extra for the workmanship of the jewellery.

Nevertheless, the discrepancy between the bribes paid in Budapest and the value of the goods eventually returned to the Jewish world was too great to be entirely explained by this fact. It was never possible to prove Arian's suggestion that Becher probably hid most of the funds. Nor could it be proved that he returned only enough to entice

Schweiger and Kasztner into testifying on his behalf at his war crimes trial. Becher, like Wilhelm Höttl, quickly became prosperous in the post-war world. He died a wealthy man in August 1995, in Bremen, Germany, and we are left to draw our own conclusions concerning the final fate of the victim loot that Becher received from Kasztner. Kasztner, who had been responsible for some of the boldest rescue negotiations during the Holocaust period, was subsequently accused of becoming altogether too close to Becher and the other top SS officials with whom he had to deal. He was at the centre of a spectacular libel trial in Israel in 1954, and in 1957 he was shot dead by a Holocaust survivor.

Appendix 2 Passenger List prepared in Brennbergbánya, March 1945 (train and motor convoy)

Dr Toldi Árpád	1898. I. 2	Kiskőrös	Previously District Governor; departmental head
Dr Toldi Árpádné	1904. VIII. 27	Hajduszoboszló	Housewife
Toldi Attila	1935. VII. 18	Szombathely	Student
Tomcsányi Aladárné	1921. III. 17	Hajduszoboszló	Housewife
Legenyei Bodnár Mária	1924. I. 3	Hajduszoboszló	Housewife
Dr Avar (Andersen) László	1907. VII. 8	Nagykikinda	Previously Mayor; departmental vice-head
Dr Avar Lászlóné	1911. III. 21	Szilágysomlyó	Housewife
Avar Tamás	1943. VII. 13	Szeghalom	–
Avar Katalin	1943. VII. 13	Szeghalom	–
Dr Z. Kiss Ernő	1899. VII. 23	Retteg	Minsterial counsellor and deputy director of Financial Directorate
Dr Z. Kiss Ernőné	1902. II. 8	Dicsőszentmárton	Housewife
Z. Kiss Ágnes	1929. IV. 5	Szeged	Student
Z. Kiss Erzsébet	1939. II. 27	Budapest	–
Demeter Dezsőné	1888. XI. 19	Emőd	Housewife
Demeter Ida	1927. II. 18	Fületelke	Housewife
Dr Mingovits István	1898. I. 5	Sepsiszentgyörgy	Royal Hungarian Financial Counsellor

Dr Mingovits Istvánné	1901. IV. 12	Budapest	Housewife
Mingovits Tibor	1923. IV. 4	Budapest	Merchant
Mingovits Tiborné	1923. VI. 3	Jászárokszállás	Accountant
Dr Boga Bálint	1888. VII. 24	Gyergyószárhegy	Presiding judge
Dr Boga Bálintné	1909. I. 27	Beszterce	Housewife
Boga Bálint	1938. I. 5	Budapest	Student
Boga Attila	1941. III. 7	Marosvásárhely	–
Dr Touttenui Tibor	1915. V. 23	Budapest	Assistant Secretary of Mining Authority
Dr Touttenui Tiborné	1913. IX. 17	Zsira	Housewife
Ritter Mária Magdolna	1934. VI. 5	Sopron	Student
Dr Zolnay Béla	1902. III. 12	Husztsófalva	Financial secretary
Dr Zolnay Béláné	1908. VIII. 21	Jászapáti	Housewife
Zolnay Béla	1930. I. 10	Gyoma	–
Zolnay Mária	1938. XII. 4	Szeged	–
Dr Tolnay Oszkár	1900. IV. 20	Léva	Chief of Audit Office
Tolnay Géza	1906. XI. 6	Aranyosmarót	Teacher
Tolnay Gézáné	1913. III. 8	Szaktalórántháza	Housewife
ifj. Tolnay Géza	1935. II. 14	Ókécske	Student
Szemere Zoltán	1885. VIII. 18	Sárosoroszi	Financial Counsellor in Audit Office
Gara Pál	1901. IX. 15	Kecskemét	Financial Counsellor in Audit Office
Biró Vilmos	1906. VI. 8	Budapest	Accountant, Ministry of Finance, and deputy director of Audit Office
Biró Vilmosné	1914. IX. 3	Budapest	Housewife
Biró Tamás	1936. VIII. 14	Budapest	Student
Biró András	1941. XII. 15	Budapest	–

Biró Róbertné	1914. IX. 8	Szolnok	Housewife
Biró Kinga	1939. IX. 9	Szolnok	–
Láng Rudolf	1900. II. 2	Budapest	Accountant
Láng Rudolfné	1899. III. 16	Marosszentgyörgy	Clerk
Domján József	1898. IV. 6	Ükk	Accountant
Domján Józsefné	1913. IX. 1	Székesfehérvár	Housewife
ifj. Domján József	1939. I. 6	Budapest	–
Domján Attila	1940. IV. 30	Budapest	–
Domján Emőke	1944. X. 6	Budapest	–
Jeszenői István	1905	Budapest	Accountant
Jeszenői Istvánné	1908	Budapest	Housewife
Jeszenői Endre	1944	Alsógöd	–
Farkas István	1874	Baja	Pensioner
Farkas Istvánné	1870	Baja	Housewife
Kóczán Elemér	1915. VII. 17	Nagysároslak	Financial Inspector
Vida Zoltán	1908	Budapest	Financial Inspector
Vida Zoltánné	1911	Siklós	Housewife
Vida Edit	1944. XII. 9	Sopron	–
Toroczkóy Tihamér	1913. V. 26	Budapest	Royal Hungarian Detective
Toroczkóy Tihamérné	1919. I. 15	Somogyvár	Housewife
Varvasovszky Emil	1928. IX. 3	Székesfehérvár	Student
özv. Dörnyei Pálné	1896	Bosnia-Novi	Housewife
Horváth Imre	1899. X. 31	Felsőireg	Revenue Officer
Horváth Imréné	1905. IX. 17	Nagyszokoly	Housewife
Horváth Matild	1934. XII. 31	Budapest	Student
Sári János László	1920. X. 3	Mezőkovácsháza	Clerk
Bognár Mihály	1926. X. 2	Budapest	Clerk (in Audit Office)
özv. Napkóri Jánosné	1872. VIII. 20	Királydarócz	Housewife
Napkóri Erzsébet	1897. XI. 19	Szolnok	Typist
Fülöp János	1909. II. 11	Szolnok	Office messenger, Finance Ministry
Fülöp Jánosné	1908. XII. 20	Taksony	Housewife

Molnár Lajos	1919. X. 25	Nick	Office messenger, Customs Department
Bernát Erzsébet	1920. IX. 5	Tiszavárkony	Housewife
Zajátz János	1908. III. 6	Pacsér	Office messenger, Customs Department
Zajátz Jánosné	1907. VI. 15	Zenta	Housewife
Csepeli Sándor	1885	Szaporca	Driver
Rucz Kálmán	1896. VIII. 11	Felsőszeli	Driver
Ercse Sándor	1907. III. 31	Sóvárad	Customs Officer
Ercse Sándorné	1911. IX. 7	Petrozsény	Housewife
Ercse Margit	1939. VI. 26	Budapest	–
özv. Kindris Jánosné	1879. VII. 7	Gencs	Housewife
Paulovits Illés	1900. IV. 20	Kisapoldor	Senior Customs Officer
ifj. Paulovits Illés	1933. VI. 10	Tiszaföldvár	Student
Szilágyi Irma	1919. VI. 10	Mánd	Housewife
Dobai Miklós	1900. IV. 10	Székelyhid	Senior Customs Officer
Molnár János	1907. I. 15	Medgyes	Customs Officer
Molnár Ignácz	1907. IX. 29	Székesfehérvár	Senior Guard, Customs
Morócz Dezső	1912. V. 24	Boba	Senior Guard, Customs
Gáspár György	1907. X. 22	Kőhalom	Senior Guard, Customs
Paszovszky Sándor	1912. XII. 22	Soroksár	Senior Guard, Customs
Szabó István	1912. IX. 14	Debrecen	Customs Guard
Orosz János	1914. IX. 5	Sepsibükszád	Customs Guard
Csiki László	1914. V. 10	Brassó	Customs Guard
Molnár Dénes	1914. IV. 21	Szentdemeter	Customs Guard
Torjai Ferenc	1914	Felsőcsernáton	Customs Guard
Boldizsár István	1914. V. 15	Sepsiszentgyörgy	Customs Guard
Kiss Árpád Ernő	1913. I. 27	Zágon	Customs Guard
Hódi Péter	1915. VI. 29	Nagymajlát	Customs Guard

Kelemen István	1916	Kézdialmás	Customs Guard
Farkas Pál	1895. XII. 20	Budapest	Customs Guard
Bartos Béla	1918. XII. 14	Brassó	Customs Guard
Csata Kálmán	1918. X. 13	Gyergyócsomafalva	Customs Guard
Fejes János	1915. XII. 28	Kovászna	Customs Guard
Zalka János	1908. X. 4	Iszkaszentgyörgy	Gendarme, Sergeant-Major
Rátkai Ignác	1914. IX. 19	Bakonynána	Gendarme, Sergeant
Fülöp Miklós	1920. X. 26	Guta	Gendarme, corporal
Kilácskó Ferenc	1920. VIII. 13	Királyrév	Gendarme, corporal
Vajda István	1919. IX. 7	Pátka	Gendarme, corporal
Edvi József	1920. X. 28	Kajár	Gendarme, corporal
Bratkó Béla	1919. X. 20	Kurtakeszi	Gendarme, corporal
Tóth János	1919. XII. 19	Tac	Gendarme, corporal
Simon Gyula	1919. VIII. 29	Sárbogárd	Gendarme, corporal
Tanács János	1919. X. 25	Etyek	Gendarme, corporal
Galla József	1917. X. 4	Udvar	Gendarme, corporal
Horváth István	1919. VIII. 3	Mezőlak	Gendarme, corporal
Gelencsér György	1919. I. 23	Szakcs	Gendarme, corporal
Sörény József	1919. I. 29	Gölle	Gendarme, corporal
Deák Árpád	1920. III. 8	Nyujtód	Gendarme, corporal
Kaposi József	1924. VII. 22	Somlóvásárhely	Gendarme, corporal
Musitz Árpád	1922. X. 2	Nyárasd	Gendarme, corporal

Kerepeczi János	1922. VI. 10	Nyujtód	Gendarme, corporal
Németh József	1920. XI. 15	Vitnyéd	Gendarme, corporal
Pinizsi József	1918. IX. 1	Balatonendréd	Gendarme, corporal
Csibi István	1919. V. 28	Gyergyóditró	Gendarme, corporal
Fekete István	1916. III. 15	Rábaszentmihály	Gendarme, corporal
Krastyenics Imre	1915. X. 29	Pozsonyeperjes	Gendarme, lance-corporal
Metykó Ferenc	1917. VII. 10	Csákvár	Gendarme, lance-corporal
Érsek László	1920. VIII. 10	Bicske	Gendarme, lance-corporal
Griell Ernő	1916. XI. 11	Zsolyombrezó	First-Lieutenant
Nagy Gábor	1923. II. 17	Tata	First-Lieutenant
Dr Veégh István	1908. XII. 25	Miskolc	Reserve artillery officer
Szotyori Nagy Tibor	1920. III. 3	Miskolc	Sergeant (?)
Szotyori Nagy Tiborné	1922. VI. 31 ?	Miskolc	Housewife
ifj. Szotyori Nagy Tibor	1943. X. 10	Miskolc	–
Ignácz András	1921. IX. 7	Hejőcsaba	Cadet Sergeant (Reserves)
Berecz Bertalan	1912. II. 21	Mezőkeresztes	Sergeant (Reserves)
Berecz Bertalanné	1921. X. 6	Egerlővő	Housewife
Berecz Zsuzsanna Eszter	1944. I. 5	Mezőkeresztes	–
Sashalmi János	1921. VIII. 17	Miskolc	Lance-Sergeant
Szabó Antal	1921. XII. 22	Besenyőtelek	Army, corporal
Haffner Károly	1921. VII. 30	Budafok	Army, corporal
Salamon Imre	1920. VIII. 28	Hámor	Army, corporal
Tóth Lajos	1921. IX. 21	Tarnaszentmiklós	Army, corporal

? János	1923. VI. 18	?	Army, lance-corporal
Mikolás János	1922. II. 17	Szerencs	Army, lance-corporal
Bakos Ferenc	1921. V. 21	Dernő	Army, lance-corporal
Dósa József	1922. VIII. 3	Vata	Army, private
Dusza István	1908. X. 8	Tard	Army, private
Gáspár György	1921. II. 9	Mezőkövesd	Army, private
Hankó János	1922. VI. 14	Szirmabesenyő	Army, private
Hornyák János	1921. X. 17	Tálya	Army, private
Igrinyi Mihály	1922. XII. 14	Poroszló	Army, private
Izsák Ádám	1921. X. 1	Solymár	Army, private
Jacsó János	1921. V. 23	Mezőkövesd	Army, private
Juhász István	1921. XI. 7	Hatvan	Army, private
Király Kálmán	1910. XI. 15	Naprágy	Army, private
Koren József	1908. IV. 26	Deresk	Army, private
Kiss János	1921. XII. 17	Legénd	Army, private
Koós Gyula	1920. IV. 26	Tornagörgő	Army, private
Kovács Gyula	1921. X. 15	Barcika	Army, private
Kovács János	1909. II. 15	Balogfalva	Army, private
Koren István	1907. VII. 10	Gömörnánás	Army, private
Kruppa Bertalan	191??. XI. 6	Bolyok	Army, private
Maloniczki Géza	1920. XII. 3	Miskolc	Army, private
Rutz Kálmán	1896. VIII. 11	Felsőszeli	Army, private
Szekeres Pál	1913. I. 4	Alsóábrány	Army, private
Varga Lajos	1922. V. 9	Diósgyőr	Army, private
Vona István	1921. X. 10	Tarnaszentmiklós	Army, private
Zelena László	1914. VI. 25	Sajókazinc	Army, private
Barta Viktor	1918. IV. 29	Csokva	Army, private
Bálint István	1921. V. 21	Mezőkövesd	Army, private
Birinyi János	1912. IX. 12	Lasztoc	Army, private
Birinyi József	1921. VII. 22	Andornaktája	Army, private
Dolák Mátyás	1911. VI. 17	Rozsnyó	Army, private
Légrádi László	1921. XI. 19	Balatonboglár	Army, private
Matyó József	1921. III. 11	Palást	Army, private
Polyák József	1921. I. 24	Palást	Army, private

Papp József	1921. V. 30	Borsodszemere	Army, private
Szamkó György	1921. XI. 27	Jolsva	Army, private
Bajusz József	1909. I. 29	Dercsk	Army, private
Warvasovszky József	1886. III. 7	Gyertyánliget	Draughtsman
Warvasovszky Józsefné	1884. III. 17	Budapest	Housewife
Felsővári Ferenc	1909. I. 3	Magyaróvár	Gendarme, Sergeant-Major (?)
Felsővári Ferencné	1912. X. 25	Balatonederics	Housewife
ifj. Felsővári Ferenc	1941. IX. 23	Budapest	–
Felsővári József Engelbert	1944. V. 31	Székesfehérvár	–
Telek Leánder	1894. IX. 13	Martonos	Customs Officer
Telek Leánderné	1890	Pozsony	Housewife
ifj. Telek Leánder	1924. V. 2	Monor	University student
Goots Béla	1913. VI. 26	Sátoraljaújhely	Customs Guard
Monostori István	1914. IX. 4	Karva	Customs Guard
Szabó István	1914. XII. 9	Söjtör	Gendarme, Sergeant-Major
Patakfalvi Sándor	1915. III. 12	Halina	Gendarme, Sergeant-Major
Horváth János VI.	1913. X. 20	Egyházashollós	Gendarme, Sergeant-Major
Gyulai Lajos	1914. X. 11	Nagyszalonta	Gendarme, Lance-Sergeant
Balogh János II.	1919. II. 25	Fertőszentmiklós	Gendarme, Lance-Sergeant
Kámán Menyhért	1914. I. 6	Gutorfölde	Gendarme, Lance-Sergeant
Hermán Gyula	1915. XII. 12	Lendvajakabfa	Gendarme, Lance-Sergeant
Molnár ??	1914. III. 17	Nagytilaj	Gendarme, Lance-Sergeant
Sándor József	1918. IX. 2	Szatmárudvari	Gendarme, Lance-Sergeant

Tóth Ferenc II.	1917. VI. 24	Karcag	Gendarme, Lance-Sergeant
Sági József	1917. V. 15	Dióslak	Gendarme, Lance-Sergeant
Kacsó Sándor	1912. XII. 3	Kisráska	Gendarme, Lance-Sergeant
Czeglédi Gábor	1916. V. 15	Ják	Gendarme, Lance-Sergeant
Béres Mózes	1913. III. 28	Sepsibodog	Gendarme, Lance-Sergeant
Kovács József	1921. IX. 21	Tiszavárkony	Corporal (?)
Dr Balogh János	1915	Jászkisér	Gendarme, Captain
Dr Balogh Jánosné	1922	Gyöngyös	Housewife
Balogh Zsolt	1943	Nyiregyháza	–
Görgényi Árpád	1897	Királd	Captain (Reserves) (?)
Dr Varga Istvánné	1924	Kisujszállás	Housewife
Kiss Béla	1894	??	Expert (?)
Füri Lajos	1913	Kispest	Journalist

(*Source*: YVA, TR-14/24)

Translated by Kinga Frojimovics and László Csősz

Notes

INTRODUCTION

1. *Képes Figyelő* ('Illustrated Observer'), 17 November 1945, p. 7.
2. *Snowbound* (1948), starring Robert Newton, Dennis Price and Herbert Lom. Based on the novel by Hammond Innes, *The Lonely Skier*.
3. *The Train* (1964), starring Burt Lancaster, Jeanne Moreau and Paul Scofield; produced by John Frankenheimer.

CHAPTER I   HUNGARY AND THE JEWS

1. R. L. Braham, *The Politics of Genocide. The Holocaust in Hungary*, vol. 1 (Columbia University Press, New York, 1994), p. 5.
2. I. Deák, 'Hungary', in H. Rogger and E. Weber (eds.), *The European Right. A Historical Profile* (University of California Press, Berkeley and Los Angeles, 1966), p. 367.
3. R. L. Braham, op. cit., vol. 1, p. 7.
4. ibid., p. 3.
5. ibid., p. 368.
6. N. Katzburg, 'The Tradition of Anti-Semitism in Hungary', in R. L. Braham and B. Vago, *The Holocaust in Hungary: Forty Years Later* (Columbia University Press, New York and Haifa, 1985), p. 4.
7. R. L. Braham, op. cit., vol. 1, pp. 8–11.
8. ibid., p. 36, n. 35.
9. I. Deák, op. cit., p. 372.
10. ibid., p. 379.
11. G. Földes and L. Hubai (eds.), *Parliamentary Elections in Hungary, 1920–1998* (Napvilág, Budapest, 1999), p. 172.
12. Gömbös was able to exploit the resignation of many career officers

following League of Nations criticism of Hungary's role in the assassination of King Alexander of Yugoslavia and the French Foreign Minister, Louis Barthou, on 9 October 1934 (R. L. Braham, op. cit., vol. 1, p. 53).

13. G. Baross, 'Hungary and Hitler', *Living History Program of University of Southern California Library* (1964); see also Braham, op. cit., vol. 1, p. 55.

14. Braham, op. cit., vol. 1, p. 123.

15. Y. Don, 'The Economic Effect of Antisemitic Discrimination: Hungarian Anti-Jewish Legislation, 1938–1944', in M. Marrus (ed.), *The Nazi Holocaust: Historical Articles on the Destruction of European Jews*, vol. 4 (Westport, London, 1989), p. 507.

16. Braham, op. cit., vol. 1, p. 126.

17. P. Sipos (ed.), *Imrédy Béla a vádlottak padján ['Béla Imrédy in the Prisoner's Box']* (Osiris-Budapest Főváros Levéltára, Budapest, 1999), p. 39.

18. N. Horthy, *Memoirs* (Simon Publications, Florida, 1957), p. 216.

19. Földes and Hubai, op. cit.

20. This account of Szálasi's thought is based on C. A. Macartney, *October Fifteenth: A History of Modern Hungary, 1929–1945* (Edinburgh University Press, 1956), vol. 1, Ch. 9.

21. M. Lackó, *Arrow-Cross Men. National Socialists, 1935–1944* (Akadémiai Kiadó, Budapest, 1969), pp. 13–14.

22. Macartney, op. cit., vol. 1, p. 165. The foremost authority on the Holocaust in Hungary, Braham, accepts Macartney's interpretation of Szálasi's anti-Jewish policy (Braham, op. cit., vol. 1, p. 65, and vol. 2, p. 945).

23. Deák, op. cit., p. 393. Deák asserts that the text is equally incomprehensible in the original Hungarian.

24. Lackó, op. cit., pp. 14–15.

25. ibid., p. 19.

26. ibid., p. 18.

27. ibid., p. 29, n. 33.

28. 'Report on Hungarian right-wing exiles in Germany', 16 August 1939 (NA, RG 242, T175, Sicherheitsdienst Archives, microfilm 542, frame 9415299-309), and 'Report on Arrow Cross Movement in Hungary', 27 April 1939 (roll 542, frame 9415265-69).

29. Lackó, op. cit., p. 36.

30. Lackó and Braham disagree on most of the details of Baky's career. Braham states that Baky openly shifted his loyalties to Pálffy only in September 1941 (Braham, op. cit., vol. 1, p. 425).

31. Lackó, op. cit., p. 41.

32. ibid., p. 55.

33. ibid., p. 63.

34. Deák, op. cit., p. 392.

35. Földes and Hubai, op. cit., p. 199.

36. Braham, op. cit., vol. 1, p. 151.

37. Don, op. cit., p. 508.

38. Act IV (1939).

39. Don, op. cit., p. 513.

40. Braham, op, cit., vol. 1, p. 159.

41. Don, op. cit., p. 515.

42. Quoted in ibid. In his *Memoirs*, Horthy wrote: 'The Jews supported each other with the solidarity of their race and earned more than 25 per cent of the national income' (p. 208). The separate question of whether the Jews, 6 per cent of the overall population, generated 25 per cent of the national wealth of Hungary, or enjoyed 25 per cent of the GNP, is unclear, and the ambiguity is interesting.

43. G. Ránki, 'The Occupational Structure of Hungarian Jews in the Interwar Period', in M. K. Silber (ed.), *Jews in the Hungarian Economy, 1760–1945* (Magnes Press, Jerusalem, 1992), p. 281. See also Y. Don, 'Patterns of Jewish Economic Behavior in Central Europe in the Twentieth Century', in M. K. Silber, op. cit., pp. 247–73 *passim*, for a discussion of Jewish occupational structure.

44. Don, op. cit. (1989), pp. 517–18.

45. G. Lengyel, 'The Ethnic Composition of the Economic Elite in Hungary in the Interwar Period', in Y. Don and V. Karády, *A Social and Economic History of Central European Jewry* (Transaction Publishers, New Brunswick, 1990), pp. 229–48.

46. M. Schmidt, 'Provincial Police Reports: New Insights into Hungarian Jewish History, 1941–1944', *Yad Vashem Studies* XIX (1987), 233–67, p. 265.

47. Braham, op. cit., vol. 1, p. 206.

48. Report of the Statistical Department of the World Jewish Congress, Hungarian Division (cited in Braham, op. cit., vol. 2, p. 1298); see also Z. Erez, 'Holocaust of Hungarian Jewry – Statistical Survey' [Hebrew], *Yalkut Moreshet* 57 (1994), 43–60 *passim*.

49. The story of Hungary's participation in the German war against the Soviet Union has been recounted elsewhere, and there is no need to repeat it here. See Macartney, op. cit., vol. 1.

50. Deák, op. cit., p. 398. Allied planes were not fired upon, and British, American and French POWs who had escaped from German camps were given refuge.

51. Baross, op. cit.

52. From Kállay's memoirs, *Hungarian Premier*, cited by N. Katzburg in his *Hungary and the Jews* (Bar-Ilan University Press, Ramat Gan, 1981), pp. 192–3.

53. ibid., p. 198.

54. 'Hungary', Military Intelligence Report (G-2), 24 November 1942 (NA, RG 165, Box 1600). Katzburg, op. cit. (1981), p. 199, gives more modest statistics, based on information published in Berlin in 1943.

55. Braham, op. cit., vol. 1, p. 258, n. 17.

56. Katzburg, op. cit. (1981), p. 200.

57. V. Ranki, *The Politics of Inclusion and Exclusion. Jews and Nationalism in Hungary* (Holmes & Meier, New York, 1999), p. 143.

58. Macartney, op. cit., vol. 2, Chs. 12 and 13 *passim*.

59. N. Petersen (ed.), *From Hitler's Doorstep. The Wartime Intelligence Reports of Allen Dulles, 1942–1945* (Pennsylvania State University Press, 1996), p. 599 (Doc. 3-37). Macartney and Braham also discuss 'Operation Sparrow'.

60. Höttl memo, 11 March, cited in Macartney, op. cit., vol. 2, p. 223, n. 1.

CHAPTER 2   DIAMONDS, GOLD AND GENOCIDE

1. Höttl is variously described as head of the Balkan section of the SD, Amt VI-E, or as head of the Hungarian department within Amt VI-E.

2. Allied counter-intelligence prepared a study of the German intelligence services that provides the classic account of the history and function of the Sicherheitsdienst. Although Amt VI first appeared in 1940 as a separate structure within the SD, the organization as a whole had been actively involved in foreign political intelligence for years. Höttl's role as head of the Amt VI-E office, responsible for Italy, the Balkans and Hungary, is specifically mentioned in this study. (PRO, WO219/5276, SHAEF G-2, Counter-Intelligence Sub-division, 'German Intelligence Services', 4 October 1944, p. 31.)

3. When Edmund Veesenmayer was interrogated by the OSS after the war, he was asked specifically about his policy differences with Höttl. Veesenmayer replied: 'Höttl's chief concern was a small group of National Socialists in Budapest with whom he was associated' (NA, RG 226, Field Station Files, London X-2, Box 55, 'Interrogation Report: Edmund Veesenmayer', 5 July 1945). During Baky's post-war trial for war crimes, Veesenmayer gave evidence that Baky 'had very good connections with Höttl' (L. Karsai and J. Molnár, *Az Endre-Baky-Jaross per* (Cserépfalvi, Budapest, 1994, p. 198), while Otto Winckelmann testified that Höttl and Baky 'were on very good terms' and 'were often together'.

4. Karsai and Molnár, op. cit., p. 83.

5. C. A. Macartney, *October Fifteenth. A History of Modern Hungary,* *1929–1945* (Edinburgh University Press, 1956), vol. 2, p. 245.

6. From the evidence of László Baky at his war crimes trial (see Karsai and Molnár, op. cit., pp. 83–4).

7. Jaross became well known for enriching himself with confiscated Jewish property and for selling protection (Macartney, op. cit., vol. 1, p. 308).

8. J. Molnár, 'Gendarmes, Policemen, Functionaries and the Jews: New Findings on the Behavior of Hungarian Authorities During the Holocaust' (unpublished paper, 1998); Macartney (op. cit., vol. 2, p. 269) states that twenty-nine out of forty were replaced.

9. G. Ránki, *1944 március 19. Magyarország német megszállása ['19 March* *1944. The German Occupation of Hungary']* (Kossuth, Budapest, 1978), p. 164.

10. Request by Police Chief of Székesfehérvár (György Székely) to Hungarian Ministry of Justice for the issue of arrest warrant for Árpád Toldi, 13 July 1946 (Budapest Municipal Archives, 1946, N3094/4-3470/946).

11. The official appointment is recorded in: Minister of War to Minister of Interior, 3 October 1939, Ministry of War Archives (HIL), 82.608/elu 20-1939. (I am grateful to László Karsai for bringing this document to my attention.)

12. Details of Toldi's career are taken from the official Gendarmerie publications *Csendőrségi Lapok, Csendőrségi Zsebkönyv* and *Csendőrségi* *Közlöny.*

13. F. Glatz, 'Hóman Bálint és a nemzetiszocialisták összeütközése Székesfehérvárott 1944-ben' ['A political clash between Bálint Hóman and the National Socialists in Székesfehérvár in 1944'], *Fejérmegyei Történeti Évkönyv* 4 (1970), 187–202 *passim.*

14. Cf. *Csendőrségi Lapok*, 'A tettes az elkövetés előtt és után' (16 April 1938, pp. 254–60, and 1 May 1938, pp. 297–302); 'Népmozgalmi nyilvántartás – csendőrségi nyilvántartás' (15 July 1940, pp. 458–62); 'A népmozgalmi nyilvántartás – közbiztonsági vonatkozásban' (1 August 1940, pp. 494–8); 'A rendkívüli fegyverhasználati jogról' (15 October 1943, pp. 610–16).

15. A. Toldi, *A bűnügyi nyomozás ['The Criminal Investigation']* (Stadium, Budapest, 1941). As this book was published at the time Toldi was promoted and began to use the academic title of 'Dr', it is probable that the publication was part of the requirements of his degree.

16. ibid., 'Csendőrök a Szovjet elleni háborúban', 15 September 1941, pp. 597–602.

17. Glatz, op. cit.

18. Evidence of Dr Lajos Kerekes, Mayor of Székesfehérvár, Székesfehérvár Police, 10 February 1947 (YVA, TR-14-24, pp. 13–14).

19. *Fejérmegyei Napló* ('Diary of Fejér County'), 12 May 1944.

20. Evidence of Dr István Ármos, Székesfehérvár Police, 6 February 1947 (YVA, TR-14-24, pp. 20–21).

21. Evidence of Dr Lajos Kerekes, Székesfehérvár Police, 10 February 1947 (YVA, TR-14-24, pp. 13–14).

22. Glatz, op. cit., *passim*.

23. Evidence of Marcell Kaári Nagy, Székesfehérvár Police, 8 February 1947 (YVA, TR-14-24, pp. 17–18).

24. Evidence of Emil Csatáry (member of the Municipal Council), Dr Lajos Kerekes, and Gita Kepes (resident), Székesfehérvár Police, 8–10 February 1947 (YVA, TR-14-24, pp. 12–20).

25. This account is based on Braham, Macartney and Lévai.

26. On the World Jewish Congress's active lobbying for Allied action to prevent the murder of Hungarian Jewry after March 1944, see Easterman to Stettinius, 28 March 1944 (NA, RG 220, War Refugee Board, McCleland Papers, Box 10, 'Relations with State Department'); and Confidential Report of Kubowitzki meeting with War Refugee Board and Grossman meeting with International Red Cross, 19 June 1944 (CZA, S26, File 1078). See also L. Kubowitzki, *Unity in Dispersion: A History of the World Jewish Congress* (World Jewish Congress, New York, 1948), p. 184.

27. R. L. Braham, *The Politics of Genocide. The Holocaust in Hungary*, vol. 1 (Columbia University Press, New York, 1994), p. 545.

28. ibid., vol. 1, p. 516.

29. E. Lévai, *Black Book on the Martyrdom of Hungarian Jewry* (ed. Lawrence P. Davis): translation of *Fekete könyv* ['This is how it happened'] (Central European Times Publishing Co., Zurich, 1948), p. 110.

30. Braham, op. cit., vol. 1, p. 547.

31. Macartney, op. cit., vol. 2, p. 285, n. 2.

32. Braham, op. cit., vol. 1, pp. 548–56.

33. OSS Research and Analysis Report 2027, 'The Jews in Hungary', 19 October 1944 (NA, RG 226).

34. Levai, op. cit., p. 102.

35. On 22 April, the day after the forced closure, Höttl obtained Baky's approval for SS experts to go through the inventory of the Jewish bookshops in Budapest in the hope of finding publications of interest to the RSHA's research institute (USHMM, 14.016, microfilm of Berlin's RG 58 (RSHA collection), vol. 34, pp. 64 and 75. I am grateful to Katrin Paehler for bringing these documents to my attention). Just as Becher was able to circumvent the

Hungarian authorities by negotiating directly with the Chorin-Weiss group, so the SS was able to rely on Höttl's links with Baky to get round the Hungarian government's attempt to keep Jewish property for themselves rather than lose it to Germany.

36. For a detailed account of the despoliation process in the Szeged region, see J. Molnár, *Zsidósors 1944-ben az V. (szegedi) csendőrkerületben ['Jews in the Fifth Gendarme District (Szeged) in 1944']* (Budapest, 1995), pp. 50–53. Molnár also points out the cynicism that lay behind the gradualism of official policy.

37. Macartney, op. cit., vol. 2, p. 284.

38. W. Höttl, *The Secret Front. The Story of Nazi Political Espionage* (Weidenfeld & Nicolson, London, 1953), p. 42; cited in Braham, op. cit., vol. 1, p. 616, n. 30.

39. Testimony of Leah Holitz (YVA Oral Testimonies, Series 03, File 6722, microfilm 033C/2311).

40. Levai, op. cit., p. 116.

41. Aladár Vozáry, *Így történt!* (Budapest, 1945), pp. 22–75. Cited in N. M. Nagy-Talavera, *The Green Shirts and the Others: a History of Fascism in Hungary and Rumania* (Hoover Institution Press, Stanford University, California, 1970), pp. 205–6.

42. Testimony of Miguel Attal (YVA Oral Testimonies, Series 03, File 10337, microfilm 033C/5568).

43. Evidence of Károly Grósz, Székesfehérvár Police, 11 February 1947 (YVA, TR-14-24, pp. 11–12).

44. Evidence of Dezső Németh, Székesfehérvár Police, 11 February 1947 (YVA, TR-14-24, pp. 15–16).

45. Eliezer Even and Benjamin Ravid, *Zakhor: Memorial Books for the Communities of Székesfehérvár and the Surrounding Area* [Hebrew] (Jerusalem, 1977), p. 51. After the war the indictment against Toldi held him responsible for the deaths of 4,000 Jews in the Fejér district as there were other deportation points in the area.

46. 'The Jews in Hungary', 19 October 1944 (NA, RG 226, OSS Research and Analysis Report 2027, p. 16). The authors of the OSS report relied on the Jewish Telegraphic Association for this information.

47. 'Memo on Situation of Jews in Hungary', 2 March 1946 (NA, RG 84, US Embassy Budapest, Box 103, File 'Anglo-American Committee of Inquiry').

48. On 31 March the Soviet-based Communist-sponsored Kossuth Radio broadcast a warning that the Germans were taking gold and jewels from the Jews. As the radio pointed out, the Germans were not only robbing the

Jews but also robbing Hungary (R. Rozett, 'Jewish and Hungarian Armed Resistance in Hungary', *Yad Vashem Studies* XIX, 1988, 276).

49. László Csősz, 'From Emancipation to Exclusion: Jewish Fate in the Jászág' (MA dissertation, Central European University, 2000).

50. I. Deák, 'Hungary', in H. Rogger and E. Weber (eds.), *The European Right. A Historical Profile* (University of California Press, Berkeley and Los Angeles, 1966), p. 403.

CHAPTER 3   COLLAPSE OF THE REICH AND *HUNGARIZMUS*

1. N. M. Nagy-Talavera, *The Green Shirts and the Others: a History of Fascism in Hungary and Rumania* (Hoover Institution Press, Stanford University, California, 1970), pp. 215–16.

2. *Fejérmegyei Napló*, 14 September 1944.

3. R. L. Braham, *The Politics of Genocide. The Holocaust in Hungary* (Columbia University Press, New York, 1994), vol. 1, p. 555.

4. As in so many other aspects of the Hungarian Holocaust, official actions preceded the formal gazetting of government policy. István Mingovits gave evidence that he received instructions to establish a department to manage Jewish property eleven days earlier, on 10 July (YVA, TR-14-24, testimony of István Mingovits, 5 October 1945). In the post-war hearing of the 'Vetting Committee', a forum to check the wartime activities of all public employees which had the authority to send a case for war crimes trial before the People's Court, Mingovits successfully established that he had a favourable working relationship with the Jewish Council in Budapest. Mingovits was considered to be a civil servant of integrity, who would not exceed official instructions out of any anti-Jewish enthusiasm. He was also considered 'ready for negotiation' – presumably to ameliorate as far as possible the intent of the confiscatory decrees. (Cf. report of the proceedings in the *Képes Figyelő* ('Illustrated Observer'), 17 November 1945, p. 6.)

5. *Képes Figyelő*, ibid.

6. Testimony of István Mingovits, 5 October 1945 (YVA, TR-14-24, pp. 109–13).

7. Papers of the Jewish Property Commissioner (*Kormánybiztos a zsidók anyagi és vagyonjogi ügyeinek megoldására*), HNA, K 498, and microfilms: *Filmtár* I-72-79; papers of the Ministry of Interior, 1944, HNA K-150, especially the papers of Department XXI ('Residential Apartment Affairs'). The following secondary sources have also been consulted: *Vádirat*

a nácizmus ellen. Dokumentumok a magyarországi zsidóüldözés törté-netéhez ['The Indictment of Nazism. Documents on the Persecution of the Jews in Hungary'], vols. 1 and 3, ed. Ilona Benoschofsky and Elek Karsai (MIOK, Budapest, 1958). I am indebted to László Csősz for summarizing these sources.

8. M. Axworthy, C. Scafes, *et al.*, *Third Axis, Fourth Ally. Romanian Armed Forces in the European War, 1941–1945* (Arms & Armour Press, London, 1995), p. 203.

9. J. Erickson, *The Road to Berlin. Stalin's War with Germany* (Weidenfeld & Nicolson, London, 1983), p. 369.

10. C. A. Macartney, *October Fifteenth. A History of Modern Hungary, 1929–1945*, vol. 2 (Edinburgh University Press, 1956), pp. 452–3.

11. ibid. Macartney points out that it was not simply a matter of German looting. His classic study of Hungary during the war years was based on personal interviews with many of the leading participants, only a few years after the war ended. As he noted: 'Herr Veesenmayer informs me that the manager of the Archduke József Ferencz's vineyards besought him for transport to take away 4,000,000 bottles of Tokaj. That the austere German refused this request is not the least tragic fact registered in this history.'

12. Nagy-Talavera, op. cit., p. 239. Different sources present other statistical breakdowns of the resources carried to the West. According to post-war internal Hungarian government assessments, they included 23,840 freight wagons, 10–12,000 vehicles, 512 river craft, and 120–150,000 horses. (Report by Géza Jankahidy, Ministry of Reconstruction, 19 November 1945: HNA, Foreign Ministry Files, XIX. J-1-k, 23/g. See also 'Survey of the Economic Situation in Hungary', published by the Hungarian Commercial Bank of Pest (n.d.), NA, RG 319, G-2 'P' files, Box 3349.)

13. M. Szabó, 'The Development of the Hungarian Aircraft Industry, 1938–1941', *Journal of Military History* 65, January 2001, 74–6.

14. Report of Squadron Leader Tupinier, Director of the Documentation Office (Bdoc) of Austria to Capitaine Lindemann, 23 September 1946 (Colmar, AUT 3180, d.510, Trésor Hongrois (1945–1953), 9991/SCE/10/PHI/RD).

15. E. J. Lévai, *Zsidósors Magyarországon ['Fate of the Jews in Hungary']* (Magyar Téka, Budapest, 1948), p. 314.

16. Memo of Andor Gellért (First Consul of Hungary in Salzburg, Delegate of the Hungarian Government to the Territories Occupied by the Allies) to Foreign Minister János Gyöngyösi, 6 February 1946 (HNA, XIX, J-1-k, 112/d).

17. Tupinier, op. cit.

18. Budapest Police interrogation report of István Mingovits and Vilmos Biró, 2 August 1945 (YVA, TR-14-24, pp. 82–9).

19. Cf. Evidence by Mingovits, op. cit., and by Illés Paulovits on 5 October 1945 (YVA, TR-14-24, pp. 104–8).

20. Fritz Kolbe, Report No. 496, 'Boston Series', OSS, NA, RG 226, Entry 210, Box 440. Kolbe, code-named 'George Wood', was a member of the German Foreign Office who voluntarily acted as a spy on behalf of the OSS. Neither the Americans nor the British fully trusted the reliability of this voluntary walk-in source, but after the war it became apparent that Kolbe's reports were authentic copies of German Foreign Office papers and that he was a genuine anti-Nazi. After March 1944 Kolbe sent dozens of documents relating to German–Hungarian relations at the highest level. The Hungarian National Bank gold was sent to the Reich, but not to the Reichsbank. The OSS informed Washington that the National Bank gold was transferred to the Reich in November 1944 (OSS-CID Report No. 125988, NA, RG 226, Box 1445, May 1945).

21. The government consisted of eight members of the Arrow Cross, three from the MEP, one Nationalist Socialist, an Imrédist and two generals. The following ministers played a role in the story of the Gold Train: Gábor Vajna (Interior), Emil Szakváry (Industry), Fidél Pálffy (Agriculture) and General Vilmos Hellebronth (Minister of Continued War Production).

22. Höttl interrogation report on Edmund Veesenmayer, 5 July 1945 (NA, RG 226, Field Station Files, London X-2, Box 55).

23. Nagy-Talavera, op. cit., p. 201.

24. ibid., p. 216, and Braham, op. cit., vol. 1, p. 423.

25. This account differs from Braham's authoritative text (op. cit., vol. 1, p. 555), and is based on the report given by László Avar in his interrogation by the Budapest Police in May 1946 (YVA, T-14-24, pp. 27–36). Avar's account is consistent with the other reports (below), and with the fact that Szálasi was forced to issue a directive on 15 January 1945 to clarify the limits of authority between the two ministries on questions of Jewish property (NA, RG 242, Seized Enemy Records: Hungarian Political and Military Records (T973), microfilm 7, frame 153). According to Avar's account, Toldi's appointment had not been gazetted in the normal way, which makes it difficult for the historian to reconstruct the different official roles of Toldi and Túrvölgyi. István Mingovits, one of the senior officials of the Property Office under Túrvölgyi, stated: 'Toldi was under the Interior Ministry, as opposed to Túrvölgyi, who was under the Ministry of Finance. In January 1945 it became Department 11 under Toldi's leadership with Avar as his deputy' (YVA, T-14-24, pp. 27–36).

26. See note 7 above.

27. Budapesti Közlöny (Official Gazette of the Hungarian Government), No. 250, Decree No. 3.840/1944.M.E. (cited in L. Karsai, 'The Last Phase of the Hungarian Holocaust: the Szálasi Regime and the Jews', in R. L. Braham and S. Miller (eds.), *The Nazis' Last Victims: The Holocaust in Hungary* (Wayne State University Press, Detroit, 1998), p. 108).

28. L. W. G. Niehorster, *The Royal Hungarian Army 1920–1945* (Axis Europa Books, New York, 1998), Ch. 11 *passim*.

29. Cited in Erickson, op. cit., p. 396.

30. For a detailed study of the forced labour deportations of Budapest Jews during the winter of 1944–1945, see Sz. Szita, *Utak a pokolból: magyar deportáltak az annektált Ausztriában, 1944–1945 ['Roads from Hell: Hungarian Deportations to Annexed Austria, 1944–1945'] (Metalon Manager Iroda, Budapest, 1991).

31. K. Frojimovics, G. Komoróczy, *et al.*, *Jewish Budapest* (CEU Press, Budapest, 1999), p. 382.

32. The total of 7,000 who died at the hands of the Nyilas during their reign in Budapest is given in Z. Erez, 'Holocaust of Hungarian Jewry – Statistical Survey' [Hebrew], *Yalkut Moreshet* 57, 1994, 43–60. Erez estimates Jewish deaths in the siege period at 10,000 during the three weeks from the encirclement of the city until the liberation of Pest (and the ghettos there) on 18 January 1945 (ibid., p. 54).

33. viz. Braham, Frojimovics.

34. Macartney, op. cit., vol. 2, p. 461.

35. Evidence by Mingovits, op. cit.

36. For a different estimate of the train's length when it left Budapest (thirty-four wagons), cf. Tupinier report, n. 14 above.

37. Protocol in YVA, M61/35.

38. Evidence of László Avar (YVA, TR-14-24, pp. 31–8).

39. *Képes Figyelő* ('Illustrated Observer'), 17 November 1945, p. 7.

40. Axworthy, Scafes, *et al.*, op. cit., pp. 313–16.

41. 'Survey of the Economic Situation in Hungary', op. cit., p. 21.

42. P. Pierik, *Hungary 1944–1945. The Forgotten Tragedy* (Aspekt, Netherlands, 1996), p. 121. Zistersdorf produced 15,000 tons a month in 1944 (USFA to War Department, P1463, 26 August 1945, RG 319, Entry 57, Box 86).

43. A. Speer, *Inside the Third Reich* (Weidenfeld & Nicolson, London and New York, 1970), pp. 434–5.

44. Erickson, op. cit., p. 446.

45. ibid., p. 515.

46. Niehorster, op. cit., p. 154.

CHAPTER 4   BRENNBERGBÁNYA

1. Testimony of László Avar to the Budapest Police, 22 May 1946 (YVA, TR-14-24, pp. 31–8).

2. Local history of Brennbergbánya was provided by Károly Kromp, the caretaker of the well-appointed small museum in the town. Born in 1927, Kromp was seventeen years old at the time of the events described here, and remembers them well. The presence of Ferenc Szálasi, the Gold Train and the large numbers of Nyilas guards left an indelible impression.

3. M. Lackó, *Arrow-Cross Men. National Socialists, 1935–1944* (Akadémiai Kiadó, Budapest, 1969), pp. 93–5.

4. Although no doubt disingenuous, Gábor Vajna, Minister of the Interior in the Szálasi government, in cross-examination during his war crimes trial in February 1946, claimed ignorance of Toldi's actions. He said that he was so uninformed of what Toldi was doing that he had 'ordered an investigation'. His evidence was met by general hilarity in the courtroom, and heckling from the public: 'Rascal! You stole it!' (E. and L. Karsai, *A Szálasi per*, Reform Printing Office, Budapest, 1988, pp. 462–3).

5. YVA, TR-14-24, 4-25-46, pp. 29–31: witness protocol of Ernő Z. Kiss to Budapest Police.

6. Details of events in Brennbergbánya during this period are based on numerous first-hand reports recorded in July and August 1945 by Avar and his associates for the American Army Counter-Intelligence Corps; Avar also prepared a written account of the events while in Lichtenegg displaced persons camp, awaiting repatriation to Hungary. In August 1945 he and a number of other officials who had been on the train appeared in Salzburg before the Hungarian Repatriation Committee, and a six-page summary of Avar's statement to the Committee was eventually sent to the Hungarian Foreign Ministry, although it was delayed for months (Andor Gellért, Chairman, Repatriation Committee, Salzburg, to Foreign Minister János Gyöngyösi: see Ch. 3, n. 16). In September 1945, Avar and his associates returned to Budapest, where they were interrogated by the Hungarian police, and the interrogations were repeated in April and May 1946. (These interrogations were unavailable to me in the Hungarian archives, but a complete copy of the substantial war crimes investigation file of the Budapest Police exists in YVA, Jerusalem. See interrogations of László Avar, István Mingovits, Vilmos Biró, and Ernő Z. Kiss, in YVA, TR-14-24.) The frankness of these testimonies might be explained by the fact that any state official who assisted in locating and repatriating displaced assets would receive an amnesty for their actions under

the fascist regime. (See Summary of Press, US Military Representative to the Allied Control Commission, Hungary, 18 July 1946, NA, RG 260, G-2 'P' Files, Box 2768.) In February 1947 the police in Székesfehérvár interviewed a number of local citizens who were acquainted with Toldi's activities there as főispán. These interviews are also to be found in YVA, TR-14-24. French military authorities in Austria also interrogated some of the participants, and these sources will be cited separately. Additional details were provided in the Kromp interview (see n. 2 above).

7. The existence of other caches is frequently alluded to.

8. Szálasi government records are deposited in Captured Enemy Records, Series RG 242, T937, in the National Archives in College Park, Maryland, USA.

9. NA, RG 242, T937, microfilm 7, frames 137–40.

10. I am grateful to Szabolcs Szita for suggesting this explanation. Dr Szita is an expert on the records of the Szálasi regime in Hungarian archives.

11. Testimony of László Avar, 22 May 1946 (YVA, TR-14-24, pp. 31–8).

12. Paulovits testimony, see Ch. 3, n. 19.

13. Interview with Kromp, Brennbergbánya, November 2000.

14. When Avar protested at the destruction of objects of value, Toldi replied that he was acting under instructions from the Minister of the Interior, Vajna, who had decided on the break-up of the jewellery and the sorting into various kinds (YVA, TR-14-24, pp. 31–8: testimony of László Avar, 22 May 1946).

15. Details from the Mingovits, Biró and Paulovits interrogations, and the Kromp interview.

16. Testimony of Janós and Mrs Zajácz, 24 August 1945 (YVA, TR-14-24, in evidence of László Avar and Béla Zsolnay, p. 101).

17. Testimony of István Mingovits, op. cit.

18. Cf. the testimony of István Mingovits, 27 October 1945 (YVA, TR-14-14, pp. 116–17). Expatriate Hungarian fascist sources, which recount the story of the Gold Train and Brennbergbánya as one of patriotic heroism in the face of marauding Russians, claim the convoy even included tractors, which towed the goods across the border (F. Fiala and L. Marschalkó, *Vádló bitófák* *['Accusing Gallows']* (Munich, 1958; reprinted Budapest, 1999), p. 107). There is one mention of 'a tractor' as part of the vehicle convoy in the eyewitness testimonies (Gyula Galambos, 6 June 1945: YVA, TR-14-24, p. 71), but the many other detailed accounts make no mention of 'tractors' at all.

19. Testimony of István Mingovits and Vilmos Biró, 2 August 1945 (YVA, TR-14-24, pp. 82–99).

20. Kromp interview: see n. 2 above. The china was abandoned, and quickly

taken by local residents. Kromp was able to recall the scene clearly, fifty-five years later.

21. R. L. Bidwell, *Currency Conversion Tables. A Hundred Years of Change* (Rex Collings, London, 1970). Relative spending power decreased between 1945 and 2000 by a factor of 10.

22. Each of the subsequent testimonies by the major participants recalls the division of the cash. See, for example, the testimonies of Avar and Mingovits.

23. There are many copies of this document in the archives. The original was found on László Avar by the American authorities, but it played an important role in the post-war Hungarian efforts to regain control of the train's contents (NA, RG 260, USFA, USACA Property Control Branch, Box 20, Hungarian Restitution Commission, to W. Hallum Tuck, PCIRO, 29 May 1948). Accordingly, copies of the document were widely distributed (cf. NA, RG 260, USFA, USACA Property Control Branch, Box 20, 28 March 1945; and YVA, M61, File 35).

24. The testimonies of the participants are inconsistent as to the exact size of the train. The number of carriages cited here is taken from Avar's interrogation by the Hungarian police, 22 and 27 May 1946 (YVA, TR-14-24, pp. 31–8). Avar's account is the most coherent and detailed.

25. Report by Mingovits and Biró (prepared for CIC), 2 August 1945 (YVA, TR-14-24, pp. 82–99).

26. Toldi, letter to Avar, 30 March 1945 (YVA, TR-14-24, p. 27).

27. Statement by Colonel Markovits, July 1945 (NA, RG 260, USFA, USACA Property Control Branch, Box 20).

28. Testimony of János Molnár, 24 July 1945 (YVA, TR-14-24, p. 81). There is some documentary support for 31 March, but greater evidence for 30 March. The question is of no consequence for the events that followed.

CHAPTER 5 INTO AUSTRIA

1. G. Ránki, E. Pamlényi, *et al.* (eds.), *A Wilhelmstrasse és Magyarország. Német diplomáciai iratok Magyarországról 1933–1944 ['The Wilhelmstrasse and Hungary. German diplomatic documents from Hungary 1933–1944']* (Kossuth Konyvkiadó, Budapest, 1968).

2. Wilhelm Höttl Interrogation File, 31 May 1945 (NA, RG 319, IRR Files, Box 617, XE000882). The SD received instructions to evacuate all confidential files from Budapest on 29 September 1944 (Circle Report Weekly Summary No. 31, 27 October 1944, NA, RG 226, Entry 210, Box 8).

3. Evidence given on 24 August 1945, together with the testimony of Avar.

The physical description fits Höttl, who, as an intelligence officer, may well not have been in SS uniform at this stage of the war.

4. The Redoubt is considered here only from the perspective of the Axis, and specifically Höttl's manipulation of the concept. There is an extensive literature on the impact of the possibility of a Redoubt on Allied thinking, and an intense debate over Eisenhower's response to that possibility. For a full discussion of Allied strategy and the Redoubt, see S. E. Ambrose, *Eisenhower and Berlin, 1945. The Decision to Halt at the Elbe* (W. W. Norton, New York, 1967), and F. H. Hinsley, *British Intelligence in the Second World War: Its Influence on Strategy and Operations* (HMSO, London, 1988), pp. 711–18 and 733–7. For a more recent discussion that focuses on the role of the RSHA in propagating the Redoubt myth, see T. Naftali, 'Creating the Myth of the Alpenfestung: Allied Intelligence and the Collapse of the Nazi Police-State', in G. Bischof and A. Pelinka (eds.), *Austrian Historical Memory and National Identity* (Transaction Publishers, New Brunswick, 1997), pp. 203–46.

5. P. Biddiscombe, *Werwolf! The History of the National Socialist Guerrilla Movement, 1944–1946* (University of Wales Press, Cardiff, 1998), p. 178. 'In February and March 1945, aerial coverage revealed no fewer than seventy instances of underground construction or the caching of stores.'

6. See the discussion in P. R. Black, *Ernst Kaltenbrunner, Ideological Soldier of the Third Reich* (Princeton University Press, Princeton, NJ, 1984), pp. 235–44.

7. W. Höttl, *The Secret Front. The Story of Nazi Political Espionage* (Weidenfeld & Nicolson, London, 1953), p. 301.

8. See the map he prepared in mid-April 1945. The map was forwarded to Washington by the OSS station in Bern (Allen Dulles to P. Horton, 19 April 1945, RG 226, Entry 210, Box 479).

9. N. Petersen (ed.), *From Hitler's Doorstep. The Wartime Intelligence Reports of Allen Dulles, 1942–1945* (Pennsylvania State University Press, 1996), Docs. 5–45, 66, 75, 98, 107, 121; J. Heideking and C. Mauch (eds.), *American Intelligence and the German Resistance to Hitler. A Documentary History* (Westview Press, Boulder, Colorado, 1996), pp. 386–91; Document 95a, 27 March 1945, Memorandum from William Donovan to Joint Chiefs of Staff: 'Approaches from Austrian and Bavarian Nazis'.

10. Naftali, op. cit., outlines Dulles's many sources of information on the Redoubt.

11. Biddiscombe, op. cit., p. 182.

12. When the Americans were able to do a head count on the non-Austrian local residents in their zone, they discovered 89,000 Hungarians, and many

other displaced persons. The population was 38 per cent above its permanent resident level (USFA to War Department, SGS813, 11 August 1945, NA, RG 318, Entry 57, Box 86). Of the 89,000 Hungarians, the Americans estimated that 40,000–50,000 would not want to be repatriated, presumably because of their association with the Szálasi regime (AusPolAd to State Department, 27 August 1945, A29, ibid.). Approximately 1,000 were Hungarian Jews liberated from concentration camps in Austria (AusPolAd to State Department, 15 August 1945, ibid.).

13. Appendix B, 'Hungarian SS "Hunyadi Division"', USFA Intelligence Summary No. 15, 15 September 1945, NA, RG 59, 740.00119 Control (Austria).

14. Biddiscombe, op. cit., p. 186. Biddiscombe cites US 3rd Army reports that the SS troops were 'receiving organized outside support obtaining supplies'.

15. G. J. Horwitz, *In the Shadow of Death. Living Outside the Gates of Mauthausen* (Free Press, New York, 1992), Ch. 7.

16. OSS Field Memorandum No. 252, 11 April 1945, 'Location of Hungarian Government Documents; Disorganization of Hungarian Communications, 1 December 1944 to 27 February 1945' (NA, RG 226, Entry 210, Box 518). The condition of the railway track system throughout Europe was an important subject for Allied intelligence in 1944–1945. The best available maps for the Hungarian and Austrian railways at that time remain those prepared for the US army in 1944. They show every track, including the narrow-gauge lines for collecting crops from individual farms (NA, RG 77, AMS M671).

17. The account of the train's journey to Hallein is based on the eighteen-page detailed testimony of István Mingovits and Vilmos Biró, prepared in late July–early August and dated 2 August 1945 (YVA, TR-14-24, pp. 82–99).

18. Testimony of Avar, 22 May 1946 (YVA, TR-14-24, p. 31).

19. Mingovits and Biró give the name as 'Wiesenbach', but as Wieselburg is the only town with a similar name on the short Wilhelmsburg–Amstetten line, they were apparently confused.

20. Perhaps for this reason Hopfgarten was spared the worst of the bombing. In 1945 only one bomb fell there, in February (T. Albrich and A. Gisinger, *Im Bombenkrieg. Tirol und Vorarlberg, 1943–1945 ['Strategic Bombing in Tyrol and Vorarlberg, 1943–1945']* (Haymon Verlag, Innsbruck, 1992, p. 322).

21. She was his second wife. According to a comment by Avar, Toldi's first wife had been Jewish (testimony of Avar, 22 May 1946).

22. Testimony of Kiss, 25 April 1946 (YVA, TR-14-24, pp. 24–36).

23. Toldi to Avar, 8 April 1945 (YVA, TR-14-24, p. 29).

24. Toldi to Avar, 10 April 1945 (YVA, TR-14-24, p. 31).

25. Testimony of Mingovits and Biro, 2 August 1945.

26. ibid.

27. Testimony of Avar, 22 May 1946.

28. Protocol of meeting of Hopfgarten, 7 p.m., 16 April 1945 (YVA, TR-14-24, p. 35).

29. Avar Report, 17 October 1945 (HNA, XXXIII-5-b, 4.d.).

30. List of valuables stored at Brennbergbánya, October 1945, ibid.

31. Evidence of Emil Csatáry to Székesfehérvár Police, 8 February 1947 (YVA, TR-14-24, pp. 21–2). The second was Ernő Griell, one of three officials engaged in sorting the most valuable goods in the bathhouse at Brennbergbánya.

32. Testimony of Mingovits and Biró, 2 August 1945.

33. Avar had actually prepared a *Marschbefehl* (transportation order) on 15 April but cancelled it the next day. He went to Kitzbühel, probably to obtain countervailing instructions from any Hungarian government authority that might have been in the area, but to no avail. So the next day the train was readied for the trip to Innsbruck. (Handwritten notes by Avar, 15 and 16 April 1945, YVA, TR-14-24, p. 34.)

34. The neighbouring town of Rattenberg was hit at the same time to ensure the total destruction of the rail bridge. Over 300 Allied bombers took part in the raid (Albrich and Gisinger, op. cit., pp. 337–9).

35. Protocol recorded at Hopfgarten on 21 April 1945, 'On opening of wagon DR. Munchen No. 91482' (YVA, TR-14-24, p. 37).

36. If this means lodging a complaint with the local police, the records of the Hopfgarten Gendarmerie contain no mention of it. In fact, Hopfgarten has chosen to forget the entire period. The police ledger for activities in the last three months of the Second World War have been removed, and a new ledger, appropriately sanitized, has been inserted. The ledger now contains no mention of the month-long stay of the Gold Train. (I am grateful to my colleague Dr Thomas Albrich, University of Innsbruck, for this information.)

37. Letter from Toldi to Avar and Sándor Ercse, March 1945 (YVA, TR-14-24, p. 22).

38. Authorization dated 7 April 1945 (YVA, M61, File 35).

39. Toldi to Avar, 23 April 1945 (YVA, TR-14-24, p. 40). The eight adults would presumably have included Toldi, Balogh, their wives, Miklós Dobai (a Finance Directorate official, acting as driver) and Lieut. Ernő Griell (see n. 31 above), as well as Toldi's two stepdaughters.

40. Testimony of Mingovits, Biró and Galambos; also protocol recorded at Hopfgarten, 24 April 1945 (YVA, TR-14-24, p. 42).

41. Toldi to Avar, 26 April 1945 (YVA, TR-14-24, p. 43). According to

Mingovits and Biró, a third Toldi letter arrived by mail, but there is no trace of it in the records.

42. Testimony of Mingovits and Biró, op. cit.

43. ibid.

44. Vajta's role in the Gold Train saga is mentioned in the Mingovits and Biró testimony, but is also supported by a later report prepared by the head of the Hungarian Repatriation Commission in Innsbruck, Dr E. Révész. Révész interviewed Vajta some years after the war and obtained some details from him about the train, although Vajta failed to mention his attempt to gain control of the treasure. (Révész's report was appendixed to a report by Viktor Schwarz on behalf of the Budapest Jewish Community, 14 January 1946, on HNA, XIX-J-1-k 112.d 46/1946 Sch/W.)

45. Testimony of Avar, 22 May 1946.

46. Toldi to Avar, 27 April 1945 (YVA, TR-14-24, pp. 45–6).

47. Receipts for the goods, and accounts of these events, are on YVA, TR-14-24, pp. 52–6.

48. Log of events, prepared at Böckstein on 6 May 1945 (YVA, TR-14-24, pp. 55–6).

49. Testimony of Mingovits and Biró, op. cit.

50. Log of activities, Böckstein station, 7 May 1945 (YVA, TR-14-24, pp. 59–60).

51. He sent a representative of the Ministry of War Production contingent to repeat the message, hoping to impress the Swiss with its urgency (Avar testimony, 22 May 1945, op. cit.). He may also have approached Vatican representatives (Mingovits and Biró testimony, op. cit.).

52. Report of Guard Duty, Böckstein, 10 May 1945 (YVA, TR-14-24, p. 62).

53. The account of the last two weeks of the war in Austria are based on C. B. MacDonald, *The Last Offensive* (US Government Print Office, Washington, DC, 1973), pp. 433–42; F. L. Gurley, 'Einmarsch der amerikanischen Armee in Westösterreich, April/Mai 1945', in M. Rauchensteiner and W. Etschmann (eds.), *Österreich 1945. Ein Ende und viele Anfänge ['Austria 1945. An Ending and Many Beginnings']* (Graz, Styria, 1997), pp. 145–56; and G. L. Weinberg, *A World at Arms. A Global History of World War II* (Cambridge, University Press, 1994), p. 817.

54. An American intelligence report laconically reported that the Hungarian SS division was lost: 'American troops captured the remaining 8,000 Hungarians, who were waiting in the Austrian mountains and were quite sure that they were in the "general territory" of Nürnberg' (USFA Intelligence Summary No. 15, 15 September 1945, NA, RG 59, 740.00119Control(Austria).

55. MacDonald, op. cit., p. 441.

56. Testimony of Colonel Markovits, July 1945 (NA, RG 260, USFA, USACA, Property Control Branch, Box 20). However, this testimony is of doubtful reliability as it is clearly tendentious on many points.

57. Testimony of Avar, 22 May 1946.

58. Toldi affidavit delivered before Colonel Henri Jung, 11 August 1945 (Colmar, AUT 3180, D. 510, Trésor Hongrois, 1945–1953).

59. Testimony of Avar, 22 May 1946. Avar may well have confused this purported delivery with the truckloads of furs that arrived at Hopfgarten in the middle of April, as reported by Mingovits and Biró.

60. Reports of gold trials, *Volkszeitung* (Innsbruck) and *Tiroler Tageszeitung*, 28 September 1946.

61. Affidavit of Colonel Toldi, 11 August 1945 (Colmar, AUT 3180, D. 510, Trésor Hongrois, 1945–1953).

62. From '679' to '110', 7 May 1945 (NA, RG 226, Entry 210, Box 375).

63. E. and L. Karsai, *A Szálasi per* (Reform Printing Office, Budapest, 1988), p. 463.

64. Liaison Department, Sûreté of Vorarlberg to Head of Security Section, Innsbruck (Colmar, AUT 3180, D. 510, Trésor Hongrois, 1945–1953), DV/2925/SP.

65. In this case, his statement that he had no idea who Toldi was. The Hungarian was introduced to him, he stated, by the Archduke Albrecht of Habsburg (a pretender to the throne of Hungary, a confidant of Himmler and a right-wing member of the Hungarian parliament), who happened to be staying at the same hotel as Höttl. (Procès verbal No. 64, Interrogation of Wilhelm Höttl on Hungarian Treasure, 25 October 1949) (Colmar, AUT 1261, Restitutions Biens Hongrois, 1948–1953, Demandes de Restitutions Nos. 394 and 395.) But if they had not met previously, then why would Toldi entrust Höttl with all the gold? It is also improbable that Höttl, who was so closely involved with the affairs of Pálffy's party, was not familiar with Toldi as főispán of Székesfehérvár.

66. Petainek or Petainchik.

67. SSU report, 'German Intelligence Service W/T contact in Switzerland', 2 June 1946 (NA, RG 226, Entry 215, Box 5, File 26051).

68. Westen had an enamel factory in Poland – an uncanny similarity to the situation of Oskar Schindler. Presumably, like all German factory-owners in Poland during the war, and again like Schindler, he had used the available slave labour. Unlike Schindler, Westen did not use this as an opportunity to save lives.

69. Procès verbal No. 63, Interrogation of Friedrich Westen on Hungarian

Treasure, 24 October 1949 (Colmar, AUT 1261, Restitutions Biens Hongrois 1948–1953, Demandes de Restitutions No. 394 and 395).

70. N. Petersen (ed.), *From Hitler's Doorstep*, op. cit., Dulles to OSS, No. 6097, 28 February 1945, and telegrams 6149, 6209, 7037.

71. 'Intermezzo in Salzburg', *Der Spiegel*, 22 April 1953, in Höttl's IRR (Counter-Intelligence) file (NA, RG 319, Box 617).

72. US Army Finance Division officers interrogated Höttl in late 1945 and 1946 while he was in American detention, suspecting that he and Westen had been involved in smuggling currency and gold to Switzerland on behalf of Ernst Kaltenbrunner, the second-in-command of the SS after Heinrich Himmler. Höttl admitted making a number of trips to Switzerland with Westen in the last weeks of the war, although he insisted that they were for the purpose of meeting Dulles (NA, RG 56, Box 239, 'Preliminary Report on External Assets of Ernst Kaltenbrunner' (n.d.)).

73. Procès verbal No. 64, Interrogation of Wilhelm Höttl on Hungarian Treasure, 25 October 1949 (Colmar, AUT 1261, Restitutions Biens Hongrois 1948–1953, Demandes de Restitutions Nos. 394 and 395; and Westen testimony, 24 October 1949, ibid.)

74. Head of the Hungarian Chancellery in Innsbruck to Head of the RRCB Division on Hungarian Treasure, 24 October 1948 (Colmar, AUT 1261, Restitutions Biens Hongrois, 1948–1953, Demandes de Restitutions Nos. 394 and 395).

75. ibid. The Vorarlberg Sûreté office subsequently established that Höttl and Westen had ties to Nigg, and that the latter was involved in the disposal of the Gold Train loot. (Commissioner of Police, Head of the French Liaison Department of the Sûreté of Vorarlberg, to the Head of the Security Section, Innsbruck, 12 September 1949 (Colmar, AUT 3180, D. 510, Trésor Hongrois (1945–1953) DV/2925/SP).)

76. Oláh was invited back to the consulate in 1948 to repeat his story (protocol prepared by Károly Oláh at the Hungarian Consulate, Bratislava, 8 December 1948, HNA, XIX. J-1-k, 23/g tétel).

CHAPTER 6   IN ALLIED HANDS

1. SHAEF to War Department, S 87263, 6 May 1945 (NA, RG 218, JCS Geographic Files 1942–1945, Box 72, Germany 386; and SHAEF to War Department, S 92053, 21 June 1945, ibid.).

2. Joel Fisher, confidential memo to General McSherry and Colonel Bernard Bernstein (Financial Department, SHAEF), 26 April 1945, in Fisher Papers.

3. For a detailed and reliable account on a subject that has attracted much sensationalism, see Greg Bradsher, 'Nazi Gold: The Merkers Mine Treasure', *Prologue*, Spring 1999, vol. 31, no. 1.

4. W. Bedell Smith to Combined Chiefs of Staff, 20 April 1945 (NA, RG 218, JCS Geographic Files 1942–1945, Box 72, Germany 386).

5. OMGUS to AGWAR, CC-1796, 30 September 1947 (NA, RG 260, OMGUS Property Division, 1945–1948, Box 5). The fate of this victim loot, known as the 'Melmer deposits' after the SS officer charged with delivering them from the extermination and concentration camps to the Reichsbank, is discussed in Ch. 10.

6. SHAEF to Combined Civil Affairs Committee, War Department, 22 June 1945, ibid.

7. An alternative site (Fraham, near Linz) is given in an early report of the discovery of the crown: HQ, USFA, to War Department, 7 August 1945 (NA, RG 319, Entry 57A, Box 86). The Mattsee location is supported by subsequent accounts of the capture of the Hungarian national relics (NA, RG 59, Entry A-15398, Box 2, File 'Crown') and is supported by recent Hungarian scholarship (see B. Illényi, 'The Adventures of the Holy Crown of Hungary', *New Hungarian Quarterly* 41, Budapest (Summer 2000), 32–61).

8. *New York Times*, 21 May 1945, p. 8.

9. Duty Logs, Böckstein, 11–14 May 1945 (YVA, TR-14-24, pp. 63–4).

10. Testimony of Mingovits and Biró.

11. Duty Logs, Böckstein, 11–12 May 1945 (YVA, TR-14-24, pp. 63–4).

12. G-2, 3rd Infantry Division, Report on Hungarian Gold Train, 16 May 1945 (NA, RG 260, USFA, USAC, Property Control Branch, Box 20).

13. 18 May 1945, p. 8.

14. Property Control Officer, Salzburg, to Commanding General, XV Corps for G-5, 21 April 1945 (NA, RG 260, USFA, USACA, Property Control Branch, Box 20).

15. Report on inspection of Gold Train, 29 May 1945, ibid. This report also mentions 'Dr Árpád Toldi, who speaks English'. As Toldi was in Dornbirn, close to the Swiss border at the other end of Austria at that time, the author of the report must have misread his notes.

16. General Townsend to AGWAR, War Department, Z-131, 9 June 1945 (NA, RG 84, Budapest Embassy, Box 60, Hungarian Property file).

17. Even twelve months after the end of the war, production in agriculture and industry was only a fraction of pre-war levels (National Bank of Hungary, 27th Annual Report, p. 10). American intelligence sources estimated that in 1947 industrial production would be at 30 per cent of its usual capacity (NA,

RG 59, 740.00119Control(Austria)/2-0946 'Disorder Reigns in Hungary', USFA Intelligence Summary No. 36, appendix B).

18. Hungarian Foreign Ministry memo to US Mission, Budapest, 18 June 1945 (HNA, XIX-J-1-k, 53 doboz, 23g). This message was conveyed by ambassador Arthur Schoenfeld to the State Department as No. 183, 19 June 1945 (RG 84, op. cit.).

19. Reports submitted to 21st Ordinary Annual Meeting of the General Assembly of the National Bank of Hungary, 27 March 1947, p. 10 (NA, RG 319, G-2 'P' Files, 1946–1951, Box 159).

20. By June 1946 the Bank of Hungary was printing 100-billion pengő notes (*Le Monde*, 4 June 1946). In the Hungarian currency reform of August 1946, 200 million pengő were exchangeable for one forint, the new unit of currency.

21. Colonel Bernstein to General Lucius Clay, Monthly Report on Financial Aspects of Allied Occupation of Germany, May 1945 (NA, RG 59, 740.0019Control(Germany)/6-2046).

22. M. Himler, *Igy néztek ki. A magyar nemzet sírasó ['This is what it looked like. The Gravediggers of the Hungarian Nation']* (St Mark's Printing Co., New York, 1958), *passim*.

23. Testimony of Avar, 27 May 1946. It has not been possible to trace the records of the 430th Detachment of the CIC for this encounter, or indeed for anything in the immediate post-war period.

24. Protocol, Werfen railway station, 19 July 1945 (YVA, TR-14-24, pp. 79–80); and Mingovits and Biró testimony, op. cit.

25. US Army guards were provided by the 242 Infantry Battalion: 'Movement of Hungarian Property from Werfen', Military Government, Land, Salzburg, to Commanding General, II Corps, 17 July 1945 (NA, RG 260, USFA, USACA, Property Control Division, Box 20).

26. For a detailed description of the cargo, see inventory, pp. 102–3.

27. 'Request for Additional Warehouse Space', Property Control Office, July 1945 (NA, RG 260, USFA, USACA, Property Control Division, Box 20).

28. Protocol at Werfen railway station, ibid.

29. Dornbirn was then a town of 20,000 inhabitants, with only a few guest-houses and no hotels. A search of their *Meldebücher* (registration books) did not uncover 'Toldi' or any aliases he was known to be using.

30. Third Army arrest report, 21 May 1945 (NA, RG 226, Field Station Reports, London X-2, Box 55); and OSS Paris to OSS Bern, No. 1326, 25 May 1945, ibid.

31. *Szabadság* ('Freedom'), 20 July 1945: article by Gyula István Révész, p. 3.

32. A long feature article on the history of the train appeared in *Képes Figyelő* ('Illustrated Observer') on 17 November 1945 (p. 7). There have been dozens

of similar articles over the years. Ironically, this issue also carried a report of the court hearing for István Mingovits (cf. Ch. 3, n. 4).

33. Dénes Csőpey, who escaped to Italy in April 1945 (NA, RG 260, Entry 211, Box 49, OSS Classified sources and methods, 9 August 1945).

34. Two independent sources mention the involvement of Czech soldiers. In a January 1946 report to the Hungarian Foreign Ministry, the DEGOB representative in Vienna (see Ch. 7), Viktor Schwartz, mentioned the arrest in the French zone of 'Czech soldiers who were looking for buried gold' (Report of the Aid Committee for Jewish Deportees, Vienna, 14 January 1946, HNA, Foreign Ministry, XIX-J-1-k 112.d 46/1946 Sch/W). French records, written two years after the event, mention Czech soldiers in a lorry, looking for the same thing (Colonel H. Jung, Head of the Control Detachment in Vorarlberg to Delegated General, Head of the Control Mission in Austria, RRCB Section – Mr Sayen. Subject: Hungarian Treasure DV/3971/CB 5242, 10 November 1947, Colmar, AUT 3180, D. 510, Trésor Hongrois, 1945–1953).

35. In a 1947 report sent to his Foreign Ministry, the Hungarian consul in Bratislava at the time refers to his investigation of Oláh's claims made in late July 1945. He did not explain *how* he investigated the existence of Hungarian gold in that part of Austria. (HNA, Report, 25 February 1947, XIX. J-1-k, 23/g tétel.)

36. K. Eisterer, 'Die Souvenirs d'Autriche vom Oberst Henri Jung', *Vierteljahresschrift für Geschichte under Gegenwarts Vorarlbergs* 47 (3), 1995, 266–72.

37. Affidavit to Colonel Jung from Colonel Toldi, 11 August 1945 (Colmar, AUT 3180, D. 510, Trésor Hongrois, 1945–1953).

38. Colonel Jung to Administrator General, French Forces in Austria, Innsbruck, 13 August 1945, ibid.

39. ibid.

40. General Cherrière to Couve de Murville, CGAAA, Paris, 15 May 1947 (Colmar, Vienne 217, Hongrie 45-55, File 5).

41. Testimony of Farkas and Balogh, No. 71, B.Doc Tyrol, 23 August 1945 (Colmar, AUT 1260, Restitutions Biens Hongrois). One year later Farkas tried to sue the authorities in order to have these goods returned to him. He did not succeed. (There are various documents in the same file.)

42. List of cases and suitcases found by Lieut. Marcel and Lieut. Boyer, 1 November 1945 (Colmar, AUT 3180, D. 510, Trésor Hongrois, 1945–1953).

CHAPTER 7 THE SURVIVORS

1. Civil Affairs Guide: 'Military Government and Problems with Respect to the Jews in Germany' 29 July 1944 (NA, RG 260, Office of the Director of Intelligence, Box 154).

2. 'Memoranda on Property of Racial or Religious Minorities Seized by the Germans or Otherwise Transferred under Duress', 10 April 1944, and 'Recommendations on Compensation for Injuries to Members of German Racial or Religious Minorities', 22 April 1944 (NA, RG 59, Lot Files, Records of Harley Notter, Box 49, Records of Economic Committees).

3. 'Note on Allocating a Share of German Reparation for Displaced Victims of Nazi Germany', 13 November 1945 (NA, RG 59, 740.00119EW/2-2045). For a full discussion of Allied policy on reparations and restitution as it affected the Jewish survivors, see Ronald W. Zweig, 'Restitution and the Problem of Jewish Displaced Persons in Anglo-American Relations, 1944–1948', *American Jewish History* LXXVIII, No. 1, September 1988, 54–78.

4. For a detailed account of the negotiations in Paris over Article 8, see 'Final Report on the Paris Conference on Reparation, November 9, 1945 to December 21, 1945', James W. Angell, 18 February 1946 (NA, RG 43, Entry 31, Box 12).

5. The State Department defined non-monetary gold for the US delegate to the Allied Gold Commission in the following terms: '[the] entire contents of boxes of valuables taken from concentration camp and political and racial victims excluding ecclesiastical articles identified as belonging to particular faith and returned to such faith, and identifiable articles which it is practicable to return to former owners. Term thus includes jewelry, stones, currency, securities, etc.' (Dean Acheson to Goldthwaite Dorr, No. 317, 2 April 1946, NA, RG 59, 740.00119EW.)

6. 'Decisions of the Reparations Conference . . .', Nehemiah Robinson, 21 January 1946 (American Jewish Archives (AJA), World Jewish Congress, Series H, File 179).

7. Louis Lipsky, American Jewish Conference, to James Byrnes, Secretary of State, 7 February 1946 (NA, RG 59, 740.00119EW/2-0746).

8. John Kenneth Galbraith, Office of Economic Security Policy, State Department, to Louis Lipsky, 18 March 1946 (NA, RG 59, 740.00119EW/2-0746).

9. Despatch 28608, US Embassy, London, to State Department, 'British Attitudes to Article Eight of the Final Act on Reparations', 3 March 1946 (NA, RG 59, 740.00119EW/3-246).

10. Gallman to State Department, No. 4224, 6 April 1946 (NA, RG 59, 501.BD Refugees/4-1646).

11. General J. Hilldring to Dr Eli Ginzberg, 10 May 1946 (NA, RG 59, 740.00119EW/5-1046).

12. 'Complete Report on Detailed Estimate of Cost in Money and Manpower for the Continuance of Displaced Persons Camps', June 1946 (NA, RG 107, Asst. Sec. of War, Correspondence of Howard Petersen, December 1945–August 1947, 383.7-386.3, Box 31).

13. Eli Ginzberg, *My Brother's Keeper* (Transaction Publishers, New Brunswick, 1989), pp. 74–5.

14. Eli Ginzberg, *Final Report on the Five Power Conference on Reparations for the Non-Repatriable Victims of German Action*, 31 June 1946 (NA, RG 165, Entry 476, Box 833, 'General Claims Law'). For the British view of the Five Power Conference, and a frank account of their failure to block Ginzberg's appointment of the Jewish Agency and the Joint as the designated operating agencies to receive the victim loot, see the memo by MacKillop, 'Allocation of a Share of Reparation to Victims of German Action', 17 June 1946 (PRO, FO 371/57744 WR1603).

15. Maurice Perlzweig, memo to Congress Office Committee, 23 January 1946 (AJA, WJC, Series H, File 179, 'Indemnification').

16. Irwin Mason to Ginzberg and State Department, No. 923, Vienna, 23 June 1946 (NA, RG 59, 740.00119EW/6-2846).

17. Mason to Ginzberg and State Department, No. 3280, Paris, 3 July 1946 (NA, RG 59, 740.00119EW/7-0346).

18. Statistics based on R. L. Braham, *The Politics of Genocide. The Holocaust in Hungary*, vol. II (Columbia University Press, New York, 1994), pp. 1296–1301; L. Varga, 'The Losses of Hungarian Jewry. A Contribution to a Statistical Overview', in R. L. Braham (ed.), *Studies on the Holocaust in Hungary* (Columbia University Press, New York, 1990), pp. 256–65; and Z. Erez, 'Holocaust of Hungarian Jewry – Statistical Survey' [Hebrew], *Yalkut Moreshet* 57 (1994), 43–60. The statistics are confused by the distinction between members of Jewish communities and those Hungarian Christian converts that the anti-Semitic laws defined as racially Jewish, and by the changing borders of Hungary.

19. R. Horváth, 'Jews in Hungary after the Holocaust: the National Relief Committee for Deportees, 1945–1950', *Journal of Israeli History* 19 (2) (1998), 69–91, gives different figures – a total of 83,331 for returnees to all of Hungary during 1945 (p. 71). The figures of Braham, Varga and Erez are based on the statistical summaries prepared by the World Jewish Congress offices in Budapest. Horváth's study is based on a wide reading of the records of the Budapest offices of the Congress.

20. Interview with Dr Shimshon Nathan, Oral History Project (hereafter OHP), Institute for Contemporary Jewry, Hebrew University, Jerusalem (File 103(4)).
21. It consisted of a wagon-load of tomato soup (interview with Dr Frigyes Görög, ibid.).
22. H. Eichler, 'New Era in Hungarian Zionism, 1945–1946', *Dapim LeHeker HaShoah* 8 (1990), p. 83.
23. Report of the Activities of the Hungarian Section of the World Jewish Congress, 18 October 1945 (AJA, WJC Series H, File 173 'Hungary – 1945').
24. Horváth, op. cit. A popular joke in Hungary after the war reflects the anti-Semitism that thrived even in post-war Hungary – 'More Jews returned from Auschwitz than were deported there.'
25. Y. Bauer, *Out of the Ashes. The Impact of American Jews on post-Holocaust European Jewry* (Pergamon Press, Oxford, 1989), pp. 136–7.
26. At one point the Joint was paying the salaries of 3,600 people (Rabbi Julius S. Fisher, memorandum for World Jewish Congress, 'Postwar Developments and the Present Position of the Jews in Hungary', AJA, WJC, Series H, File 173).
27. By the end of 1949, 57,000 people were still receiving direct aid from the JDC. The Joint's programme was terminated early in 1952, following increasing Communist harassment.
28. Ferenc Nagy, the second prime minister of Hungary after the war (1946–1947) and leader of the Smallholders Party, attributes the riots to provocation by regional Communist Party officials hoping to gain the sympathy of the local population (F. Nagy, *The Struggle Behind the Iron Curtain* (Macmillan, New York, 1948), pp. 245–9). Eichler, op. cit., supports Nagy, adding that the Communist Party was also trying to lose the stigma of being a party led by Jews (p. 85). See also the discussion in S. Reuveni, 'Antisemitism in Hungary in the Years 1945–1946' [Hebrew], *Yalkut Moreshet* 43–44 (1987), 177–200 *passim*.
29. NA, RG 84, US Embassy, Budapest, Box 13, File 'Anglo-American Committee of Inquiry'. The report was prepared especially for this committee, and was dated 24 February 1946.
30. An additional 55,000 surviving converts of Jewish origin were not polled as to their emigration plans.
31. The actual migration of Hungarian Jewry for the period 1945–1946 was approximately 18,000 (Eichler, op. cit., p. 99). As late as 1947 an internal JDC report stated that 75 per cent wished to leave (cited in Bauer, op. cit., p. 140). The number of Jews who left Hungary (illegally) in 1948–1949 was approximately 30,000 (Bauer, p. 148).

32. The total number of illegal immigrants during 1946–1948 was 72,000. Approximately half of them came from the Allied zones of occupation in central Europe, and the rest from Romania and Bulgaria.

33. Term invented by the US army to describe this population movement. The policy was never formally committed to paper as it would have been a slap in the face to the British. But it was consistently pursued by the American occupation authorities, and they communicated their intentions unofficially to the Jewish organizations through the Adviser on Jewish Affairs to the Commanding Officer of the US Forces (Rabbi Philip Bernstein) and through the assistant to General John H. Hilldring, Assistant Secretary of State for Occupied Areas, Herbert Fierst (interview with the author).

34. T. Albrich, *Exodus durch Österreich. Die Jüdischen Flüchtlinge, 1945– 1948 ['Exodus through Austria. Jewish Refugees, 1945–1948']* (Haymon Verlag, Innsbruck, 1987), and T. Albrich (ed.), *Flucht nach Eretz Israel. Die Bricha und der jüdische Exodus durch Österreich nach 1945 ['Flight to Israel. The Bricha and the Jewish Exodus through Austria after 1945']* (Studien Verlag, Innsbruck, 1998), *passim*.

35. Gideon Ruffer changed his name to Rafael. Rafael became a professional diplomat in Israel's Foreign Ministry, and was for many years Director-General of the ministry.

36. Gideon Rafael ms. (18 pp.), undated (CZA, S25, File 10719).

37. Petition by the Central Bureau of Hungarian Jews Temporary Managing Committee, 20 December 1945 (HNA, Foreign Ministry, XIX-J-1-k 112.d. 134 KHJ-946).

38. Munkácsi and Stöckler to the American Legation, 20 December 1945 (NA, RG 84, Box 65, File 'Jewish Property'). The same document can be found at HNA, Foreign Ministry, XIX-J-1-k 2529/1949.

39. Schoenfeld to State Department, Despatch No. 478, 31 October 1945 (NA, RG 84, Box 60, 'Hungarian Property in US Zones').

40. Munkácsi and Stöckler to the American Legation, 18 February 1946 (NA, RG 84, Box 103, File 'Jewish Property').

41. Memo by László Ferencz on the history of the Gold Train, 8 February 1949 (HNA, Foreign Ministry, XIC-J-1-k 112.d 70.280/1947).

42. Memorandum, 4 February 1946 (HNA, XIC-J-1-k 40.307/4 112.d 120/ 46 Sch/W). The records of the Jewish community, including those of DEGOB, were seized by the Hungarian Secret Police in the early 1950s, and only selected parts of the collection survived. With the fall of communism in Hungary in 1989 the Secret Police records were moved to the Hungarian National Archives, including the records of the community.

43. Ruffer (Rafael) to Eliezer Kaplan, Treasurer, Jewish Agency, 19 March

1946 (CZA, S53/1654). It is interesting that a copy of this letter is also in the papers of the Board of Deputies of British Jews, suggesting that it was circulated among a number of organizations (Greater London Record Office, ACC: 3121, C11/7/3b/6).

44. ibid.

45. David Ben-Gurion Diaries, Munich, 30 January 1946 (Ben-Gurion Archives, Sde Boker).

46. ibid., Frankfurt, 1 February 1946. In the three days Rafael travelled with Ben-Gurion, the Gold Train was frequently discussed.

47. Extract of letter from Ruffer (Rafael), Frankfurt, 2 February 1946 (CZA, S25, File 5197).

48. Ruffer (Rafael) to Eliezer Kaplan, Treasurer, Jewish Agency, 19 March 1946, op. cit.

49. Frigyes Görög interview, see n. 51 below.

50. Between 1945 and 1952, when it was forced to close its offices in Budapest, the Joint spent $49,585,870 in Hungary, 14.4 per cent of its overall budget (*JDC Annual Reports*, 1945–1952, New York).

51. These included discreet supplies of penicillin from the USA for the wife of one of the (communist) generals of the Hungarian armed forces. She had been raped by a Russian soldier and contracted venereal disease. Antibiotics were a rare commodity in the post-war world, and the Joint's ability to obtain them in America won it friends in Hungary. (Interview with Dr Frigyes Görög, director of the JDC Budapest office, 1945–September 1947, OHP, March 1968.) In March 1946 six boxes of sulphathiozole tablets, costing $136 – an astronomical price at the time – were sent to the Jewish community in Budapest (Kurt Grossman to Siegfried Roth, AJA, WJC, Series H, File 173, 'Hungarian Section', 1947).

52. The fact that there were many Jews among the Hungarian communists did not guarantee a favourable reception. Like the Christian converts, the communists of Jewish origin took pains to distance themselves from the Jewish community and to hide their Jewish roots. (In the convoluted ethnic politics of central and eastern Europe, this is the reason why the Jewish communists were suspected of encouraging the anti-Jewish mass demonstration of workers in Diósgyőr-Miskolc. The same communists of Jewish origin, including Rákosi, led the anti-Zionist and anti-Semitic show trials that swept the Soviet bloc in 1951–1953.)

53. *Ha'aretz*, Supplement, 17 January 1997, pp. 25–6.

54. Interview with Shimshon Nathan (OHP, 103 (4), pp. 30–31).

55. Ferenc Nagy, prime minister of Hungary, to the Jewish Agency, 10 May 1946 (CZA, S25/5197).

56. Interview with Shimshon Nathan, Oral History Project, Institute for Contemporary Jewry, Hebrew University, Jerusalem, 103 (4).

57. Rafael to Eliezer Kaplan, Treasurer, Jewish Agency, 7 February 1949, CZA, S25, File 10119.

58. Ernest Marton to Leon Kubowitzki, 15 March 1946 (AJA, World Jewish Congress, Series H, File 174 'Hungary 1946'). Marton stated that the 'experts' were brought in from Milan by order of General Clark, but there are no other documents corroborating this claim. On the question of the future fate of the Gold Train, Marton informed the Congress leadership that the leaders of the Jewish community in Budapest agreed that 'the Jewish fortune brought out of Hungary . . . can under no circumstances be returned to Hungary in its entirety, but should be used for Jewish communal causes . . . for the emigration, settlement and integration in Palestine of those Jews who will hopefully leave Hungary soon and in large numbers'. Gerhard Riegner, the Congress representative in Geneva, sent the organization's head office a similar letter to that by Marton. He mentioned the $300 million, and the fact that the Hungarian community did not want the victim assets returned to Hungary. (Riegner to Maurice Perlzweig, Leon Kubowitzki and Nehemiah Robinson, 28 February 1946, HUC, World Jewish Congress, Series H, Box 175, File 'Hungary 1946'.)

CHAPTER 8   GOLD AND POLITICS IN WASHINGTON

1. 'Russian Statement on the Hungarian Economy', US Embassy to State Department, No. 1302, 23 April 1946 (NA, RG 59, 864.50; cited in FRUS, Vol. VI, 1946).

2. B. Zhelitski, 'Postwar Hungary, 1944–1946', in N. Naimark and L. Gibianskii (eds.), *The Establishment of Communist Regimes in Eastern Europe, 1944–1949* (Westview Press, Boulder, Colorado, 1997), p. 76. American official sources in 1947 believed that Hungary was lagging badly in the schedule of payments ('Memorandum: Reparations Obligation' (draft), NA, RG 43, Box 141).

3. Despatch No. 946 from Vienna (USFA) to State Department, 14 March 1946 (NA, RG 59, 740.00119Control(Austria); USFA to WBS, Paris, OMGUS and USFET P-7901, 9 May 1946, RG 260, OMGUS, Restitution Branch, 1945–1948, Box 5; and USFA to WAR COS OPD, 5 June 1946, RG 260, USFA, USACA, Property Control Branch, Box 21).

4. Intelligence Research Report, OCL 3773, 24 July 1946 (NA, RG 43, Box 99, 'Council of Foreign Ministers').

5. Frigyes Görög interview, see Ch. 7, n. 51.

6. SSU Report, 'Hungary's Stand on Hungarian Wealth in the American Zones', 7 February 1946 (NA, RG 226, Box 623, File 11). Interestingly, the French occupation authorities in Austria received similar reports of Hungarians who did not want Hungarian assets returned to Hungary (ACC to CGAAA, 4 June 1946, Colmar, Vienne 116, Biens Étrangers en Autriche, Hongrie 45-52 (1946–1950)).

7. Schoenfeld to State Department, A-203, 26 February 1946 (NA, RG 59, 740.00119EW/2-2646). Schoenfeld was quoting from the communist daily, *Szabadság*.

8. Joint Chiefs of Staff to General McNarney and General Clark, WARX 85965, 29 November 1945 (NA, RG 218, JCS Decimal files, Box 6/1).

9. Vienna to State Department, for Joint Chiefs of Staff, No. 65, 16 January 1946 (NA, RG 218, JCS Decimal Files, Box 6/1). The incident with the 'repatriation commission' had taken place in August 1945.

10. A fourteen-page summary list is on HNA, XIX, J-1-k, 23/g, 40.259/4/ 1946.

11. SWNCC Paper, 20 February 1946 (NA, RG 59, 740.00119EW/2-2046), and JCS to McNarney and Clark, WARX 99226.

12. Amended by War Office to USFET, OMGUS and USFA, WR-92218, 22 June 1946.

13. OMGUS to War Department, No. 1929, 23 March 1946, and USFA to War Department, No. 5687, 31 March 1946 (JCS Decimal Files, Box 6/3).

14. John Erhardt, US Political Representative in Vienna, to the State Department, Despatch No. 946, 13 March 1946, Enclosure No. 3, 'Hungarian Displaced Property in Austria' (NA, RG 59, 740.00119Control(Austria)/ 3-14-46).

15. State–War–Navy Coordinating Committee, 16 March 1946 (NA, RG 218, JCS Decimal Files, Box 6/3).

16. War Office to Generals McNarney, Lucius Clay and Mark Clark, WARX 91471, 15 June 1946 (NA, RG 218, JCS Decimal Files, Box 6/4).

17. Lieut. Walter Treece, Chief, Property Control Branch, memo on Werfen Train Property, 14 March 1946 (NA, RG 260, USACA, USFA, Property Control Branch, Box 20); 'Disposition of Werfen Train', Lieut. F. J. Raines to Commanding General, USFA, 29 July 1946, and 'Transfer of Accountability', 13 June 1947, ibid.

18. Property Control Branch to Military Government Detachment, Salzburg, 8 June 1946 (NA, RG 260, USFA, USACA, Property Control Branch, Box 20).

19. Ambassador Schoenfeld to State Department, No. 1206, 27 June 1946 (NA, RG 59, 740.00119EW).

20. Memo, European Affairs Bureau, State Department, 1 July 1946 (NA, RG 59, 800.515/7-146).

21. Robert Murphy to State Department, No. 1622, 28 June 1946 (NA, RG 59, 740.00119EW).

22. US Legation, Budapest, to State Department, No. 1939, 13 September 1946, ibid.

23. McNarney to General Weems, US Representative on Allied Control Commission, Budapest, 2 August 1946 (NA, RG 260, OMGUS Restitution Branch, 1945–1948, Box 2).

24. War Department to USFA, 29 May 1946, W 89481 (NA, RG 260, USFA, USACA, Property Control Branch, Box 20). After Rafael obtained Nagy's letter, he wrote to Nahum Goldmann, the Jewish Agency representative in Washington, suggesting that the matter be brought to the attention of the State Department (Rafael to Goldmann, 24 May 1946, CZA, S53/2128). Goldmann immediately approached the State Department for details about the train, only to be informed that the Department could find no official reports about it. So they asked USFA for details (Goldmann to Shertok, 28 May 1946, in files of GLRO, BODBJ, Acc:3121, C11/7/3b/6).

25. USFA, USACA to War Department, 4 June 1946, P 9355, ibid. It is interesting to note the dynamics of government in Washington – within a week this confidential telegram was leaked to the World Jewish Congress (Irving Dwork, WJC Washington Office, to Nehemiah Robinson, 12 June 1946: AJA, WJC. Series H, Box 173, File 'Hungary – 1946').

26. Goldmann to Shertok, cable, 12 June 1946 (CZA, S53/2128).

27. He met a World Jewish Congress delegation in New York, and probably other Jewish groups too (Hungarian Consul, New York City, to Congress, 17 June 1946 (AJA, WJC, Series H, File 173, Hungary-WJC, Authorities, 1945–1948)).

28. Goldmann to Eliezer Kaplan, Jewish Agency Treasurer (visiting London), 25 June 1946 (CZA, Z6/268).

29. Ruffer (Rafael) and Berl Locker to Stöckler, 14 June 1946 (CZA, S53/2128).

30. Stöckler and Munkácsi (on behalf of the Central Board of Jews in Hungary), Imre Reiner and Samu Kahan-Frankel (Orthodox Community), and Mihály Salamon and László Nagy (Hungarian Zionist Federation) to the Jewish Agency, and to the Joint, 16 July 1946 (copy on AJA, WJC, Series H, File 173).

31. Schoenfeld to State Department, 14 August 1946, No. 1544 (NA, RG 84, US Embassy, Budapest, Box 103, Jewish Property).

32. Rafael received a full account of the internal community debate on

the terms of the response to his telegram from the head of the Zionist Office in Budapest (Shimshon Nathan to Rafael, 8 September 1946, CZA, S53/2128).

33. Frigyes Görög interview, see Ch. 7, n. 51.

34. N. Katzburg, 'Between Liberation and Revolution: Hungarian Jewry, 1945–1948', in Y. Gutman and A. Saf, *She'erit Hapletah, 1944–1948. Rehabilitation and Political Struggle* (Yad Vashem, Jerusalem, 1990), p. 133; J. Gordon, 'Hungary', *American Jewish Yearbook*, American Jewish Committee, New York, 51 (1950), 362–3; and Nathan interview.

35. David Wahl memo, 'Meeting on Peace Treaties' (CZA, American Jewish Conference Papers, C7, Box 30). The meeting was between the State Department and delegations from the American Jewish Conference and the World Jewish Congress.

36. Treaty of Peace between the Allied Powers and Hungary, 10 February 1947, Paris (NA, RG 43, Box 99).

37. S. J. Roth, 'Indemnification of Hungarian Victims of Nazism: An Overview', in R. L. Braham and A. Pok (eds.), *The Holocaust in Hungary. Fifty Years Later* (Columbia University Press, New York, 1997), p. 742.

38. Roth to Nehemiah Robinson, 4 April 1947 (AJA, WJC, Series H, Box 174, File 'Hungary – Jewish Rehabilitation Fund').

39. Joseph Schwartz, the highly respected director of the Joint's welfare programme in Europe, conveyed this to General Hilldring at the State Department (Boukstein to Kaplan, 17 September 1946, CZA, Z6/79), and Lieut.-Colonel Marget, Chief of Finance Division of USFA, argued the point strongly in a USFA cable to the War Department (draft cable in reply to WARX 98112, 29 August 1946, NA, RG 260, USFA, USACA, Box 21).

40. Moses Leavitt to Secretary of State Byrnes, 6 November 1946 (NA, RG 59, 840.48, Refugees).

41. Memo by Hickerson, 'Refugee Problem – Financial Aspects', State Department, 2 June 1946 (NA, RG 59, 501.MA).

42. Mark Clark to War Department for Assistant Secretary of War, P-0563, 29 June 1946 (NA, RG 165, CAD, Refugee Program Messages, Box 857).

43. There is an extensive literature in English and Hebrew on the Jewish displaced persons. Y. Bauer, *Out of the Ashes. The Impact of American Jews on Post-Holocaust European Jewry* (Pergamon Press, Oxford, 1989); L. Dinnerstein, *America and the Survivors of the Holocaust* (A. S. Hyman, New York, 1982); *The Undefeated* (Gefen, Jerusalem, 1993); these cover different aspects of their history.

44. War Department to USFA, USACA, WARX 93184, 2 June 1946 (NA, RG 260, Property Control Branch, Box 21).

45. State Department to US Embassy, London, 26 June 1946, No. 5015 (NA, RG 260, Civil Affairs Department, Refugee Program Messages, Box 857).

46. Joel Fisher was a SHAEF expert on foreign currency and gold. He joined IGCR in September 1946 and left in 1947, when he joined the Joint. On the State Department role in his appointment to IGCR, see Boukstein to Kaplan, 23 October 1946 (CZA, Z4/10098). Fisher's role within the IGCR is discussed in Ch. 10.

47. Sir Herbert William Emerson, GCIE, KCSI, CBE, Governor of the Punjab, 1933–1938, High Commissioner for Refugees, League of Nations, 1939–1946, and Director of the Intergovernmental Committee on Refugees, 1939–1947.

48. State Department papers on NA, RG 59, 740.00119EW, 14 August 1946. Instructions to OMGUS and USFA were issued by the War Department (telegram no. WARX 98112) on 23 August (NA, RG 260, USFA, USACA, Property Control Branch, Box 21).

49. Schoenfeld to State Department, No. 1544, 14 August 1946 (NA, RG 84, Box 103, 'Jewish Property' file).

50. Marget, draft reply to WARX 98112, 29 August 1946 (NA, RG 260, USFA, USACA, Property Control Branch, Box 21).

51. Noel Hemmendinger, memo to General Hilldring, 3 September 1946 (NA, RG 59, 740.00119EW).

52. See Department of State *Bulletin*, 4 August 1946, p. 229.

53. General Weems, chief US member of the ACC, to War Department, Z-3683, 9 August 1946 (FRUS, 1946, vol. 6, pp. 329–30).

54. 'Text of Memorandum on Hungary', *New York Times*, 25 September 1946.

55. Irving Dwork, WJC Washington Office, to Arieh Tartakower, WJC New York, 2 September 1946 (AJA, WJC, Series H, Box 174, File 'Hungary – 1946').

56. Nehemiah Robinson to Irving Dwork, 4 September 1946, ibid.

57. 'Outline for discussion at Executive Committee', 5 September 1946, David Wahl, American Jewish Conference, David Wahl Private Papers; also 'Minutes of Meeting between Joint, Jewish Agency, World Jewish Congress, American Jewish Committee and the American Jewish Conference', 10 September 1946 (AJA, WJC, Series H, Box 174, File 'Hungary – 1946'); and Maurice Boukstein to Eliezer Kaplan, 17 September 1946 (CZA, Z6/79).

58. Fierst memoirs, paragraph 51, Philip Bernstein Papers, University of Rochester; and author interview, Washington, DC, January 2001; Wahl to I. L. Kenen, 24 September 1946, David Wahl Papers; and Boukstein to Kaplan, 21 October 1946 (CZA, S53, File 1669).

59. State Department paper, 'Definition of Non-Monetary Gold Pursuant to Article 8 of the Paris Reparations Agreement', 28 October 1946, circulated at SWNCC 336 (NA, RG 353, LM 54, roll 28).

CHAPTER 9 BETWEEN PARIS AND BUDAPEST

1. Eli Ginzberg to State Department, No. 2918, 17 June 1946 (NA, RG 59, 740.00119EW).

2. Simon Wiesenthal, then a member of the Central Committee of Liberated Jews in Upper Austria, wrote a detailed summary of the information known about the train, based on Avar's testimony of August 1945, to the Swiss offices of the World Jewish Congress and to the Jewish Agency. (See Wiesenthal to S. Silberschein, Geneva, 17 July 1946, YVA, M9, Silberschein Papers; and Wiesenthal to G. Ruffer (Rafael), 2 February 1946, CZA, S53/1659. In both of these, he refers to previous letters he sent in October and again in December 1945.)

3. As late as 1947 Jewish Agency officials were still searching for 'eight wagons' from the Toldi train that they believed had ended up in the French zone. (See, for example, Boukstein to André Blumel, 20 January 1947, CZA, Z6, File 89.)

4. Note verbale presented by the Hungarian MFA to the French Legation, Budapest, 18 March 1946 (French Foreign Ministry Archives, MAE, Y 44-49 Carton 11, Dossier 9 (vol. 56), Droit International Public et Droit de Guerre).

5. Allied Control Commission to Commissaire Général des Affaires Allem-andes et Autrichiennes (CGAAA), 4 June 1946 (Colmar, Vienne 116, Biens Étrangers en Autriche . . . Hongrie 45-52, 1946–1950).

6. Williamson, US Political Advisor's Office, Vienna, to State Department, draft telegram, 5 October 1946 (NA, RG 260, USFA, USACA, Property Control Division, Box 21).

7. UNRRA, French zone, Austria, to UNRRA HQ, Vienna, 31 January 1946 (UN, P.A.G.-4 (UNRRA), 3.0.1.0.2.0:18). There was one camp run by the JDC in Gnadelwald, near Innsbruck, and small Jewish displaced persons communities in Hohenems and Bregenz. On the other hand, a significant number of Hungarian fugitives and displaced persons were there, but as ex-enemy aliens they were not entitled to the assistance of the IGCR. (Report made by General Bethouart to Massigli (French ambassador in London), 20 November 1945, MAE, Europe 1944–1960, vol. 1: Sous-Série Autriche, EU 44-60: Autriche Z, Carton 516, Série 3 (vol. 9).)

8. Henri Gauquie to MAE, No. 57, 21 June 1945 (MAE, Europe 1944–1960,

vol. 1: Sous-Série Hongrie, Dossier 24, Relations Bilaterales: France–Hongrie, December 1944–January 1949).

9. France undertook to supply agricultural equipment, raw materials and textiles worth FFr 150 million in exchange for Hungarian produce and pharmaceuticals worth FFr 100 million (*Szabadság*, 15 June 1946). This agreement was extended to FFr 1 billion in 1947, and to FFr 3 billion in December 1949 (*Le Monde*, 7 December 1949).

10. Note by Henri Paul Chargueraud (Director of Accords Techniques, Quai d'Orsay), Reference 2131/AT, 'Non-monetary Hungarian Gold', 21 August 1946 (MAE, Direction des Affaires Economiques et Financières, Sous-Série Direction des Accords Techniques, Dossier 97, 547-2-1-5-1).

11. J. Hilldring to Patrick Malin, IGCR, 19 November 1946 (NA, RG 59, 740.00119EW).

12. 'Monetary gold, non-monetary gold and the Tripartite Gold Commission', Library and Research Division, No. 12, Foreign and Commonwealth Office, 11 May 1997.

13. Chargueraud to Administrative Convention Direction, 21 August 1946, Reference 2131/AT, Subject: Non-monetary Hungarian Gold, Direction des Affaires Économiques et Financières (MAE, Sous-Série Direction des Accords Techniques, Dossier 97, 547-2-1-5-1).

14. *New York Times*, 6 October 1946, p. 41.

15. US Embassy, Paris, to French Foreign Ministry, Note 2085, 19 December 1946 (MAE, Direction des Affaires Économiques et Financières, Sous-Série Direction des Accords Techniques, Dossier 97, 547-2-1-5-1. The evasive French reply of 28 December 1946 is on NA, RG 43, Entry 319, Box 13).

16. US Delegation, Council of Foreign Ministers, Moscow, 19 April 1947, to State Department, No. 1479 (NA, RG 43, Entry 319, Box 13).

17. US Embassy, Paris, to Quai d'Orsay, No. 2531, 13 May 1947 (NA, RG 84, Paris Embassy 1947, files 711.3–711.9, Box 435); US Embassy to Quai d'Orsay, Memorandum on Non-Monetary Gold, 13 June (MAE, Direction des Affaires Économiques et Financières, Sous-Série Direction des Accords Techniques, Dossier 100, 547-2-1-5-10); and No. 2652, 26 June 1947 (NA, RG 84, Paris Embassy 1947, files 711.3–711.9, Box 435).

18. War Department to USFET, 22 August 1947 (NA, RG 59, 840.48).

19. Goldthwaite Dorr, US representative, Tripartite Gold Commission, to State Department, No. 1540, 5 October 1947 (NA, RG 59, 800.515, Box 4236).

20. Chargueraud to Alphand Schweitzer, 21 April 1947, No. 2167; and Memo on Reparations to Non-Repatriable Victims of Nazi Aggression, 6 November 1947 (MAE, Direction des Affaires Économiques et Financières, Sous-Série Direction des Accords Techniques, Dossier 100, 547-2-1-5-10).

21. Chargueraud internal memo, ref. 2219, 26 August 1947, ibid. The State Department was well aware of France's position, but apparently chose not to answer it (Caffery, US Embassy, Paris, to Secretary of State, No. 2359, 15 June 1947, NA, RG 59, Lot 53, D 307, Papers Relating to IRO, Box 16).

22. François de Panafieu, internal memo, 1 September 1947 (MAE, Direction des Affaires Économiques et Financières, Sous-Série Direction des Accords Techniques, Dossier 100, 547-2-1-5-10).

23. See correspondence from the French Embassy, London, 29 December 1947 and 12 January 1948, ibid.; British policy is discussed in K. Unwin, Commercial Department, British Embassy, Paris, to G. B. W. Woodroffe, Foreign Office, London, 23 September 1947 (FO 944, File 252).

24. Lewis Douglas, US Embassy, London, to Secretary of State, No. 3911, 17 July 1947 (NA, RG 59, Lot 53D307, IGCR Files, Box 16).

25. On 21 February and again 25 August 1947. (Stöckler and Reiner to French Foreign Ministry, MAE, Direction des Affaires Économiques et Financières, Sous-Série Direction des Accords Techniques, Dossier 100, 547-2-1-5-10.)

26. General Cherrière to the General Administrator, Chief of the Military Government of the French Occupation Zone in Austria – Innsbruck. Subject: Hungarian Property (2406 CE/RE/RR), 24 July 1946 (Colmar, AUT 3180, D. 510, Trésor Hongrois, 1945–1953).

27. RRCB to CGAAA, 26 September 1946 (Colmar, Vienne 116, Biens Étrangers en Autriche . . . Hongrie 45-52, 1946–1950).

28. ibid., 2 October 1946.

29. This account is based on the records of the police investigation and the court protocols (Colmar, Tribunal Gouvernement Militaire, Dossier Judiciaire, Affaire Schwenninger/Traffic d'Or, AUT 4176 D. 1405, files 1–22). Cf. also 'An Insidious Gold Treasure', *Volkszeitung*, 26 September 1946; 'Gold Treasure Found Near Schnann', *Tiroler Tageszeitung*, 25 September 1946; 'Gold Treasure Trial Before French Court', ibid., 26 September 1946.

30. General Cherrière to Commanding General, French Forces in Innsbruck, 5 January 1947 (Colmar, Vienne 116, Biens Étrangers en Autriche . . . Hongrie, 1946–1950).

31. Invoice of delivery, 11 January 1947 (Colmar, AUT 3180, D. 510, Trésor Hongrois, 1945–1953); and (12805/DM) Delegated General, Head of the Control Mission to the Commander of the Gendarmerie in Austria. Subject: Transfer of important archives from Innsbruck to Paris, 10 January 1947, ibid.

32. The Jewish organizations were individually officially informed by letters from Assistant Secretary of State General John Hilldring on 14 January 1947 (NA, RG 59, 840.48 Refugees).

33. See, for example, Boukstein to André Blumel, 20 January 1947 (CZA, Z6, File 89).

34. One of the main defendants at the Schnann trial.

35. Note from Hungarian Embassy and Hungarian Restitution Commission, 27 November 1947 (MAE, Direction des Affaires Économiques et Financières, Sous-Série Direction des Accords Techniques, Dossier 97, 547-2-1-5-1).

36. Alfred Cobban, *A History of Modern France*, vol. 3 (Penguin, Harmondsworth, 1965), p. 208.

37. For a succinct summary of this long and tedious diplomatic fight, see Jefferson Caffery, US ambassador to France, to Jean Chauvel, Director-General of French Foreign Ministry, 16 January 1948 and 23 January 1948, and the French reply to the US Embassy, 31 January 1948 (NA, RG 84, Paris Embassy, Special records, 711.9, Box 25).

38. US Representative, Allied Control Commission, Budapest, to US Military Attaché, Paris, Z-4967, 11 March 1947 (NA, RG 260, OMGUS Restitution Branch, 1945–1948, Box 5).

39. Headed by István Vásárhelyi, the Under-Secretary of State in the Hungarian Ministry of Finance. The French negotiator was François de Panafieu, Director of Accords Techniques at the Quai d'Orsay.

40. Protocol signed between Hungary and France, with accompanying letter, 19 February 1948 (MAE, Direction des Affaires Économiques et Financières, Sous-Série Direction des Accords Techniques, Dossier 25(b), 528-5-1).

41. The Hungarians honoured their part of the deal with alacrity. By late June 1948 Hungary had returned 4,428 freight wagons in 92 separate transports (Latour, French Embassy, Budapest, to Head of RRCB Division, Vienna, ML/GC/D461, 23 June 1948, Colmar, AUT 1260, Restitutions Biens Hongrois).

42. See, for example, 'French Participation in Safehaven Negotiations', Despatch No. 299, US Embassy, Madrid, to Secretary of State, 25 May 1948 (NA, RG 59, 800.515).

43. Keyes, USFA, to US Military Attaché, Budapest, P-1283, 14 February 1948 (NA, RG 84, Budapest, Box 158, File 'Hungarian Property').

44. *Le Monde*, 21 February 1948.

45. Memorandum of talks at French Embassy, Budapest, between Marcel Latour, Commercial Attaché, and Charles Cook of the US Embassy, Budapest, 2 March 1948 (NA, RG 84, Budapest, Box 158, File 'Hungarian Property').

46. MAE to French Embassy, Budapest, 2 March 1948 (MAE, Direction des Affaires Économiques et Financières, Sous-Série Direction des Accords Techniques, Dossier 97, 547-2-1-5-1).

47. French Embassy, Budapest, to MAE, 20 March 1948, ibid.

48. Chief of French Control Mission, Austria, to French High Commissioner,

Executive Committee, Reparations and Restitution Branch, Subject: Hungarian Treasure, CB/15.166, 25 February 1948 (Colmar, AUT 3180, D. 510, Trésor Hongrois, 1945–1953).

49. Report of Property restored to the Hungarian Government, 26 June 1948, ibid.

50. Defector account, 8 February 1949 (JDC, NYC, AR45/64, Box 532A, 'Hungarian Gold Train'). This account claims that the Jewish victim loot included 2,400kg of gold, which was more than the sum estimated by the French appraisers.

51. *Szabadság*, 6 June 1948. Sent as enclosure to Despatch No. 515 from US Legation, Budapest, to State Department, 11 June 1948 (NA, RG 84, Box 158, File 'Hungarian Property').

52. Cf. Budget speech by Minister of Transport, Ernő Gerő, quoted in *New York Times*, 30 December 1948.

53. Memo of meeting with Miklós Nyárádi, prepared by Dr Imre Reiner, 18 June 1948 (HNA, XXIII-5-b, 4.d, pp. 110–13).

54. The American Jewish Committee representative was Eugene Hevesi. See Eli Rock, JDC, NYC, to Kurt Wehle, JDC, Paris, No. 2335, 17 May 1949 (JDC, NYC, AR 45/64, File 532A).

55. Andrew Friedman, Paris Office, Notice for File, 31 January 1949 (JDC, Givat Ram, Jerusalem, Geneva IV, File 10/1A: 'General Reparations: Hungarian Gold Train').

56. 'Memorandum upon the Actual Status of Restitution to Jews in Hungary', 3 January 1949 (JDC, NYC, AR 45/64, File 532A).

57. Jewish Telegraphic Agency, 1 February 1949.

58. Reiner memo, see n. 53 above.

CHAPTER 10   NEW YORK CITY

1. The author was given generous access to Joel Fisher's private papers. For that, and a lengthy interview with Mr Fisher, I am grateful.

2. See, for example, Fisher to Moses (Moe) Leavitt (vice-chairman of the Joint in New York), November 1946, and Fisher to Fierst, 10 December 1946, Fisher Papers; Fisher to Fierst, 16 February 1947, ibid.; Fisher to Fierst, 27 and 28 May 1947, ibid. Emerson prepared a paper in February 1947 setting out some of the policy differences between his approach and that of his Jewish officials (Emerson note, 12 February 1947, CZA, A444).

3. Abba Schwartz to Emerson, memo, 28 November 1946 (CZA, A444). The State Department supported Fisher's position on this, and Emerson was forced

to restrict the use of funds derived from victim assets to the sole benefit of persecutees, Jewish or non-Jewish (Schwartz to US Embassy, London, 27 January 1947, NA, RG 59, 840.48 Refugees).

4. Schwartz to Emerson, 'Report on Conferences with OMGUS Officials in Berlin and Frankfurt', 24 December 1946 (CZA, A444).

5. OMGUS to AGWAR, 30 September 1947, C-1796 (NA, RG 260, OMGUS Property Division, 1945–1946, Box 5).

6. Over fifty years later, the official responsible for dealing with this part of the non-monetary gold property was too distraught to discuss it.

7. Schwartz to Emerson, 'Report on Conferences January 7–14 with OMGUS officials in Germany' (CZA, A444); and Finance Division, HICOG, Frankfurt, to State Department, No. 99, 14 July 1950 (NA, RG 59, Lot 53D307, records relating to the IRO, Box 14, IRO Subject Files).

8. General rules defining coins and currency as either monetary or non-monetary were set out in instructions from Dean Acheson to Robert Murphy, OMGUS, No. 814, 16 April 1947 (NA, RG 59, Lot 53D307, Records Relating to IGCR, Box 16). The application of this ruling to the Gold Train was made a few weeks later. (James Garrison, Chief, Reparations, Deliveries and Restitution Division, USACA, USFA, Subject: Inventory of Movable Property Comprising 'Werfen Train', 16 May 1947, NA, RG 260, Property Control Division, Box 20.)

9. Schwartz to Emerson, 'Report on Conferences with USFA Officials in Vienna and Salzburg', 14 to 23 and 26 January 1947 (JDC, NYC, AR45/64, Files 532A).

10. The chief of the Restitution, Deliveries and Reparations Division of USFA, James Garrison, explained that the paintings in the warehouse had been seized by the US army from a schloss in southern Austria. Baroness Weiss was allowed to examine the paintings, but could not identify any of them as belonging to her family. (Garrison to Military Government, Vienna, 5 November 1947.) The warehouse was a repository for many cultural items seized by the US forces in 1945, and not just the Gold Train goods.

11. Inventory of Judaica on Hungarian Train, 19 January 1948 (NA, RG 260, Property Control Branch, Box 20). The inventory of religious items was prepared by US army chaplain Captain Oscar Lipshutz.

12. Lieut.-Colonel Raymond Gunn to Property Control Branch, 20 January 1948, ibid.

13. Single stamps in books and booklets, stamp dealers' stock-blocks, sheets, airmail sets cancelled and uncancelled (good to excellent condition), whole sheets of uncancelled stamps, fine collections, used envelopes of philatelic value, miscellaneous dealer stocks, Hungarian cancellations, albums in

various conditions, covers and postal cards, single stamps in bundles and filing cabinets ('no value'), philatelic literature – sixteen crates, total value $35,600. (Description from the 'Joint Army–IGCR Inventory and Appraisal Forms', NA, RG 260, USFA, USACA, Property Control Branch, Miscellaneous Correspondence, Box 7.)

14. Schwartz to Emerson, 'Report on Conferences with USFA Officials in Vienna and Salzburg', see n. 9 above.

15. Report by Joseph Schwartz, European Director of Joint, to Joint Headquarters in New York, 9–12 June 1947 (JDC, NYC, AR45-64, File 4391).

16. Imre Reiner to Quai d'Orsay, 21 February 1947 and 25 August 1947 (MAE, Direction des Affaires Economiques et Financières, Sous-Série Direction des Accords Techniques, Dossier 100).

17. Captain Howard Mackenzie, Property Control, to Reparations, Deliveries and Restitution Division, USACA, USFA, Subject: Inventory of Movable Property Comprising 'Werfen Train', 22 May 1947 (NA, RG 260, Property Control Division, Box 20).

18. Lieut.-Colonel Raymond Gunn to Reparations, Deliveries and Restitution Division, USACA, USFA, Subject: Inventory of Movable Property Comprising 'Werfen Train', 18 August 1947, ibid.

19. See, for example, memo 'Transfer of Accountability and Responsibility for Property Released from the Property Control Warehouse, Salzburg', 13 June 1947, ibid.

20. Gideon Rafael, 'Conversation with Yehuda Gaulan on the Hungarian Property in Salzburg', 16 July 1947 (CZA, S25, File 10719). It is highly unlikely that Gaulan would have witnessed such blatant theft.

21. Gideon Rafael, 'Memorandum on Meeting with Arthur Marget', 17 September 1947, ibid.

22. William Schwartzmann, Business Enterprise Subsection, 'Alleged Theft or Diversion of Werfen Train Property', 15 July 1947 (NA, RG 260, Property Control Division, Box 20).

23. These details from Kenneth Alford, *The Spoils of War. The American Military's Role in the Stealing of Europe's Treasures* (Birch Lane Press, New York, 1994), pp. 90–93.

24. JAG papers from Alford. The author wishes to thank Ken Alford for generously giving him access to these and other papers from his research collection. Mr Alford's interpretation of the documents is very different from that offered here.

25. See T. Albrich, *Exodus durch Österreich ['Exodus through Austria']* (Haymon Verlag, Innsbruck, 1987), *passim*.

26. Stanley Nowinski manuscript, 'The Will to Live' (JDC, NYC, Nowinski file).

27. 'Influx and Departure of Jewish Refugees in US Zone, Austria' (NA, RG 338, Entry 11013, Box 36, File 383.6).

28. Stanley Nowinski's role was acknowledged in 1973 when he was brought to Israel as an official guest.

29. Yehuda Gaulan (Golan) to Eliezer Kaplan (Jerusalem), 11 June 1947 (CZA, S53, File 1669).

30. Report of Hungarian Embassy, Bern, 10 October 1947 (HNA, XIX-J-1-k 112.d ad.4777/47).

31. 'Non-monetary Gold for Victims of Nazism', PCIRO press release, 19 December 1947.

32. US Consulate, Bremen, to State Department, Despatch No. 1046, 11 December 1947, and Robert Murphy to State Department, Despatch No. 7, 5 January 1948 (NA, RG 59, 800.515).

33. 'Interim Progress Report of the Director-General of the IRO on the Program of Allocation of a Reparations Share to Non-Repatriable Victims of German Action, July 1947–September 1948', p. 11 (NA, RG 59, Lot 53D307, Box 14).

34. 'List of Diamonds and Terms and Conditions of Tender', 15 September 1948 (NA, RG 59, Lot 53D307, Records Relating to IRO, IRO Subject File, 1946–1952, Box 14).

35. Receipt for last shipment of Hungarian Gold Train silver, 17 February 1948, ibid.

36. Lieut.-Colonel Raymond Gunn, 'Inventory of Judaica Items Ex Werfen Train', 20 January 1948 (NA, RG 260, USFA, USACA, Property Control Branch, Box 20).

37. There may have been more – No. 1,544 was the highest crate number traceable in the archival records.

38. The transport documents for the last shipment described it as 'the eighth shipment of Werfen Train property disposed of through PCIRO for use in local DP camps'. (Raymond Gunn, 'Eight Werfen Shipments', 16 January 1948, NA, RG 260, USFA, USACA, Property Control Branch, Box 20.)

39. Protocol of meeting, 'Proposed Disposition of the Hungarian Gold Train', 29 January 1948 (NA, RG 59, Lot 54D331, Box 2).

40. US Legation, Budapest, to Hungarian Foreign Ministry, No. 168, 24 March 1948 (NA, RG 84, Budapest, Box 158, File 711.5 DPs); Hungarian Foreign Ministry to US Legation, No. 1270, 12 April 1948 (sent to USPO-LAD, Frankfurt, No. 38, April 13), ibid.; and US Legation, Budapest, to Secretary of State, No. 936, 10 June 1948 (NA, RG 59, 740.00119EW).

41. Many of them were personal friends of W. Hallam Tuck, Emerson's successor and head of the IRO. The chairman of the committee was Colonel Ray C. Kramer.

42. Ray Kramer to Merchandizing Committee, 13 August 1948 (CZA, A444).

43. Details of the merchandizing phase are in the Abba Schwartz Papers in the Central Zionist Archives, Jerusalem.

44. State Department memorandum, 'Merchandizing Advisory Committee', 28 June 1951 (NA, RG 59, Lot 53D307, Box 14).

45. IRO press release on Reparations Funds Disbursements, 1 April 1949 (JDC, NYC, AR 45/64, File 532A).

46. Abba Schwartz to Moe Leavitt, 8 September 1949, ibid.

47. State Department internal memo, 'Reparations Payments to IRO as of 20 April 1951' (NA, RG 59, Lot 53D307, Box 14).

CHAPTER 11   AFTERMATH OF WAR

1. Hungarian Restitution Commission, Innsbruck, to Head of the RRCB Division. Subject: Hungarian Treasure: Restitution Demands, No. 395/1948, 18 June 1948 (Colmar, AUT 3180, D. 510, Trésor Hongrois, 1945–1953); and Hungarian Restitution Commission, Innsbruck, to Head of the RRCB Division. Subject: Hungarian Treasure: Restitution Demands 394–395, No. 644/1948, 24 October 1948 (Colmar, AUT 1261, Restitutions Biens Hongrois 1948–1953).

2. See Ch. 5.

3. Note on Hungarian Treasure, 10 January 1950, ibid.

4. Interrogation reports on Friedrich Westen, 24 October 1949, and Wilhelm Höttl, 25 October 1949: see Ch. 5, nn. 65 and 69.

5. Commissioner Emile Dabonville to the Head of the Security Section, Innsbruck, 12 September 1949. Subject: Cases of Gold and Jewellery, commonly called 'Hungarian Treasure', DV/2925/SP, Trésor Hongrois, 1945–1953 (Colmar, AUT 3180, D. 510).

6. Der Spiegel, 'Intermezzo in Salzburg', 22 April 1953.

7. Note for the Head of the Property Control Section. Subject: Hungarian Treasure, 5.771/SP/CAB, 7 October 1953 (Colmar, AUT 1261, Restitutions Biens Hongrois 1948–1953).

8. The information presented here is based on CIA and CIC files made available in April 2001 as part of the large-scale declassification of Second World War-related material mandated by the 1998 Nazi War Crimes Disclosure Act (NA, RG 319, IRR Personal Files, Box 617, Höttl file and Höttl

CIA file. I am grateful to Miriam Kleiman for bringing this material to my attention). See also 'Intermezzo in Salzburg', *Der Spiegel*, op. cit. This in-depth study of Höttl makes the same accusations against him as those in the CIA files. The material was probably leaked to the German magazine.

9. In 1946 the NKVD, predecessor of the KGB, confiscated all records of the Gendarmerie and took them to Moscow. The Gendarmerie had played such a criminal role in the deportation of the Hungarian Jews that the Soviets would certainly have found much compromising information in these records – and with it, the ability to coerce the loyalty of the incriminated rural police to the post-war communist regime. The files relating to part of Toldi's career vanished with all the rest. Further, the files for the period of his service in the regular army, prior to transfer as an officer of the Gendarmerie, which should be housed today in the archives of the Hungarian Ministry of Defence, have vanished – unaccountably. Two separate attempts were made to trace the files during 2000 with the assistance of Hungarian colleagues, but the files were reported as 'missing'. (I am indebted to Dr László Karsai of the University of Szeged for information concerning the Gendarmerie files.)

10. Order of Investigation: People's Prosecutor to the Political Department of the Budapest Headquarters of Hungarian Police requesting investigation against Dr Árpád Toldi, 11 March 1946, Budapest Municipal Archives, 3094/ 1.N.1946; and 8248/1 Head of Justice Department to the Commissioner of the French High Tribunal in the Tyrol–Vorarlberg region, 19 March 1946, C.G. 949: Árpád Toldi (Colmar, AUT 2273 – 949).

11. The French Legation in Budapest informed the Quai d'Orsay that the fact Toldi was living freely in Innsbruck was the subject of press comment in Hungary (Legation to Quai d'Orsay, 22 April 1947, MAE, Y 44-49, Carton 11, Dossier 9 (vol. 56), Droit International Public et Droit de Guerre).

12. Commissioner of Police, Head of the French Liaison Detachment of the Sûreté of Vorarlberg to the Head of the Security Section, Innsbruck, DV/2925/SP, 12 September 1949 (Colmar, AUT 3180, D. 510, Trésor Hongrois, 1945–1953).

13. 'Hungarian Gold Train', anonymous report, probably written by Simon Wiesenthal (CZA, A444, Abba Schwartz Papers. No date). There is no serious evidence to prove that this was true.

14. E. J. Lévai, 'The War Crimes Trials Relating to Hungary', *Hungarian-Jewish Studies*, ed. R. L. Braham, New York, II, 1969, p. 279.

15. Cf. p. 114.

16. Reports by Dr Gyula Szilvay, ex-president of the Hungarian Foreign Trade Office, 16 December 1945, February 1946 and 12 August 1947 (HNA, Series XIX.J-1-k, 23/g tétel).

17. See transcripts of United States–Hungarian negotiations, meetings 1–25, in NA, RG, Entry A15398, Box 1, 'Hungarian Claims'.

18. US Embassy, Budapest, to State Department, 20 November 1967, *Foreign Relations of the United States, 1964–1968*, vol. XVII – *Eastern Europe*, pp. 315–17.

19. Rafael (Ruffer), Geneva, to Moshe Shertock, Jerusalem, 14 July 1947, *Political Documents of the Jewish Agency*, vol. 2, January–November 1947, ed. Nana Sagi (Jerusalem, 1998), pp. 446–7.

20. Dr Péter Feldmájer, 'Bitter Restitution' [Hungarian], *Szombat*, July 1999.

21. Article by Merenyi Miklós, *Népszabadság*, 13 August 1992. In 1993 Merenyi wrote a series of additional articles on the subject. (I am indebted to Mr Paul Kertész of Tel Aviv for bringing these articles to my attention.)

22. US Legation, Budapest, to State Department, A-380, 15 June 1948 (NA, RG 59, 800.515).

CHAPTER 12   CONCLUSION:
FANTASIES OF WEALTH

1. See G. Lengyel, 'The Ethnic Composition of the Economic Elite in Hungary in the Interwar Period' (1990); G. Ránki, 'The Occupational Structure of Hungarian Jews in the Interwar Period' (1992); Y. Don, 'The Economic Effect of Antisemitic Discrimination: Hungarian Anti-Jewish Legislation, 1938–1944' (1989); and Y. Don, 'Patterns of Jewish Economic Behavior in Central Europe in the Twentieth Century' (1992). Details of all these articles can be found in the Bibliography.

2. In October 1946 Sándor Ercse, one of the most senior Property Directorate officials on the train, surrendered two kilograms of gold and 250 gold Napoleon coins to the Hungarian Restitution Commission in Innsbruck (report of 25 October 1946, to Hungarian Foreign Ministry, HNA, XIX, J-1-k, 23/g tétel). Presumably Ercse wanted to benefit from an amnesty offered by the Hungarian government. It is safe to assume that the other 'guardians' of the loot on the Gold Train also took steps to protect against future contingencies before they left the train.

APPENDIX 1: THE BECHER DEPOSIT

1. Yehuda Bauer, *Jews for Sale? Nazi–Jewish Negotiations, 1933–1945* (Yale University Press, New Haven and London, 1994), Chs. 11–13.

2. Ronald W. Zweig, 'Feeding the Camps: Allied Blockade Policy and the Relief of Concentration Camps in Germany, 1944–1945', *Historical Journal* 41, 3 (1998), 825–51 *passim*.

3. On five separate occasions between 1946 and 1948 he testified on behalf of Becher and other top SS personalities involved in the ransom schemes. Kasztner's role as head of the Aid and Rescue Committee continues to attract heated controversy (see S. Barri (Ishoni), 'The Question of Kasztner's Testimonies on Behalf of Nazi War Criminals', *Journal of Israeli History* 18, nos. 2–3 (1997), 139–66 *passim*; Y. Weitz, *Ha-Ish sh'Nirzach Pa'amayim* ['The Man Who Was Murdered Twice'] (Keter, Jerusalem, 1995); and K. Müller-Tupath, *Reichsführers gehorsamster Becher. Eine deutsche Karriere* ['The Reichsführer's Obedient Becher. A German Career'] (Aufbau-Verlag, Berlin, 1999).

4. Herbert Katzki (Joint) and Roswell McClelland (War Refugee Board, Bern) to Brigadier-General William O'Dwyer (War Refugee Board, Washington), 27 April 1945 (NA, RG 59, 840.48 Refugees).

5. The inventory itemizes the contents of twenty-nine bags of valuables (CZA, A140, File 251). Schweiger, in his joint report with Kasztner (see below), recounted that Becher had removed the bags from the six boxes, and disposed of the boxes.

6. Affidavit by Schweiger and Kasztner, 21 October 1945, Bern (NA, RG 59, 840.48 Refugee/46-0809).

7. Kasztner to Melech Neustadt, Tel Aviv, 7 November 1945 (CZA, L17, File 170).

8. Memorandum: 'Jewish National and Public Monies and Valuables of Hungarian Jews', 9 December 1945 (CZA, S25, File 5179).

9. Testimony of Captain Karl Kittstein, G-2, 3rd Army. Kittstein was asked about his talks with Mayer in September 1946, when the State Department was attempting to reach a decision about the fate of the Becher Deposit (NA, RG 59, 840.48 Refugees, 18 September 1946).

10. Report to Committee on Claims, Simon Shargo, 9 December 1946 (JDC, Jerusalem, Geneva IV-325A).

11. Kurt Becher Erklärung, 29 July 1946 (NA, RG 59, 840.48 Refugees).

12. The research of Shoshana Barri indicates that the Jewish Agency was interested in Becher's cooperation for other reasons as well. They believed

that he could help them hunt down and convict Adolf Eichmann and the Mufti of Jerusalem (op. cit., pp. 152–4).

13. The Joint recently commissioned a committee of inquiry to examine its record on this matter. The author was allowed restricted access to the confidential report of the Arad Committee (JDC, New York, 2000).

14. Memorandum of meeting with Eliezer Kaplan and Saly Mayer in Geneva, 9 January 1947 (JDC, NYC, File 532A).

15. General J. Hilldring to Henry Monsky, 14 January 1947 (NA, RG 59, 840.48 Refugees).

16. Dr Dagobert Arian to Eliezer Kaplan, report on Becher Deposit, 13 March 1947 (CZA, L17, File 170).

17. Kasztner (in Geneva) to Chaim Posner, Director of the Jewish Agency Office, Geneva, 30 April 1947 (CZA, L17, File 170).

18. Eliezer Kaplan to Walter Butler, JDC Legal Department, Austria, 23 November 1947, ibid.

Sources

ARCHIVES

Hungary

Hungarian National Archives
Budapest Municipal Archives

Israel

Yad Vashem Archives
American Jewish Joint Distribution Committee (European Office)
Ben-Gurion Heritage Center
Central Archives for the History of the Jewish People
Central Zionist Archives
Hebrew University, Jerusalem (Institute for Contemporary Jewry, Oral History Project)

United States

National Archives
American Jewish Archives (Cincinnati)
American Jewish Joint Distribution Committee (New York office)
The Citadel, Charleston (Mark Clark Papers)
Eisenhower Library (Bedell-Smith Papers)
Roosevelt Library
Truman Library (Bernard Bernstein Papers)
United Nations Archives (UNRRA), New York City
United States Holocaust Memorial Museum Archives
University of Minnesota (Max Lowenthal Papers)
University of Rochester (Philip Bernstein Papers)

France

Archives Nationales
Archives du Ministère des Affaires Étrangères, Colmar
Archives du Ministère des Affaires Étrangères, Paris
Banque de France

England

Public Record Office
Jewish Board of Deputies (London Metropolitan Archives)

PRIVATE PAPERS

Herbert Fierst
Joel Fisher
Abraham Hyman
Gideon Rafael (Ruffer)
Abba Schwartz
David Wahl

NEWSPAPERS

Csendőrségi Lapok (1938–1944)
Fejérmegyei Napló (1944)
Haladás (1946–1947)
Harc (1944)
Képes Figyelő (1945)
Le Monde (1945–1948)
Népszabadság (1992, 1999)
New York Times (1945–1948)
Palestine Post (1945–1948)
Szabadság (1945, 1948)
Tiroler Tageszeitung (1946)
Új Élet (1945–1946, 2000)
Új Szó (June, 1994)
Világ (1945–1946)
Volkszeitung (Innsbruck) (1946)

INTERVIEWS

Herbert Fierst
Joel Fisher
Eli Ginzberg
Abraham Hyman
Károly Kromp
David Rohlbein (telephone)
Abba Schwartz

Bibliography

OFFICIAL PUBLICATIONS

Foreign and Commonwealth Office, Great Britain, *Nazi Gold: Information from the British Archives*, Historians, Library and Records Department (LRD), No. 11, London, September 1996

Foreign and Commonwealth Office, Great Britain, *British Policy Towards Enemy Property During and After the Second World War*, Historians, LRD, No. 13, London, April 1998

Foreign Relations of the United States, 1964–1968: Vol. XVII, *Eastern Europe*

William Slany, United States Department of State, *U.S. and Allied Efforts to Recover and Restore Gold and other Assets Stolen or Hidden by Germany During World War II. Preliminary Study*, Washington DC, May 1997

William Slany, United States Department of State, *U.S. and Allied Wartime and Postwar Relations and Negotiations with Argentina, Portugal, Spain, Sweden, and Turkey on Looted Gold and German External Assets and U.S. Concerns about the Fate of the Wartime Ustasha Treasury* (Supplement to Preliminary Study), Washington DC, June 1998

UNPUBLISHED PAPERS

Csősz, László, 'From Emancipation to Exclusion: Jewish Fate in the Jászág' (MA dissertation, Central European University, 2000)

Molnár, Judit, 'Gendarmes, Policemen, Functionaries and the Jews: New Findings on the Behaviour of Hungarian Authorities During the Holocaust' (paper delivered at Columbia University, October 1998)

Molnár, Judit, 'Activities of the Hungarian Jewish Councils as compared with other European Jewish Councils' (paper delivered at the Institute for Holocaust Studies, Yad Vashem, Jerusalem, April 1999)

SECONDARY SOURCES

Albrich, T., *Exodus durch Österreich. Die Jüdischen Flüchtlinge, 1945–1948* ['*Exodus through Austria. Jewish Refugees, 1945–1948*'] (Haymon Verlag, Innsbruck, 1987)

Albrich, T., and A. Gisinger, *Im Bombenkrieg. Tirol und Vorarlberg, 1943–1945* ['*Strategic Bombing in Tyrol and Vorarlberg, 1943–1945*'] (Haymon Verlag, Innsbruck, 1992)

Albrich, T. (ed.), *Flucht nach Eretz Israel. Die Bricha und der jüdische Exodus durch Österreich nach 1945* ['*Flight to Israel. The 'Bricha' and the Jewish Exodus through Austria after 1945*'] (Studien Verlag, Innsbruck, 1998)

Alford, K., *The Spoils of War. The American Military's Role in the Stealing of Europe's Treasures* (Birch Lane Press, New York, 1994)

Ambrose, S. E., *Eisenhower and Berlin, 1945. The Decision to Halt at the Elbe* (W. W. Norton, New York, 1967)

Axworthy, M., C. Scafes, et al., *Third Axis, Fourth Ally. Rumanian Armed Forces in the European War, 1941–1945* (Arms & Armour Press, London, 1995)

Barkan, E., *The Guilt of Nations. Restitution and Negotiating Historical Injustices* (W. W. Norton, New York and London, 2000)

Baross, G., 'Hungary and Hitler', *Living History Program of University of Southern California Library* (1964)

Barri (Ishoni), S., 'The Question of Kasztner's Testimonies on Behalf of Nazi War Criminals', *Journal of Israeli History* 18, nos. 2–3 (1997), 139–66

Bauer, Y., *Out of the Ashes. The Impact of American Jews on Post-Holocaust European Jewry* (Pergamon Press, Oxford, 1989)

Bauer, Yehuda, *Jews for Sale? Nazi–Jewish Negotiations, 1933–1945* (Yale University Press, New Haven and London, 1994)

Beer, S., 'Early CIA Reports on Austria, 1947–1949', in G. Bischof and A. Pelinka (eds.), *Austrian Historical Memory and National Identity* (Transaction Publishers, New Brunswick, 1997), pp. 247–59

Beer, S., 'Salzburg nach dem Krieg. Beobachtungen des US-Geheimdienstes OSS/SSU über Österreich 1945' ['Postwar Salzburg. The Surveillance of US Intelligence Agencies OSS/SSU in Austria, 1945'], *Mitteilungen des Gesellschaft für Salzburger Landeskunde* 139 (1999), 117–221

Benoschofsky, I., 'The Position of Hungarian Jewry after the Liberation', in R. L. Braham (ed.), *Hungarian-Jewish Studies*, vol. 1 (Columbia University Press, New York, 1966), pp. 237–60

Biddiscombe, P., *Werwolf! The History of the National Socialist Guerrilla Movement, 1944–1946* (University of Wales Press, Cardiff, 1998)

Bidwell, R. L., *Currency Conversion Tables. A Hundred Years of Change* (Rex Collings, London, 1970)

Black, P. R., *Ernst Kaltenbrunner, Ideological Soldier of the Third Reich* (Princeton University Press, Princeton, NJ, 1984)

Bradsher, Greg, 'Nazi Gold: The Merkers Mine Treasure', *Prologue* 31, no. 1 (1999)

Braham, R. L., 'The Rightists, Horthy and the Germans: Factors Underlying the Destruction of Hungarian Jewry', in B. Vago and G. Mosse, *Jews and Non-Jews in Eastern Europe* (Israel Universities Press, Jerusalem, 1974), pp. 137–56

Braham, R. L., *The Politics of Genocide. The Holocaust in Hungary*, 2 vols. (Columbia University Press, New York, 1994)

Braham, R. L., and A. Pok (eds.), *The Holocaust in Hungary: Fifty Years Later* (Columbia University Press, New York, 1997)

Braham, R. L. (ed.), *Genocide and Retribution* (Kluwer-Nijhoff, The Hague, 1983)

Bungert, H., 'A New Perspective on French–American Relations during the Occupation of Germany, 1945–1948: Behind-the-Scenes Diplomatic Bargaining and the Zonal Merger', *Diplomatic History* 18 (3) (1994), 333–52

Carl, H., 'Liechtenstein und das Dritte Reich. Krise und Selbstbehauptung des Kleinstaates' ['Liechtenstein and the Third Reich. Crisis and Self-Assertion of Small States'], in Volker Press and Dietmar Willoweit (eds.), *Liechtenstein – Fürstliches Haus und staatliche Ordnung* (R. Oldenbourg Verlag, Munich, 1987)

Cobban, A., *A History of Modern France*, vol. 3 (Penguin, Harmondsworth, 1965)

Deák, I., 'Hungary', in H. Rogger and E. Weber (eds.), *The European Right. A Historical Profile* (University of California Press, Berkeley and Los Angeles, 1966)

Dinnerstein, L., *America and the Survivors of the Holocaust* (A. S. Hyman, New York, 1982)

Don, Y., 'The Economic Effect of Antisemitic Discrimination: Hungarian Anti-Jewish Legislation, 1938–1944', in M. Marrus (ed.), *The Nazi Holocaust: Historical Articles on the Destruction of European Jews*, vol. 4 (Westport, London, 1989)

Don, Y., 'Patterns of Jewish Economic Behavior in Central Europe in the Twentieth Century', in M. K. Silber (ed.), *Jews in the Hungarian Economy, 1760–1945* (Magnes Press, Jerusalem, 1992), pp. 247–73

Don, Y., and V. Karády, *A Social and Economic History of Central European Jewry* (Transaction Publishers, New Brunswick, 1990)

Eichler, H., 'New Era in Hungarian Zionism, 1945–1946', *Dapim LeHeker HaShoah* 8 (1990), 81–102

Eisterer, K., 'Die Souvenirs d'Autriche vom Oberst Henri Jung', *Vierteljahresschrift für Geschichte under Gegenwarts Vorarlbergs* 47 (3) (1995), 266–72

Eisterer, K., *La Présence Française en Autriche (1945–1946). Occupation–Denazification–Action Culturelle* (Université de Rouen, 1998)

Erez, Z., 'Holocaust of Hungarian Jewry – Statistical Survey' [Hebrew], *Yalkut Moreshet* 57 (1994), 43–60

Erez, Z., 'Mátyás Rákosi versus Zionism and the State of Israel', *Shvut* n.s. 1, 17–18 (1995), 332–41

Erickson, J., *The Road to Berlin. Stalin's War with Germany* (Weidenfeld & Nicolson, London, 1983)

Fiala, F., and L. Marschalkó, *Vádló bitófák ['Accusing Gallows']* (Munich, 1958; reprinted Budapest, 1999)

Földes, G., and L. Hubai (eds.), *Parliamentary Elections in Hungary, 1920–1998* (Napvilág, Budapest, 1999)

Frojimovics, K., G. Komoroczy, *et al.*, *Jewish Budapest* (CEU Press, Budapest, 1999)

Gillis, F., and H. Knopf, *The Reparation Claim of the Jewish People* (pamphlet; The Jewish Agency, Tel Aviv, 1944)

Ginzberg, E., *My Brother's Keeper* (Transaction Publishers, New Brunswick, 1989)

Glatz, F., 'Hóman Bálint és a nemzetiszocialisták összeütközése Székesfehérvárott 1944-ben' ['A political clash between Bálint Hóman and the National Socialists in Székesfehérvár in 1944'], *Fejér megyei Történeti Évkönyv* 4 (1970), 187–202

Gordon, J., 'Hungary', *American Jewish Yearbook* (American Jewish Committee, New York, 51 (1950)), 361–5

Gurley, F. L., 'Einmarsch der amerikanischen Armee in Westösterreich, April/Mai 1945', in M. Rauchensteiner and W. Etschmann (eds.), *Österreich 1945. Ein Ende und viele Anfänge ['Austria 1945. An Ending and Many Beginnings']* (Graz, Styria, 1997)

Heideking, J., and C. Mauch (eds.), *American Intelligence and the German Resistance to Hitler. A Documentary History* (Westview Press, Boulder, Colorado, 1996)

Henry, M., *The Restitution of Jewish Property in Central and Eastern Europe* (American Jewish Committee, New York, 1998)

Himler, M., *Így néztek ki. A magyar nemzet sírasó* ['This is what they looked like. The Gravediggers of the Hungarian Nation'] (St Mark's Printing Co., New York, 1958)

Hinsley, F. H., *British Intelligence in the Second World War: Its Influence on Strategy and Operations* (HMSO, London, 1988)

Horst, Carl, 'Liechtenstein und das Dritte Reich. Krise und Selbstbehauptung des Kleinstaats', in Volker Press and Dietmar Willoweit (eds.), *Liechtenstein – Fürstliches Haus und staatliche Ordnung: geschichtliche Grundlagen und moderne Perspektiven* (R. Oldenbourg, Munich, 1988).

Horthy, N., *Memoirs* (Simon Publications, Florida, 1957)

Horváth, R., 'Jews in Hungary after the Holocaust: the National Relief Committee for Deportees, 1945–1950', *Journal of Israeli History* 19 (2) (1998), 69–91

Horwitz, G. J., *In the Shadow of Death. Living Outside the Gates of Mauthausen* (Free Press, New York, 1992)

Höttl, W., *The Secret Front. The Story of Nazi Political Espionage* (Weidenfeld & Nicolson, London, 1953)

Höttl, W., *Einsatz für das Reich* ['Devoted Service for the Reich'] (Bublies Verlag, Koblenz, 1997)

Hyman, A. S., *The Undefeated* (Gefen, Jerusalem, 1993)

Illényi, B., 'The Adventures of the Holy Crown of Hungary', *New Hungarian Quarterly* (Budapest) 41 (Summer 2000), 32–61

Institute of Jewish Affairs, *European Jewry Ten Years After the War* (New York, 1956)

Jacobmeyer, W., *Vom Zwangsarbeiter zum Heimatlosen Auslander* ['From Forced Labourers to Stateless Foreigners'] (Vanderhoeck & Ruprecht, Gottingen, 1985)

Karasik, M., 'Problems of Compensation and Restitution in Germany and Austria', *Law and Contemporary Problems* 16 (1951), 448–68

Karsai, E., and L. Karsai, *A Szálasi per* (Reform Printing Office, Budapest, 1988)

Karsai, L., 'The Last Phase of the Hungarian Holocaust: the Szálasi Regime and the Jews', in R. L. Braham and S. Miller (eds.), *The Nazis' Last Victims. The Holocaust in Hungary* (Wayne State University Press, Detroit, 1998)

Karsai, L., 'The People's Courts and Revolutionary Justice in Hungary, 1945–1946', in István Deàk, Jan Gross and Tony Judt (eds.), *The Politics of Retribution in Europe* (Princeton University Press, Princeton, NJ, 2000)

Karsai, L., and J. Molnár, *Az Endre-Baky-Jaross per* ['The Trial of Endre, Baky and Jaross'] (Cserépfalvi, Budapest, 1994)

Katzburg, N., *Hungary and the Jews* (Bar-Ilan University Press, Ramat Gan, 1981)

Katzburg, N., 'The Tradition of Anti-Semitism in Hungary', in R. L. Braham and B. Vago, *The Holocaust in Hungary: Forty Years Later* (Columbia University Press, New York and Haifa, 1985)

Katzburg, N., 'Between Liberation and Revolution: Hungarian Jewry, 1945–1948', in Y. Gutman and A. Saf, *She'erit Hapletah, 1944–1948. Rehabilitation and Political Struggle* (Yad Vashem, Jerusalem, 1990)

Knight, R., 'Restitution and Legitimacy in Post-War Austria, 1945–1953', *Leo Baeck Yearbook* 36 (1991), 413–41

Kubowitzki, L., *Unity in Dispersion: A History of the World Jewish Congress* (World Jewish Congress, New York, 1948)

Kuklick, B., *American Policy and the Division of Germany. The Clash with Russia over Reparations* (Cornell University Press, Ithaca and London, 1972)

Kursietis, A. J., *The Hungarian Army and its Military Leadership in World War II* (Axis Europa Books, New York, 1999)

Kurtz, M. J., *Nazi Contraband. American Policy on the Return of European Cultural Treasures, 1945–1955* (New York and London, 1985)

Lackò, M., *Arrow-Cross Men. National Socialists, 1935–1944* (Akadémiai Kiadó, Budapest, 1969)

Lehrman, H., 'Hungary: Liberation's Bitter Fruit', *Commentary* 1 (1945), 28–33

Lehrman, H., 'Austria: Way-Station of Exodus', *Commentary* 2 (6) (1946), 565–72

Lengyel, G., 'The Ethnic Composition of the Economic Elite in Hungary in the Interwar Period', in Y. Don and V. Karady, *A Social and Economic History of Central European Jewry* (Transaction Publishers, New Brunswick, 1990), pp. 229–48

Lévai, F., *Black Book on the Martyrdom of Hungarian Jewry*, ed. Lawrence P. Davis (Central European Times Publishing Co., Zurich, 1948)

Lévai, J., *Zsidósors Magyarországon ['Fate of the Jews in Hungary']* (Magyar Téka, Budapest, 1948)

Lévai, J., *Eichmann in Hungary* (Pannonia Press, Budapest, 1961)

Macartney, C. A., *October Fifteenth. A History of Modern Hungary, 1929–1945*, 2 vols. (Edinburgh University Press, 1956)

MacDonald, C. B., *The Last Offensive* (US Government Print Office, Washing, DC, 1973)

Marrus, M. R., *The Unwanted. European Refugees in the Twentieth Century* (Oxford University Press, New York and Oxford, 1985)

Molnár, J., *Zsidósors 1944-ben az V. (szegedi) csendőrkerületben ['Jews in the Fifth Gendarme District (Szeged) in 1944']* (Budapest, 1995)

Moses, S., *Jewish Post-War Claims* (pamphlet; The Jewish Agency, Tel Aviv, 1944)

Müller-Tupath, K., *Reichsführers gehorsamster Becher. Eine deutsche Karriere ['The Reichsführer's Most Obedient Becher. A German Career']* (Aufbau-Verlag, Berlin, 1999)

Naftali, T., 'Creating the Myth of the Alpenfestung: Allied Intelligence and the Collapse of the Nazi Police-State', in G. Bischof and A. Pelinka (eds.), *Austrian Historical Memory and National Identity* (Transaction Publishers, New Brunswick, 1997), pp. 203–46

Nagy, F., *The Struggle Behind the Iron Curtain* (Macmillan, New York, 1948)

Nagy-Talavera, N. M., *The Green Shirts and the Others: a History of Fascism in Hungary and Rumania* (Hoover Institution Press, Stanford University, California, 1970)

Niehorster, L. W. G., *The Royal Hungarian Army 1920–1945* (Axis Europa Books, New York, 1998)

Novák, A., 'Zionism in Mature Age: The Zionist Movement in Hungary After World War II' [Hungarian], *Múlt és Jövő* 2–3 (1998), 89–106

Petersen, N. (ed.), *From Hitler's Doorstep. The Wartime Intelligence Reports of Allen Dulles, 1942–1945* (Pennsylvania State University Press, 1996)

Pierik, P., *Hungary 1944–1945. The Forgotten Tragedy* (Aspekt, Netherlands, 1996)

Ránki, G., *1944 március 19. Magyarország német megszállása ['19 March 1944. The German Occupation of Hungary']* (Kossuth, Budapest, 1978)

Ránki, G., 'The Germans and the Destruction of Hungarian Jewry', in R. L. Braham and B. Vago, *The Holocaust in Hungary: Forty Years Later* (Columbia University Press, New York and Haifa, 1985)

Ránki, G., 'The Occupational Structure of Hungarian Jews in the Interwar Period', in M. K. Silber (ed.), *Jews in the Hungarian Economy, 1760–1945* (Magnes Press, Jerusalem, 1992), pp. 274–86

Ránki, G., E. Pamlényi, *et al.* (eds.), *A Wilhelmstrasse és Magyarország. Német diplomáciai iratok Magyarországról 1933–1944 ['The Wilhelmstrasse and Hungary. German diplomatic documents from Hungary 1933–1944'* (Kossuth Könyvkiadó, Budapest, 1968)

Ranki, V., *The Politics of Inclusion and Exclusion. Jews and Nationalism in Hungary* (Holmes & Meier, New York, 1999)

Reuveni, S., 'Antisemitism in Hungary in the Years 1945–1946' [Hebrew], *Yalkut Moreshet* 43–44 (1987), 177–200

Robinson, N., *Spoliation and Remedial Action* (Institute of Jewish Affairs, New York, 1962)

Roth, S. J., 'Indemnification of Hungarian Victims of Nazism: An Overview', in R. L. Braham and A. Pok (eds.), *The Holocaust in Hungary. Fifty Years Later* (Columbia University Press, New York, 1997), pp. 733–55

Rozett, R., 'Jewish and Hungarian Armed Resistance in Hungary', *Yad Vashem Studies* XIX (1988), 269–88

Rubin, S., and Abba P. Schwartz, 'Refugees and Reparations', *Law and Contemporary Problems* 16 (3) (1951), 379–94

Sagi, N. (ed.), *Political Documents of the Jewish Agency*, vol. 2, *January–November 1947* (Hassifrya Hazionit, Jerusalem, 1998)

Schmidt, M., 'Provincial Police Reports: New Insights into Hungarian Jewish History, 1941–1944', *Yad Vashem Studies* XIX (1987), 233–67

Schoenfeld, A. H. F., 'Soviet Imperialism in Hungary', *Foreign Affairs* 26 (3) (1948), 554–66

Sipos, P. (ed.), *Imrédy Béla a vádlottak padján ['Béla Imrédy in the Prisoner's Box']* (Osiris-Budapest Főváros Levéltára, Budapest, 1999)

Sjöberg, T., *The Powers and the Persecuted. The Refugee Problem and the Intergovernmental Committee on Refugees (IGCR), 1938–1947* (Lund University Press, 1991)

Smith, Jr., A. L., 'A View of US Policy Toward Jewish Restitution', *Holocaust and Genocide Studies* 5 (3) (1990), 247–59

Speer, A., *Inside the Third Reich* (Weidenfeld & Nicolson, London and New York, 1970)

Stark, T., *Hungarian Jews During the Holocaust and After the Second World War, 1939–1945. A Statistical Review* (Columbia University Press, New York, 2000)

Szabó, M., 'The Development of the Hungarian Aircraft Industry, 1938–1941', *Journal of Military History* 65 (January 2001), 53–76

Szita, Sz., *Utak a pokolból: magyar deportáltak az annektált Ausztriában, 1944–1945 ['Roads from Hell: Hungarian Deportations to Annexed Austria, 1944–1945']* (Metalon Manager Iroda, Budapest, 1991)

Szöllösi-Janze, M., *Die Pfeilkreuzlerbewegung in Ungarn. Historischer Kontext, Entwicklung und Herrschaft ['The Arrow Cross Movement in Hungary. Historical Context, Development and Rule']* (R. Oldenbourg Verlag, Munich, 1989)

Toldi, A., *A bűnügyi nyomozás ['The Criminal Investigation']* (Stadium, Budapest, 1941)

Varga, L., 'The Losses of Hungarian Jewry. A Contribution to a Statistical

Overview', in R. L. Braham (ed.), *Studies on the Holocaust in Hungary* (Columbia University Press, New York, 1990), pp. 256–65

Weinbaum, L., *Righting an Historic Wrong: Restitution of Jewish Property in Central and East Europe* (Institute of the World Jewish Congress, Jerusalem, 1995)

Weinberg, G. L., *A World at Arms. A Global History of World War II* (Cambridge University Press, 1994)

Weitz, Y., *The Man Who Was Murdered Twice* [Hebrew] (Keter, Jerusalem, 1995)

Zhelitski, B., 'Postwar Hungary, 1944–1946', in N. Naimark and L. Gibianskii (eds.), *The Establishment of Communist Regimes in Eastern Europe, 1944–1949* (Westview Press, Boulder, Colorado, 1997), pp. 73–92

Zweig, R. W., 'Restitution and the Problem of Jewish Displaced Persons in Anglo-American Relations, 1944–1948', *American Jewish History* LXXVIII (1) (1988), 54–78

Zweig, Ronald W., 'Feeding the Camps: Allied Blockade Policy and the Relief of Concentration Camps in Germany, 1944–1945', *Historical Journal* 41, 3 (1998), 825–51

Index